The Idea of Europe

The creation of the European Union and the progressive integration of the European states have raised serious questions about the existence of a distinctive European identity. If there is something that distinguishes all Europeans, no matter their national or local differences, what is it, and how is it being changed by recent events? This book addresses these questions in essays that range from ancient Greece to the end of the twentieth century. They discuss matters of politics, law, religion, culture, literature, and even affectivity. In the massive literature of European integration, no other book takes such a long historical perspective, and none other deals directly with the question of identity.

Anthony Pagden is a professor of history and political science at The Johns Hopkins University. He is the author of many books on the history of European social and political thought and of Europe's links to the non-European world.

D1470722

WOODROW WILSON
CENTER SERIES

Michael J. Lacey, editor, *Religion and Twentieth-Century American Intellectual Life*

Michael J. Lacey, editor, *The Truman Presidency*

Joseph Kruzel and Michael H. Haltzel, editors, *Between the Blocs: Problems and Prospects for Europe's Neutral and Nonaligned States*

William C. Brumfield, editor, *Reshaping Russian Architecture: Western Technology, Utopian Dreams*

Mark N. Katz, editor, *The USSR and Marxist Revolutions in the Third World*

Mary O. Furner and Barry Supple, editors, *The State and Economic Knowledge: The American and British Experiences*

Michael J. Lacey and Knud Haakonssen, editors, *A Culture of Rights: The Bill of Rights in Philosophy, Politics, and Law—1791 and 1991*

Robert J. Donovan and Ray Scherer, *Unsilent Revolution: Television News and American Public Life, 1948–1991*

William Craft Brumfield and Blair A. Ruble, editors, *Russian Housing in the Modern Age: Design and Social History*

Nelson Lichtenstein and Howell John Harris, editors, *Industrial Democracy in America: The Ambiguous Promise*

Michael J. Lacey and Mary O. Furner, editors, *The State and Social Investigation in Britain and the United States*

Hugh Ragsdale, editor, *Imperial Russian Foreign Policy*

Dermot Keogh and Michael H. Haltzel, editors, *Northern Ireland and the Politics of Reconciliation*

Joseph Klaits and Michael H. Haltzel, editors, *The Global Ramifications of the French Revolution*

René Lemarchand, *Burundi: Ethnic Conflict and Genocide*

James R. Millar and Sharon L. Wolchik, editors, *The Social Legacy of Communism*

James M. Morris, editor, *On Mozart*

Blair A. Ruble, *Money Sings: The Changing Politics of Urban Space in Post-Soviet Yaroslavl*

Continued on page following index

WOODROW WILSON
INTERNATIONAL CENTER FOR SCHOLARS

Lee H. Hamilton, Director

BOARD OF TRUSTEES

Joseph A. Cari, Jr., Chair; Steven Alan Bennett, Vice Chair. Public Members: James H. Billington, Librarian of Congress; John W. Carlin, Archivist of the United States; William R. Ferris, Chair, National Endowment for the Humanities; Roderick R. Paige, U.S. Secretary of Education; Colin L. Powell, U.S. Secretary of State; Lawrence M. Small, Secretary, Smithsonian Institution; Tommy G. Thompson, U.S. Secretary of Health and Human Services. Private Citizen Members: Carol Cartwright, John H. Foster, Jean L. Hennessey, Daniel L. Lamaute, Doris O. Matsui, Thomas R. Reedy, Nancy M. Zirkin.

WILSON COUNCIL

Steven Kotler, President. B.B. Anderson, Charles S. Ackerman, Cyrus A. Ansary, Charles F. Barber, Lawrence E. Bathgate II, Joseph C. Bell, Richard E. Berkowitz, Thomas J. Buckholtz, Conrad Cafritz, Nicola L. Caiola, Raoul L. Carroll, Scott Carter, Albert V. Casey, Peter B. Clark, William T. Coleman, Jr., Michael D. DiGiacomo, Donald G. Drapkin, F. Samuel Eberts III, J. David Eller, Sim Farar, Susan R. Farber, Barbara Hackman Franklin, Morton Funger, Chris G. Gardiner, Eric Garfinkel, Bruce S. Gelb, Alma Gildenhorn, Joseph B. Gildenhorn, David F. Girard-diCarlo, Michael B. Goldberg, William E. Grayson, Raymond A. Guenter, Verna R. Harrah, Carla A. Hills, Eric Hotung, Frances Humphrey Howard, John L. Howard, Darrell E. Issa, Jerry Jasinowski, Brenda LaGrange Johnson, Dennis D. Jorgensen, Shelly Kamins, Anastasia D. Kelly, Christopher J. Kennan, Michael V. Kostiw, William H. Kremer, Dennis LeVett, Harold O. Levy, David Link, David S. Mandel, John P. Manning, Edwin S. Marks, Jay Mazur, Robert McCarthy, C., Stephen G. McConahey, J. Kenneth Menges, Jr., Philip Merrill, Jeremiah L. Murphy, Martha T. Muse, Della M. Newman, Paul Hae Park, Gerald L. Parsky, Michael J. Polenske, Donald Robert Quartel, Jr., J. Steven Rhodes, John L. Richardson, Margaret Milner Richardson, Edwin Robbins, Philip E. Rollhaus, Otto Ruesch, B. Francis Saul III, Timothy R. Scully, J. Michael Shepherd, George P. Shultz, Raja W. Sidawi, Deborah Siebert, Thomas L. Siebert, Ron Silver, William A. Slaughter, Norma Kline Tiefel, Mark C. Treanor, Christine M. Warnke, Pete Wilson, Deborah Wince-Smith, Herbert S. Winokur, Jr., Joseph Zappala.

ABOUT THE CENTER

The Center is the living memorial of the United States of America to the nation's twenty-eighth president, Woodrow Wilson. Congress established the Woodrow Wilson Center in 1968 as an international institute for advanced study, "symbolizing and strengthening the fruitful relationship between the world of learning and the world of public affairs." The Center opened in 1970 under its own board of trustees.

In all its activities the Woodrow Wilson Center is a nonprofit, nonpartisan organization, supported financially by annual appropriations from the Congress, and by the contributions of foundations, corporations, and individuals. Conclusions or opinions expressed in Center publications and programs are those of the authors and speakers and do not necessarily reflect the views of the Center staff, fellows, trustees, advisory groups, or any individuals or organizations that provide financial support to the Center.

The Idea of Europe
From Antiquity to the European Union

Edited by

ANTHONY PAGDEN
The Johns Hopkins University

WOODROW WILSON CENTER PRESS

AND

CAMBRIDGE
UNIVERSITY PRESS

CAMBRIDGE UNIVERSITY PRESS
Cambridge, New York, Melbourne, Madrid, Cape Town, Singapore,
São Paulo, Delhi, Dubai, Tokyo, Mexico City

Cambridge University Press
32 Avenue of the Americas, New York, NY 10013-2473, USA

www.cambridge.org
Information on this title: www.cambridge.org/9780521795524

WOODROW WILSON CENTER
1300 Pennsylvania Avenue, N.W., Washington, DC 20004-3027

© Woodrow Wilson Center 2002

This publication is in copyright. Subject to statutory exception
and to the provisions of relevant collective licensing agreements,
no reproduction of any part may take place without the written
permission of Cambridge University Press.

First published 2002

A catalog record for this publication is available from the British Library

Library of Congress Cataloging in Publication data
The Idea of Europe : from antiquity to the European Union / edited by Anthony Pagden.
p.   cm. – (Woodrow Wilson Center series)
Includes bibliographical references and index.
ISBN 0-521-79171-5 – ISBN 0-521-79552-4 (pbk.)
1. Europe – Politics and government.   2. European federation.   3. Nationalism – Europe.
4. Europe – Civilization.   5. Europe – Ethnic relations.   6. Political culture – Europe.
I. Pagden, Anthony.   II. Series.
D105 .I34   2001
940 – dc21   2001025960

ISBN 978-0-521-79171-7 Hardback
ISBN 978-0-521-79552-4 Paperback

Cambridge University Press has no responsibility for the persistence or
accuracy of URLs for external or third-party internet websites referred to in
this publication, and does not guarantee that any content on such websites is,
or will remain, accurate or appropriate. Information regarding prices, travel
timetables, and other factual information given in this work are correct at
the time of first printing but Cambridge University Press does not guarantee
the accuracy of such information thereafter.

BLACKBURN COLLEGE
LIBRARY

Acc. No. BB52518

Class No. UCL 940 PAG

Date 5 · 11 · 2012

For Félix and Sebastian, citizens of Europe
Anthony Pagden

Contents

Acknowledgments

The idea for this book originated with an invitation from James Morris, at that time with the Woodrow Wilson Center, to present the first in a series of public lectures on the idea of Europe. What have subsequently become the chapters by J. G. A. Pocock, James Tully, and Biancamaria Fontana all began as lectures in the same series. I would like to thank James Morris not only for this initiative but also for organizing and hosting a conference at the Center that brought together a number of the other contributors to discuss the future shape and direction of the volume. This was sponsored with the generous support of the Andrew W. Mellon Foundation and the United States Federal Conference Fund. I owe a special debt of gratitude to Susan Nugent who has been a constant source of assistance in any number of ways during the long and often torturous period of the book's gestation, to Joe Brinley for all his patience and encouragement, and to Patricia Katayama and Barbara de Boinville for their care in preparing the text for publication. Two anonymous readers for Cambridge University Press made a number of suggestions that have greatly helped to improve the volume. Finally, I would like to thank José Maria Hernández for his friendship and for having reminded me of the presence of the "smaller nations" in Europe, and Giulia Sissa, another good European, who has influenced greatly what I think on this, and many other topics, and who has saved me from innumerable errors.

Anthony Pagden

Introduction

ANTHONY PAGDEN

Today, as the older territorial and national boundaries of the world become increasingly uncertain, the quest for national and transnational identity has intensified. This, as Talal Asad observes in chapter 10, is a fairly recent phenomenon, the product of "the individual's social locations and psychological crises in an increasingly uncertain world." Previously, anxieties about identity tended to afflict only states of relatively recent creation—the so-called "new states" in Africa and Asia in particular— and areas of massive and diverse emigration such as the United States.[1] The states that made up "Europe," however, had supposedly been of such antiquity and undisputed cultural homogeneity that their members rarely troubled to ask themselves who they were.[2] But the experience of two world wars, combined with ever-increasing migration for political, economic, or broadly cultural motives across the rapidly dissolving frontiers of Europe, have forced upon Europeans the uneasy sense that their self-confidence in knowing just who they are is almost certainly unfounded.

This volume traces from the ancient world to the present the determining features of what might count as a collective "idea" of Europe as a political and cultural domain. This is not, of course, a linear history. No such history could be written. Our objective is rather to identify the concerns and convictions, the shifting discursive practices and the different languages, political, cultural, and economic, of which all identities are constituted. The contributors represent different disciplines—history, anthropology, political science, the law—as they do different intellectual styles. Some (J. G. A. Pocock, Talal Asad, and James Tully in particular)

---

[1] On identity in the "new states," see Clifford Geertz, "After the Revolution: The Fate of Nationalism in the New States," in *The Interpretation of Cultures* (New York: Basic Books, 1973), 234–54.

[2] See Thomas Risse and Daniela Engelmann-Martin's chapter in this volume.

look at Europe from beyond Europe, and their gaze is highly critical of both what Europe has been and what it is now becoming. Others (Ariane Chebel d'Appollonia, Luisa Passerini, Thomas Risse and Daniela Engelmann-Martin, Biancamaria Fontana), while accepting the obvious burdens and contradictions of the European past, are cautiously hopeful about the possibilities of a new and happier European future. The volume offers no attempt to solve Europe's current dilemmas. Its purpose is rather to add an historical voice to a conversation that has been going on within Europe and outside for several decades, a conversation that will shape a new, potentially exciting, potentially threatening, political, cultural, and social order. Most of us, whether we belong to Europe itself or (like some of the contributors to this volume) to other parts of the "Western" world, which Europe has played such an important role in shaping, will have to learn to live with this order. It is time we also came to understand it.

For decades there has been within Western Europe an ever-insistent suspicion that the days of the nation-state are numbered. This, at least for the foreseeable future, is largely an illusion. Politically and institutionally the state remains the final term of reference. As the general enthusiasm for the unification of Germany demonstrated, the state is still capable of arousing a great deal of popular attachment, even among one of the most Europhile of Europe's peoples.[3] In the minds of such East German politicians as Wolfgang Thierse, former leader of the Eastern SPD and subsequently speaker of the German parliament, there may be an insoluble link between unification and "Europeanization." But if his position is to be at all coherent, Thierse's vision of the future United States of Europe must still be one in which the individual states retain a great measure of their former identity as nations.[4]

Even if the nation-state is not about to vanish, the erosion of its effective powers within what now constitutes the European Union has been considerable. As Philip Ruttley explains in his essay on the process of unification after 1945 (chapter 11), the institutions of the Union, the European Commission, the European Parliament, and the European Court of Justice have, as the "Euroskeptics" bitterly complain, greatly diminished the authority of local assemblies and national judiciaries.[5] Beyond Europe, too,

---

[3] Andrés de Blas Guerrero reminds us of this point in chapter 14.

[4] In their chapter Risse and Engelmann-Martin write that "the 'United States of Europe' are not seen as a unitary state with a strong central government, but as a distinctively federalist order.... The model is the Bonn republic, not Paris and the Fifth Republic."

[5] See William Wallace, "Rescue or Retreat? The Nation State in Western Europe, 1945–93," in Peter Gowan and Perry Anderson, eds., *The Question of Europe* (London–New York: Verso, 1997), 21–46.

"globalization" has shrunk the operational capacity of the state by transferring a great deal of its previous informal authority to private, and necessarily multinational, institutions.

All of this is obvious enough. Whether you view it with dismay or pleasure depends on which side of a number of political and cultural fences you happen to sit. All people, not only Europeans, must share some anxiety over whether the successor to this now long-standing political and social institution will turn out to be a mega-state, a federation of minor states, or merely a political corporation. In the midst of this shifting political landscape, most of the peoples of Europe are participants in a vast and far-ranging political, economic, and cultural experiment. No one has any clear idea of the outcome. But, as Thomas Risse and Daniela Engelmann-Martin stress, it will be—indeed, if it is to succeed, it must be—dependent upon the image of a newer and better political order, one that ultimately can replace the older alignment of peoples. This alignment dates back to the Congress of Vienna, and, as Biancamaria Fontana argues in chapter 5 on the legacy of the Napoleonic wars, it set the scene for many of the divergences and contradictions that still beset the attempt to create a united Europe. Most, too, will recognize that some of the divisions in Europe established even earlier by the confessional struggles of the sixteenth and seventeenth centuries—divisions between Protestants and Catholics, between an industrialized, capitalist, and predominantly republican North and a largely agricultural, quasi-feudal if not exactly monarchical and ultimately backward South—are vanishing and that in their place a new sense of what it means to be European is slowly and uncertainly emerging. The very thought that it might be useful to talk of a *European* identity, which even those who most abhor the idea do so if only reactively, has become a source of anxiety.

GOVERNMENT

That there exists such a place as Europe has been evident to those who inhabit it since the fourth century BCE if not earlier. At first "Europe" designated a vague geographical region distinguished less by what it was than what it was not. In time, however, this sense of difference, of being unlike the other regions into which the world was divided, became more distinct. One feature of this difference, which in various ways has remained constant over time, is the belief that Europeans have always pursued roughly similar political ends. The forms of government adopted by the different peoples of the continent have, of course, varied widely.

But all of the governments have subscribed to the idea that freedom of individual choice and protection by a universal system of law was the necessary condition for what the Greeks defined as "the good life." From the Greek geographer Strabo in the first century CE until Montesquieu in the eighteenth, observers of the peculiar identity of Europe have fastened upon some conception of liberty as the defining feature of all the societies of Europe—or at least, as J. G. A. Pocock in his pluralist view of Europe rightly insists—all the societies of the Christian Latin West.[6] This belief in liberty has been most closely identified with the republican and democratic traditions that originated in ancient Greece. In Europe, claimed Machiavelli, "although there have been some kingdoms, there have been many republics." The peoples of Asia and Africa, by contrast, had only ever lived under princely rule. Machiavelli was being unduly optimistic even at a time—the late fifteenth century—when the republican tradition was still a powerful force within Italy. But even if most of Europe has, for much of its history, been ruled by monarchs, they have generally accepted two basic principles: first, that their subjects were free persons, in the sense of not being their personal property; second, that although the laws they enacted might be nothing other than the expression of their will, all rulers were nevertheless bound by a higher legal order. This legal order was, it is true, held to be derived from God and immanent in nature rather than dependent upon the legislative will of the majority, and for that reason was infinitely malleable. But since the natural and divine law provided a court of final appeal that was beyond the reach of even the mightiest ruler, it constrained the power of kings. In the end these two principles provided the ideological grounding for the revolution that would alter the conception and the practice of power within Europe at the end of the eighteenth century and would bring into being a world that was and would remain, despite the restorations of the nineteenth century, fundamentally republican.

There was also the generally shared belief that power, although it derived from God, was conferred upon kings by a contract with the people. The force of this contract (and its nature) varied greatly. But no European monarch in theory wielded personalized or unfettered power. The history of social life, and the political realities of most (if not all) European states since the collapse of the Roman Empire, might suggest that such conceptions of the sources of authority had very little enduring significance. Freedom, even under the law, was the freedom only of the few.

---

[6] On this point see also my chapter and the one by Biancamaria Fontana.

(It excluded in most cases most women and all children.) The existence of slavery was accepted as part of nature, and even the emphasis of Christianity on the equality of all human beings in Christ (if not in society) did little to change this. Martin Luther famously warned Christian slaves against "stealing themselves" away from their rightful Muslim masters. The possibility for self-determination on the part of the vast majority of the population was further constricted by systems of land tenure and indenture, and by semisacred hierarchies based on kin and patrimonial succession. Nevertheless, ideologies associated with a contractualist view of political association, in particular after the great religious and civil disturbances of the sixteenth and seventeenth centuries, exerted a constant pressure on all the European monarchies, which not infrequently led to open warfare and in some cases the death of the ruler himself. And in most cases these ideologies drew their inspiration from forms of Greek and Roman republicanism. Belief in a monarch's divine origins or "divine right" was never anything but unstable.

Some kind of republicanism had, therefore, always been a presence in the politics of early modern Europe. But it was the emergence of the Dutch republic and its enormous political and commercial success that led, as Hans Blom explains (chapter 4), to a new kind of political idiom, one that was essentially modern and commercial. The merchants Pieter and Johann de la Court, the philosopher Baruch Spinoza, and (in a rather different idiom) the humanist Hugo Grotius all stressed the need for a form of government that would not, as the republics of the ancient world had supposedly done, demand the involvement of the entire citizen body in the life of the state. Instead, through the rule of law and government by a representative elite, it would protect the interests, in particular the economic interests, of the citizen body. In the highly modified shape of modern liberal democracy, the Dutch reevaluation of the republican creed has, of course, proved to be triumphant—as well as triumphalist.

The history of belief that the constitutional state, based upon representation and universal suffrage, is a determining feature of European political life began with the emergence, after 1648 in England, of what Montesquieu identified as a quasi-republican government "hidden beneath" a monarchy. It then passed through the various republicanisms of Jefferson, Rousseau, and Kant, to the liberal monarchism of Benjamin Constant and Tocqueville, Wilhelm von Humboldt, John Stuart Mill, and Giuseppe Mazzini—to name but a few. Today its most powerful defenders are North American, but it has, for the entire "Western" world, become normative. Failure to conform to the standards of what the

Chinese leader Deng Hsiao Ping called contemptuously the "bourgeois liberal republic"[7] is what excluded Spain and Portugal from inclusion in the original European Economic Community, and it is at least one of the reasons for Turkey's continuing exclusion from the European Union.

Of course, not all Europeans have consistently taken this view. The English liberal historians of the nineteenth century had such an understanding of the history of England but not of most of continental Europe. The narratives of Jules Michelet and Louis Adolphe Thiers, by contrast, claimed for the French Revolution a transformative phase that in some sense had restored Europe to its ancient foundations within an essentially republican tradition. On these accounts, monarchies—or at least the would-be absolutist monarchies of Louis XIV, Charles II, and Frederick the Great—were aberrations in a story that reached from the Greek city-states to the Europe of nations created after the Congress of Vienna.

Today, however, another dimension has been added, one we owe to Kant. It has become, as James Tully says in his critical assessment of European constitutionalism (chapter 15), a "regulative idea" during the two centuries since the publication of *Perpetual Peace a Philosophical Sketch* in 1795. This is the assumption that all "modern" states (by which is generally meant Western and thus ultimately European states) can form themselves into some kind of league. In the past such leagues have usually been the response to some possible exterior threat (as indeed was the case in Kant's hypothetical future "great federation"). The European Union, although it was not in origin defensive (the planned European Defensive Council of the 1950s came to nothing), was also conceived with the initial intention of preventing further conflict between the European states.[8]

The possibility of any kind of federal structure, however, was based upon the assumption of common political practices and values by the member states. In Kant's case these were the values of what he called the "representative republic," a term that has widely been assumed to correspond, *mutatis mutandis*, to modern social democracy. In Kant's view the true "cosmopolitan constitution" would become possible only once all the societies of the world were ruled by republican and representative governments. This has led to the claim, now a commonplace of international relations theory, that not only do liberal democracies not go to

---

[7] See John Dunn, "The Identity of the Bourgeois Liberal Republic," in Biancamaria Fontana, ed., *The Invention of the Modern Republic* (Cambridge: Cambridge University Press, 1994), 206–25.

[8] See David McKay, *Federalism and the European Union: A Political Economy Perspective* (Oxford: Oxford University Press, 1999), 3–36.

war with one another, they also actively cooperate for one another's well-being. This—the capacity for international cooperation—has become, in Tully's words, a "normative standard against which many people organize and evaluate forms of political association in Europe and throughout the world." Like so many other "regulative ideas," this is at best an illusion. That the democratic states of *western* Europe have not gone to war with one another cannot be taken as normative. The democratic or quasi-democratic republics of Africa, the Indian subcontinent, and Latin America have rarely shown any reluctance to make ferocious wars against their neighbors. Nor, of course, have the new democratic and quasi-democratic states of Eastern Europe.

The obvious empirical weakness of the idea has not detracted from its great influence in the creation of the idea of modern Europe as a continent that, if it only adheres to the principles of liberal democracy, will never collapse into internal warfare. The initial and prime objective of "Europe" as a political (and economic) conception is to ensure peace—an objective it shares with Kant's cosmopolitan order. The founders of what was to become the European Economic Community sought above all to suppress the horrors of two world wars, initiated by Europeans and fought between European states and their overseas dependencies. The consequences of the second war continue to have a momentous impact on European consciousness.[9] The concern to create a Europe that would no longer be prey to internal conflict has been the foundation of many postwar foreign policy objectives. This has sometimes reached apocalyptic levels, as Risse and Englemann-Martin show, in particular among the Germans, and to a lesser degree the Italians, as the perpetrators of much of the horrors associated with nationalism in Europe. The German chancellor, Helmut Kohl, went so far as to argue in 1997 that the success of the European Monetary Union (EMU) was "a question of war and peace" and Joschka Fischer, a Green party leader in the Bundestag at the time, claimed that "the only alternative to an early start of the Euro was a return to the European past of power balancing and nationalism."[10] Kohl and presumably Fischer both knew, as had Kant, that a union based solely upon mutual economic interests—the "commercial society" of the eighteenth century—or a union organized merely for defense would never be

---

[9] Alan S. Milward, *The European Rescue of the Nation State* (London: Routledge, 1994), 4.

[10] Risse and Engelmann-Martin observe that in Germany "the new Europe is seen primarily as a stable peace order in almost Kantian terms of a 'pacific federation' combining cooperation with external partners with liberal democracy internally."

sufficiently compelling in the long run to suppress the murderous instincts of humankind.

Only what Kant called "the ideal civil constitution" could achieve that. Kant's "universal cosmopolitan existence ... as the matrix within which all the original capacities of the human race may develop" was firmly located, however, in the future. It was, as he said, a "sweet dream." But the modern conception of "Europe" is no dream. If Romano Prodi is right, it might bring into being a community that is, in Prodi's words, "more open to civil society and to the citizen body, less obsessed with party pride and more concerned with bringing together diverse positions in a project of government which will operate at all levels," than was any of its more ideological predecessors.[11]

Like the intellectual architects of today's Europe, Jean Monnet, Robert Schuman, and Altiero Spinelli, Kant was looking for a way to reduce the possibilities for conflict between sovereign bodies. Unlike them, however, he had his gaze fixed upon the entire world. But in practice his "cosmopolitan right" could have applied only to Europe because he sought a union of states and, in the opinion of many, true states have been the dominant mode of political association, at least before the nineteenth century, only within Europe. This belief in the uniqueness of the state, like every other component of the discourse of European exceptionalism, has its origins in the ancient Greek, and later Roman world. In his massive attempt to capture the unique identity of European civilization, the great German sociologist Max Weber identified the ancient conception of "citizenship" as the defining feature of the modern state. As Wilfried Nippel explains in chapter 6, this involved the creation of a community "which he [Weber] calls *Verbrüderung* (confraternity), a community based on artificially created and freely willed mutual ties, not on consanguinity." This community, furthermore, conferred identity upon all those who entered into it. It was, that is, transformational, and as such it could change over time, which, in Weber's view, the kin-based civilizations of the other great polities of the world, China and India, could not do.

The "state"—the Greek *polis* and the Roman *civitas*—determined the shape of all future political associations in what has come to be called "Europe." After the collapse of the Roman world, however, somewhat different political arrangements came into existence: free city-states, prince-bishoprics, independent bands of knights, military orders, a Church whose

---

[11] Romano Prodi, *Un'idea dell'Europe. Il valore Europe per modernizzare l'Italia* (Bologna: Il Mulino, 1999), 8.

power and influence reached into most parts of the continent, and an Empire whose emperor was only the "first among equals" (*primus inter pares*). But the modern nation-state, as a concept, emerged out of the sixteenth-century ambition to define, in William Chester Jordan's words, a "national essence, never actually lost but hidden sometimes under the debris of anarchy and, at other times, under Catholic and Imperial universalism" (chapter 3). It emerged, too, from an increasing need to establish a world of security after the confessional conflicts that devastated much of the continent between 1562 and 1648. This could be achieved only by limiting—and consolidating—the sovereignty of national rulers. As J. G. A. Pocock observes (chapter 2), the familiar "Enlightened narrative" that makes gunpowder, the printing press, and the compass seminal inventions tends to be associated with the discovery of America, but "for Voltaire and Hume and Robertson, they had a prior importance—their role in the creation of powerful military monarchies controlling their own resources, pursuing their own policies, and capable of acting independently of the papal Church."

Although most of the new military states were feudal or semifeudal monarchies, they had to be ruled by monarchs who were, in principle, impersonal. Only a supreme and impersonal state could guarantee not merely independence from the papal Church but continuing stability in the face of the new ideological threats produced by the division of Christendom into two antagonistic camps.[12] This simultaneous centralization and impersonalization of political power distinguished the European states from such non-European sovereign bodies as the Ottoman or Ming empires.

The independence of the new states reinforced by this form of power created a far greater fragmentation of the continent—politically, religiously, economically, and ultimately culturally—than had been the case. The "persistent localism" that had characterized the European world in the Middle Ages at a nonelite level was now buttressed by a political ideology endorsed by all but a few. Since the days of the Emperor Augustus's new Rome, there has been a vision of a future in which "Europe" would acquire some kind of unity. Paradoxically, one of the most distinctive political features of the continent—the modern state—resulted in what was, and in certain respects still remains, the main obstacle to its unification.

---

[12] See Quentin Skinner, "The State," in Terence Ball, James Farr, and Russell L. Hanson, eds., *Political Innovation and Conceptual Change* (Cambridge: Cambridge University Press, 1989), 90–131.

THE LEGACY OF EMPIRE

The formation of the European state accompanied the creation of Europe's modern overseas empires. In the Middle Ages, as William Jordan reminds us, although persistent localism was the condition of most Europeans, this did not entirely cut them off from the recognition that they were also "part of a wider world." Internationalism was a necessary consequence of the increased contact between the states of Europe as they struggled to establish themselves as states, and of the ever-increasing encounter of Europeans with the worlds beyond Europe. From the sixteenth century until the first decades of the twentieth, European overseas expansion and European imperialism were broadly conceived in terms of the triumph, not merely of one ethnic group over another, but of one political system, belief, and (crucially) one vision of the world over all others. Europeans managed to establish some measure of political ascendancy in nearly every part of the globe in this period. In 1800 the European imperial powers occupied or controlled some 35 percent of the surface of the planet, by 1878 they had taken 67 percent, and by 1914 more than 84 percent.[13] This astonishing success may be attributed—as Michael Herzfeld (chapter 7), Luisa Passerini (chapter 9), and I (chapter 1) point out—to the conviction that understanding the world and shaping it to meet Europeans' ends were related projects. Most Europeans conceived of themselves as "individualists," even if, until the twentieth century, they lacked the language in which to do so. As Michael Herzfeld reminds us, "individualism" also was a concept exported by Europeans to their settler populations overseas— in particular to the British colonists in North America. Europeans were property owners, not as members of a group, but as persons. Their individualism was, in Herzfeld's words, "grounded in the relationship between property ownership and selfhood." A belief in the ability to own discrete parts of the globe is by no means restricted to Europe. But it is doubtful that many other peoples have made it so central to their understanding of what humanity is.

Therefore, the history of the European and subsequent "Western" domination of the planet is not merely the consequence of a superior technology. It is also the triumph of a conception of the world, one which assumed that the European scientific tradition from Aristotle to Newton had correctly interpreted the globe as a place for the forceful expropriation of human potential. Philosophy thus became associated with science in ways

---

[13] Paul Kennedy, *The Rise and Fall of the Great Powers* (New York: Macmillan, 1987), 148–9.

that were unique or so, at least, it seemed. That it was the Europeans who had seen this most clearly meant that it was the Europeans who had, in a quite specific sense, inherited the earth. Others might know how to live on it, but only Europe possessed the "Faustian power" to reconstruct it in its own image. This, too, has become a "regulative idea," and it, too, is founded on very shaky empirical and historical foundations. Before the first decade or so of the nineteenth century, the European powers had very little superiority either intellectually or technologically over the peoples of Asia, even when measured by their own criteria.[14] Yet the association of science with philosophy—or, to put it more crudely, with reason—has contributed more than any other conception to bringing "Europe together as a unity," in the words of the German philosopher Hans-Georg Gadamer.[15]

This, too, has a history, as I try to explain in chapter 1. It is a history that acquires its most compelling and enduring modern form in the eighteenth-century Enlightenment, in a project that linked the quest for individual autonomy and secularization with the most sustained bid to understand, and through science to control, the external world of nature. At one level the "Enlightenment project" can be read as another extension of the universalist ambitions of the ancient world. Just as the Romans had exported a concept of civilization and the Christians a concept of Christianity (as the belief not only in the redemptive power of Christ but also the way of life to be lived by St. Paul's *homo renatus*), so the secular thinkers of the Enlightenment and their heirs exported an idea of humanity as individual, transformative, and property-owning—an idea that inevitably involved a large measure of concern for the burdens of history. In the link between philosophy and science, reaching out to "others"—albeit with the ambition to transform them into ourselves—has been as much a part of the European colonial inheritance as the exploitation and enslavement of others.

This has created a double imposition for most modern European states: the need to repudiate their imperial past while clinging resolutely to the belief that there can be no alternative to the essentially European liberal democratic state. Any attempt at something different is either (like Marxism) doomed to economic failure or (like the various forms of religious fundamentalism) ultimately tyrannical. Talal Asad (chapter 10) is

---

[14] See, in particular, Jack Goody, *The East in the West* (Cambridge: Cambridge University Press, 1996).

[15] Hans-Georg Gadamer, "The Diversity of Europe: Inheritance and Future" [Die Vielfalt Europas, Erbe und Zukunft] in Hans-Georg Gadamer, *Education, Poetry and History: Applied Hermeneutics*, trans. Lawrence Schmidt and Monica Reuss (New York: State of New York Press, 1992), 224. See also Luisa Passerini's chapter in this volume.

surely right in saying that "Europe's colonial past is not merely an epoch of overseas power that is now decisively over. It is the beginning of an irreversible global transformation that remains an intrinsic part of 'European experience' and is part of the reason that Europe has become what it is today." His relative pessimism about the possibility of Muslims finding any place for themselves within European societies that claim to be pluralist (and at many levels clearly are) is not unfounded. A true European Union, that is, may need not only compelling cultural symbols and representative political forms in order to persuade the Danes and the British that what they are being asked to identify with is as much "their" Europe as it is the Europe of the French or the Germans; it also may need sufficient adaptability to provide a common *patria* for Algerians and Malays, Muslims and Hindus.

Jacques Derrida has argued, *a propos* of this aspect of the European Union's future, that there can be no cultural identity that is "identical with itself," for it is in the nature of a "culture that it is not identical with itself."[16] Pluralism, the successor to Kant's cosmopolitanism, is aimed precisely at making cultures "not identical with themselves" in this way. But the difficulty still remains. Even Derrida's formulation—perhaps, most especially Derrida's formulation—belongs to a European conception of the self sustained ultimately by an intrinsically European set of political values. Any claim that constitutional equality necessarily implies a form of "difference blindness" cannot be other than a reflection of the values of one particular, and in this case hegemonic, culture.[17]

That pluralism, like most other generalized conceptions, is the product of a specifically European intellectual environment must be especially obvious to Muslims, who now constitute the largest single immigrant group in Europe. As William Jordan makes clear in chapter 3, modern pluralism—however secularized the conception might be in most Enlightenment thinkers—depends, as does any idea of the unity of European culture, upon a continuing Christian tradition. Add to this the fact that from the tenth century until the dismemberment of the Ottoman Empire in the nineteenth, Islam had been Europe's most constant "other," in terms of religion, and politically and culturally, as the expression of various kinds of "oriental despotism," it is easy to see how a "European" Muslim might appear to be virtually an oxymoron. As Asad says in his chapter, "in the contemporary European suspicion of Turkey, Christian history, enshrined

---

[16] Jacques Derrida, *L'Autre Cap* (Paris: Les Éditions de Minuit, 1991), 16–17. See also the rather different interpretation offered by Luisa Passerini in her chapter.

[17] See Tully's chapter in this volume.

in the tradition of international law, is being reinvoked in secular language as the foundation of an ancient identity."

WAR AND COMMERCE

Europe's first modern overseas empires came into being at the moment when a series of predominantly civil wars had divided it along confessional lines. From the beginning of the Wars of Religion in France in 1562 until the end of the Thirty Years War in 1648, the whole continent was engaged in almost ceaseless conflict. The Treaty of Westphalia of 1648 achieved an albeit precarious balance of power between the various national states of Europe. It established that religion would henceforth be not a papal but a national issue, and it put a final end to the Church's role as arbiter in international affairs. It also set up a division, which has survived to this day, between an increasingly wealthy Protestant North and an increasingly impoverished Catholic South. Before the reformation, as Henri de Saint-Simon lamented, at a time (1815) when the Congress of Vienna was seeking to create a new equilibrium among the European powers, Europe shared a common culture and a common set of institutions; after Westphalia it became two huge federations permanently at odds with one another.[18] One of the objectives of the projects to unify Europe that emerged in the post-Napoleonic era was to undo the deleterious effect of Westphalia while preserving the peace that a "Europe of Treaties" had been able to achieve, if only precariously.

The confessional wars of the sixteenth and seventeenth centuries were the first modern conflicts in which the belligerents were divided—if not always consistently—along broadly ideological lines. They were also the first wars to be fought, as were all subsequent European conflicts, both within and beyond Europe. The Dutch struggle for independence from Spain—the Eighty Years War, as the Dutch called it—involved at one time or another most of the major European powers, and it was conducted not only in Europe, but also in the Americas and in Asia. As the historian Charles Boxer has said, it was the "first world war," and it ensured that all subsequent rivalries between the European states would be played out in a global arena. As Talal Asad (chapter 10) nicely remarks, although in

---

[18] Henri de Saint-Simon, "De la réorganisation de la société européenne ou de la nécessité et des moyens de rassembler les peuples de l'europe en un seul corps politique en conservant a chacun son indépendance nationale" [October 1814], in *Oeuvres de Claude-Henri de Saint-Simon* (Slatkine Reprints [of the Paris edition of 1868], Geneva 1977), 1:161–2.

another context, "Europe did not simply expand overseas; it made itself through that expansion."

The Treaty of Westphalia put an end to the confessional sources of conflict between the European powers and in a sense ensured the triumph of the secular state in the international arena. The Treaty of Utrecht of 1713, however, achieved (in J. G. A. Pocock's words) "a 'Europe' that had outgrown barbarism, fanaticism, and conquest" and in its place established "a republic or confederation of states held together by treaties to which wars were merely auxiliary, and by a common system of civilized manner communicated everywhere by commerce." Until 1945 at least, Europeans may have been one of the most consistently belligerent groups of peoples anywhere in the world. But, as with many of the general aspects of modern European history, the opposite was true as well: a perennial quest for an ideal of eternal universal peace, based upon what the Leiden philosopher Franco Burgersdijk in the sixteenth century called an "Imperium Oecumenicum"—an ecumenical empire.

The desire for world peace was, of course, nothing new. It had been one of the major objectives of the fifteenth- and sixteenth-century humanists, of Erasmus and Juan Luís Vives. But before the seventeenth century it had never been pursued with quite such insistence and with such possibilities of ultimate success, or so it seemed to contemporaries. This desire for world peace resulted in a series of ambitious projects: the Duc de Sully's "Grand Design" of 1620, Emeric Cruce's *Le Nouveau Cynée* of 1623, the Abbé de St. Pierre's *Projet pour rendre la paix perpetuelle en Europe* of 1712, and Immanuel Kant's *Perpetual Peace* of 1795. None of these projects, except Kant's, which as I have said was always a condition of future time, were understood, even by their authors, as serious political objectives. As Voltaire complained of the Abbé de St. Pierre's *Projet*, it could no more exist among princes "than it could among elephants and rhinoceroses, or between wolves and dogs." But like Kant's *ius cosmopoliticum*, they were "regulative ideas," ideas that kept the conception of a possible peace among nations alive during periods of seemingly interminable warfare.

Even the persistent belief that a war between commercial nations could only ever be, in Diderot's telling phrase, "a fire that destroys them all"[19] could not achieve the kind of world desired by champions of the commercial society from Montesquieu to Benjamin Constant. Neither could the Treaty of Paris of 1763 that brought to an end the Seven Years

---

[19] From one of the passages that Diderot wrote for the Abbé Guillaume Raynal's *Histoire philosophique et politique des etablissemens et du commerce des Européens dans les deux Indes*, 10 vols. (Geneva, 1781), III, 205.

War—perhaps the most intense of the struggles between European nations conducted overseas—achieve it, nor the Congress of Vienna, nor even the Treaty of Versailles. But by the middle of the eighteenth century an order had been established. This order was based to a high degree upon the common experience of overseas expansion and of maritime commerce. For all the cultural and political differences that separated North from South, it still seemed possible that Europe might aspire to some common heritage, some common sense of self. This is what Edmund Burke meant by "the great vicinage of Europe."[20] As J. G. A. Pocock explains here, it was also why Burke looked upon the French Revolution with such horror. The ideological aspirations of the revolutionaries seemed intent to destroy the polite world of eighteenth-century commerce and to replace it with scarcely modernized versions of the fanatical convictions that had torn Europe apart in the sixteenth century.

Eighteenth-century commerce, the "commercial society," seemed to many to be not merely a means of ending warfare within Europe, but also a device for transforming the older European empires into more benign forms of human association. By the 1780s, Britain had already fought and lost one colonial war, and Spain was rushing headlong into another. The European capacity for overseas domination, once conceived as such a significant component of her identity, was now increasingly looked upon as a curse. Despite the confidence in the intellectual achievements that made it possible, empire itself had never been regarded as an unconditional blessing. The great Spanish theologians of the sixteenth century, Francisco de Vitoria and Domingo de Soto, first raised the question of the legitimacy and the moral consequences of limitless expansion. Ever since then there had existed a powerful argument that overseas conquests were inevitably as destructive for the imperialists as they obviously were for their victims.[21] In the second half of the eighteenth century, this moral unease intensified, both because of the obvious threat created by the ever-present rivalry between the imperial powers and because of the growing awareness that in a modern society, bound together by what the Marquis de Mirabeau called "the universal confraternity of trade," nothing that

---

[20] Edmund Burke, "First Letter on a Regicide Peace," ed. R. B. McDowell, in Paul Langford, ed., *The Writings and Speeches of Edmund Burke* (Oxford: Oxford University Press, 1991), 9:250. On Burke's invocation in this context of the Roman law of vicinity, see Jennifer M. Welsh, "Edmund Burke and the Commonwealth of Europe: The Cultural Bases of International Order," in Ian Clark and Iver B. Neumann, eds., *Classical Theories of International Relations* (London: Macmillan Press, 1996), 173–92.

[21] See Anthony Pagden, *Lords of All the World: Ideologies of Empire in Spain, Britain, and France, c. 1500–c. 1800* (New Haven and London: Yale University Press, 1995), 156–77.

took place overseas could fail to have some influence—generally malign—on what occurred in Europe.[22]

This moral anxiety found its best-known and certainly its most powerful expression in Kant. James Tully (chapter 15) argues that although Kant "roundly denies" that European imperialism is in any sense "right," he endorses the general conviction that it moves in "the direction of nature and history and the precondition of an eventual just national and world order." For Kant, however, European imperialism is essentially a thwarted objective. True, as Tully insists, Kant fully endorses the traditional view of the non-European world's need for what Tully calls "cultural self-understanding." As Kant said in the *Idea for a Universal History with a Cosmopolitan Purpose*, "the political constitution of our continent . . . will probably legislate eventually for all the other continents." But it is also clear that Kant's cosmopolitan ideal could come about only once the habits displayed by "the civilised states of our continent, especially the commercial states . . . in *visiting* foreign countries and peoples (which in their case is the same as *conquering* them)" had been finally abandoned.[23] The vision of a cosmopolitan order was, of course, no less essentially "European" than the first European empires had been, but it would at least be one that recognized the rights of all peoples, Europeans and non-Europeans alike, to determine their own ends as autonomous human agents. Although Kant nowhere says this, the vision would extend to everyone access to that "Faustian power" for so long believed to be a defining feature of Europe alone.

Kantian cosmopolitanism had its origins in an ambition to transmute, to "transvaluate," the older European imperial ambitions. Yet it also, although in ways that Kant himself could only have deplored, became the inspiration behind the quest for a new kind of domination. In this Tully and Asad have good reason to be suspicious of the possible consequences of the so-called Enlightenment project. Kant had looked toward revolutionary France to provide the political model for the new Europe, which, as he saw it in the 1790s, could only be republican and federal. The Marquis de Condorcet had looked in the same direction, even as that revolution was about to put an end to his life. Like the final stage of Kant's *Cosmopolitan History*, the "Tenth period" of Condorcet's *Esquisse d'un*

---

[22] Marquis de Mirabeau, *L'Ami des hommes, ou traité de la population* (The Hague, 1758), 3:176–7.
[23] *The Metaphysics of Morals*, ed. Mary Gregor (Cambridge: Cambridge University Press, 1991), 158. See also "Perpetual Peace: A Philosophical Sketch," in *Kant Political Writings*, ed. Hans Reiss (Cambridge: Cambridge University Press, 1991), 106–7.

tableau historique des progrès de l'esprit humain is a vision of a republican order that would eliminate all further conflict within Europe and all military domination beyond. Similarly, Napoleon, although he abandoned republicanism as a constitutional form of government, retained the view that his administration, "wise and liberal," would bring the same degree of peace and civilization to the continent as the realization of Kant's *ius cosmopoliticum* was intended to bring to the entire world.[24] Like Kant, Napoleon saw his "empire" as a modern version of the confederacies of ancient Greece, and his imperial venture remained, in Fontana's words (chapter 5), "inextricably bound to the revolutionary heritage and with it the universalizing tradition of the Enlightenment." Napoleon's conception of a universal European order was, of course, one that was to be united under a single national sovereign. In this respect, at least, it had much in common with the subsequent attempts of the German Romantics— Novalis, the Schlegel brothers, Adam Müller, even fitfully Madame de Staël—to revive the idea of the old Germanic *Reich* as the instrument of European unification. But just as few Europeans who were not French wished to see themselves incorporated into the Napoleonic empire, so few who were not "Goths" were eager to see a European federalism, in Müller's words, "wearing German colours."[25]

Napoleonic and Proto-Germanic imperialism were not, however, the only discourses of unity offered. "Nationalism," which became the single most powerful language in the postrevolutionary world (and has remained so until this day), could also be harnessed to the older belief in the civilizing and unifying power of commerce. In nineteenth-century Europe, in the aftermath of the Napoleonic wars, a new pluralism arose. It was based less on the kind of annihilation of the historical memory that the French Revolution has supposedly effected and which Ernest Renan believed necessary for the new nationalism, than on a reworking of the Enlightenment vision of a cosmopolitan order sustained by commerce.[26]

Benjamin Constant gave the most powerful expression to this new pluralism. In Constant's view, as Biancamaria Fontana explains (and Edmund Burke had understood), the revolutionaries, and their ideologues from Rousseau to Saint Just, had attempted to destroy the very real freedom that eighteenth-century commercial society had achieved. In its place they

---

[24] See Biancamaria Fontana's chapter in this volume.

[25] Adam Müller, *Die Elemente der Staatskunst* (Wien–Leipzig: Wiener lierarische anstalt, 1922), 26–9.

[26] Ernest Renan, "L'oubli et je dirais même, l'erreur historique sont un facteur essentiel de la création d'une nation," in *Qu'est-ce qu'une nation?* (Paris, 1882).

had installed the fiction of a society based upon virtue and a common will. They had sought to replace a sense of the nation as a *patria* (as, in Constant's words, "a vivid attachment to the interests, the way of life, the customs of some locality") with "a factitious passion for an abstract being, a general idea stripped of all that can engage the imagination and speak to the memory."[27] Constant's vision was of an identity based upon loyalty to a common place, where the ties were ones of friendship and kin, and of a shared way of life, rather than the empty abstraction that the Revolution had created. Beyond that men should be true only to their moral objectives. This vision was by no means consistent. But Constant's larger ambition was always, in Fontana's words, for a "Europe of commerce and freedom—where money fled from the constraints of national frontiers, and individuals refused to fight for a cause they did not understand or left their country in search of a better lifestyle or more liberal government."[28]

Like Montesquieu before them (and to some degree Kant), the post-revolution liberals in France hoped that commerce would do what conquest had tried and failed to do: bring homogeneity out of diversity yet without destroying diversity itself. Like Montesquieu, they stressed the variety of the peoples, cultures, and traditions that existed side by side in Europe.[29] The same was true of the Italians Giuseppe Mazzini and Carlo Cattaneo, the Greek Rhigas Velestinlis (as Ariane Chebel d'Appollonia explains in chapter 8), and the Albanian Teofan Noli. This was to be a nationalism based not upon exclusion, but upon a community of cooperative states with strong national identities.

The possibility, at least, of a union with a difference has remained one of the main objectives of all subsequent pan-European projects. If the excesses of the Jacobins ruptured the earlier Enlightenment ambitions for a cosmopolitan world ruled by the interests of commerce, the two world wars performed a similar operation on the post-Napoleonic liberal vision of a "community of peaceful, commerce-oriented European nations united against despotism."[30] When the European Economic Community was created in 1958, it also sought to establish peace, and a security against Europe's all-too-obvious tendencies toward illiberal politics, through a commercial union. Europe, wrote Altiero Spinelli in 1947,

---

[27] In addition to Fontana's chapter in this volume, see Fontana, "The Shaping of Modern Liberty: Commerce and Civilisation in the Writings of Benjamin Constant," *Annales Benjamin Constant* 5 (1985): 2–15.

[28] See Fontana's chapter in this volume.

[29] See Fontana's chapter; see also Montesquieu, *De l'Esprit des Lois*, Bk. VI, chap. 1.

[30] See Fontana's chapter in this volume.

had been the "pre-eminent centre of the diffusion of civility throughout the world." It had achieved this position, however, in spite of the fact that throughout its history it had itself been subjected to almost ceaseless "internecine conflicts." A peaceful federalized Europe would therefore constitute the "greatest possible step towards world peace which can be achieved in the present circumstances."[31]

Not only had the Revolution and the Revolutionary Wars threatened to destroy forever the world of free commercial states. They had also made possible another kind of imperialism overseas, one that lacked all the ecumenical ambitions that Constant and others had had for a future postimperial Europe. The great empires of the nineteenth century—the British, the French, the Dutch, the German—although outwardly possessed of many of the trappings of neoclassical universalism that had marked the "first" European settlements in America, were as much the creations of a new nationalism as Napoleon's European empire had been. Unlike most of their early-modern predecessors, however, these new overseas ventures evolved out of former commercial enterprises. The Dutch, the British, and to a lesser degree the French East India Companies had all begun as limited seaborne organizations occupying "factories" that were overwhelmingly multinational and that operated in areas where the Europeans were one group of foreign merchants among many. The ambitions of the British East Indian Company, for instance, had their origins in the same commercial distrust of colonization that Edmund Burke and Adam Smith had voiced about the British Empire in America. Gradually, however, these modest settlements were transformed into colonies; in the British and Dutch cases, they came finally to constitute the basis for a new imperial project.[32] When in 1858 the British Crown imposed direct rule over India, this represented precisely the seizure of power by a centralized bureaucratic state from a group of largely independent "aristocratic republicans." In the attempt to safeguard their privileges, the directors of the East India Company even resorted to the language of country-party opposition that the American revolutionaries had used seventy years before. After the 1880s the new European nations began another period of fierce overseas competition that would only be resolved finally—and one hopes irrevocably—by the two world wars. Since the early seventeenth

---

[31] Altiero Spinelli, "Gli Stati Uniti d'Europa," in Sergio Pistone, ed., *Una Strategia per gli Stati Uniti d'Europa* (Bologna: Il Mulino, 1989), 41.

[32] K. N. Chaudhuri, *The Trading World of Asia and the English East-India Company, 1660–1760* (Cambridge: Cambridge University Press, 1978); and P. J. Marshall, *Trade and Conquest: Studies in the Rise of British Dominance* (Aldershot: Variorum, 1993).

century, imperial successes provided the European peoples with a sense of their own collective identity as creators and technologists. Those very successes have also provided the most powerful reason for competition between them.

A MODERN EUROPEAN IDENTITY

Europeans, therefore, have more than a shared past; they have a shared history of antagonisms to overcome. The present attempt to fabricate a modern European identity must be able to obliterate not only the now remote struggles for control of Europe or for empire overseas, but also the more immediate experience of two world wars, in particular of World War II. For the exiled members of the German Social Democrats and the Christian Democrats in the 1930s and 1940s, as well as for countless other liberals across Europe at that time, "Europe's 'other' was Nazi Germany."[33] Now, for the first time, western Europeans are confronted by a need to create for themselves a new postwar political culture. It now matters what being "European" is and is not.

The European Union, and any future federalized "United States of Europe" (should such a thing come to be), cannot survive unless, as Ariane Chebel d'Appollonia (chapter 8) argues, it can generate some level of attachment to itself as a new political project. More than a vision of a "just political and social order," in Risse and Engelmann-Martin's words, is needed. What is required is a vision of a political and social order that is more just and economically, culturally, intellectually, and aesthetically more compelling than the order currently prevailing in any of the independent nation-states. Peoples, in short, do not willingly surrender their cultural and normative allegiances to their nation or their political system in order to exchange it for one that is neither better nor worse. They do so only in the hope of a brighter future. As Philip Ruttley explains in chapter 11 on the juridical development of the Union, the original EEC treaty, the Merger Treaty of 1965, made this plain in stressing the intention of the Community to promote "a harmonious and balanced development of economic activities" with a view to "raising the standard of living and the quality of life."

To say that people are likely to endorse the conception of a new Europe only if that can provide an improved "quality of life" is not to conflate

---

[33] See Risse and Engelmann-Martin's chapter as well as Tony Judt, "The Past is Another Country: Myth and Memory in Post-war Europe," *Daedalus* 121 (1992): 4.

(in Friedrich Meinecke's old but still serviceable distinction) the *Staatsnation* with the *Kulturnation*.[34] One of the basic tenets of European nationalism was (and in many places still is) that "the boundaries of the state must correspond to those of the nation" (Talal Asad's words). Nation-building, particularly in the postcolonial world, has been conceived as "striving to make culture and polity congruent, to endow a culture with its own political roof, and not more than one roof at that."[35] But it is not necessarily so. Shocked by the Terror and faced with the prospect of nascent German nationalism at the end of the eighteenth century, Goethe urged upon his countrymen the salutary image of a culture of many "voices" with many political centres in place of a single nation-state. This vision was reiterated by the novelist Günter Grass when, after 1989, he found himself confronted with the spectre of another quest for a unified German state. And what applies so markedly to Germany, applies for the other nations of Europe. Today we are learning to live in a world in which the nation-state, although still robust, may not be the final stage in some long historical experiment. It may turn out to be only one political agency among many. If the European Union is to work at all, Europeans will have to accept that it is perfectly possible to be, say, French or Spanish while being ruled from Brussels or Strasbourg by multinational institutions. In a sense the only secure defense against the dangers of nationalism is to ensure in this way that the "cultural-state" and the "nation-state" are kept separate.

I therefore disagree with the general principle behind James Tully's claim in chapter 15 that "the equal recognition and respect of their cultural identities require different institutions of self-government." By "their," Tully refers to the position of the remaining Aboriginal peoples of the world—precisely the victims of European imperialism. Unlike the Europeans who are without their consent being asked to *share* only political sovereignty, the Aboriginal peoples have been deprived of sovereignty of any kind, and under alien legal systems that they did not understand. Self-determination for them is clearly an unquestionable right. (It is perhaps less clear, however, that the language in which that right is pressed should be, once again, that of European nationalism merely because the rights of the peoples in Asia and Africa who have succeeded in gaining self-determination were also made in that language.)

---

[34] Friedrich Meinecke, *Weltbürgertum und Nationalstaat. Studien zur Genesis des deutschen Nationalstaates* (Munich-Berlin: Druck un Verlag von R. Oldenbourg, 1915), 124–57.

[35] Ernest Gellner, *Nations and Nationalism* (Ithaca, New York: Cornell University Press, 1983), 43.

Within Europe any claim to an indissoluble communality between state and culture can be nothing other than an impediment to the political union, the plurality in unity—*e pluribus unum*—that is as much the objective of the new Europe as it was in the eighteenth century of the new America. Furthermore, within postwar Europe, as within Kant's ideal confederation, all the states have more or less the same type of government. Certainly all are committed to the principles of liberal democracy. (What will happen in this respect when the Union expands toward the East—as it must surely do—is still an open question.) As Saint Simon saw at the time of the Congress of Vienna, a unity something like the one that he believed to have existed in Europe before the Reformation could be recreated only if it replaced the force of religious belief by the politics of liberalism, and the institutions of the Church by those of parliamentary democracy.[36] So long as our political institutions are roughly comparable, we have no need to invest those institutions with the features of our culture, nor do we need to insist that all of us who share a common culture—an increasingly difficult position for any modern Europe state to maintain—should be ruled only by "our" people.

Euroskeptics who claim that the legislative and political activities of the Union are a threat to local cultural difference take a rigidly undifferentiated and highly impoverished view of what a culture is. French "culture" is more than a dedication to unpasteurized cheeses, and "British"—or more accurately "English"—culture is more than the desire to ride in double-decker buses. And can any people's cultural identity be seriously compromised by the disappearance of so recent a creation as the deutschemark? Of course, as Thomas Risse and Daniela Engelmann-Martin argue (chapter 13), the dedication to the mark is a dedication to the prime symbol of German resurgence after World War II. The Deutsche Mark, however, cannot be described as an integral part of German *culture*. More serious might be the British claim—although it has never been expressed as such—that *not* participating in, for instance, a charter of human rights was, as integral a part of British culture as an unwritten constitution. Once again culture is assumed to be static and whole, whereas most cultures are, as James Tully has argued elsewhere so powerfully, constantly evolving and endlessly porous.[37]

---

[36] Saint-Simon, "De la réorganisation de la société européenne," 165–8.
[37] See James Tully, *Strange Multiplicity: Constitutionalism in an Age of Diversity* (Cambridge: Cambridge University Press, 1995), 11–15, and his chapter in this book.

Despite this porousness, despite the learning in the past two decades of the kind of differences that create antagonism and impede recognition, some sense of "national identity" remains a significant part of the lives of most Europeans. Christine Korsgaard's definition of identity as "a description under which you value yourself" suggests that cultures possess the same capacity for autonomous self-reflection as citizenship is supposed to possess.[38] But it is hard to see how this can be case. Belonging to a culture, having an identity of any kind, necessitates limiting choice in ways that can only be partly voluntary. In all cultural exchanges there is always more than one actor. I do not choose my culture or even have it thrust upon me. I choose it, or I accept it, in the presence of a third party, in the gaze of someone. This is the point of Rousseau and Kant's roughly similar accounts of the origins of all society. It is our desire for recognition by all those whom, in Kant's words, we "cannot *bear*, yet cannot *bear to leave*," which first drove our ancestors to form societies and which continues to constitute our place within them.[39] A similar difficulty arises with Tully's hope that "a citizen or a people will be the bearer of more than one culture, of multiple cultural identities" (chapter 15). To have a cultural identity in the first place is to pledge allegiance to the "power of cultural imposition." A citizen who could literally elect to be, say, German or Portuguese, or who could choose to be some mixture of Portuguese and German, would first have to have some position from which he or she could make such a choice. She would have to be a cosmopolitan in the most literal sense. And having been that, it is hard to see why such a person would wish to become either Portuguese or German. It is equally difficult to see by what route she would realize that choice. Of course, many people—international monetary agents and merchant banks are largely staffed by them—speak several languages with equal ease and share several cultural features. But that, at least for the purposes of building a new European identity, is not the same thing as being a "bearer of more than one culture."

To create a genuinely transnational identity, a genuinely European "culture," means blending the features of existing European cultures into a new whole. To claim, as Agnes Heller has done, that there is not now, and by implication never can be, a "European culture"—that "there is Italian and German music, there is Florentine and Venetian painting, but

---

[38] Christine Korsgaard quoted by Tully in his chapter.
[39] "Idea for a Universal History with a Cosmopolitan Purpose," in *Kant Political Writings*, 44.

there is no European music and no Europen painting"—requires one to take a very restricted view of what might count as "European."[40] Paradoxically seen from within Europe, the differences that separate German from Italian culture are easy enough to perceive. Viewed from, say, Japan, those differences will seem less obvious than the similarities. Viewed from Europe there may be no such thing as a "European culture." Viewed from Japan there clearly is. What the new Europe must generate is a sense of belonging that retains the Japanese eye-view, a sense of belonging that can perceive diversity while giving allegiance to that which is shared. Of course, what is to be shared will have to be rather more developed, rather more obvious than it is at present. It will have to be capable of inspiring a similar degree of attachment to "Europe" as the older nationalism did to the nation. It will have, that is, to create a sense of belonging that is not merely imposed from outside. As Ariane Chebel d'Appollonia points out in chapter 8, however, the concern with European issues, even within the more Europhile of nations, is still low. (One example is the low turnout in European elections.) For most in today's Europe, "Europe" has as much resonance as "France" or "England" or "Castile" would have had for a sixteenth-century farmer. That need not, however, be a serious impediment to the eventual elaboration of a more compelling image of Europe than the one that exists at present. Attachment has always been a relative affair. Most peoples everywhere care more for their locality than they do for their nation, and more for their nation than they do for any larger and more abstract notion such as "Europe." But that is not to say that identity with "Europe" is an impossible objective. Nor is it the case, as most of the critics of "Europe" have supposed, that alliegiance to "Europe" must preclude or over-rule allegiance to, say, Spain or Italy. In certain highly specific instances, the interests of "Europe" will take precedence over those of Athens or Dublin: they do so already, just as there have always existed conflicts between national and regional interests. To share sovereignty is not to surrender it.

AGENCIES OF IDENTITY

Constructing from local identities a universal identity—and the political culture required to sustain it—involves assembling and reordering pieces of national myths and histories to form new ones. These have to be made

---

[40] Agnes Heller, " Europe: An Epilogue?" in Brian Nelson, David Roberts, and Walter Veit, eds., *The Idea of Europe: Problems of National and Transnational Identity* (New York and London: Berg, 1992), 23–4.

up as we go along. As Michael Herzfeld says in chapter 7, "selfhood is deeply invested in claims on emblematic symbols of restricted availability." At present these symbols are barely available for Europe. To ask an individual, let alone an entire people, to be "European" is not like asking an immigrant to the United States to become "American." However fluid, volatile, and precarious American national identity might be, it exists, if only as a vaguely existential notion, prior to the arrival of the immigrant. Over time she will have a considerable impact upon what being "American" involves, but she is not being asked to participate in the initial process of self-definition. She acquires a flag, an anthem, a rhetoric of self-presentation, a system of laws and courts, and a political culture. Although many of those things also exist for Europe, they are, as Chebel d'Appollonia points out, still rudimentary. How many people know the words of the European "national" anthem, or even that such a thing exists? Nearly all the symbols of European unity are forced to compete with the much more familiar national versions. These versions, as Herzfeld suggests, are all too often conceived as a form of property that leads to the "reification of culture as a national possession." Once made in this way into a possession, local cultures become very hard to surrender.

Creating a modern European identity has, therefore, little in common with the processes used by the only other modern peoples who have been faced with a similar need to create or fabricate an identity for themselves: the settler and indigenous populations of the former European colonies in the Americas or the indigenous populations of the former European colonies in Africa and Asia. Both these groups constructed "imagined communities"—in Benedict Anderson's now celebrated term—that were American, or Argentinean, or Nigerian, or Pakistani out of a *bricolage* of cultural symbols and beliefs.[41] At the same time they struggled to build a political order that would both reflect and sustain the aspirations of their new societies. They had their own narratives of foundation, most of which were inscribed in histories of liberation from their colonial masters and embodied in national heroes: Washington, Bolívar, Gandhi, Nehru, Sukarno, Kenyata, or, from a slightly different perspective, Nasser and Castro.

Although the new Europe also has its origins in the resolution of conflict, this conflict has only been internal. There can be, therefore, no "national" heroes (close as Jean Monnet comes to being one), no

---

[41] Benedict Anderson, *Imagined Communities: Reflections on the Origin and Spread of Nationalism*, rev. ed. (London–New York: Verso, 1991).

stirring narratives of independence or origination. (Who could be moved by the story of the creation of the European Coal and Steel Foundation?) The history of Europe is the collective history of all its parts. Inventing the European community involves imagining Europe *as* a community, and this, as Herzfeld suggests, depends on all its members recognizing the similarities they do share. The nineteenth-century French historian François Guizot, in Herzfeld's words, "got around this difficulty by arguing, in effect, that what made Europeans all alike was their shared capacity for being different." Although this—like the possibility that Europeans have for situating themselves firmly within some wider world—provides for a measure of self-description, it is hardly the basis for a distinctive culture.

The question remains: who, or what, is to be the agent of the new self-awareness? Clearly—if we are to maintain the necessary distinction between *Staatsnation* and *Kulturnation*—it cannot be the state. But it cannot be the Church, the family, or the parish either. Cultural values are, as Jürgen Habermas has argued, "always components of intersubjectively shared traditions," and because of this "the revision of the values used to interpret needs and wants cannot be a matter for individuals to handle monologically."[42] If, as the European Court of Justice has ruled, the Union is a "Community not only of States but also of peoples and persons" equally subject to a common rule of law, then what must eventually be required is a new mode of citizenship.[43] And this can be achieved only in the course of a dialogue between those involved. As Thomas Risse and Daniela Engelmann-Martin (chapter 13) and Elie Cohen (chapter 12) stress, the difficulty in actual practice is that all the attempts to "construct Europe," and with it a notion of European citizenship, have been the work of elites—elites composed of "experts" whose work has generally been conducted behind closed doors.

Philip Ruttley (chapter 11) demonstrates just how much of the process of integration has been a juridical one. In this, too, the Union is unlike any previous political creation. Whereas all the former colonial states were constitutional creations (as is the EU), their constitutions were a general expression of identity among the people. In the United States the constitution has acquired sacral status. In some cases—gun control, for instance—this has led to a degree of fetishization that has impeded the development of the community for which it was written. In parts of Africa

---

[42] Habermas quoted by Tully in chapter 15.
[43] The European Court of Justice is quoted by Ruttley in chapter 11. See also Tully's chapter.

and Asia constitutions written by one ethnic group have been used to tyrannize another. But nowhere, except in Europe, has the "constitution" been the creation of a series of treaties that, by their sheer complexity, have been made inaccessible to the bulk of the population in whose name they have been drafted.

In chapter 12 Elie Cohen traces the history, and vicissitudes, of the Single European Currency, perhaps the most contentious, and potentially most hazardous, attempt to create a new European social and political community. Here what Herzfeld calls the "capacity of ordinary social actors to recast and reconfigure received orthodoxies" is severely restricted. What the "ordinary social actor" does (informed or more often misinformed by his or her national press) is to recast the received orthodoxy as a form of conspiracy. The institutions of the Union, and the increasingly complex languages that sustain them, are beyond the range of most of the peoples of the various nation-states. Public debate on "the question of Europe" is lamentably restricted in most European countries and virtually nonexistent in some such as Britain. This is due not only to public apathy fueled by the habitual secrecy of all state bureaucracies. It is also due to the complexity, and the unfamiliarity, of much of the current political structure of the Union. Structurally, at least, the European Parliament bears little resemblance to national parliaments anywhere in the world. The European Court of Justice is primarily an institution whose purpose is to adjudicate decisions made by functionaries who are not subject to democratic accountability. This is because, as Philip Ruttley explains, they come from bureaucratic cultures in which efficiency is valued over accountability, and because they have no equivalents in any existing democratic society. The European Court of Justice is far closer to the U.S. Supreme Court than to any European judicial body. It has the essentially political power to extend the power of community institutions, most specifically that of the European Parliament, and, staffed largely by judges with marked federalist sympathies, it has been responsible, in Ruttley's words, for "nudging forward" the process of European unification.

If "Europe" is to become the location of political as well as cultural allegiance, it will need to be far better understood than it is. It will need, as Habermas has insisted, the kind of dialogue that exists, if sometimes only fitfully, within most democratic states—namely, the dialogue between the citizens and the institutions of the state and among the citizens themselves. That this is also an objective shared by most of the builders of Europe is, as Ruttley argues, evident from the terms of the treaties of Maastricht (1992) and Amsterdam (1997). These require that all decisions taken within the Union be made "as openly as possible." They call for the advancement of "freedom, security, and justice," and they have committed the Union to a struggle against discrimination on grounds of "sex, race, ethnic origin, religion, belief, disability, or sexual orientation." The treaties have made, in Ruttley's word, the "ever closer union among the peoples of Europe an integrative process flowing in only one (federalist) direction." As yet, however, despite these good intentions, the dialogue, when it does occur, tends to be between the representatives of the member states, rather than between "the rulers"—however defined—and "the people"—however understood—of the Union.

What will finally come about if any wider dialogical situation does emerge is still uncertain. It must surely be not just another political identity, but a new kind of identity, as nationalism was in the nineteenth century. Already, in the words of the European Court of Justice, the European Union "constitutes a new legal order within international law." If the Union is to make that legal order into something with which all those who live by it can identify, it will have to learn to do without local heroes and without an historical narrative based upon significant moments of creation. It will, in short, have to be capable of transforming "internationalism" and "cosmopolitanism" from the vague yearnings they currently are into more concrete, more persuasive modes of civil and political association.

To do that, the peoples of Europe will have to abandon the ancient concept of sovereignty as, in Hobbes's phrase "incommunicable and inseparable."[44] They will need to be able to accept that a parliament composed of representatives of various nationalities does indeed *represent* each of those nationalities and is not, as some seem to think, an organ of a federation run in the interests of a single national group. Parliamentary representation has always been limited and fragmentary, and few national parliaments have been a source of enduring national awareness, except perhaps in the imagination of those who live by them. But they can provide a focus of political concern and political loyalties. Therefore, there is no obvious reason why, as Chebel d'Appollonia suggests, a European Parliament should not come to represent a distinctive Europeanness shared by Greeks, Germans, and French alike. In order to do that, however, it would have to be something rather more distinctive

---

[44] Thomas Hobbes, *Leviathan*, ed. Richard Tuck (Cambridge: Cambridge University Press, 1991), 127.

than the current European Parliament. Its relative powerlessness with respect to the European Commission rightly arouses concern about the degree to which it can be said to represent those who vote for it. As Ruttley points out, the executive power of the Commission and the judicial activism of the European Court of Justice conflict with the beliefs of some states, most obviously Britain and Denmark, on "the separation of powers and the noninterventionist nature of the judiciary." Both the Commission and the European Court of Justice are essentially French creations. Their ideological origins are to be found in the ambition of eighteenth- and nineteenth-century rationalists, from Francois Quesnay to Saint-Simon, for a "despotism" of the law, for a rational and efficient administration that would ultimately dispense with the messiness, brutality, and particularism of politics.[45] But neither enlightened despotism nor the attractions of Alexander Pope's "whatever's best administered is best" can create a place of loyalty or offer a source of political identity.

The European Union may evolve into something more than the extension of national administrative structures and nationalist sentiments to a multinational geographical area. In the process of establishing what is already a quite new federal structure, Europe may create a new politics, one in which identity expressed in collective terms ceases to be of much political significance. It is fully possible to conceive of a federalism in which the citizens can agree on those matters that touch them all—defense, security, welfare, communications, and so on—with no concern for the origins of the people who act in their name. The close association between politics and culture, and the assumption that both are determinants of something called "identity," are after all a creation of the postrevolutionary representative state. It is possible to think of politics in the same context as identity, only if you believe that politics—and politicians—actually represent *you*. This is frequently taken to mean allowing another to stand in for you. This, in turn, requires that this person not merely act in your name and on your behalf but also in some sense resemble you: speak your language, share your tastes, share the same moral imperatives or (where this is of concern) the same religious beliefs. But, as Benjamin Constant argued in his famous essay entitled "The Liberty of the Ancients Compared with that of the Moderns," the evolution of modern societies, which were largely commercial and generally liberal, made it necessary to

---

[45] See the comments by Tony Judt, *A Grand Illusion? An Essay on Europe* (New York: Penguin Books, 1996), 115.

distinguish between the private person, the "private citizen," and the public actor.[46] Modern liberty was not like the "ancient" liberty that Rousseau had imagined and Robespierre and St. Just had tried to make a reality. That was a liberty in which the citizen was obliged to subsume his—and it was always his—private person into the collective identity of the state. With hindsight it is obvious that what Constant in 1819 believed the modern states of Europe (and the United States of America) were on the verge of becoming has still to be realized fully. True, with the collapse of the Soviet Union, there are no longer any Rousseauian republics left in Europe. But nationalism, various forms of modern communitarianism, and the resurgence in some places of a new kind of "republicanism" as a substitute for the old Marxism still carry with them traces of what Bernard Williams has called "St. Just's illusion."[47]

It is by no means clear that the European Union has the possibility—or the collective will—to create for itself a new kind of federalism. But by insisting that persons from various cultural backgrounds can represent each other, by emptying (as far as possible) most kinds of political discourse of moral or religious referent, and by severing "culture" from the nation, the European Union has established principles upon which Constant's "modern republic" could finally be built. J. G. A. Pocock may well be right in saying that the Union must inevitably transform individuals from citizens into consumers, and that "Europe, the cradle of the state, may be about to discover what it is like to do without it"—although not perhaps in the way he intends.

"Doing without the state" may sound sinister to those who have every reason to be content with belonging to large, powerful, and centralized political societies. But there are those, and they are by no means culturally insignificant, who have everything to gain from total immersion in a new European sense of self. As Luisa Passerini (chapter 9) explains, for feminists such a Rosi Braidotti or Ursula Hirschmann "being European" can mean turning the "historical contradictions of a European identity" into "spaces of critical resistance to hegemonic identities of all kinds."[48]

What is true at the personal level may be true at the community level—although here the benefits to be gained are far less certain. Attempts at

---

[46] *The Liberty of the Ancients Compared to that of the Moderns*, a speech delivered to the Athénée Royale in Paris in 1819, in Benjamin Constant, *Political Writings*, ed. Biancamaria Fontana (Cambridge: Cambridge University Press, 1988), 309–28.

[47] Bernard Williams, *Making Sense of Humanity and Other Philosophical Papers, 1982–1993* (Cambridge: Cambridge University Press, 1995), 135–50.

[48] Quoted in Luisa Passerini's chapter.

totalitarian centralization in some parts of Europe, primarily Italy and Spain, have heightened regionalism, a form of "nationalism" within the state, which has now spread to other states (France and Britain, for example), which were once thought to be wholly stable communities. Most separatist or semiseparatist groups from Scotland to Sicily have seen in Europe a means of establishing their claims against central governments now viewed as "foreign" powers. Catalans and Basques, Lombards and Piedmontese, can agree to be European more easily than they can agree to be either Italians or Spanish. Members of both the Welsh and Scottish nationalist parties are eager to present themselves as good Europeans, and to avail themselves, wherever possible, of the institutions of the Union against those of the parliament in Westminster.

The problem with this, however, is that the Europe imagined by nationalists and proto-nationalists alike does not yet exist, as Andrés de Blas Guerrero explains (chapter 14), and it is highly unlikely that an assembly of autonomous regions will be in a position to bring it about. As Giuseppe Mazzini observed in the late nineteenth century of the first movement toward a consolidated, if not yet united, Europe, the creation of pan-national Europe could only be the creation of the nation itself. Instead of gaining increased self-hood (which, rather than political or economic advancement, is primarily what they seek), the small nations of Europe will find themselves increasingly marginalized by the larger ones. It is highly unlikely that Scotch or Catalan will become community languages, any more than Irish has. If the Union increases toward the East, which it surely must, this can only disadvantage still further the interests of the small nations, which will find themselves similarly swamped by larger and more powerful voices.

The European Union, like the EEC, has largely been created by states in their own image, as Ruttley shows. Politically, the Union is a unique institution. It has the exterior shape of a confederation of states but features of a nation-state. Like the federal government of the United States, it possesses an international legal personality (as does any state), and it can enter into diplomatic relations with sovereign states (as can other states). And as its critics frequently point out, the Union, in many crucial areas, has usurped the independent legislative powers of its member states. In this respect, as Michael Walzer has pointed out, it differs markedly from the older European empires, which generally tolerated a variety of different legal cultures within their midst. Practices that were formerly tolerated within individual member states will inevitably become unacceptable within the legal order of the Union, with some far-reaching social consequences.[49] The hope, therefore, that a structure whose purpose is to bring about the end of the nation-state in its present form would be able to offer Europe's "smaller nations" the kind of antiquated national identity most of them seek, would seem to be at best a vain one.

None of the essays in this volume pretends to offer a consolidated vision of the future. Whether one shares the optimism of the federalist or the scepticism of those who still hope that "Europe" will remain little more than an economic expression, one can detect a very gradual transition from a Europe of competing and frequently hostile nations to a "Union" of peoples. (This transition, however, is not as slow as some suppose. It is doubtful that even Monnet and Spinelli could have hoped for the degree of integration implied by the Maastricht Treaty.) As Friedrich Nietzsche had seen more than a century ago, the speed of modern communications, the rapid dissolution of the artificial boundaries between the peoples of Europe, could only lead, or so he passionately hoped, to the "abolition of nations." The Europe of Nietzsche's "Good European" may still be a thing of the future. But the "idea" of Europe is very much with us now.[50]

[49] Michael Walzer, *On Toleration* (New Haven and London: Yale University Press, 1997), 49.
[50] Friedrich Nietzsche, *Human, All Too Human: A Book for Free Spirits*, trans. R. J. Hollingdale (Cambridge: Cambridge University Press, 1986), 174–5.

1

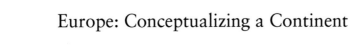

Europe: Conceptualizing a Continent

ANTHONY PAGDEN

The identity of "Europe" has always been uncertain and imprecise, a source of pride for some and hatred or contempt for others. Like all identities it is a construction, an elaborate palimpsest of stories, images, resonances, collective memories, invented and carefully nurtured traditions. It is also particularly elusive because continents, far more than nations, tend to be simply geographical expressions. In recent times, postcolonial times, collective identities—at least in the face of opposition—have become commonplace elsewhere. But before the nineteenth century few would have said that they were "Asian" or "African," and—something that the peoples of the United States tend to forget—"American" has always been carefully qualified in virtually every language but English. Only Europeans have persistently described themselves, usually when faced with cultures they found indescribably alien, to be not merely British or German or Spanish but also European: "we Europeans" (*nos Europai*), as the English philosopher Francis Bacon said in 1623.[1]

Because it is collective, there are those who have argued that any such thing as a "European" identity is, at best, an illusion. "Europe" now exists as an economic, and increasingly political, entity. But this has no wider cultural or affective meaning. It merely describes the signatory states of the Maastricht Treaty. Yet if that is all Europe was now, or had ever been, the Maastricht Treaty would never have come into being. For behind the limited, practical conditions that have brought together a series of postwar states on the continent of Europe into a loose federation lies a very long history.

The origins of this history are to be found in a fictional but forever compelling story, one of abduction, and of a metamorphosis. It is the

---

[1] Francis Bacon quoted in John Hale, *The Civilization of Europe in the Renaissance* (London: HarperCollins, 1993), 3.

story of Europa, daughter of Agenor, king of the city of Tyre on the coast of Sidon. One fine day she was carried off by Zeus, transformed into a white bull. Zeus deposited her, and ravished her, on the shore of the continent that would bear their offspring and her name. This is the myth. As with all myths, however, there is another more mundane version. It was suggested by the Greek writer Herodotus and later seized upon by the early Christian theologian Lactantius, eager to debunk and demystify such unsettling erotic fantasies from the ancient world. In this version Cretan merchants abduct Europa in a ship shaped like a bull and take her to be a bride for their king Asterius. Since the Cretans are what later generations would come to call "Europeans," and Europa herself an Asian woman, her abduction was taken by all Asians to be an affront. Later the Trojans, also a people of what we now call Asia Minor, seize a (not wholly unwilling) Helen, wife of Menelaus, in revenge. In turn, Menelaus's brother, Agamemnon, raises an army, crosses the sea, and begins the most celebrated war in European history. The Persians, Herodotus tells us (and "Persians" is his shorthand for all the peoples of Asia), found this tale of abduction puzzling. "We in Asia," they say, "regarded the rape of our women not at all," thus establishing an enduring Asian cultural stereotype, "but the Greeks all for the sake of a Lacedaemonian woman mustered a great host, came to Asia and destroyed the power of Priam. Ever since then we have regarded the Greeks as our enemies."[2] What in myth had been a divine appropriation becomes in mythopoeic history a tale of the hatred between two continents, a hatred that would burn steadily down the centuries, as the Trojans were succeeded by the Phoenicians, the Phoenicians by the Ottoman Turks, and the Turks by Russians.

No myth, however, is as simple as that. Most myths are tales of metamorphoses where everything is not merely not all it seems but is frequently its very opposite. For fleeing from the ruins of Troy, with his father Anchises on his back and leading his son Ascanius by his hand, comes Aeneas, who years later will land on the shores of Latium and found the city and the state of Rome. It is Rome that will be the true creator of "Europe." But Rome, too, will try to shed its mythopoeic "oriental" identity. When Virgil, in the first century CE, came to write the *Aeneid* under the emperor Augustus, he told another story that would preserve the link with Troy while at the same time effacing all traces of Trojan identity. In the twelfth and final book of the poem, the gods, who have

---

[2] *Histories*, I, 3–4.

(as gods do) taken different sides in the struggles between the invading Trojans and the native Latins, decide to bring the war to an end. Juno, who has supported the Latins, finally agrees to allow the two peoples to intermarry and thereby create a new race. But she insists that his new race will look like the Latins, will dress like the Latins, will speak like the Latins, and their customs—their *mores*—will be Latin. All they will preserve of their oriental ancestors will be their gods, for those gods were also the gods of the Greeks, and the common patrimony of all humankind.[3] Europe, which will fashion itself for generations in opposition to Asia, has always owed to Asia its historical origins.

This sense of double ambiguity survives even the collapse of the political structures of the Graeco-Roman world and the dominance of Graeco-Roman origin myths. Christianity was to provide Europe with much of its subsequent sense of both internal cohesion and its relationship with the rest of the world, and Christianity began as an Asian religion. "Jesus Christ, who is the way the truth and the life, has long since given the Bill of Divorce to ingrateful Asia where he was born and of Africa the place of his flight and refuge, and has become almost wholly European," wrote Samuel Purchas, the English propagandist for the settlement of America, in 1625 in an attempt to secure the glory of Christ's apostolate, and of the overseas mission, exclusively for Europe.[4] "Almost wholly" because not even Purchas could entirely discount the existence of the Greek and Russian Churches and their failure to submit to the authority of the Papacy or, as the English fitfully hoped, convert to Protestantism. The fact that the undeniably Christian adherents of Greek Orthodoxy had for long been under Ottoman rule, and thus fully absorbed into Asia, remained an additional reminder of the alien origin of Christianity. Greek and Russian Christianity, as J. G. A Pocock reminds us in this volume, would always be a threat to any sustained attempt to fabricate a single European identity with a single origin.

Thus an abducted Asian woman gave Europe her name; a vagrant Asian exile gave Europe its political and finally it cultural identity; and an Asian prophet gave Europe its religion. As Hegel was later to observe, Europe was "the centre and end" of History, but History had begun in Asia: "characteristically the *Orient* quarter of the globe—the region of

---

[3] *Aeneid*, XII, 808–42. I would like to thank Maurizio Bettini for drawing this passage, and its significance, to my attention.

[4] Samuel Purchas, *Hakluytus Posthumus or Purchas his Pilgrimes, Contayning a History of the World, in Sea Voyages and Lande-Travells by Englishmen & Others*, 5 vols. (London, 1625), I, 45.

origination."[5] The course of civilization, like that of empire and the sun itself, moves inexorably from East to West.

In the beginning, however, the world was divided not into two but three: Europe, Asia, and "Libya," as Africa was generally called (although as Herodotus, the first to travel well beyond the limits of his own home and who reveled in the oddities of the behavior of those he found there, complained, with characteristic Greek misogyny, he could not conceive "why three names, and women's names at that, should have been given to a tract which is in reality one)."[6] For most Greeks the difference between what they called Europe—by which they frequently if not consistently meant Hellas, the lands around the Aegean Sea—and Asia or Africa would remain, as it had been for Aeschylus, one not only of climate and disposition, but also of race (*ethnos*). Herodotus, however, had understood that "Europe" had no natural frontiers and that, as most subsequent cosmopolitans came to realize through experience, cultures are never so incommensurable as their members often like to suppose. If "Europe" had come to acquire an identity, it was always one that had to accommodate the uneasy realization that not only were the origins of Europe non-European, but that no one could establish with any precision where Europe stopped and Asia and Africa began.

If this geographical uncertainty meant that the landmass of Europe could not be said to be at the center of the world, it still could be placed at the center of some other conceptualization of the environment. For the Greeks and their Roman heirs, the means of establishing a relationship between them and the rest of humanity frequently rested upon a complex theory of climate and physical environment. The northern parts of the world, according to this theory, were inhabited by peoples whose inhospitable climates had made them brave and warlike, but also uncouth, unthinking, and—to use the Latinized term that will become central to all modes of European self-fashioning—"uncivilized." Those who lived in the South—the Asians—were, by contrast, quick-witted, intelligent, but also lethargic, slow to act, and ultimately corrupt—a claim that became in time another enduring stereotype of the "Oriental." Europeans (then the peoples of the Mediterranean), living as they did midway between these extremes, are the mean. This conception of Europe, much modified it is true, but still insistent on the radical distinction between North and South, retained its imaginative force until at least the nineteenth century.

---

[5] G. W. F. Hegel, *The Philosophy of History*, trans. J. Sibree (New York: Dover Publications, 1956), 99–101.

[6] *Histories*, VII, 104.

(The current use of the terms by the United Nations and international aid agencies to mean, roughly, the "developed" and the "developing" worlds is perhaps unintentionally a continuation of the same distinction.) Even Hegel, writing in the 1830s from the viewpoint of an intellectually and culturally emergent North, could still speak confidently of the Mediterranean as the "uniting element" of "three quarters of the globe" and "the centre of World-History"—once, that is, he had relegated America firmly to the domain of the future, "where in the ages that lie before us, the burden of the World's History shall reveal itself."[7] As late as the 1960s, the great French historian Fernand Braudel was able to refer (with no trace of irony) to the Mediterranean as the "radiant centre" of the entire globe, "whose light grows less as one moves away from it, without one's being able to define the exact boundary between light and shade."[8]

"Europe," wrote the first-century Greek geographer Strabo, in the earliest surviving attempt to demonstrate and explain the continent's perception of its superiority over all others, "is both varied in form and admirably adapted by nature for the development of excellence in men and governments." The two instincts in man (the peaceable, which Strabo significantly called the "agricultural and the civilized," and the warlike) live in Europe side by side, and "the one that is peace-loving is more numerous and thus keeps control over the whole body."[9] In Strabo's account the Greek dialectic between the world of nature (*physis*) and that of men (*nomos,* a term that relates to law and custom or as we would say "culture") has been resolved in Europe and only in Europe.

Because of this harmony, Europe becomes—in another image that has survived unbroken to this day—the home of liberty and of true government. The Greeks, Herodotus tells us, are the most free of peoples, because, unlike the Asians, they are subject, not to the will of an individual, but only to the law. European society might have had many forms of government, some of them decidedly less liberal than others, but centuries later Voltaire echoed an enduring commonplace when he claimed that the continent constituted a "kind of great republic divided into several states," all of which were united in having "the same principle of public law and politics, unknown in other parts of the world."[10] As Montesquieu

---

[7] Hegel, *The Philosophy of History,* 86.
[8] Fernand Braudel, *La Méditerranée et le monde méditerranéen a l'époque de Philippe II,* 2d ed. (Paris: Armand Colin, 1966), 2 vols., I, 168.
[9] Strabo, *Geography,* 2.5, 26.
[10] Quoted in Denys Hay, *Europe: The Emergence of an Idea* (Edinburgh: Edinburgh University Press, 1968), 123.

had remarked some years earlier, most of Europe (he was a little uncertain about Spain) is ruled by "custom" (*les moeurs*); Asia, and the still darker regions of Africa and America, by despots.[11]

The rule of law, restraint through custom rather than will, was responsible for the fashioning of societies that provided a space for individual human action, while at the same time ensuring that such action was rarely capable of reducing society to a state of simple anarchy. From this we will see the descent of the notion that all human improvement depends upon conflict, that human beings are, by their nature, competitive creatures, and that only those societies that know how to harness what Kant in the late eighteenth century called man's "unsocial sociability" instead of attempting to suppress it will flourish.[12] As Machiavelli noted, the power of the Roman Republic had derived from the opposition between the Senate and the plebians and not from the exercise of a common will, as so many had supposed.[13] There was from the beginning the conviction, which the modern democratic societies of the West have inherited, that this vision of the world was in the long—if not always in the short—run suitable for all peoples everywhere and that its cultural power was irresistible. This assumption could have emerged only within a collection of societies, which, while being in many significant respects very different from one another, shared the sense of a common identity.

How the highly chauvinist Greeks could speak of themselves as members of a larger grouping of peoples, which must have included non-Greek speakers and thus, in the Greek understanding of the term, "barbarians," is probably impossible to determine. The Greeks, however, had always been peoples on the move (*poluplanês*)—"extreme travellers." Some time in the fifth century BCE, Herodotus traveled to Egypt and Libya, to Babylon and the Phoenician city of Tyre, even to southern Russia, and reported extensively on what he had found there. Phythagoras, the great sixth-century mathematician, journeyed from his native Samos to Egypt and Crete before settling finally in Croton in southern Italy, and the earliest of the ancient geographers, Hecateus of Miletus, visited Egypt even before Herodotus had. By the third century, the rhetorician Isocrates could

---

[11] *De l'esprit des lois*, VIII, 8, *Oeuvres complètes de Montesquieu*, ed. Roger Caillois (Paris: Gallimard, 1951), 2 vols., II, 356.

[12] *Idea for a Universal History with a Cosmopolitan Purpose*, in Hans Reiss, ed., *Kant: Political Writings* (Cambridge: Cambridge University Press, 1971), 44–5.

[13] See Quentin Skinner, "Machiavelli's *Discorsi* and the Pre-humanist Origins of Republican Ideas," in Gisela Bock, Quentin Skinner, and Maurizo Viroli, eds., *Machiavelli and Republicanism* (Cambridge: Cambridge University Press, 1990), 121–41.

confidently declare that being a Hellene was no longer a matter of blood or racial origin, but one of culture and education.[14]

This sense of a possible communion with all the peoples of the inhabited world (*oikoumene*) may have been due, as Strabo suggests, to the fact that Europe could provide for itself all "the fruits that are best and that are necessary for life and all the useful metals" and imported only luxury goods, "species and precious stones" that he says dismissively "make the life of persons who have a scarcity of them fully as happy as those who have them in abundance."[15] Only *Europe* as a continent, crisscrossed by trade routes from East to West, could do this, but none of the many disparate peoples of the Mediterranean could do it alone. Life was so difficult for those peoples that they could survive only by developing the great commercial networks that would become the basis of their future expansion far beyond the limits of Europe. Because of the intense competition that persisted among them, they were all forced into the political unions called the *symmachiai* and *sympoliteiai* that dominated the later world of the Greek city-states, until at the battle of Chaeronea in August 338, Philip of Macedon swept it away altogether. This combination of strength and dependency made the recognition of a shared political culture difficult to withhold. "The cities of Ancient Greece," wrote Edward Gibbon of the origins or modern Europe,

were cast in the happy mixture of union and interdependence which is repeated on a larger scale, but in a looser form, by the nations of modern Europe; the union of religion, language, and manners which renders them spectators and judges of each others' merits; the independence of government and interests, which asserts their separate freedoms, and excites them to strive for pre-eminence in the career of glory.[16]

This political culture was centered upon a unique form of life: the city. Of course, as in most other civilizations, the vast majority of the populations of Europe actually lived and worked in the countryside until well into the nineteenth century. For most of the rural peoples of Europe, and the illiterate majority in the cities themselves, identity was a question of attachment to microcommunities: the parish, the village, the guild, sometimes the country, the *pays* (or what the Castilians aptly called the *patria*

[14] Francois Hartogth, *Mémoires d'Ulysse: Récits sur la frontière en Grèce ancienne* (Paris: Gallimard, 1996), 12–13.

[15] Strabo, *Geography*, 2.5, 26.

[16] Edward Gibbon, *The History of the Decline and Fall of the Roman Empire*, ed. David Wormersley (London: Penguin Books, 1995), I, 106.

chica, the "small homeland"), only rarely the nation, and never, one sus-
pects, such an abstract cultural grouping as "Europe." But for the literate, intellectual elites who had far more in common with similar groups
from other nations than they did with their own peasantry, the spaces
beyond the city walls were, until they became sentimentalized in the mid-
eighteenth century, largely invisible. What Voltaire mockingly called "the
supposed savages of America" were in his view indistinguishable from
those savages one met every day in the countryside, "living in huts with
their mates and a few animals ceaselessly exposed to all the intemperance
of the seasons."[17]

Despite its dependence upon agriculture, despite the real distribution
of its populations, Europe, as a collection of social and political groups
with a shared and historically-determined culture, was conceived as overwhelmingly urban. Our entire political and social vocabulary derives from
this fact. "Politics" and "polity" have their root in the Greek term *polis.*
Similarly, "civil," "civility," and "civilization" have their origins in the
Latin word *civitas,* which describes the same spatial, political, and cultural entity. Both *polis* and *civitas* became, in time, abstract nouns, sometimes translatable as "the state" or the "commonwealth," and definable
in abstract terms. But originally they belonged to a semantic field that
described the urban space itself, and a close association between urban
ways of life and true "civility" persists to this day. Cities were, of course,
by no means unique to Europe. Like all else that defines European culture,
the walled, largely self-governing urban space had originated in Asia.

With the rise of Athens after the sixth century, an association in the
European political *imaginaire* began to form between an urban environment and a particular way of life. Man, said Aristotle, was *zoon
politikon*—quite literally an animal "made for life in the polis." True,
he was not the only such animal. Bears and ants were observed to be
similarly sociable. But his—and in the Greek world it was always his—
way of being in the world was for him not merely the best attainable
existence. It was what the Greeks called "the good life," the only life in
which it was possible for man to achieve his ends *as* a man, to achieve
that elusive goal that Aristotle termed *eudaimonia,* his Latin, Christian
translators, "blessedness," and later writers rendered as "happiness," or
by the clumsy term employed by many modern philosophers, "human
flourishing."

---

[17] Voltaire, *Essai sur les moeurs et l'esprit des nations,* ed. R. Pomeau (Paris: Classiques
Garnier, 1990), 2 vols., I, 23.

Furthermore, true *politeiai* were like the persons who inhabited them, autonomous entities. They were places of *autarkeia*, or self-sufficiency, self-governing, autonomous; they were what in the Latin Aristotelian tradition came to be called "perfect communities." This is also the moral force behind Strabo's claim that Europe was, unlike Asia, "self-sufficient" in foodstuffs since the ability to provide for one's own material needs suggests a high degree of personal autonomy. Little wonder that for Aristotle there could be no life beyond the limits of the city but that of "beasts and Gods."[18] Because humans, unlike both beasts and Gods, were guided by rules, by laws and customs, the city was also the source of law. Those who lived within it had to abide by its rules. Beyond was the wilderness, what later writers would describe as "the state of nature." All humans began in this condition, and all humans are constantly threatened by it. In the Greek worldview, and in the conceptions of generations of Europeans, to live in the state of nature, to live like a "barbarian" or a "savage," meant living as something less than human. The polis was, in this way, a bounded space. But it was also conceived as a community that could even transform all those who entered it. Aristotle—to whom we owe much of what we now know about the place of the polis in Greek life, although he celebrated the city of Athens and wrote her political history—was an outsider by birth.

This identification of a distinctive European communal life with a specific environment reached its peak with the effective domination of the whole of what we now call Europe, and much of Asia, by the greatest city of them all: Rome. Like the Greek cities to which it was heir, Rome was the source of law, the place of custom, *mores*, which in the poet Virgil's punning vision was now encircled and protected by its massive walls (*moenia*).[19] Unlike the Greek city-states, Rome (particularly after the collapse of the Republic) depended heavily for its political identity and continuing survival on the vast areas of Europe and Asia over which it exercised authority. Thus, to a far greater degree than its Greek antecedents, it welcomed outsiders within its walls, and—at least during the periods when this particular civic community offered stability, security, and the access to world power—it proved to be enormously attractive. "It might be said," wrote James Wilson as he reflected upon the possible future of the United States as a new Rome in the West, "not that the Romans

[18] Aristotle, *Politics*, 1253 a 1–29.
[19] Bellum ingens geret Italia, populosque feroces
contundet moresque viris et moenia ponet
Aeneid 1, 263–4.

extended themselves over the whole globe, but that the inhabitants of the globe poured themselves upon the Romans."[20]

It is, therefore, unsurprising that by the first century CE, this "Roman Empire," which was merely an extension in space of the city of Rome, the poet Horace's "Prince among Cities" (*princeps urbium*), had come to be identified simply with "the world," the *orbis terrarum*.[21] After the establishment of the Emperor Augustus's new regime in 27 BCE, these imperial longings became formally expansionist to the point where Rome was transformed—imaginatively at least—into a "world-state," bounded in Virgil's words only by *Oceanus*.[22] This did not mean that the Romans ignored the actual existence of the rest of the globe, nor that they ever seriously aspired to full domination over it. Indeed, they possessed a lively and sophisticated ethnographical curiosity about the peoples who inhabited the lands beyond the frontiers of the empire. It meant that, for the Romans, the peoples of these other worlds, the Syrians, for instance, or the Chinese, had no separate identity as communities—much less as political powers—as the Romans conceived such things. When, in the second century, the Emperor Antonius Pius was addressed as "Lord of all the World" (*dominus totius orbis*), this merely gave legal expression to long-held Roman belief that, whether those who lived beyond their borders recognized it or not, the political realm of Rome and the human genus had been made one.[23]

Rome, however, was not only a political realm. It was also the embodiment of the Stoic belief in the possibility of a single law for all humanity. If the Greeks gave Europe the philosophy and the mathematics that made possible its subsequent scientific development, the Romans gave it its legislative habits. Although the concept of Europeans as law-governed peoples originated in Greece, it was the Romans who elevated the law to the place it still holds today—as the sole guarantor of the continuity of "civilization," however we choose to define that emotive term. Much of this was swept away during the Gothic invasions that followed the collapse of the Roman Empire. In the outer fringes of the empire, Germanic customary law came to replace Roman law. But despite these changes, that law remained, and remains, the single most unifying feature of the

[20] "Lectures on Law: XI Citizens and Aliens," published in 1790–1, can be found in *The Works of James Wilson*, ed. Robert Green McCloskey (Cambridge, Mass.: Harvard University Press, 1967), 2 vols., II, 581.
[21] Horace, *Odes*, IV.3, 13.   [22] Virgil, *Aeneid*, 1, 286–7.
[23] *Digest* XIV, 2.9. See Claude Nicolet, *L'Inventaire du monde: Geographie et politique aux origines de l'empire romain* (Paris: Fayard, 1988), 28.

continent. Edmund Burke, good European that he was, offered an image of a world of independent states united as a common culture, based upon "the old Gothic customary [law]...digested into system and disciplined by the Roman law," in every part of which it would be possible for a European to feel at home.[24] For this reason the creation of a single legislative order for the whole of Europe remained an ambition of the most powerful of Europe's rulers from the Emperor Justinian in the sixth century, through Philip II of Spain and Louis XIV to Napoleon. In somewhat muted form, this ambition is held by the European Court of Justice today.

After the triumph of Christianity, ancient Greek and Roman notions of exclusivity were further enforced by Christians' insistence upon the uniqueness both of the Gospels and of the Church as a source of moral and scientific authority. Custom, in Lactantius's words, had been "made congruent with religion." Christianity was thought of as spatially coextensive with the Roman Empire. The world, the *orbis terrarum*, thus became, in terms of the translation effected by Pope Leo the Great in the fifth century, the *orbis Christianus* or, as it would be called in the European vernaculars, "Christendom." As late as 1761, such a relatively hostile witness as Jean-Jacques Rousseau conceded that "Europe, even now, is indebted more to Christianity than to any other influence for the union...which survives among her members."[25] It was a union he frequently abhorred but from which he could never quite escape.

The scattered, diverse, and plural cultures of the ancient world that constitute what we now call Europe shared, therefore, a single identity as so many places of "human flourishing" bound together by a common system of law. When they gradually converted to Christianity, they acquired a common religion and a common cult. They also shared a language: Latin. Although, after the fourth century, Roman institutions, Roman architecture, and Roman literature gradually lost their power to unite Europe in a common culture, and the concept of a single body of citizens vanished altogether, Latin survived as the language of the Church and the learned elites of Europe until well into the eighteenth century. As the Italian Republican Carlo Cattaneo noted in 1835, Europe possessed four unifying

---

[24] Edmund Burke, *Two Letters Addressed to a Member of the Present Parliament on the Proposals for Peace with the Regicide Directory of France* [hereafter, *Letters on the Regicide Peace*], in *The Writings and Speeches of Edmund Burke*, ed. Paul Langford et al. (Oxford: Oxford University Press, 1981–1991), IX, 248–9.

[25] *Écrits sur l'abbé de Saint Pierre*, in *Oeuvres complètes de Jean-Jacques Rousseau*, ed. Bernard Gagnebin and Marcel Raymond (Paris: Bibliothèque de la Pléiade, 1964), III, 566.

features: the power of the former imperial authority, the Roman Law, Christianity, and the Latin language.[26]

Latin, however, was almost wholly a written language, and even then it was largely confined to the clergy and the lay intelligentsia. Few could, or did, actually speak it. Even the professoriat, who were bound by statute in most of the universities of early-modern Europe to deliver their lectures in Latin, spoke for the most part in a curious hybrid version of the language and when excited frequently lapsed for long periods into the vernacular. Diplomatic Latin became restricted after the 1520s to polite formulae, and writers on the increasingly important science of diplomacy, such as Ottaviano Maggi, stressed the need for living languages—although in his *De Legato* of 1566 he did so in Latin. Most of educated Europe before the eighteenth century was multilingual. Rulers, such as the Holy Roman Emperors, governed peoples speaking a bewildering number of languages. Charles V was said to have spoken Spanish to God, French to his mistress, and German to his horse. Many European languages—Breton, Provencal, Arrogance, Walloon, Piedmontese—are now minority tongues that have long been made subservient to a national vernacular. But throughout most of the early-modern period, these were the dominant and in some cases the official languages of the regions in which they were spoken. Making oneself understood as one passed from one territory to another was of crucial importance.

Since few could hope to speak all the major languages of Europe, most educated Europeans shared the conviction that there should exist a spoken tongue that, if not as universal as Latin had once been, should be widely understood. In the sixteenth century this became Italian, the language in which Dante, two centuries before had, in a self-conscious break with tradition, decided to write his great poem. Italian was the language of literature and as such as familiar to the learned elite as English is today. Michael de Montaigne learned Italian, although his father had brought him up in an entirely Latin-speaking household, and when he crossed the Alps, he changed the language of his journal from French to Italian. On returning through the Mon Cernis pass, he noted, in French, "here French is spoken, so I leave this foreign language in which I feel competent but ill-grounded."[27] By the late seventeenth century, because of Louis XIV's effective political domination of mainland Europe, French had become the language of diplomacy and the courts, and the language in which

---

[26] Carlo Cattaneo, *Sulle Interdizioni israelitiche*, ed. G. A. Belloni (Rome: Sestante, 1944), 56–8.
[27] Michel de Montaigne, quoted in Hale, *The Civilization of Europe*, 162.

educated Germans, such as Gottfried-Wilhelm Leibniz, wrote when they were not still writing in Latin or, in Leibniz's case struggling to devise a "universal system of characters" capable of "expressing all our thoughts" be we Frenchmen or Assyrians.[28] And French remained dominant until the end of the eighteenth century.

Despite the religious, cultural, and linguistic unity they had given to the continent, neither the Roman Empire, nor Christendom was, of course, identical with "Europe." Much of the Roman Empire lay in Asia and in North Africa. Christianity had begun as an Asian religion, and the first Christian churches had been established on the North African littoral. After the fall of Rome, however, and the subsequent attempt under Charlemagne to rebuild the empire in the West, the notion of "the world" shrank until it covered little more than what is today continental Europe. Charlemagne, although frequently claiming some kind of world sovereignty, called himself *pater europae*—"the father of the Europeans." The Emperor Charles V, who in the early sixteenth century came closer than any ruler before or since to uniting Europe under one sovereign, was addressed as *totius europae dominus*—"lord of all Europe"—an obvious allusion to Antoninus Pius's claim to be *dominus totius orbis*.

For all this self-confidence, however, "Europe" was, and always had been, a highly unstable term. No one has ever been certain quite where its frontiers lie. Only the Atlantic and the Mediterranean provide obvious "natural" boundaries. For the Greeks, Europe had sometimes been only the area in which the Greeks lived, a vaguely defined region that shaded into what was once Yugoslavia in the North and is still Turkey in the South. For most, however, Europe had a larger, more indeterminate geographical significance. It was seen as the lands in the West, whose outer limits, the point at which they met the all-encircling *Okeanos,* were still unknown. Beyond Europe lay Asia and Africa. Africa, South of the Atlas mountains, was dark and unimaginable and remained so, despite the Portuguese exploration and settlement of large areas of the western shores, until the nineteenth century. Only the North coast, which had once been part of the Roman Empire and from the fifteenth century was the home of Barbary pirates and the focus of disastrous crusading ambitions by the Portuguese and the Spaniards, was *terra cognita*. North Africa, however, was a frontier region where Berber states and Ottoman client rulers posed a constant threat to the settled places of Christendom until the extinction

---

[28] Leibniz, quoted in Stephen Toulmin, *Cosmopolis: The Hidden Agenda of Modernity* (Chicago: University of Chicago Press, 1990), 100.

of Turkish hegemony in the Mediterranean in the late seventeenth century. All along the southern coast of Italy and Spain were strings of fortifications to guard local populations against the continual threat of Islamic incursions. These might be brief, but they could also be deadly. When in 1544 Francis I of France allowed the Turkish fleet to winter at Toulon, he was not merely giving assistance to the enemies of Christ (and, more to the point, of the Emperor Charles V). He was dissolving a centuries-old antagonism. He was allowing Asia into Europe.

If Europe's southern frontiers were in this way indeterminate, her eastern ones were forever undecided. Poised between eastern Europe and the recognizable Orient was the unsettling presence of Russia. Russia, sometimes friend, more frequently foe, threw into stark relief the fact that Europe was a culture, a shared way of life, rather than a place. Russia had many of the features of a European society, and it was undeniably Christian. Yet because of its vast size and the fact that so much of it had been ruled for so long by nomadic peoples who were clearly not European, it lay beyond the formal limits of Romanized "civilization." While it remained, in this way, stubbornly an oriental despotism, Russia rested firmly within Asia, the backward barbaric empire of the steppes. But once, in the eighteenth century, its rulers took to wearing silk brocade and conversing in French, it became inescapably Europeanized. In their ambition to subjugate Europe, the Russians, Rousseau declared, had themselves been subjugated. Peter the Great, the first of the Czars to "modernize," which meant "Europeanize," the Russian Empire, was described by Montesquieu as "having given the manners of Europe to a European power."[29] His successor, the Empress Catherine the Great, declared at the beginning of the reforming constitutional code she had devised (the Nakaz) that "Russia is a European Power."[30] (Catherine, however, was German born and French educated and Russian only by marriage.) But if the Russia of Peter and Catherine was "in," as far as the rest of Europe was concerned, it was only partially so. Frederick the Great of Prussia was not alone in denying the empire of the Czars any lasting place among what he described significantly as "the civilized nations of Europe."[31] When seen in this way from the heartlands of Europe, Russia could appear distinctly "other." When set, however, against the image of the true

---

[29] Montesquieu, De l'esprit des lois, XIX, 14.

[30] Denis Diderot, "Observations on the Instruction of the Empress of Russia to the Deputies for the Making of the Laws," in Denis Diderot, Political Writings, ed. John Hope Mason and Robert Wokler (Cambridge: Cambridge University Press, 1992), 85.

[31] Quoted in Denys Hay, Europe: The Emergence of an Idea, 2d ed. (Edinburgh: Edinburgh University Press, 1968), 125.

Orient, she appeared, if only fleetingly, European. When William Pitt, during the Ochakov crisis of 1791, proposed sending British troops to help the Sultan resist the Czar, Edmund Burke responded angrily: "What have these worse than savages to do with the powers of Europe, but to spread war, devastation and pestilence among them?" Russia, if only briefly, had thus joined the "powers of Europe."[32]

Because of this ambivalence, which survives to this day, the "official" frontier to the East, always a faintly absurd notion, was forever on the move. At the end of the fifteenth century it advanced steadily from the Don, where it had been fixed for a thousand years, to the banks of the Volga; by the late sixteenth century it had reached the Ob; by the nineteenth, the Ural and the Ural mountains. In the twentieth it finally came to rest on the banks of the river Emba and the Kerch.[33] Despite this juggling with geography and the literalness with which geographers from Fra Mauro in the 1450s to the All-Union Geographical Society in the 1950s have treated what is, in fact, a cultural frontier, despite Catherine's efforts and the absorption in the nineteenth century of the Romanovs into the families of the crowned-heads of Europe, Russia has always been incorporated into Europe imperfectly. After the creation of the Soviet Union, that tenuous sense of similarity vanished once again, and communism rapidly became for many Europeans, in particular those close to the Soviet borders, yet another manifestation of the Oriental "other." Today things are beginning to change, if only gradually. East-German politicians, such as Lothar De Maizière, conceive of a "common European house" that will "supersede the old divisions" so that "a greater Europe from the Atlantic to the Urals [will] again takes shape."[34] But the Germans feel a special responsibility toward the rest of East Central Europe. Europeans from farther West remain diffident and suspicious. Eastern Europe's uncomfortable proximity to Asia and its linguistic and religious separateness (made the most striking in the Russian case by the use of the Cyrillic alphabet) reinforce the belief that the East belongs on the far side of some unmarked but clearly perceptible frontier.

If European society was, and remains, one broadly committed to a life of civility, it is also one in which identity has been closely associated

---

[32] Quoted in Jennifer Welsh, *Edmund Burke and International Relations: The Commonwealth of Europe and the Crusade against the French Revolution* (New York: Macmillan, 1995), 78.

[33] See W. H. Parker, "Europe: How Far?" in *The Geographical Journal* 126 (1960): 278–97.

[34] De Maizière quoted by Risse and Engelmann-Martin in chapter 13.

with ownership. Citizenship in Europe has long been restricted to property owners. (Until very recently jury service in Britain—the obligation of the citizen to participate in the judiciary process—was restricted to house owners.) Even the French Revolution could be conceived by some, Tocqueville and Taine among others, as the product rather than the source of modern property relations.[35] The right to property could be established in a number of ways: by autochthony, by inheritance, by purchase, or by what in Roman law was called prescription—that is, prolonged and unchallenged possession. But the question for most early-modern theorists was how to establish property rights as a feature not only of the civil law, but also of the law of nature. One of the basic claims of the latter was that all humankind had been granted an equal share in the earth. Inequality was a feature of the divisions of the races of the world into different peoples and thereafter of the creation of political societies. How then had the first men acquired the right to divide up God's earth among themselves? The answer to this question, which still plays a significant role in the European definitions of land rights, drew on the Greek conception of the potentiality of nature.

In a celebrated passage in the *Second Treatise on Government*, John Locke argued that mankind had acquired possession of the earth by laying "out something upon it that was his own, his labour." So that he "thereby annexed to it something that was his Property, which another had not Title, nor could without injury take from him."[36] It was thus man's "labour"—precisely, that is, his *techne* (skills)—that established his right to secure for his personal use alone a portion of what was significantly called "Adam's plenty." In Emeric de Vattel's *Le Droit des gens, ou principes de la loi naturelle appliqués à la conduite et aux affaires des nations et des souverains* of 1758, which became a textbook on the natural law in the late eighteenth century, the disposition to acquire property in this way is turned into a definition of what it is to be human—the imposition, in Hegel's understanding, of the subjective "will" on the "objective world of nature." "The cultivation of the soil," wrote Vattel,

is *an obligation imposed upon man by nature* [emphasis added]. Every nation is therefore bound by natural law to cultivate the land which has fallen to its share.... Those peoples such as the Ancient Germans and certain modern Tartars who, though dwelling in fertile countries, disdain the cultivation of the soil and

---

[35] Donald R. Kelley, *Historians and the Law in Postrevolutionary France* (Princeton: Princeton University Press, 1984), 126.

[36] *Locke's Two Treatises on Government*, ed. Peter Laslett (Cambridge: Cambridge University Press, 1960), 309.

prefer to live by plunder, fail in their duty to themselves, injuring their neighbours and deserve to be exterminated like wild beasts of prey.[37]

As Talal Asad observes in this volume, European history "becomes a history of continuously productive actions defining as well as defined by Law."

Men were thus encouraged to see in the natural world a design of which they were the final beneficiaries. "Art itself," as the eighteenth-century Scottish social theorist Adam Ferguson was later to observe, "is natural to man. . . . [H]e is destined from the first age of his being to invent and to contrive."[38] But not precisely all men. The European sense of superiority, of having been singled out, first by nature, then by God, to play a special role in the history of creation, derived from the conviction that only those who dwelt in the kind of law-governed free urban communities of which "Europe" was constituted would ever be likely to possess the capacity to harness nature to their purposes. The others, the "barbarians," ground down by the demands of their rulers and thwarted in every attempt to express their individual selves, remained forever in unenlightened herds. In Europe the arts were, in the full sense of the term, "liberal." And if these, too, had begun in Asia, in Babylon and Egypt, it was only in Europe that their potential had been realized. "The liberal arts," wrote a complacent Samuel Purchas, "are more liberal to us, having long since forsaken their seminaries in Asia and Africa."[39]

It is this, too, which led to the assumption that science would always be superior to simple force. In Herodotus's view it had been their skills, their *techne*, which had allowed the vastly outnumbered Spartans to defeat the Persians.[40] Generations of later Christian apologists represented the Turks as an enslaved, archetypical Asian, people, descendants of the Scythians, who had been denied not merely freedom of action by their rulers, but also all access to knowledge.[41] Their military success, like those of the Persians before them, had been due in part to their ferocity and in part to the weakness and intellectual poverty of their opponents. Throughout the sixteenth century, when successive Christian intellectuals called

---

[37] *Le Droit des gens ou principes de la loi naturelle appliqués à la conduite et aux affaires des nations et des souverains* [1758], ed. James Brown Scott (Washington: Carnegie Foundation, 1916), 3 vols., III, 37–8.

[38] Adam Ferguson, *An Essay on the History of Civil Society*, ed. Fania Oz-Salzberger (Cambridge: Cambridge University Press, 1995), 12.

[39] Purchas, *Hakluytus Posthumus or Purchas his Pilgrimes*, I, 17.

[40] Herodotus, *Histories*, IX, 61.

[41] See James Hankins, "Renaissance Crusaders: Humanist Crusade Literature in the Age of Mehmed II," *Dumbarton Oaks Papers*, 49 (1995): 111–207.

upon their rulers to bury their differences and mount a crusade against the Turk, the claim was always that European, Christian, science could never fail against Asian ignorance. And when, beginning in the thirteenth century, Europeans set out to persuade the world of the truth of their religion, they assumed a self-evident association between knowledge and belief. The European capacity to span an open space using an arch was said to have instantly persuaded one Peruvian chieftain of the truth of Christianity. The Jesuits who traveled to China in the late sixteenth century took with them clocks, astrolabes, telescopes, clavichords, Venetian prisms, and suction pumps. If, the argument went, the European God had taught the Europeans how to devise such ingenious things, the European God must be the true one. The Chinese, however, had other conceptions of the necessary relationship between technology and religious belief. While grateful for the clocks, they declined the offer of the Gospel. This refusal to accept the obvious led the most famous of the Jesuits, Matteo Ricci, to declare that "they have no logic" and the Chinese to accuse the missionaries of indulging in "countless incomprehensible lines of reasoning."[42]

After Columbus's discovery of America and the rounding of the Cape of Good Hope (famously declared by Adam Smith to be "the two greatest and most important events recorded in the history of mankind"),[43] the European belief in the capacity of European science to dominate the world became even more assertive. Both these oceanic journeys had been made possible by the use of the compass and the skill of European navigators and cartographers. Only those whom Purchas described as "we in the West" had been able to achieve such triumphs. Asians and Africans had been capable of limited navigational feats. But only the Europeans had managed to cross oceans, to settle and to colonize. Only the Europeans had "civilized" peoples from distant and inferior worlds. In a famous engraving by Johannes Stradanus of 1589, Amerigo Vespucci is shown drawing aside a curtain to reveal the "America" whom he will have named, and thus in some sense created. In this image of the first moment of contact, Vespucci is represented with an astrolabe, the symbol of his empowering knowledge in his hand. America, in recumbent allusion to Vespucci's own image of the continent as an ever-available female, is raising herself half-naked from the long sleep of her ignorance.

---

[42] Jacques Gernet, *China and the Christian Impact: A Conflict of Cultures*, trans. Janet Lloyd (Cambridge: Cambridge University Press, 1982), 242–3.

[43] Adam Smith, *An Inquiry into the Nature and Causes of the Wealth of Nations*, ed. R. H. Campbell, A. S. Skinner, and W. B. Todd (Oxford: Oxford University Press, 1976), 2 vols., II, 626.

From the early sixteenth to the late eighteenth century images of the four continents appeared in the most unlikely places. They were reminders both of the newly acquired vision of a vastly enlarged world and of Europe's triumph over so much of it, a triumph that only the sciences and the arts had made possible. Take one striking but representative example. On the ceiling of the stairway hall of the Trappenhaus, the residence of the Prince-Bishops of Wurzburg, a princely family in no way associated with transoceanic navigation, the great eighteenth-century Venetian artist Giambattista Tiepolo depicted in lavish detail each of the four continents. They are so arranged that no matter where the viewer stands, *Asia, Africa,* and *America* can only be seen in relation to *Europe*. The allegorical figure of *Asia* is shown seated on an elephant, *Africa* on a camel, and America on a crocodile—menacing, languid, and amphibious. Only *Europe* sits on a throne instead of an animal, and only *Europe* is surrounded, not by the natural produce of the continent she represents, but by what its peoples have created, by the attributes of the arts, of music and painting, the sciences, and the technology of warfare. Furthermore, *Europe* is the point from which all the other figures must be viewed. As Svetlana Alpers and Michael Baxandall wrote, to look at *Europe* "one should look *from Europe*" for "*Asia, Africa* and *America* are depicted in their relation to *Europe. Europe* is the rubric, the initial code."[44] This is why in Cesare Ripa's *Iconologia* of 1603, a work that provided artists with a easy set of iconographic rules, readers were instructed to depict Europe wearing a crown "to show that Europe has always been the leader and queen of the whole."[45] Thus an abducted Asian princess had become, as she appears in Sebastian Münster's *Cosmographia* of 1588, a Queen.

The shrinking of the frontiers in this way gradually forced upon the European consciousness a greater sense of the boundaries that lay between them and the rest of the world. But this did not, except for the very few, result in any greater sense that the assumed superiority of the continent over all others might be unwarranted. Montaigne's skepticism—which drew some of its inspiration from his awareness of non-European cultures as well as from the diversity of cultural practices within Europe—led to a form of cultural pluralism. In the hands of the natural law theorists of the seventeenth century, Hugo Grotius and Samuel Pufendorf in

---

[44] Svetlana Alpers and Michael Baxandall, *Tiepolo and the Pictorial Imagination* (New Haven and London: Yale University Press, 1994), 154.

[45] *Iconologia overo Decrittione d'imagini delle virtù, vitij, Afetti; Passione humane, Corpi celesti, Mondo e sue parti* (Padua, 1611), 356.

particular, the awareness of the diversity of the world beyond Europe did much to shatter the idea that that law of nature was more or less identical with the customs practiced by the peoples of Europe. Even the information that was available by the end of the seventeenth century on such an "advanced" and complex civilization as China did little to shake the belief that, taken as a whole, European civilization was not doing very much better than any of the available alternatives. To believe otherwise is to mistake the force of Montaigne's irony for approval. Similarly, the uses to which Voltaire put the Chinese sacred histories—which seemed to demonstrate that there were centuries that the biblical narrative of the creation could not account for—were largely directed against the absurd claims of the Christian Church rather than at the broader cultural worlds that have always sustained it.

What Burke called "the great vicinage of Europe" might no longer be the source of nature's laws, but for most Europeans it remained the only place of true civility, of free men living in secure urban communities under the rule of law. The rest of humanity served out its days under tyrannies governed according to the caprice of individual rulers, or in nomadic or seminomadic groups never far from the primordial "state of nature." By the late seventeenth century this sense of exceptionality had found expression in a stadial theory of history. In this universal narrative all human societies begin as hunter-gatherers. They then become pastoralists, less mobile than their predecessors but still, as Montesquieu phrased it, "unable to unite."[46] Finally, they invent agriculture, and this in time transforms them into city dwellers and traders, into modern, civilized, social beings. For all the great social theorists of the seventeenth and eighteenth centuries—which in this volume James Tully subjects to such searching criticism—the final stage ("commercial society") represented the highest possible human attainment on a trajectory through which all the peoples on the globe were bound to pass. The commercial society was one that had forsaken ancient violence (or so it was hoped) for benevolent, enlightened communication, for the transaction not only of goods but also of beliefs, habits, and ideas. The commercial society was one, or so its proponents believed, that could finally dispense with colonization in favor of harmonious transnational cooperation, one in which the less civilized peoples of the world would welcome the "civilizers"—not as conquerors and despoilers but as intellectual and moral liberators. The peoples of America, Africa, Asia, and other "distant countries seem to be waiting

---

[46] Montesquieu, *De l'esprit des lois*, XVIII, 11, *Oeuvres Complètes de Montesquieu*, II, 537.

only to be civilized and to receive from us the means to be so, and find brothers among the Europeans to become their friends and disciples," enthused the Marquis de Condorcet in 1793, at the very moment that the order he was celebrating was about to vanish.[47]

The ability, whether the consequence of environment or divine will, to control the resources of the natural world, to make them work for the greater good of humankind, had given Europe its assumed superiority among the peoples of the world. This is the origin of the belief, which is still shared by many, that Europe or "The West" or "The North" is somehow exceptional. As much as we all may regret it, for long periods of its recent history, the West has exercised technological and political mastery over much of the rest of the world. Just as the ability to do this derived substantially from a specific set of convictions embedded in particular ways of life—from a specific culture—so the record of those achievements has served to define that culture.

Europeans are, I suspect, unusual in sharing in this way a sense that it might be possible to belong to something larger than the family, the tribe, the community, or the nation yet smaller and more culturally specific than "humanity." If the Chinese, the Japanese, the Koreans, or the Singhalese now sometimes choose to identify themselves as Asians, this is because European notions of ethnicity, and the domination of the world economy by European concepts of exchange, have compelled them to do so. Similarly, the peoples of, say, Uganda and Congo—themselves the products of European impositions—are highly conscious of belonging to a continent called "Africa" largely because European colonization, and the marks of European racism, have obliged them, for motives of economic and political survival, to speak of Africa, from Libya to the Transvaal, as if it were the bearer of a common cultural identity. Yet being African in Africa or Asian in Asia provides only the loosest cultural or political cohesion and at most levels no cohesion at all.

I am not endorsing any kind of European exceptionalism. All the peoples of the world are the outcome of the combination, dispersal, and recombination, through warfare and the pursuit of subsistence, of myriad diverse groups of peoples. China, which is larger than Europe, was not inhabited by one ethnic group either. Nor was Assyria, Elam, Urartu, Persia, ancient Mexico, or Inka Peru. But these were ethnic states. They invited (or compelled) the outsiders whom they conquered into their homelands

---

[47] Marquis de Condorcet, *Esquisse d'un tableau historique des progres de l'esprit humain*, ed. Alain Pons (Paris, 1988), 269.

and absorbed them into the dominant ethnic community. What is unusual about "Europe" is that it has for long possessed an identity as a cultural space where there have been and continue to be frequent political unions. It has never, however, constituted a single state, much less a single ethnic group.

The modern European Union has, in one sense, changed all that. The notion that "Europe" might become not merely a loose association of communities sharing an indeterminate common culture, but instead a political union of states is hardly new. From the Duc de Sully's Grand Design of 1620 to the fitful projects, which begin to appear after the 1840s, for a United States of Europe, there has existed a continuous objective to create a European federation that would finally put an end to intracontinental warfare and enhance the welfare of all the peoples of the region. Only since 1945, after what the Spanish writer and statesman Salvador de Madariaga once described as Europe's two great "civil wars," has this project had any chance of being realized.[48] Despite the single market and the single currency, despite ever-increasing convergent political and legal institutions, the vagaries and uncertainties that once hung over the notion of a single European identity hang there still. Europe will never be an ethnic community, nor even the "mega-state" that the opponents of the Union so fear it might become. But the European Union and—should it ever come about—the "United States of Europe" will surely come closer than any political order has ever done before to establishing just what it means to be a "European." When it does it will be the embodiment of a vision that reaches back nearly three millennia.

---

[48] *Portrait of Europe* [*Bosquejo de Europa*] (New York: Roy Publishers, 1955), 23.

2

Some Europes in Their History

J. G. A. POCOCK

I shall try to give some answers to the questions "What is Europe?" or rather "What do we mean by Europe?" The second question implies that "Europe" is something we have invented, and there is a habit at present of putting the words "the invention of" before the name of anything we want to discuss. This implies that there is nothing to discuss except the reasons, very likely discreditable, that have led others to invent whatever it is and impose their construction upon us, so that the point of discussion is to liberate ourselves from the construction by subverting the dominant paradigm, as the bumper stickers urge us to do. This is, of course, a very healthy skepticism, and I intend to adopt it in this essay. I do, in fact, perceive that a construction called "Europe" is being invented and imposed upon me in language that suggests that I must accept it without asking too many questions about what exactly it is, and I am very skeptical about the motives with which this is being done. I like to characterize myself as a Euroskeptic, in the proper sense of the term; meaning that I am skeptical, indeed, about the use of "Euroskeptic" to denote that sort of person. Why is it being suggested that we cannot be a skeptic about Europe without being a fanatical opponent? When that sort of thing happens, it is usually because a word is being used so as to block all critical thought about it, and we may want to ask who is using it in that way and from what motives.

Equally, I do not want to suggest that there is nothing to study here except constructions in the mind, framed with discreditable intentions. I have no difficulty in accepting "Europe" as a reality as well as a construction; many things in human history can be both at once. When I set foot in "Europe," I know that I am there and not in America or in some other place; that is, I am in a certain place, a configuration of land and water, not just the sum of the maps that have been drawn of it, and I am in a certain complex of human cultures and human histories constructed by human effort of one sort and another. They have been constructed, however, by so many humans doing and meaning so many different things that the process of construction becomes a kind of reality and cannot just be reduced to a limited number of constructions and inventions waiting for us to come and deconstruct them.

I want, then, to describe ways in which the word "Europe" has been used—necessarily by people acting in history—and how those ways have grown and spread until the word has reached the point of being used to denote, first, a continent and, second, a civilization. I am skeptical about both these ways of using it. I hold "Europe" to be only part of a continent and only part of a civilization, but the word has been used to denote, and to bring together, a great many things that are important in human experience, and it is important to see what these have been and are. In the last analysis I am conscious that as a New Zealander I am not a European. I am, therefore, looking at "Europe" from the outside; I am not committed to it.

THE GEOGRAPHICAL CONCEPT OF "EUROPE"

Let us start with some "geography." The word suggests land, and human beings, of course, are land animals. But for some thousands of years they have been seafaring animals as well, and if, like me, you come from an island group situated in the vast distances of the Pacific Ocean, you know that the seas are bigger than the continents, and that what we call the Planet Earth could just as well be called the Planet Water. It should come as no surprise, then, that the invention of continents was the work of humans who had left the land and were looking back at it from the sea.

The original distinction took shape in a saltwater area of very limited size, with land masses all around it. I refer, of course, to the Aegean Sea, the part of the Mediterranean that today lies between Greece and Turkey. The ancient peoples who used that sea and lived around it became aware of what we call the Bosphorus, the narrow waterway that connects the Aegean with the larger and, to them, less-known Euxine or Black Sea. They developed myths and folktales that had the effect of giving the name "Europa" to lands lying West of the Bosphorus and the name "Asia" to lands lying East of it. At the same distant time, a third name, or rather a pair of names, appeared to denote another coast and its hinterlands lying well to the South of the Aegean. One of these, "Egypt," was the Greek Aegean term for the peoples of the Nile valley and its delta, an immensely ancient and literate people who could give their own accounts of who they were and where they came from. The other word, "Africa," tended to move westward, away from the Egyptians, and adhere to other coastlands—also known as Libya, Mauritania, and so on—with which the Aegean Greeks and Phoenicians came in contact as their ships explored the Mediterranean basin.

Once we start talking about the movement of words from one coastland and hinterland to another, we have begun talking about geography and cartography: the description of configurations of land and water and their reduction to spoken and written words and image. Over many centuries— perhaps more than twenty from start to finish of the mapping process— the Aegean words "Europe," "Asia," and "Africa" moved outward from the coastlines to which they had originally been applied and traveled deeper and deeper into the hinterlands behind them until finally they reached the opposite seacoasts of these hinterlands and became the names of what were by then called continents. There is a process in the history of geography by which the word "continent" comes to denote a landmass of very great size, possessing a well-defined maritime perimeter, and linked to other continents either by a single narrow isthmus—as Africa is joined to Asia and the two Americas to one another—or not at all, as in the cases of Australia and Antarctica, the two island continents in the southern hemisphere.

The anomaly in our typology of continents—an anomaly that shows how Aegean and Mediterranean concepts still dominate our thinking— consists in our persistent habit of listing Europe as one of the seven continents, when it does not comply with the above definition at all precisely. There is a disjunction between the ancient and medieval practice of distinguishing the parts into which the earth was divided and the modern postnavigational practice of mapping and listing the continents. "The continent of Europe" is a product of the Mediterranean need of a term to describe the lands West of the Bosphorus. It is also the product of the exceptionally self-centered and world-dominating outlook developed by a civilization that took place in those lands. The notion of a "continent" was formed in that civilization but does not fit its own self-description as "the continent of Europe."

In the sixteenth century there were in circulation many copies of a map and image of "Europe, the first part of the earth in the form of a virgin." It was shaped by the rule of the Habsburg family over Spain, the Netherlands, the German Empire, and Austria, and showed "Europe" as a crowned woman, whose head was the Iberian Peninsula and whose heart was situated at Prague. Her left arm was the peninsula of Denmark, and she held a scepter ruling over the Baltic and the North Sea; her right arm was the peninsula of Italy, with which she grasped the island of Sicily, as an imperial orb giving power over the Mediterranean. The skirts of her robe floated freely over vast and indeterminate regions, between the Black Sea and the Baltic, to which the draftsman affixed such names as Scythia, Muscovy, and Tartary.

One can see that the mapmakers have been pushing the Baltic as far East and the Black Sea as far North as they dare, hoping to bring them close enough to each other to justify the description of Europe as a continent, but it is not possible to link Europe to Asia by a narrow isthmus with sea on either hand. Europe is not linked to Asia so much as it is an extension of it, a peninsula or subcontinent like that of India. Even then there is no huge mountain barrier like that of the Himalaya, separating the peninsula from the rest of the continent that we might call Eurasia. The skirts of the imperial robe float over an enormous plain in which there are neither seas nor mountains, nor any natural frontier at all. Subsequently, there arose the habit of terminating Europe at the Ural Mountains, which marked no important climactic or cultural or political characteristics. It is another characteristic of the Habsburg map that it can touch only the coasts of Scandinavia North of the Baltic, as of Africa South of the Mediterranean. One might almost say that Scandinavia is a separate peninsula of the Eurasian continent and that Europe is another. When Scandinavia came to be considered part of Europe is a historical question.

The formation of "Europe" was not quite complete in 1760 when Voltaire, who though a great historian was not a great scholar, wrote his *History of Russia under Peter the Great*. Certainly, he wrote to celebrate the work of Peter and his successors in bringing Russia into the civilization he thought of as European; but at the same time he is inclined to include Sweden, Baltic Germany, Poland, and Russia in an area he called simply "the north" (*le nord*) and did not consider fully European. And what is more, Voltaire remarks that if you situate yourself imaginatively about the Sea of Azov, just East of the Crimean, you cannot tell where Europe leaves off and Asia begins. It would probably be better to abandon both terms, expanding the term *le nord* into *terres boreales* or *terres arctiques*, corresponding (he says) to "the *terres australes* and *antarctiques* which we use in speaking of the great continent we believe to exist in the southern hemisphere." Very soon after Voltaire wrote this, European navigators in the Pacific dissolved the southern continent into the two island continents called Australia and Antarctica, perhaps confirming the presumption that continents must be situated in the ocean. But we have not given up the practice of describing Europe as a seventh, or rather as the first, "continent," though we have long known perfectly well that its eastern aspect does not separate it from Asia but establishes a continental heartland in which all frontiers, physical or cultural, are essentially indeterminate. This tells us a great deal about the civilization that has grown up in "Europe" and calls itself by that name, and we have now to turn from "Europe" as a continent to "Europe" as a civilization.

The word "Europa" was in use in the Roman empire but was not used self-descriptively; Rome may have known that it was in Europe but did not characterize itself as European, since the word was not used that way. The reason for this was that the Roman empire was not continental but Mediterranean. It was formed by the hegemony of a central Italian people over all three of the coastlands—Asian, African, and European—first defined in the ancient Mediterranean and has been carried deep into the hinterlands behind each: in Asia as far as Armenia and Mesopotamia, in Africa as far as the cataracts of the Nile and the Sahara, and in Europe by a series of conquests (first over the Iberian peninsula, then beyond the Western Alps into Gaul and Britain and the delta of the Rhine, and finally over a series of provinces along the Danube from modern Switzerland to modern Romania). The poet Ovid found himself exiled to the shore of the Black Sea, on the edge of Voltaire's *le nord*, which he thought of as Scythia, not as Asia. In central Germany the Romans were closer than they knew to the vast indeterminacy of Eurasia.

Now what we call "Europe" is a civilization, rather peninsular and transalpine than Mediterranean in any comprehensive sense, created in the last group of Roman provinces after the disintegration of a unified Roman empire. That disintegration—Gibbon's famous *Decline and Fall*—came about in stages. The first, most "European," and to him for various reasons the most prominent, was the collapse of Roman control over the far western provinces, and over Italy itself, which happened when an upheaval originating in nomadic central Eurasia caused German peoples to move over the Danube and Rhine in greater numbers than the Romans could absorb. This extinction of the empire "in the West" was Gibbon's primary theme, both because it happened first and because he was preoccupied, as a European, with the rise of the feudal kingdoms and the papal church. But it was followed, two centuries later, by an even greater event, when a religious revolution in the Fertile Crescent led to the Muslim Arab conquest of most of Roman Asia and all of Roman Africa, from Egypt West to Spain: the destruction of Mediterranean cultural unity, which has never quite recovered.

The conquest produced a double separation of "Europe" from the other Mediterranean hinterlands: the western provinces went their own way, and the empire that survived was based in Constantinople, with one foot in ancient Asia and the other in ancient Europe, one East and the other West of the Bosphorus, which had originally separated the two. Four and then eight centuries later still, Islamicized Turks from Central Eurasia began and ended the conquest of Arab Asia and Egypt, and of Byzantine Asia and Europe; the princedom of Muscovy set itself up as the Third Rome, the heir of Byzantium; and this completed a process by which the concept of "Europe" migrated irreversibly to the far western provinces. As a result, we are no longer quite sure whether the former Byzantine world (ex-Ottoman or ex-Soviet) belongs in "Europe" or not, and the great indeterminacy of "Europe's" eastern borderlands has taken on a cultural as well as a geographic significance.

The geographical concept of "Europe" has moved West, to the point where it defines an Atlantic peninsula by calling it a continent. Similarly, the historical concept of "Europe" has migrated, to the point where everything we mean when we say "the history of Europe" refers to the history of the political and religious culture—the highly distinctive civilization—that arose in the far-western Latin-speaking provinces of the former Roman empire. This has become what we mean by "Europe," and its history is what we mean by "the history of Europe." The lands to which the term "Europa" was originally applied—Thrace, Macedonia, Illyria, the more modern Bulgaria, Albania, and Serbia—those which the Byzantine emperors considered their European "themes" or provinces—are in our minds only marginally European, inhabited by uncouth warring tribes whose history is not ours and whose problems are none of our business.

We are no doubt very wrong in having this perception, but we do have it, and it is important to understand how we have acquired it. In the western provinces lost by the Romans to a diversity of German-speaking settlers, two things happened. The Christian Church acquired the formidable organization of papal authority, and the barbaric kingdoms acquired the formidable feudalism of heavy-armored horsemen. All this happened a long way from the sophisticated urban societies of the Greeks, Arabs, and Iranians, but the consequences have been such that the narrative of history was stolen from them. In his book significantly entitled *The Making of Europe,* Robert Bartlett has examined how it happened that this far-western culture—feudal, papal, monastic, Latin—began in the eleventh and twelfth centuries to expand aggressively. It expanded westward at the expense of Celtic peoples, beyond England into Wales and Ireland;

eastward at the expense of Slavic and Finno-Ugrian peoples, beyond Saxony into the heartlands of the European peninsula; and southeast-ward at the expense of the Byzantine empire and the increasingly Turk-dominated Arab Khalifat, in the far less stable and enduring enterprise of the Crusades. It was the last expansion that led the Greek historian Anna Comnena to write that all the western barbarians had marched across Europe to Asia. She also refers to the mainly Frankish and Norman cru-saders as "Celts," which tells us that she is using what old Greek and Latin terms she can find to describe far-western phenomena, and that there is no reason why she should think of herself as either European or Asian. She is a Roman. It has not yet happened that the new Latin civilization—to Anna Comnena purely barbaric—can claim a monopoly of the word "Europe" and a monopoly of history by calling itself by that name.

The episode of the Crusades did not last. The expansion of "Europe" into the Slavic heartlands altered the historical map by creating what we think of as the problem of "Central Europe." Certain Catholic provinces of Latin culture were created—among Lithuanians, Poles, Czechs, Hun-garians, Croats—and they share that "European" history that is the his-tory of the Latin papacy and empire and their aftermath. These peoples exist in close proximity with other peoples—Russians, Ukrainians, Serbs, Greeks, and Turks—whose history is not Latin and whom we may think of as Europeans or not as we choose. The point is that we have to choose and do not quite know how to choose.

The eastward expansion of the western Latins entered that broad zone where there is neither a maritime nor a terrestrial frontier permitting us to say where "Europe" leaves off and "Asia" begins. In this zone—once known to geopolitical theorists as the Heartland of the World Island—the Latin civilization that came to call itself "Europe" found itself with-out any fixed cultural, ecclesiastical, or political frontiers either. To the Southeast, the lands originally called "Europe" passed increasingly from Greek Orthodox to Turkish Muslim control, culminating in the tempo-rary Ottoman conquest of Catholic-Protestant Hungary in 1526. In the indefinitely extensible heartlands between the Baltic and the Black Sea, the contact between Latins and Greeks was overwhelmed in the thir-teenth century by Mongol power, which deeply affected the history we call Russian and left Poland and Lithuania vulnerable to Crimean slave-raiders well into the seventeenth century.

Is all this history "European" or not? It depends on what we want to say, and on whether we want to decide what we want to say. History since

1989 suggests that "we"—whoever "we" are—would rather not have to decide. Is this the product of a prudent awareness that "Europe" has no frontiers in the East or of some deeper weakness of will?

THE ENLIGHTENED NARRATIVE

I now return to the history we all know, more or less, and describe as the history of "Europe." When did it begin to be said that "Europe" had a history, and when did it begin to be implied that all history was the history of Europe? A good answer—though like all good answers an oversimplification—can be given by fastening on the great historians of the eighteenth century, the Age of Enlightenment: on Voltaire, Gibbon, Hume, Robertson, and the extraordinary partnership of Raynal and Diderot. They were the ones who set about defining "Europe" as a secular civilization and supplying it with a secular history and an age of modernity.

Writing history for them was a weapon against the Church, Protestant as well as Catholic, and in consequence they wrote a history of the Church designed to reduce it to secular history. The weakness of the Roman empire, for them, had coincided with the rise of the Church, and there was a polemic against the history of Greek philosophy, because the Christian theology that gave the Church authority had been shaped in the old Greek East, in Alexandria and Antioch and Constantinople. Islam, which the Enlightened historians rather admired, had progressively destroyed that Greek world. But in the far western provinces lost to the Franks, Saxons, and Normans, a new Latin theology had arisen, designed to buttress the universal jurisdiction of the Pope and to make the Latin church the greatest enemy ever faced by the authority of human society over itself. Gibbon wrote that the beginnings of modern history should be sought in the eighth century A.D., when the papacy allied itself with the Frankish kingdom that became the empire of Charlemagne. Notice that he is using "modern" to mean "not ancient" (and therefore Christian). He has not reached the point of using it to mean "not medieval" (and therefore no longer wholly Christian). For all of these historians there had followed a long struggle between the empire and the papacy, each created by the other. A climax occurred about 1300, when the papacy called in the French Angevins to defeat the Hohenstaufen in Italy, and the French kings defeated Pope Boniface VIII and removed the papacy from Rome to Avignon. History as seen by French scholars and publicists now removed its center from the Church Universal to the kingdom of France, not universal but hegemonic.

This was a history of feudal as well as clerical power. The Crusades figured as the ultimate lunacy of both. It was, of course, a wholly Latin history dominated by an obsession with the Pope. Greek Orthodox history, which we might want to call "European" on the grounds that it continued Christian and Roman history in a non-Latin way, was excluded from it once the Byzantines were driven out of Italy. Gibbon declared that he could find nothing in Byzantine history except its fall that deserved more than a summary and that it was better to study the far more dynamic peoples—Latins and Normans in the West, Arabs and Turks in the East, Bulgars and Russians in the North—who had supplanted it. Latin history contained its own dynamic. Its external enemies remained external, and even its critical expansions into Spain, Ireland, Scandinavia, and "Central Europe" remained peripheral to the struggle between church and civil society, which had happened nowhere else. Here is the germ of the idea that history happens only in Europe, while other peoples never change.

The Enlightened narrative proceeded to the late fifteenth century, when "Europe" could be said to have become "modern" in the sense of "not medieval." It began emerging from the feudal and clerical, barbaric and religious, culture that has enveloped it ever since Charlemagne, or since Constantine. This was partly a result of the recovery of pre-Christian classical culture—for which, significantly, "Europe" was supposed to have been indebted to the fall of Constantinople and the extinction of Byzantine civilization. But also it was the result of a series of technological innovations—gunpowder, the compass, and the printing press—unknown to the ancients. We associate these with the discovery of the New World, but for Voltaire and Hume and Robertson, they had a prior importance—their role in the creation of powerful military monarchies controlling their own resources, pursuing their own policies, and capable of acting independently of the papal Church. Once there were several of these monarchies, "Europe" could be said to have endowed itself with a states-system, whose *raison d'état* and *jus gentium* took the place of the political theology of empire and papacy, and this states-system, or system of international relations, began to become the definition of "Europe" itself.

The great Edinburgh historian William Robertson wrote of "Europe" as an entity that had pre-existed the Romans, been half-destroyed and yet half-civilized by Roman conquest, flung into barbarism half-redeemed by religion when the Roman empire collapsed, and a millennium later emerged into conditions under which a civilized religion could again exist. All these were events in the history of "Europe." Their culmination occurred, for Robertson, with the empire of Charles V, which seemed to threaten "Europe" with a new universal empire but, in fact, ushered in the age of reason of state, when the French monarchy, resisting the Habsburg dynasty, and the English monarchy, adapting itself to this struggle, began educating "Europe" in the conduct of secular power. The balance of power was "Europe," and "Europe" was the balance of power. It was Spanish and French, English and Burgundian, German within the structure of the Holy Roman Empire. It was seldom Polish and never really Central European at all. Its energies were turned inward on the problems of Latin civilization, and the explosion of that civilization into Mexico and Peru belonged, said Robertson, in a history that would have to be written separately.

In 1780, in their great *Philosophical and Political History of the Two Indies*, Raynal and Diderot had already begun to write the history of the Europeans' conquest: first, of the planetary ocean, which had brought them in contact with all the cultures in the world simultaneously, and, second, of the two American continents, which was leading to the creation of European societies existing beyond Europe. The discovery of America, said Hume, marked the true beginning of "modern history." Robertson, however, confined his history to the first half of the sixteenth century and did not continue it through the seventeenth. Unlike Voltaire and Hume, he chose to avoid the Wars of Religion. The Enlightened mind saw Lutheranism, Calvinism, and Anabaptism as the reverse side of the medal to the papacy they sought to destroy: religious fanaticism threatening civil authority in a new way. Voltaire and Hume did not see the Wars of Religion as ending at the Peace of Westphalia in 1648; they were preoccupied with their after-effects, the Wars of the Fronde in France, the Wars of the Three Kingdoms in the British islands.

These wars carried the story into Voltaire's *Age of Louis XIV*, the first and most central of his historical writings. Voltaire saw "Europe" emerging from the last phase of religious fanaticism into an age of Enlightened sociability fostered by both courtly monarchy and commercial refinement. A peripheral debate was carried on by those who held that Louis XIV had threatened "Europe" with another universal empire like that of the Romans. In their view the states-system constituting Europe was achieved only when his adversaries brought him to terms (or he them) at the Treaty of Utrecht in 1713. French and Scottish historians could agree that Utrecht had achieved a "Europe" that had outgrown barbarism, fanaticism, and conquest. It was a republic or confederation of states held together by treaties to which wars were merely auxiliary, and by a common system of civilized manners communicated everywhere by commerce; a

European economic community, in fact, but one composed of states whose sovereignty was the precondition of their capacity for commerce.

This was the "Europe"—the civilization of states, commerce, and manners—that we so misleadingly call the *ancien regime* (it was totally and self-consciously modern) and that Edmund Burke, writing in the 1790s, declared had been destroyed by two disastrously regressive events: the French Revolution and the partition of Poland. The first occurred at the very heart of Enlightened "Europe." What was disastrous about it was that it had restored the climate of fanaticism and returned "Europe" to its climate during the Wars of Religion, with ideology taking the place of theology. The second event occurred nearer the periphery, in what we have been calling "Central Europe." To understand its meaning to Burke, it may help to recall that the great Enlightened histories were mostly written just before, during, or just after the Seven Years War (the French and Indian War) of 1756–63. This war enlarged a "European" war into a global struggle and in the process modified the concept of "Europe" itself. The system founded on the Treaty of Utrecht was in essence an Anglo-French Consortium, with Spain, the Netherlands, and Austrian-dominated Germany and north Italy as auxiliaries. The Seven Years War, however, transformed this system in two ways. West of the Atlantic, a struggle for empire in North America and the Caribbean became so far-reaching that the historians Raynal and Diderot could propose that wars for power in Europe were now dominated by wars for oceanic commerce and empire. They set out to write the first history of the world-system created by "European" conquest of the ocean, arguing that Europeans were still barbarians who had not fully escaped from the Middle Ages and asking whether even an Enlightened system of global free trade could improve them. This is the first history that tries to view "Europe" in its global setting, but it is still the maritime far-west of the peninsula they are looking at. France, they declare, is "at the center of Europe" because it lies between the Atlantic and the Mediterranean. They probably mean that "Europe" has been defined by France.

East of, let us say, the river Elbe, the other face of the Seven Years War enlarged the limited warfare of the system founded on Utrecht into a struggle between three military empires: the Austrian, the Prussian, and the Russian. The Central European space in which their war went on merged into the vaster space in which "Europe" and "Asia" can no longer be told apart—Voltaire's *le nord*, created by such far-reaching processes as the decline of the Ottoman Empire and the transformation of the Russian state by Peter the Great and his successors. Voltaire's history of Russia, which I quoted earlier, is the major response of Enlightened historiography to all this. He sees Peter as creating a "European" state, fit to take part in the treaties and commerce of "Europe." Voltaire even imagines that contacts between Russia and the Ch'ing emperors will induce China to take part in this system. He believes that Russia and China between them will domesticate the Central Asian steppe and end that phase in world history when Huns or Mongols might dominate or destroy the settled civilizations around them. This is to imagine "Europe" as "tomorrow the world." Voltaire is enraged by Rousseau's insistence that Peter did too much damage to the customs of his subjects, so that sooner or later the Europeanized Russian state will collapse and the Tartars will return to Europe. But if the far western imagination did not travel all the way to China and Kamschatka, it might stop on its own doorstep. Gibbon, having carried his history to the fall of Constantinople in 1453, could, in principle, have gone on to the greatness and decline of the Ottoman Empire and the politics of its Austrian and Russian successors. But there is no Enlightened history of Central and Eastern Europe, none that offers to explain the partition of Poland. Gibbon chose instead to return to his starting point amid the ruins of the Capitol and write three chapters on the city of Rome under the popes as far as the Renaissance. The imagination of Catholic-Protestant-Enlightened "Europe" always came home to its deeply critical concern with itself.

Enlightened "Europe"—the states-system of the Treaty of Utrecht—has been principally a set of political and cultural arrangements imposed by the maritime states of the Atlantic coastlands. It was brought to an end— if we follow Burke's analysis—by two series of events. The first was the revolution in the maritime states themselves—France, the Netherlands, perhaps Ireland, but never Britain—and in their extensions beyond the Atlantic to English, French, and Spanish America, a world that Burke's *Annual Register* (a journal that he edited) included under the heading "History of Europe," but which Raynal and Diderot showed was hard to fit into European notions of history. The second event was the growth of military empires in the great spaces where Europe shades into Eurasia, which, by partitioning Poland, indicated their power to redefine the states-system that "Europe" recognized as part of itself but that existed in a world western Europeans found very hard to recognize or understand.

In his book *Inventing Eastern Europe: The Map of Civilization on the Mind of the Enlightenment*, Larry Wolff describes how eighteenth-century Europeans, as they traveled beyond Germany into Catholic Poland, Orthodox Russia, and the still Ottoman Balkan Peninsula, felt themselves to have quite suddenly entered an alien and archaic world of vast distances, enserfed peasantries, and brutal petty officials—a world that corresponded all too easily to their received notions of "oriental despotism." This last concept was not exclusively an invention of maritime imperialism, though of course it was that. It also reflects the encounter of "Europe" on its open eastern frontier with forms of government derived from the Ottoman or Mongol empire or shaped by these empires as they withdrew; it was a problem for the British in India whether they were going to join the family of military empires or attempt something different. The indeterminacy of Europe in the East, however, may help explain the rather strange way in which Larry Wolff's pages are pervaded by the notion that western Europeans ought not to have evaluated central and eastern Europe as they did, that it is not for "Europeans" to decide who is "European" and who is not. This reflects the deeply confused way in which we now think about cultural identity, but it also reflects the fact that the decision is difficult to make or to avoid. Should we say that the affairs of former Yugoslavia ought to be arranged by "Europe" because they are part of it? Or should we say that this area is a barbaric frontier (or rather a collision of archaic frontiers in a world still barbaric), which it is better to avoid trying to control? Should an empire seek to assimilate its barbarians or to exclude them? If we reply that it should not have defined them as barbarians in the first place, the question arises of the terms in which it ought to have understood them. The lands originally called "Europa" are those in which "Europe" experiences a continuing problem in defining itself.

ANOTHER "EUROPE" IN HISTORY

But this is to anticipate the history of "Europe" since the end of the Enlightened settlement. That was succeeded by the transitory if spectacular Napoleonic interlude, when the revolutionary empire of France over Latin Europe proved itself very nearly capable of dominating the three military monarchies of Europe's eastward expansion. The resistance of Austria, Russia, and the maritime empire of Britain over the Atlantic and Mediterranean led the French empire to overreach itself, collapse, and be succeeded by an attempt to restore that "Europe" of several states linked by treaty and trade in which Enlightened thinkers had seen the security of civilization. But this "Concert of Europe," heir to the early-modern states-system, had to be guaranteed by, and therefore had to include, the eastward military monarchies themselves: Prussia, Austria, Russia (but not the Turkish empire, seen as barbaric, oriental, decadent, and on the way to relegation to the colonial world over which "Europe" ruled). The technology of industrialism transformed the old empires and republics into formidably unified military states capable of conscripting their entirely willing citizenries into great national armies. An era of great states, great wars, and great revolutions can be said to have lasted, rather neatly, from 1789 to 1989, and the United States and Japan to have played their parts in it. In the history of "Europe," we take as cardinal the two world wars of the twentieth century in which the German empire-state twice proved that it could simultaneously threaten to dominate the Netherlands (thus provoking war with France and Britain on the ancient battlegrounds of historic "Europe") and Poland and Ukraine (thus provoking war with Russia about that great debatable land that geopoliticians used to proclaim the Heartland, declaring that whoever ruled it ruled the world). Both the world wars were so destructive to "Europe" that they produced huge systemic collapses and the intervention of the continental superstates created by European settlements beyond "Europe": the United States of America and the Eurasian empire of Russia. After 1945, and for the greater part of my adult lifetime, it was a commonplace among the most trendy historians to say that the European age had ended, and "Europe" itself had been partitioned by the intercontinental superpowers. This prediction has been falsified, and something calling itself "Europe" has emerged and claimed a dominant role.

The European Economic Community, then the European Community, and then the Union—the names by which it has progressively called itself—seems to display a series of characteristics. First, it has remained a Franco-German consortium, a series of arrangements designed to ensure that France and Germany will not again go to war by inducing them to merge their institutions and economies to a point where this ceases to be possible. This laudable aim could not be pursued without drawing in adjacent populations in Italy and the Low Countries, and so forth. The economic benefits of Germany's industrial recovery, and other countries', were such that many were willing to join in the enterprise. But the enterprise entailed inducing democracies to give up their sovereignty—which is to say their capacity for self-government. The strategy adopted from the start was described by one Quebec statesman as tempting lobsters into the lobster pot, inducing them to take the first step, and then revealing to them that it was irrevocable, so that no way remained but forward. There is no phrase commoner in the rhetoric of Europeanism than "we—or you— have no other choice," language reused in the United States when the

North American Free Trade Agreement was being mooted. When I hear it said that the separate histories of the Irish or British, French or Spanish, German or Scandinavian (but not yet Polish or Hungarian and certainly not, for the foreseeable future, Russian) merge in the history of something called "Europe," which has not been written yet, I wonder what this indeterminacy means, and I think we had better set about writing that history and seeing how it comes out when we do. There are numerous ways of writing it, and none will be final.

Second, the institutionalization, and the creation of a mystique, that went with the idea of a union to be called "Europe" went on in the era of the Cold War, the Iron Curtain, and the partition of Europe. This partition, by which the Soviet Union hoped to protect its domination of the Heartland, and its own unity, ran well west of the indeterminacies of that region and cut deep into Latin "Europe." It separated Lutheran East Germany from Catholic West Germany, and Catholic Poland, Hungary, and Czechoslovakia from the western Europe of which they might be considered extensions. In the era of partition, "Europe" was far from clear what it intended to do about the central and eastern "Europes," apparently lost to Soviet domination. Its ideology was never in practice what it was in principle: an affirmation of Catholic-Protestant-Enlightened "Europe" against the Orthodox-Muslim Europes and "Eurasia" now ruled by a semi-Enlightened Russia. Turned westward, the ideology of "Europe" became the instrument of a dispute with its other protector: France and Germany, the losers in the Second World War, against the United States as the principal victor, and also against Britain while that state continued to belong to the maritime world of the British Commonwealth and the "special relation." A sense of defeat in that set of relationships led the United Kingdom to accede "Europe." Since "Europe" has not allayed that sense of defeat, the British relationship to it remains deeply ambivalent. I speak, of course, as a citizen of the former Commonwealth, but I do so without hesitation. "Europe" must see itself as a new Norman Conquest, the Channel Tunnel as a revival of the camp at Boulogne in 1805. The power of the Napoleonic bureaucracies, now serving the international market, seeks to extend itself over the British Isles.

If "Europe" was a product of the partition of "Europe," it has had to survive the end of that partition and the downfall, not only of the Soviet Union, but perhaps also of the Russian state created by Peter and Catherine and their successors. The door is wider open than at any time in recent history toward those areas where "Europe" has no frontiers, and any attempt to withdraw them or extend them must be equally arbitrary—toward the old Heartland where Catholic-Protestant-Enlightened "Europe" shades into Orthodox-Muslim-Communist Eurasia, and toward the ancient original "Europa" now known as the Balkan Peninsula, whose problems are still those created by the expansion and contraction of the Ottoman Empire. Among the innumerable alarming features of this situation—in which the possible disappearance and the possible renewal of Russian great-power capacity appear equally threatening—occurs the thought that "Europe" may now be what "Germany" formerly was: an imperial power secure in the Atlantic coastlands but obliged to attempt imperial control in one or both of the great marchlands to the East. In times gone by this role entailed great-power rivalries and world wars. Unless a Russian great power revives, these should not occur again, but the history of European and American dealings with former Yugoslavia brings to light one more characteristic of contemporary "Europe," of which I want to say something before concluding.

CONCLUSION

We have considered two eras in which "Europe" was defined as a largely economic entity and doing so was designed to put an end to periods of destructive war. The first was the era of Enlightenment from 1713 to 1789, when "Europe" was presented as a republic of states held together by commerce, succeeding and terminating the Wars of Religion and the threat of universal monarchy. The second is our own. Whereas the Enlightened theorists invented "Europe" as a system of states in which the partnership of civil sovereignty and civil society was necessary to commerce and the spread of manners, we, apparently, are committed to the submergence of the state and its sovereignty, not in some pan-European or universal confederation, but in a postmodern era in which the global market demands the subjugation of the political community and perhaps of the ethnic and cultural community also; we are to give up being citizens and behave exclusively as consumers. This is why the European Union is ineffective as an empire. An organization designed to break the will of the state to govern itself necessarily reduces its own will to use military power to police its own frontiers, notably when these lie in parts of the world where only will can establish where these frontiers lie. The question for the new century is whether we will retain any capacity to govern ourselves by political means. Unfortunately, the power to decide on the use of military force cannot be detached from the retention of the former capacity as completely as we should like. Europe, the cradle of the state, may be about to discover what it is like to do without it.

BIBLIOGRAPHICAL NOTE

I shall not attempt an extensive footnoting of this chapter. It is one of several essays in which I seek to examine the meaning of "Europe." The others are "Deconstructing Europe," *History of European Ideas* 18, no. 3 (1994): 329–46; "Vous autres Européens—or Inventing Europe," *Acta Philosophica* 14, no. 2 (1993): 141–58 (published by the Slovene Academy of Sciences, Liubliana); and "Notes of an Occidental Tourist," *Common Knowledge* 2, no. 2 (1993): 1–5, 8–18.

The works cited in the text include Robert Bartlett, *The Making of Europe: Conquest, Colonization, and Cultural Change, 950–1350* (Princeton: Princeton University Press, 1993); *The Alexiad of Anna Comnena* (Penguin Classics, 1969); and Larry Wolff, *Inventing Eastern Europe: The Map of Civilization on the Mind of the Enlightenment* (Palo Alto, Calif.: Stanford University Press, 1994). I cite three Enlightened histories by Voltaire: *Le Siècle de Louis XIV* (available in English as *The Age of Louis XIV*), *Essai sur les Moeurs et l'Esprit des Nations,* and *Histoire de Russia sous Pierre Le Grand.* I also cite the following histories: Guillaume-Thomas Raynal, *Histoire philosophique et politique des établissements et du commerce des Européens dans les deux Indes,* with additions by Denis Diderot; David Hume (works available from Liberty Classics, Indianapolis); William Robertson, *History of the Reign of the Emperor Charles V* (Bristol: Thoemmes Publishers, 1998); Edward Gibbon, *History of the Decline and Fall of the Roman Empire* (London: Allen Lane: Penguin Press, 1994), critical edition by David Womersley.

3

"Europe" in the Middle Ages

WILLIAM CHESTER JORDAN

In the great thirteenth-century collection of poems and songs known as the *Carmina Burana*, one of the longer specimens of the versifier's art opens with the phrase "Cum in Orbem Universum," poetically captured in English as "Song of the Vagrant Order." The song takes its starting point from the Latin imperative *Ite* (Go forth) and describes the wandering lives of priests, monks, and deacons who bolt their duties. As the poem continues, the poet characterizes other social groups as travelers, often doing so with a hard and biting sarcastic edge. Besides priests, monks, and deacons, the wanderers include adolescents and soldiers, tall men and short men, and scholars. A description repeated in the song—although not in precisely the same words—identifies the band of vagabonds in territorial terms. At one point the poet describes them as Austrians, Bavarians, Saxons, and Easterners; at another he sings of Bohemians, Germans, Slavs, and Italians:

> Give to any folk you meet
> Reasons for your questing.
> As that men's peculiar ways
> Seem in need of testing.[1]

In other words, the poet advises the wanderer to respond to questions about his purpose by an affirmation of the virtues of cosmopolitanism. Individual ways—the ways of Austrians or Italians—have to be tested against the habits, loves, and hatreds of other people.

In this chapter I reflect on the idea of Europe in the High Middle Ages, the period from about 1050 to 1350. My principal focus is on one

I wish to thank my friend and colleague Anthony Grafton, professor of history at Princeton University, for his close reading of an earlier version of this essay.
[1] *The Goliard Poets: Medieval Latin Songs and Satires*, trans. George Whicher (New York: New Directions, 1949), 273–9.

prominent characteristic of European civilization in this period—namely, the tension between cosmopolitanism, like that lauded in the song quoted earlier, and intense localism. This theme obviously owes much to current concerns that are greeting the emerging unity of Europe among which the grim persistence of its ethnic and religious hatreds is one of the most important.

The fundamental discussion throughout is political: the emergence of large units of organization whose power and persistence were always tested by local loyalties and outright resistance to central authority. This political theme should not obscure two similar themes, one economic and one ecclesiastical. In the economic sphere I will look at the growth of markets and interregional and international trade. The sheer growth of population, the spread and growth of towns (especially in Italy), and the place of the crusades in this wide vision and reality of European identity are addressed as well, albeit in rather broad strokes. In the ecclesiastical sphere the emphasis will be on the cosmopolitan character of "scholasticism," a term that encompasses the curriculum, method of study, and philosophical concerns of the intellectual elite of Europe. The medium of scholastic discourse was the Latin language, and thanks to cosmopolitan patterns of appointment to elite church and educational offices, scholasticism was the dominant mode of professional thinking and learning from the Atlantic Coast to the Carpathian Mountains. Academic careers, like that of Saint Thomas Aquinas, sent Italians to study in Germany and teach in Paris; administrative careers, like that of Saint Anselm of Aosta, sent southerners to monastic posts in northern duchies and to episcopal offices in England.[2] The system of papal legates, nuncios, and judges-delegate, the pope's eyes and ears in even the most distant provinces of the church, knitted together the whole in an impressive, if fragile, pan-European administrative network. Over against this cosmopolitanism stands the relative self-sufficiency of the village economy, the extreme parochialism of rural priests and of the inmates of minor religious establishments, and the often restrictive impulses associated with concerns for family and lineage.

At the chronological end of the story, as we shall see, the balance on all fronts shifted back toward parochialism. Academic and administrative careers, like that of Lanfranc, William the Conqueror's friend, would become rare. Lanfranc, an Italian from Pavia, spent time in Bec in

---

[2] For what we know of the career of Thomas Aquinas, see *The Life of Saint Thomas Aquinas: Biographical Documents*, ed. and trans. Kenelm Foster (London: Longman, Green and Co., 1959); on Anselm, see G. R. Evans, *Anselm* (London: Chapman, 1989).

Normandy governing a major monastery and ended his career as the great-est churchman in England as archbishop of Canterbury. His career was extraordinary in his own time but almost unthinkable in the late Middle Ages, say, after 1350 or so.[3] Overextension by the papacy and the "feudal states" of northern Europe would reveal the systemic weaknesses of both. And the shocks of war, famine, and plague destabilized the entire array of European political, economic, and, indeed, cultural systems. Nonethe-less, an ideal of unity survived along with vestiges of the old cosmopoli-tanism. It has never died, and now many hope it is irreversibly in the ascendant.

No theme, even one as comprehensive as the tension between the local and the cosmopolitan, can adequately cover three hundred years of history in Europe, but this one is perhaps better than most. It includes the contin-uing role played in Europe by the Scandinavians through their diplomatic alliances, military contributions to the crusades, active engagement in Baltic and North Sea trade with Scotland, England, the Hanse towns, and among themselves, long after the Viking invasions were over, the only time a reader ordinarily encounters Scandinavians in any general consideration of the Middle Ages. Spain (or, more properly, the Spains), if there were more space in this chapter, would come in and out of the story in a way that this region rarely does in traditional pictures of medieval develop-ment. Focusing on the recruitment and attraction of soldiers and settlers from North of the Pyrenees to reconquer territories from the Muslims and to resettle the conquered land stresses Spain's ties to Europe as a whole. In the same way the diplomatic and marriage alliances of Spanish aristocrats and the activities of Iberian merchants (Portuguese and Castilian traders in England; Catalonian throughout the Mediterranean) point to Spain's integration into a manifestly European civilization.

EUROPE

The first issue that needs to be addressed is terminological. People who thought about toponymy at all, even mapmakers who thought about it all the time, rarely used the word Europe (Latin, *Europa*) to describe the geographical or cultural entity we now call Europe.[4] The word of choice

---

[3] For Lanfranc's career, see Margaret Gibson, *Lanfranc of Bec* (Oxford: Clarendon Press, 1978).

[4] Benjamin Braude, "The Sons of Noah and the Construction of Ethnic and Geographical Identities in the Medieval and Early Modern Periods," *William and Mary Quarterly*, 3d series, 54 (1997): 109.

among the dominant groups in society, at least from the eleventh century on, was *Christianitas* (Christendom). We may learn a great deal from this fact. Europe was where Latin Christians—Roman Catholic Christians—dominated the political and demographic landscape.[5] A profound divide, symbolized by the mutual excommunication of pope and patriarch of Constantinople in 1054 and made unbridgeable by westerners' occupation of Constantinople (1204–61) following the Fourth Crusade, separated Catholics from Greek or Orthodox Christians in Russia, the Balkans, and the Greek peninsula and archipelago. Regions in North Africa and the Near East, once ruled by Christians and still having substantial sectarian Christian populations (Copts in Egypt, for example), had come under the political and demographic dominance of Muslims. Even when Palestine and its environs temporarily succumbed to Christian political control and military occupation in the aftermath of the First Crusade (1096–1100), Catholic Christians remained a demographic minority among other Christians in the Near East.

When people spoke of Christendom geographically in, say, the year 1250, they meant the totality of regions we would now call Iceland, Scandinavia, the British Isles, France, most of Spain and Portugal, all of Italy, the Low Countries, Germany, Austria, Poland, Hungary, Bohemia, Moravia, Slovakia, and Croatia. In all these regions the dominant political power was vested in avowed Roman Catholic Christians, and the clear demographic edge lay with this *Glaubensvolk*.[6] Within these regions Jews constituted numerically, if not symbolically, an insignificant minority. The number of Muslims was dwindling (even in the Christian kingdoms of Spain and in southern Italy and Sicily where the Muslim population was largest). The political power of Muslims was negligible. Pagans were being subjugated in the Northeast (what we would now call Finland, Estonia, Latvia, and Lithuania) by Catholic Christians, although the process was not entirely successful. The resistance of the Lithuanians was especially spectacular and, for a very long time, effective; in 1387, though under significant military pressure, their ruler would accept Catholic Christianity voluntarily for diplomatic reasons, not because of any crushing

---

[5] See Gerard Delanty, *Inventing Europe: Idea, Identity, Reality* (London: Macmillan, 1995), 10, 16–17, 34–6, 38–42.

[6] The term *Glaubensvolk*, used in the way I have used it, is an adaptation of Ulrich Haarmann's terminology. His comparative treatment of Christendom and Islam in the Middle Ages and the tensions between cosmopolitanism and "nationalism" is highly recommended; "Glaubensvolk und Nation im islamischen und lateinischen Mittelalter," *Berlin-Brandenburgische Akademie der Wissenschaften: Berichte und Abhandlungen* (Berlin: Academie Verlag, 1996), 2:161–99.

military defeat or demonstration of insurmountable western technological and logistical superiority. He would acquire the throne of Catholic
Poland in the bargain.[7]

POLITICAL DEVELOPMENTS

Since the sixteenth and seventeenth centuries, when scholars began the
serious study of the Middle Ages, the rise of the state or attempts to discern the peculiar genius of the nation have been at the center of their
concerns. Seeking after Eternal France—the essence of France—was, for
example, largely a sixteenth-century innovation.[8] This centrality of concern about the state and nation in medieval studies arose because of an
almost manic preoccupation with the balance of power among states.
Scholars wondered how the political units that negotiated the balance of
power had come about. What were their so-called natural borders? Did
a people who constituted a nation have to be one in religion or sect, language, traditions, and in some way lineage?[9] Out of a preoccupation with
these questions came "patriotic ideologies" that, in the case of France, for
example, might sustain people even in the worst of times—civil war, invasion, social revolution.[10]

To a degree, the surviving sources seemed to point in this direction for
research. Royal clerks had created the greatest archives of documentary
sources, but the church was not far behind with its zealously preserved
and voluminous documentary and chronicle sources.[11] The editing of the
ecclesiastical sources usually had less to do with a disinterested wish to

---

[7] Although it does not deal with the later phases of the struggle, S. C. Rowell's wonderful
book (*Lithuania Ascending: A Pagan Empire within East-Central Europe, 1295–1345*
[Cambridge: Cambridge University Press, 1994]) describes the pagan Lithuanians' greatest successes.

[8] Ernst Kantorowicz, *The King's Two Bodies: A Study in Mediaeval Political Theology*
(Princeton, N.J.: Princeton University Press, 1957), 79, n. 89.

[9] See Colette Beaune, *The Birth of an Ideology: Myths and Symbols of Nation in Late-
Medieval France*, trans. Susan Huston, ed. Frederic Cheyette (Berkeley and Los Angeles:
University of California Press, 1991), 310–25, for an adept summary.

[10] See Robert Mandrou, *Introduction to Modern France, 1500–1640: An Essay in Historical
Psychology*, trans. R. E. Hallmark (New York: Holmes and Meier, 1976), 125–6. For a
slightly earlier period, see Beaune, *Birth of an Ideology*, 302–8.

[11] France led the way here with the two massive collections (the first of royal documents,
the second of ecclesiastical records). See *Recueil des historiens des Gaules et de la France*,
24 vols., ed. Martin Bouquet and others (Paris: 1734–1904); the *Imprimérie* has varied
in its publishing history, depending on the nature of the regime (*Imprimérie Royale,
Imprimérie Impériale, Imprimérie Nationale*). On the church see *Gallia christiana in
provincias ecclesiasticas distributa*, 16 vols. (Paris: 1715–1865). Its editor and publisher
was the Congrégation de Saint-Maur.

investigate church history than with a desire to show that the distinctive form that ecclesiastical history took in this country or that one had much to do with the irreducible national essence of its people, language, and culture. The history of the church was a purposive handmaiden to the history of the state.

In seeking the roots of Frenchness or whatever national essence the scholars of the sixteenth and seventeenth centuries were seeking, they discovered something quite unsettling and called it "feudalism." The term now is under attack: historians question whether they should apply a word coined by seventeenth-century controversialists to a world like Europe in the High Middle Ages.[12] What they called feudalism reflected their recognition of the intense fragmentation of loyalties around the rulers of great fiefs or other large units of property in the medieval past. Given their teleological concerns with how kingdoms developed, they searched for keys to explain how great rulers domesticated feudalism and its plethora of lords by transforming it into a tight and neatly hierarchical system of government. It was this system of government under a powerful king, they believed, that allowed the national essence (never actually lost but hidden sometimes under the debris of anarchy and, at other times, under Catholic and Imperial universalism) to blossom in their own age.

Despite their teleologies, these controversialists and early scholars were right about many things. They were right in discerning a tension between the multiplicity of governing units (like castellanies, viscounties, counties, and duchies) and the idealistic universalism of the political theorists and theologians of the Middle Ages. For many of the great intellectuals of the twelfth and thirteenth centuries, there was never much doubt that there should be and eventually would be only one faith and only one *Imperium*.

Below the level of the great thinkers and the great lords of kingdoms, duchies, and counties, there was a bewildering variety of local cultures.[13] They might be clan-based, as in Scotland and Ireland, or caste-like, as in Wales, or male-dominated but otherwise far more egalitarian, as in Scandinavia. Most people would have expressed their deepest loyalties in a vocabulary dominated by these local realities. But the sources most accessible to sixteenth- and seventeenth-century scholars spoke hardly a word about these multiple worlds. Despite present-day sensitivity in the historical profession to the plight of the lowly and the desire to fill the

---

[12] Susan Reynolds, *Fiefs and Vassals: The Medieval Evidence Reinterpreted* (Oxford: Oxford University Press, 1994).

[13] For a useful overview, see Susan Reynolds, *Kingdoms and Communities in Western Europe, 900–1300* (Oxford: Clarendon Press, 1984).

silences, the lack of sources remains the great barrier to any simple reconstruction of the so-called authentic voices of subordinate groups in the European Middle Ages.

The diversity of material life among the various groups that occupied the landscape in the High Middle Ages underscores the fragmentation endemic in society.[14] Basic facts of medieval demography suggest widely disparate densities of population and a great unevenness in the incidence of towns. Agricultural technologies varied because of the many different soil types, not to mention the gross differences in the topography and hydrography between northern Europe (well-watered and cold) and southern Europe (dry and hot).

Still the attraction of and adherence to an ideal of universalism stimulated an arresting cosmopolitanism that transcended the narrow loyalties of village and town and even the wider loyalties of lordship and kingdom. It ripped boys and men (and girls and women, although to a far lesser extent) out of their parochial networks and transformed their lives and the life of society at large. A girl from Domrémy, a tiny village on the Saône far from anyone's heartland, would think thoughts about France and England and the church of God that would change the world. We know of her, of course, as Joan of Arc.[15] Economic developments were crucial to this possibility.

THE ECONOMY

Underpinning these developments was the booming population in Europe.[16] It is hard to explain why population began to rise, steeply and steadily, around the year 1100 or perhaps slightly before. Although massive external invasions had come to an end, there was no long period of internal peace in Europe. England suffered various forms of disorder, perhaps even some anarchy, during the first half of the twelfth century, and civil wars as well as wars with France occupied productive resources for much of the late twelfth and thirteenth centuries in England. In addition to petty internal wars and the long struggle with England, France endured the bitter conflict known as the Albigensian Crusade. The Holy

---

[14] For a brief introduction to this subject, see Hans-Werner Goetz, *Life in the Middle Ages from the Seventh to the Thirteenth Century*, ed. Steven Rowan, trans. Albert Wimmer (Notre Dame, Ind.: University of Notre Dame Press, 1993), 9–23.

[15] For a readable biographical study, see Marina Warner, *Joan of Arc: The Image of Female Heroism* (New York: Alfred A. Knopf, 1981).

[16] Philippe Contamine and others, *L'Economie médiévale* (Paris: Armand Colin, 1993), 141–6, 211–14.

Roman Empire drifted in and out of civil war over and over again, and partly because of the repercussions in Italy of the German emperor's disputes with the popes over their respective political and spiritual powers, it is not easy to see why the peninsula's population grew significantly.

It is possible, of course, that unusual spells of mild weather in the growing season improved harvests and nutrition and encouraged or at least permitted larger families. It is possible, too, that changes in field systems, the diffusion of established technologies like the heavy plow in the North, new methods of crop rotation, and the introduction of new crops, especially beans and peas, or their diffusion on a grand scale, had similar effects. These positions have been strenuously argued by generations of scholars, but they remain largely conjectures. What is fact is simply the take-off in population. Gross estimates see a rise from about 25 million Europeans in the year 1100 to 80 million or more by the year 1300.[17]

The growth of population, most of it in the countryside, stimulated the spread of rural markets. Recent estimates see a peak in the creation of periodic markets in the thirteenth century throughout the British Isles and in region after region on the continent. Some of these regions, like Germany, had ten times as many markets in 1300 as thay had in the eleventh century. This expansion permitted the movement of labor, goods, and money more efficiently and in a more widely flung network or series of economic networks than had ever existed in the North of Europe before or had been in existence in southern Europe since the fall of the Roman Empire.

Southern Europe led the way, especially in the growth and sophistication of towns.[18] Northern Italy, particularly Lombardy and Tuscany, were to provide Europe a cradle for bourgeois values. By the end of the thirteenth century, Florence, Milan, Genoa, and Venice had populations close to 100,000. Only Paris and perhaps London, in the North, were comparable. The demand for provisions created by these urban agglomerations in Italy and unevenly elsewhere (along the Baltic Coast, in Flanders, on the eastern shore of the Iberian peninsula, to name the most important places where towns flourished) stimulated food production and industry in all their hinterlands.

---

[17] Unless otherwise noted, the information in this paragraph and the next several on the structures of society, the role of technology, the influence of markets, and other aspects of the economy is from my book *The Great Famine: Northern Europe in the Early Fourteenth Century* (Princeton, N.J.: Princeton University Press, 1996), 43–8, 87–96, 127–34.

[18] In general, see Contamine, *Economie médiévale*, 185–94.

The magnitude of the growth of population, the rapid proliferation of rural markets that ensued, and the urban resurgence led to the development of increasingly dense networks of regional and international trade. As a result, by the year 1300 prices and wages in the economy of Europe were genuinely responsive to supply and demand, despite the continuing moral hegemony of the doctrine of the just price, one aspect of which stressed the sin of charging high prices for subsistence goods in times of extreme scarcity. By the end of the thirteenth century, even eastern Germany and western Poland had insinuated themselves in the international trade networks dependent on the existence of these markets. In the year 1300 rye from Brandenburg was available for sale in Flanders. Although the crusades to the Holy Land were in no sense primarily economic ventures, they indirectly testify to the networks by which products of the East came to the West and vice versa in a seemingly endless rhythm of exchange.[19]

What was the converse of these economic developments? For every merchant—or man with dusty feet, as he was picturesquely named in the Middle Ages—traveling a road that led from Italy through the Alpine passes North to Germany or traversing the sun-baked routes from the Mediterranean ports of Spain and southern France to the cities of the plains, there were scores of petty retailers who never saw more than two or three marketplaces in their lives. For them the word "silk" or the plethora of words for exotic spices would remain only words. Yet at least they knew the words. When one sees today pictures from the Third World, where poor people, apparently isolated from the global community, wear sweatshirts emblazoned with the logos and legends of the Chicago Bulls or the Dallas Cowboys, one recognizes that isolation is relative. The same may be said of rustics and artisans, like Peter Saracen, a man dwelling in a medieval village in the heartland of western Europe, say the mountains of Auvergne in central France, far from the real Saracens, the Moors, living on the Spanish frontier or the Muslims besieging the crusaders' outposts in Syria. In the thirteenth century someone knew that the people of this village were part of an adventure that pitted Christians and Saracens in deadly combat a thousand miles away. One need not believe that Peter Saracen had any sympathy for Saracens merely because he bore the name, anymore than wearers of American sweatshirts in Lebanon today

---

[19] Jonathan Riley-Smith, "Early Crusaders to the East and the Costs of Crusading, 1095–1130," in *Cross Cultural Convergences in the Crusader Period: Essays Presented to Aryeh Grabois on His Sixty-Fifth Birthday*, ed. Michael Goodich and others (New York: Peter Lang, 1995), 237–57.

necessarily love the United States. But, like Peter Saracen of Auvergne, they know they are part of a wider world.[20]

THE ECCLESIASTICAL WORLD

That world was defined by the Latin church. Universalism—incorporation of all people through baptism in the Christian community, irrespective of color, ethnic origin, place of settlement, or previous beliefs—was a central element of the ideology and objectives of the Catholic church. The twin legacies of early medieval missionary activity before the year 1000 and of monastic reform in the eleventh and twelfth centuries provided the conditions for translating ideology into practice. The earlier medieval missions had aimed to increase the sheer territorial expanse of Christianity.[21] Famous examples include the sixth-century mission to the Anglo-Saxons, sponsored by the papacy, which brought England into the Catholic fold and the ninth- and tenth-century missions to the Scandinavians and other northern peoples culminating in their general conversion. These missionary activities, in one sense, made Christianity a genuinely European-wide religion.

The second impulse, after universalism, was monastic reform. It is usually, though perhaps exaggeratedly, associated with the great monastery of Cluny in Burgundy and the other houses in the Cluniac order that nurtured an idyllic vision of the organization and dignity of the clerical community.[22] What the reform accomplished was the creation of centers or locations, including Cluny, for the dissemination of this idyllic vision of Catholic universalism. Out of the ferment of monastic reform arose a largely new form of the institutional church, one that looked down upon localism in favor of central—indeed papal—control. In the end the papacy came to be seen by many reformers as the best guarantor of Catholic universalism and, partly in response to this, papal spokesmen arrogated to the office of the pope wide authority in managing religious affairs and protecting the freedom of the ecclesiastical community.

---

[20] The real "Petrus Sarraceni" of Auvergne may be encountered in a judicial action recorded in the thirteenth-century *Enquêtes administratives d'Alfonse de Poitiers*, ed. Pierre-François Fournier and Pascal Guébin (Paris: Imprimérie Nationale, 1959), 154.

[21] For a breathtaking evocation of the period, see Peter Brown, *The Rise of Western Christendom: Triumph and Diversity, A.D. 200–1000* (Oxford: Basil Blackwell, 1996).

[22] For a reasoned evaluation of the subject, with due emphasis on German developments, see C. H. Lawrence, *Medieval Monasticism: Forms of Religious Life in Western Europe in the Middle Ages* (London and New York: Longman, 1984), 80–92.

This transformation occurred in the late eleventh and twelfth centuries and was seemingly secure in the thirteenth. A 1994 book on Pope Innocent III, the pope who reigned at the turn of the twelfth/thirteenth century, can use the subtitle *Leader of Europe* without apparent irony.[23] The achievement of papal monarchy came at a great price, however.

Violence resulted from the attack on extreme forms of sacred kingship. Hitherto, the dominant theory had vested power over the church and churchmen in the king or emperor. In the eleventh century ecclesiastical reformers contested the theory. The struggle between emperor and pope that ensued, usually referred to as the Investiture Controversy, turned on the alleged right of the former to confer the staff and ring on newly elected bishops.[24]

The staff and ring were the symbols of spiritual, not secular, authority. The staff represented the bishop's right to bring the errant sheep back into the fold. In other words, it meant the bishop could exercise the magisterium—to say what the Catholic faith was—and to enforce his view against heretics. The staff also represented the power to beat away wild dogs and wolves, enemies of the Christian faith from outside the fold, and to sanction the use of force for the protection of the Christian faithful. The ring symbolized the marriage of the bishop to his diocese, his unbreakable union with the people whom he protected, served, and loved.

No king or emperor, the radical reformers argued, had any right to bestow such authority. The church rested firmly on the foundation of the apostles and their successors, the bishops. ("Thou art Peter and upon this rock I will build my church.") Only bishops ought to bestow the powers symbolized by the staff and ring on bishops-elect.

The problem was that, for centuries, customs had grown up contrary to this view. The reform movement of the eleventh century challenged these entrenched customs. As the leader of the reform party pointed out, "Christ did not say I am custom, but I am Truth." Civil wars in Germany and confrontations in other countries resulted in hard-fought victories for the ecclesiastical reformers' position. But they also undermined *political* universalism. As a result of this struggle, the claim of the Holy Roman Emperor to universal secular rule eroded. The weakening of Imperial

---

[23] Jane Sayers, *Innocent III: Leader of Europe, 1198–1216* (London and New York: Longman, 1994).

[24] Uta-Renate Blumenthal, *Investiture Controversy: Church and Monarchy from the Ninth to the Twelfth Century* (Philadelphia: University of Pennsylvania Press, 1988). On the parameters of reform, see Giles Constable, *The Reformation of the Twelfth Century* (New York: Cambridge University Press, 1996).

control in northern Italy where it had once been strong is the clearest example of this reality.

One can characterize the discourse of those who debated problems of the internal organization of the church, church-state relations, and doctrinal and legal matters as "scholastic." Scholasticism was supranational, like the language of its expression, Latin. The adjective "scholastic," of course, covers many sins and obscures many nuances, but to some extent the word is a good one, for it emphasizes the general role of schools and, most important for our purposes, the specific role of the schools of higher learning as institutional sites for the production and exchange of knowledge.[25]

The number of universities even by the year 1250 was very small: Bologna in northern Italy, Montpellier in southern France, Paris in northern France, Oxford in England, and a handful of others. Although the number of universities or places of general studies (*studia generalia*) was small, or perhaps because their number was small, they were truly international institutions.[26] They were also valuable in providing training for future administrators of churches and principalities. Therefore, there was a vested interest over time for individual princes and towns to have their own "local" universities. The late Middle Ages would see a profound undermining of early university cosmopolitanism.[27] Although pretensions to cosmopolitanism never vanished, localism began to prevail toward the end of the fourteenth century. I am tempted to see a parallel in my home institution, Princeton. Scholars there talk often of their contributions and loyalty to the *world* of learning, but the university motto is "Princeton in the *nation's* service."

---

[25] The title of R. W. Southern's *Scholastic Humanism and the Unification of Europe*, I: *Foundations* (Oxford: Basil Blackwell, 1995) promises more than the book delivers, but it should be remembered that this is only the first volume of a projected trilogy. Happily, the introduction to volume one (pages 1 to 13) does offer an informed, not to say impassioned, defense of the universalism of scholasticism, precisely the point I am trying to make in this chapter.

[26] The divisions of their student bodies into *nationes* demonstrates that the word "cosmopolitanism" obscures, even in the early stage of the universities' history, certain centrifugal tendencies.

[27] Alan Cobban, "Reflections on the Role of Medieval Universities in Contemporary Society," in *Intellectual Life in the Middle Ages: Essays Presented to Margaret Gibson*, ed. Lesley Smith and Benedicta Ward (London and Rio Grande, Ohio: Hambledon Press, 1992), 234: "Whereas several of the early universities, including Bologna, Paris, Montpellier and Salamanca, had been cosmopolitan centres of learning which transcended national boundaries and local allegiances, universities of the later medieval period were founded by kings, princes and city authorities as symbols of national, provincial or civic prestige. Stripped of their supranational character, universities were viewed increasingly as integral parts of political territorial units, designed to serve the requirements of national institutions and to be of benefit to the local community."

Latin was the universal language of the higher schools and of university life in general.[28] "In castles and towns" men who were enemies of Peter Abelard said of his books, "they replace light with darkness." They perceived his books to be dangerous not only for their content but also for their reach: "they pass from one race to another, and from one kingdom to another." They "cross the oceans, they leap over the Alps...they spread through the provinces and the kingdoms."[29] In many places this structure of diffusion remained intact in the universities until the eighteenth century. When Christian Thomasius started to lecture in German instead of Latin at the University of Leipzig in 1687, the event, the first of its kind, was a shock and caused a scandal.[30] It also sounded the death knell—the inevitable collapse—of Latin as the universal language of university instruction.

To be sure, even in the thirteenth century, when Latin was providing a glue binding the intellectual elite in universities and the universal church, the vernaculars were providing a basis for a countervailing localism.[31] The early influence of churchmen in newly Christianized, northern European governments had made Latin the official language of record in many courts and administrative bureaus. In the thirteenth century this monopoly collapsed; in the fourteenth, Latin was in retreat except as tradition and prestige required it in certain kinds of records and transactions. In the fourteenth century and later, however, the languages of pleading in the hundreds of new courts across Europe and the languages of recording the decisions were vernacular.

As literatures began to emerge or re-emerge in vernaculars in the twelfth and with a vengeance in the thirteenth and fourteenth centuries, distinctive regional or national traditions and genres emerged. Latin literature became learned literature, the literature of high theology, ethics, political theory, jurisprudence, and natural philosophy. It was somewhat remote,

---

[28] For perceptive brief analyses of the use of Latin in the Middle Ages, see the essays on the "Varieties of Medieval Latinity," in *Medieval Latin: An Introduction and Bibliographic Guide*, ed. F. A. C. Mantello and A. G. Rigg (Washington, D.C.: Catholic University Press, 1996).

[29] Quoted in C. Stephen Jaeger, *The Envy of Angels: Cathedral Schools and Social Ideals in Medieval Europe, 950–1200* (Philadelphia: University of Pennsylvania Press, 1994), 239. For other examples of scholastic cosmopolitanism, see 16.

[30] On Christian Thomasius, sometimes characterized as the author of the second German Reformation, see Werner Schmidt, *Ein vergessener Rebell: Leben und Wirken des Christian Thomasius* (Munich: Eugen Diederichs Verlag, 1995).

[31] On the problematic status of the vernacular in France, see Gabrielle Spiegel, *Romancing the Past: The Rise of Vernacular Prose Historiography in Thirteenth-Century France* (Berkeley and Los Angeles: University of California Press, 1993), 66–7.

at best, if not absolutely divorced from everyday life, except when school-boys forced to learn it wrote scurrilous screeds.

> Stilus nam et tabule
> sunt feriales epule,
> et Nasonis carmina
> vel aliorum pagina.
> (Pen and ink and copy-book,
> How funereal they look;
> Ovid's songs, how dull with age,
> Still more any other's page.)[32]

The lively literature of stories and novellas, love poetry and satires, and personal letters among middling people found expression in the vernacular. It is true that one vernacular enjoyed a privileged status and, with that, a certain cosmopolitan flair. This was French.[33] Many people spoke versions of it as a native language across what we would call northern France, as did the nobility and gentry in England and the administrative elite in southern France. Many commercial and military types throughout the Mediterranean spoke a *lingua franca* that built itself on the skeletal structure of the language of Paris, a fact that owes much to the prominence of northern Frenchmen and women in the crusades. In an Italian jail at the end of the thirteenth century, Marco Polo dictated the famous tale of his Asian travels in a form of merchants' Franco-Italian that literate upper-class persons living almost anywhere on the northern shores of the Mediterranean might have puzzled out.[34]

Among the upper classes, facility in French continued to be common long after the Middle Ages; among those who aspire to Culture with a capital C, a French word or phrase, properly pronounced in conversation, seldom hurts even now. But otherwise regional and national vernaculars steadily displaced Latin and French in the late Middle Ages, ultimately reducing Latin to a "dead language" (the phrase is common in English from the Enlightenment on) and leaving French in Europe to the French and some of their Belgian, Swiss, and (a few isolated) Italian neighbors.

---

[32] *Goliard Poets*, 223. The reference to Ovid's songs is explained by the fact that students improved their Latin by memorizing and imitating a very sanitized version of the poems.

[33] R. A. Lodge, "Language Attitudes and Linguistic Norms in France and England in the Thirteenth Century," in *Thirteenth Century England*, IV, ed. P. Coss and S. Lloyd (Woodbridge, Suffolk: Boydell Press, 1992), 78.

[34] The manuscript history of Marco Polo's *Travels* is complex. The most likely linguistic circle of the original was a variety of French. See *The Travels of Marco Polo*, ed. M. Komroff (New York and London: Liveright, 1953), xxv.

In the High Middle Ages it was different. Bearing written messages in Latin, the pope at Rome delegated men to represent his dignity across Europe. These legates, nuncios, and judges-delegate provided the essential and routine links between the universal papacy, centered at Rome, and the most distant parts of Christendom.[35] Chosen for their intelligence, loyalty to the pope and papal monarchy, diplomatic skills, and energy, these men moved comfortably from one region to another. John of Abbeville, a town in northern France, was papal legate in Spain in the 1220s. Guala Bicchieri, the Italian, was sent by Pope Innocent III (an Italian who had studied in Paris) to be papal legate in England, and he served on the triumvirate that governed the northern kingdom after the death of King John in 1216.

Careers like these were standard, even for men who did not reach the very top of their professions. Giles of Verracclo was born in Monte Cassino in Italy. His first serious appointment in the church was as archdeacon of Thessalonika in Greece in 1218. The next year he traveled more than a thousand miles to serve as archdeacon of Ely in the Fenland of East Anglia in England. Through the early 1220s he was a presence at the papal curia in Rome and served successively as papal legate to Croatia (1229), nuncio to Hungary (1230), and nuncio to Apulia in southern Italy thereafter.[36]

In the early fourteenth century the pattern continued.[37] Thomas of Strasbourg, born in Hagenau in Germany, attended schools in Strasbourg and Padua. He served the Augustinian Order in Venice (1332), in Paris (1335–9), and in the Rhineland and Swabia (1354–7). Hermann of Schildesche, schooled in northern Germany, taught in western and central Germany at Magdeburg and Erfurt and served his order for nearly a decade in Paris before returning to eastern Germany to finish his career. There is no reason to multiply what could easily become a thousand examples.

---

[35] For a precise exposition of the differences among these offices, see Richard Schmutz, "Medieval Papal Representatives: Legates, Nuncios, and Judges-Delegate," *Studia Gratiana* 15 (1972): 441–63. The differences do not affect the point I am making in the text.

[36] Nicholas Vincent, "The Election of Pandulph Verracclo as Bishop of Norwich (1215)," in *Historical Research: The Bulletin of the Institute of Historical Research* 68 (1995): 154–5.

[37] On the examples I cite, see Christopher Ocker, *Johannes Klenkok: A Friar's Life, c. 1310–1374* (transactions of the American Philosophical Society, vol. 83, pt. 5; Philadelphia, 1993), 5, n. 9. Parallel examples may be found in the foreign appointments to the Scottish prelacy in the High Middle Ages. See Bruce Webster, *Medieval Scotland: The Making of an Identity* (London: St. Martin's Press, 1997), 113–31.

The opposite kind of career, one that would make a native cleric into a papal legate in his native land, was still rare. By the fourteenth century this pattern became more common and eventually came to dominate. The archbishop of Canterbury, to give one example, would have legatine powers bestowed on him because of his office and rank in the English church in the late Middle Ages. The problem was that a system originally designed to bring the disparate parts of the Catholic church into obedience with Rome was more likely in the Renaissance and on the eve of the Reformation to reinforce divisions within Christendom and dissent from the papacy. Instead of men like John of Abbeville and Guala Bicchieri, the later system produced men like Cardinal Wolsey, the ill-fated English prelate with the office of legate in England during the reign of Henry VIII.

Yet even at its heyday in the thirteenth century, the cosmopolitanism of career patterns and of other linkages in the church was in tension with the local interests of churchmen with far more restricted outlooks. There were thousands and thousands of monasteries and priories (small, dependent houses) in Europe. Most of the administrators of these institutions necessarily focused their attention on events and problems within about a five- or ten-kilometer radius of their buildings and estates. They often resented the time that they had to spend going to local and provincial councils to report on their activities to the powerful men, often aliens because of the cosmopolitanism of the church, who flourished in the network described earlier.[38] They even more deeply resented having to pay the taxes and levies that made it possible to sustain the universal church and to carry out transnational, indeed supranational, projects like crusades. To be sure, there were those among them who looked with envy at the career patterns, the contacts, the power, and the prestige of the men who claimed to be governing the world, but envy unfulfilled ate away, like a cankerworm, at the vaunted unity of the Catholic church. And sometimes anti-alien feeling spilled

---

[38] See Nicholas Vincent, *Peter des Roches: An Alien in English Politics, 1205–1238* (Cambridge: Cambridge University Press, 1996), 37. Vincent extends this observation to the consequences of cosmopolitan recruitment to secular governmental offices: "Unfortunately for the aliens themselves, the very fidelity and cosmopolitanism that earned them gratitude and reward from the crown were the selfsame factors that served to heighten their unpopularity." More generally on the growth of anti-alien feeling in the thirteenth century (including the promulgation of legislation against aliens in England, for example), see D. A. Carpenter, "King Henry III's 'Statute' against Aliens: July 1263," in *The Reign of Henry III* (London and Rio Grande, Ohio: Hambledon Press, 1996), 261–80.

over into violence, pitting alien churchmen against natives and their lay allies.[39]

By the end of the Middle Ages, certainly by the fifteenth century, the faultlines in such unity as there was became major fissures. Heresy was a serious problem, but one that churchmen confronted continually and in an urgent way from the twelfth century onward.[40] What made dealing with heresy more difficult in the late Middle Ages was a distressing turn of events, the so-called Babylonian Captivity of the Church.[41] In the early and mid-fourteenth century (1305–76), the popes ruled from Avignon rather than from Rome. Ostensibly papal officials justified their reluctance to reside in Rome by invoking the appalling political conditions of the eternal city. But the shift of residence to Avignon, coming as it did in the wake of a humiliating papal confrontation with the French crown, contributed to the widespread perception that the popes had come under the domination of France. It did not help to overcome this perception that the men chosen as popes in the seventy-odd years of the captivity were Frenchmen.

The Great Schism (1378–1417), initiated by an attempted return of the papacy to Rome, was of equal importance in undermining its moral authority, a pillar of its claim to universal obedience. The schism produced two lines of popes and thus divided Christians according to those loyal to the Roman and allegedly more independent line and those who supported the Avignonese papacy, stigmatized by its enemies as a French puppet. The dispute would end in compromise, but the legacy of that compromise was almost as dangerous as the schism itself. The decision to yield to the judgment of an ecumenical council seemed to some observers to support the troubling assertion, already debated in the two centuries before, but now given great urgency, that a council was superior to the pope.[42] Conciliarism, as a movement and an ideology, was not defined by this radical interpretation of its meaning. Moderate conciliarists merely argued that in the peculiarly difficult circumstances of the early fifteenth century, recourse to a council made sense. Moderates did not champion

---

[39] Vincent, *Peter des Roches*, 303.

[40] Malcolm Lambert, *Medieval Heresy: Popular Movements from the Gregorian Reform to the Reformation* (Cambridge, Mass.: Basil Blackwell, 1992).

[41] On the late medieval church and the problems treated in this and the next paragraph, see Francis Oakley, *The Western Church in the Later Middle Ages* (Ithaca, N.Y.: Cornell University Press, 1979).

[42] On the origins of conciliarism, see Brian Tierney, *Foundations of the Conciliar Theory: The Contribution of the Medieval Canonists from Gratian to the Great Schism* (Cambridge: Cambridge University Press, 1955).

the end of universal papal monarchy or the devolution of doctrinal authority, although a century later, because of the Reformation, both came to be, to some degree, accomplished facts.

CONCLUSION

In the High Middle Ages there was a strong and creative tension between cosmopolitan values and local concerns, universalism and parochialism. This chapter has concentrated on the political, economic, and ecclesiastical aspects of medieval life, but others are equally revealing. Recently, for example, Manlio Bellomo has argued for a commonality (a *ius commune*) of legal principles and terminology that existed in a symbiotic relationship with local legal systems (*iura propria*) in high medieval Christendom. He has suggested, too, that this commonality survived the birth of modernity and persisted until the nineteenth century. In his view scholars have been remiss in their aberrant fascination with local particularities of the law, a fascination that has blinded them to the fundamental unity of medieval European civilization.[43]

The artistic component of the tension between cosmopolitanism and localism, another feature of this story, is as fascinating as the political, economic, religious, and legal components. In the twelfth century there emerged a distinctively European style in architecture. French in origin, the Gothic became the cutting-edge style of artistic production in the twelfth century from northern Britain to the Holy Land and from Spain and Italy northward to the Baltic Coast. It continued as the exemplary style for at least two centuries.

Recent research, however, emphasizes two points, First, local conditions put constraints on the international style, thereby stimulating the birth of new and distinctive regional styles. Second, indigenous styles sometimes enjoyed a syncretic relationship with the Gothic without being dominated by it. Sometimes these styles continued their lively growth through the twelfth and thirteenth centuries independent of Gothic influences.[44] What was true of architecture was true of styles in painting and glass that flourished in the Ile-de-France and are sometimes thought to have swept away everything in their path as they became the European standard. No such failure or weak-willed retreat occurred, despite a

---

[43] Manlio Bellomo, *The Common Legal Past of Europe, 1000-1800*, trans. Lydia Cochrane (Washington, D.C.: Catholic University Press, 1995).

[44] Jean Bony, *French Gothic Architecture of the Twelfth and Thirteenth Centuries* (Berkeley and Los Angeles: University of California Press, 1983), 249–50, 411–63.

certain degree of stylistic coherence that drew on French models and is discernible in thirteenth- and fourteenth-century European painting and stained glass.[45]

The point is that a set of ideals about the proper ordering of life culminated in a spectacularly overarching attempt in the High Middle Ages to create institutions and practices that allowed those ideals, grouped under the twin rubrics of cosmopolitanism and universalism, to be achieved. Nothing was so difficult as to sustain this achievement in the twelfth and thirteenth centuries against the pressures of a persistent localism, itself perpetuated by the relative technological and logistical primitiveness of the coercive forces at the center. But the ideals, and to some extent the institutions and practices, endured in the face of localism. Greater challenges had to be faced toward the end of the thirteenth century and in the fourteenth century as a result of regional patriotism and the multiple crises at the center of papal government such as the Babylonian Captivity and the Great Schism. And one might add as well the extraordinary natural and man-made disasters that affected all European life in the fourteenth and fifteenth centuries: famines, persistent class warfare in the countryside and in the towns, not to mention the multiple attacks of plague and of other pestilences.[46] Under these pressures many Europeans continued to affirm the unity of their culture and their common purpose. This is nothing short of remarkable. European unity today is faced with far fewer contradictions. It may emerge victorious in the long struggle with parochialism and prejudice—as long as the idealists and bureaucrats of unity do not in their hope, or perhaps in their hubris (coercive power is much stronger now), aim quite so high as their predecessors did in the High Middle Ages.

---

[45] Meredith Lillich, *The Armor of Light: Stained Glass in Western France, 1250–1325* (Berkeley and Los Angeles: University of California Press, 1994). See her cautionary remarks on pages 221 and 321–2 as well as her views on resistance to and regional adaptation of Parisian styles in painted and stained glass. Her examples come from western France.

[46] The bibliography on these problems is immense. In particular, see *Europa 1400: Die Krise des Spätmittelalters*, ed. Ferdinand Seibt and Winfried Eberhard (Stuttgart: Klett-Cotta, 1984).

4

The Republican Mirror: The Dutch Idea
of Europe

HANS W. BLOM

In 1622 Pieter de la Court, who was both a cloth manufacturer in Leiden and, together with his brother Johann, one of the most influential political and economic theorists of the seventeenth century, set out the principles of the *Interests of Holland and West-Friesland* in the book that bore this title. In it he described the political institutions and policy aims of the Dutch predominantly in terms of the economic conditions of their society. Profitable occupations, thriving markets, and a numerous population were among the main attributes of what he believed to be the "welfare of the people." The main sources of welfare were, he believed, to be found in fishing and trade, and in particular maritime trade. These occupations were well suited to the actual conditions of the Low Countries, provided an income for many, and attracted people from abroad to add to the population, thereby helping to establish the conditions for even greater welfare. The political institutions appropriate to sustain this economy could be easily summarized as religious tolerance and responsible government.

De la Court maintained that the freedom of the individual was essential to promote profitable economic activities, since only by consulting one's self-interest would citizens be able to make the right choices. The epitome of freedom is to have the opportunity to think for oneself and to learn from one's mistakes. Religious dogmatism frustrates such a development, while bringing the church's interference with the proper ways of politics in its wake. Moreover, responsible government is mainly a matter of the ruling elite being tied to the interest of the people at large.

This might be most easily understood in the Harringtonian sense of electing the elite from among the most important class of society. Although for his English contemporary and fellow republican James Harrington that class was the landowners, for de la Court it could only be the merchants. De la Court was not naïve about this connection. He did not believe that there will automatically be a correspondence of interests between rulers and citizens engaged in comparable occupations. His model was rather that of how best to divide a cake: one party cuts it, the other chooses first. Rulers must be prevented from the misuse of their power by being responsible to the law, and to their successors. Free citizens, a political order geared to further the conscious pursuit of self-interest, and an adequate macroeconomic structure are de la Court's guarantees for promoting public well-being.[1]

In his analysis de la Court seems to take for granted that Holland represents a coherent economic unity. He emphasizes its natural conditions (lack of local resources and therefore the necessity to trade, maritime location and thence the necessity for maritime occupations) as its uniform characteristic and the nation's boundaries determined by this characteristic. At the same time, however, de la Court defends the superiority of the republican form of government in a discussion of ancient and modern political regimes. Monarchies and oligarchic aristocracies for various reasons are less likely to promote the people's welfare, whatever the circumstances. The close connection between "market" and "polity" is thereby subsumed under a more general theory of political efficiency. It is this combination that suggests itself as an argument against Machiavellian expansionist republicanism, and indeed there is a very noticeable irenical tone to the writings of this Dutch merchant and publicist.

The connection between de la Court's general republicanism and his understanding of the specific interests of Holland is based on the insight that national boundaries in general correspond to the unique national characteristics of each individual market-cum-polity: a notion of the international state-system as an interdependence of individual variety. Peace should result from each country's understanding that war is only meant to satisfy the desire for the glory of monarchs and is always detrimental to the interests of the people. From this perspective a vision of Europe ensues that is both realistic and irenical, together allowing for national differences and peaceful cooperation.

De la Court was a practical man. He was an independent but devout Protestant, who understood the frailty of man and articulated a political

---

[1] Literature in English on de la Court—in particular from a contextual perspective—is scarce. For a first introduction, see Noel Malcolm, "Hobbes and Spinoza," in *The Cambridge History of Political Thought, 1450–1700*, ed. J. H. Burns (Cambridge: Cambridge University Press, 1991), 530–57.

theory in accordance with that understanding. He was not a self-conscious philosopher. But he profited from contemporary philosophy. (His sister was married to the Leiden Cartesian philosopher Adriaan Heereboord.) Later, philosophers, most famously Spinoza, elaborated on his practical political works.

He did have an axe to grind, however. His political ambition was to weaken dogmatic Protestantism and to provide arguments for a government by the States without the *Stadhouder*. Contemporary critics referred to de la Court, son of a Flemish immigrant, as the "Walloon," who tried to introduce unacceptable novelties into Dutch politics. They poked fun at him and quoted the arch-republican Hugo Grotius in their support. Some decried him as a "new Cromwell" or the "Quaker from Leiden." Nevertheless, all agreed with him that while politics is about the well-being of the people, the principle of politics is self-interest.

In what follows I propose to show how this "commercial" republicanism came about and what it implied for the Dutch perspective of the European order. It was, of course, Montesquieu who first pronounced the verdict on the fate of republicanism that by now has become commonplace: since republics depend on civic virtue (that is, the preference of the public interest over private interests) and commercial republics depend on equality, classical republics will be unable in the long run to withstand corruption in this world of vanity, and commercial republics will always ultimately succumb to luxury. For Montesquieu republics require the constant challenge of external threat if they are to maintain their civic spirit.[2] Monarchies, on the other hand, thrive on ambition, luxury, and reason of state. This is obviously contrary to de la Court's picture of a republic.

The question I will attempt to answer in this essay is thus twofold: Does there, in fact, exist an essentially modern and commercial republicanism that, contrary to Montesquieu's diagnosis, is able to survive the threat of corruption and "luxury"? And secondly, can we model our notion of Europe on this republicanism rather than on the image of the nation-state that Montesquieu offers as an alternative? In an attempt to answer these questions, I will first provide an interpretation of Dutch republicanism, including its view of Europe, and then, in the light of this, analyze the debate over the possibility of a "republican" Europe.

Dutch republicanism integrated the arguments of the reason-of-state theorists and replaced civic humanism with the language of self-interest.

---

[2] See, in particular, Montesquieu, *De l'esprit des lois*, III, 7; IV, 5; VIII, 5; VII, 2–4; XX, 5.

It was out of tune with the generally megalomaniac and millenarian notions prevalent in many of the other states in Europe—of which the Spanish Habsburgs are an early, and Napoleon a later, case. It also was at odds with the republican critics of "Divine Right."[3] I propose to discuss Dutch republicanism in more detail by drawing attention to the political discussions of the late 1610s—to which Grotius was an important contributor—and late 1640s—the debates leading up to the Peace of Westphalia in 1648—in order to describe the context for important political notions that emerged in the debates around de la Court and Spinoza in the 1660s and 1670s. In conclusion, I will take up the issue of the reflection of the idea of Europe in the mirror of Dutch republicanism.

My basic presupposition is that the idea of Europe is strongly related to the political economy of Europe. Bernard Mandeville, writing in the 1720s, rightly understood that what was needed was a new synthesis of reason of state, self-preservation, and Christian morality (or humanity, for that matter). Insofar as present-day Europe is still attempting to achieve a secularized form of this synthesis, one has every reason to follow de la Court and his contemporaries in their quest.

As a theme in early-modern politics, nonparochialism was developed in republicanism—not necessarily in civic humanism as opposed to natural law theory (*iusnaturalismo*), as J. G. A. Pocock maintains, but rather in republicanism as a discourse.[4] "Republicarians" have been necessarily concerned with the "international" ramifications of their political models precisely because they have a linkage conception of politics. Traditionally, this latter attribute has been regarded as related to warfare, along classical Machiavellian lines: to defend one's liberty, one must be prepared to expand the limits of one's state because foreign competitors need to be eliminated and because the desire for glory needs to be satisfied in order to maintain civic virtue. With the advent, however, of a broader and more culture-oriented conception of civic life (education, learning, religion, commerce), the republican notion of linkage acquired a different tone. Different conceptions of "unity in diversity" sprang up, as in the eighteenth-century notion of a "Republic of Letters." Attempts were

---

[3] For a discussion of this line of republican argument in relation to de la Court, see the introduction to Algernon Sidney, *Court Maxims Discussed and Refelled*, ed. H. W. Blom, E. O. G. H. Mulier, and R. Janse (Cambridge: Cambridge University Press, 1996), MS 1663–4.

[4] See, for example, Quentin Skinner, *Liberalism* (Cambridge: Cambridge University Press, 1998); Hans W. Blom, *Causality and Morality in Politics: The Rise of Naturalism in Dutch Seventeenth-Century Political Thought* (Rotterdam, 1995).

made, on the one hand, to define human nature and, on the other, to rephrase the value of national distinctions. This allowed for a new, republican understanding of sovereignty as an attribute of the polity or *respublica*. It stressed the reality of sovereignty as an adaptive system of human interaction rather than its legal formality.

A republican understanding of Europe became henceforth an enlargement upon this theme. As Pieter de la Court phrased it:

> In a word, all consists in this, Whether they that enter into a League, have a common Interest to avoid or obtain that which they have both in their Eye. [But if that common interest is absent,] Words, Hand, and Seal... hold no proportion to preponderate and resist the Ambition, Covetousness, Lust, Rage, and Self-conceit of great Princes....Ambition exceeds all other Affections...[s]o that the best way is not to trust them, and then we shall not be cheated....Which is quite contrary in all Republics, where the Rulers and Magistrates being first educated as common Citizens, must daily converse with their Equals or Superiors, and learn that which is just, otherwise they would be compelled to their Duty by the Judge, or other Virtuous and Powerful Civil Rulers....Custom is a second Nature, which is not easily altered....[A] Republican Government in all Countries of the World...would be much more advantageous to the People than a Government by a single Person.[5]

THE RISE OF DUTCH REPUBLICANISM

The construction of this Dutch republican perspective on Europe did not come about as the result of a conscious process, nor did it depend upon the arrogance of uncontested success or the establishment of a new orthodoxy. It was rather the outcome of particular circumstances, of a particular cultural climate, of party conflict, and of philosophical achievements. The ideology of Dutch republicanism came into being through the channels of dissent and criticism. Its essentially contested nature made it no less central to Dutch politics, nor less influential abroad. Without this republicanism, William III might never have joined forces with Jewish bankers and English dissenters and set sail for England.[6] Bernard Mandeville might never have been persuaded that paradox lay at the basis of all social relations. The Scots, in particular Adam Smith,

---

[5] Pieter de la Court, *True Interest and Political Maxims of the Republick of Holland and West-Friesland: Written by John de Witt and Other Great Men in Holland* (London: 1702). This is a translation of *Aanwysing der heilsame politike gronden en maximen van de republike van Holland en West-Vriesland* (Leiden/Rotterdam: Hakkens, 1669), 258, 259, 262, 375.

[6] See D. J. Roorda, *Rond Prins en patriciaat. Verspreide opstellen* (Weesp: Fibula, 1984), 172ff.

might never have devised a theory of moral sentiments to complement the Grotian natural system of liberty.[7] French philosophical dissent—from Stouppe, Fontenelle, and Vauvenargues to Diderot—was greatly influenced by Spinoza and the republicanism associated with him.[8] Similarly, the roots of German idealism are to be found in Spinoza and in the "Spinozan Platonist" François Hemsterhuis.[9] The republicanism behind these influences may not always be straightforwardly political. A more generous interpretation of republicanism, however, will help in understanding the commerce of Dutch ideas in the making of a broadly European political culture.

The creation of the Dutch Republic has been dated to 1579, the year when the defense union of the "United Provinces" against Spain was concluded in the city of Utrecht, or to 1609, the year when the Spanish Crown accepted a truce with its rebels (the Twelve Years' Truce), or to 1648, the year of the Peace Treaty of Westphalia which finally ended all conflict between the Spanish Hapsburgs and the Low Countries. The first of these years—1579—would seem to be the most appropriate, if only because it gave rise to the growing political self-consciousness apparent in the works of Dirck Coornhert, Grotius, and many lesser figures of the early years of the seventeenth century. The period after Westphalia has been called the "republican era," and it, too, produced outstanding political thinkers, among them John de Witt, Pieter de la Court, and Spinoza. It was in these years that William III, prince of Orange, successfully reclaimed the *Stadhoudership* after the French invasion of 1672–4 and went on to become king of England in 1688–9. In many respects the eighteenth century witnessed a consolidation of republicanism and its general acceptance by society.[10] The Batavian revolution of 1787 was a prelude to the 1795 proclamation of the Batavian Republic. The aftermath of that republic in the years between 1795 and 1814 led to the conviction that a

---

[7] On Mandeville, see Douglas Den Uyl, "Passion, State, and Progress: Spinoza and Mandeville on the Nature of Human Association," *Journal for the History of Ideas* 14 (1987): 481–98; Hans W. Blom, "The Dutch Ideology of Consumption" (Paper presented at a conference on "The Consumption of Culture/The Culture of Consumption," Werkgroep Achttiende Eeuw, Rotterdam 20–21 November 1997).

[8] See, for example, *Mémoires de Jean de Witt, grand pensionnaire de Hollande*. The Hague, 1709 (translation of de la Court's *Aanwysing*); A. Ch. Kors, *Atheism in France, 1650– 1729. II: Naturalism and Disbelief* (Princeton: Princeton University Press, 1995).

[9] Rüdiger Otto, *Studien zur Spinozarezeption in Deutschland im 18. Jahrhundert* (Frankfurt am Main: Königshausen & Neumann, 1994); Winfried Schröder, *Spinoza in der deutschen Frühaufklärung* (Würzburg: Königshausen & Neumann, 1987).

[10] See Hans Blom, "The Republic's Nation: Republicanism and Nationalism in the Dutch Eighteenth Century" (paper presented at *The Eighteenth Century Conference*, Dublin, July 1999).

constitutional monarchy fitted best with the Dutch republican tradition. And in that sense the Netherlands remains a republic to this day.[11]

The political institutions of the United Provinces were complex and remained virtually unchanged during the two centuries of their existence.[12] The defense federation created to secure independence from Spain had conceded a considerable measure of autonomy to the cities and provinces. The States General, on the other hand, and in particular the pensionary of Holland, who acted as "secretary-general" to the States General, obtained a major policy influence in foreign affairs and commercial policy. As the prime nobleman of Holland, the *Stadhouder*, appointed by the States of each province, held an eminent position in the States General. Only members of the House of Orange have been the *Stadhouder*, a function they generally combined with that of captain-general of the army. The navy was led by professional admirals, supervised by commissioners of the States General. In addition, the admiralties, the chartered companies, and the Water Boards were important and largely independent public organizations with special jurisdictions and the right to levy taxes. Historians have often remarked that the Republic lacked an adequate concept of sovereignty. In doing so, they overlook the republican value of the dispersion of sovereignty that necessarily accompanied this "polyarchy." It thus seems inadequate to label the Republic a federal state, if only because it possessed no detailed regulation of the respective rights and duties of its different parts.[13]

Throughout the seventeenth and eighteenth centuries the terms "liberty" and "republic" were highly contested concepts.[14] From the early years of the Revolt (1568–1648) to the final Patriot debates of the last decades of the eighteenth century, they functioned as the foci of discussion rather than as a source of agreed principles. The debates over the nature of the "free republic" nicely illustrate the contested character of "liberty" and "republic" as well as the evolving republican discourse. The first debate developed between 1610 and the early 1620s at almost the same time as the Twelve Years' Truce (1609–21) in the eighty-year-long struggle with Hapsburg Spain, and it took the form of a conflict over the practicalities of religious tolerance. This conflict between Arminians

---

[11] For this history see Jonathan Israel, *The Dutch Republic: Its Rise, Greatness, and Fall, 1477–1806* (Oxford: Oxford University Press, 1995).

[12] See J. L. Price, *Holland and the Dutch Republic in the Seventeenth Century: The Politics of Particularism* (Oxford: Clarendon Press, 1994).

[13] See Blom, *Causality and Morality*, ch. 2.

[14] See, for example, Henry Méchoulan, *Amsterdam au temps de Spinoza: Argent et liberté* (Paris: Presses Universitaires de France, 1990).

and Gomarists apparently centered on the issue of predestination, but the burgeoning aristocratic republicanism of politicians like Grotius was also at stake. The conflict resulted finally in the defeat of the Grotian faction and thus paved the way not only for Grotius's epochal *De iure belli ac pacis*, but, more importantly at the time, it forced the intellectual elite to come to a common ideological understanding of the issues of human nature and the nature of politics. As a consequence, in the 1620s a Neostoic Aristotelianism and the mixed constitution became the dominant republican model.

The second debate took shape in the years around 1650, accompanying first the preparation and conclusion of the Treaty of Westphalia (1648) and the subsequent execution of Charles I and the early death of William II of Orange in 1650. The publication in 1651 of the young Lambertus van Velthuysen's defense of Hobbes's *De Cive* was, in a sense, its apogee and marked the advent of a new phase in the republican debate. Still haunted by what many regarded as the triumph of Calvinist orthodoxy in the final years of the truce, the republicans made a new attempt to articulate the relationship between the moral and the political, between the people and their rulers. Here, the intellectual achievements of the 1620s were put to a more radical use, in particular in the interpretations of Grotius's *De iure belli*.

Whereas Grotius had discussed the nature of international politics in terms of perfect rights, van Velthuysen wanted to show how to deal with imperfect rights in morality and politics. Unusually for a defendant of Hobbes, van Velthuysen stressed the fact that morality admits of degrees and yet in all its imperfection constitutes the basis for any form of sociability. Moreover, it was precisely in his understanding of an historically evolving sociability that van Velthuysen found an essential point of reference for political rule. Thus, it was van Velthuysen who set the agenda for the republican version of the great debate between the Grotian and Hobbesian understanding of sociability, which today is better known in the terms set by Samuel Pufendorf and his followers.[15] This move toward a concept of sociability acquired political momentum with the rise of a "bourgeois reason of state," that is, of a realist view of republics based on self-interest.

The third debate was set off by the publications of Pieter and Johan de la Court from 1660 onwards and culminated in Spinoza's *Tractatus Theologico-politicus* (1670) and *Tractatus Politicus* (1677). This was the

---

[15] For a discussion of van Velthuysen, see Blom, *Causality and Morality*, chs. 4 and 5.

closest that the republican debate came to being rephrased in commercial terms, de la Court taking "commerce" to mean economic exchange, and Spinoza, something closer to moral communicability. In many respects Spinoza and de la Court were pursuing much the same argument within the republican debate. On the issue of commerce, however, they parted company. They both accepted wholeheartedly the evolutionary perspective on morality, but their ensuing conceptions of enlightened self-interest differed. Although neither of them would endorse laws against luxury, de la Court believed that the individual, while eschewing bankruptcy, is free to enjoy his private indulgences; Spinoza, on the other hand, reckoned luxury a failure of understanding. Although Spinoza was convinced that laws cannot prevent luxury, he sincerely believed that the rational man would endeavor to be useful to his fellowman and attempt to articulate a common moral ground. Bernard Mandeville, for his part, attempted to bring together the two approaches: he demanded that "a Golden Age must be as free for acorns as for honesty."[16] It is one of the merits of this republican discourse that it found the means to keep the space for disagreement open and to allow a continuing debate on the distinctions between the public-private and moral-political/economic. This flexibility was to be an important rhetorical factor in the evolution of the linkage conception of European politics.

THE FAILURES OF HUMANIST, ARISTOCRATIC REPUBLICANISM, 1609–29

The Leiden philosopher Franco Burgersdijk was well known for his compendia of Aristotelian logic, metaphysics, and moral and political thought.[17] In 1623 he asked his student-readers whether it was reasonable to hope for a universal and eternal peace in this world.[18] The answer was straightforward. We may hope for eternal peace because this follows "from Holy Scripture, human reason and the consensus of all the wise." The means to achieve this eternal peace is what Burgersdijk calls the

---

[16] Bernard Mandeville, *The Grumbling Hive: or, Knaves Turn'd Honest* (London: Sam. Ballard, 1705).

[17] Moti Feingold, "The Ultimate Pedagogue: Franco Petri Burgersdijk and the English Speaking Academic Learning," in *Franco Burgersdijk (1590–1635): Neo-aristotelianism in Leiden*, ed. E. P. Bos and H. A. Krop, vol. 1 of *Studies in the History of Ideas in the Low Countries* (Amsterdam/Atlanta, Ga.: Rodopi, 1993), 151–65.

[18] Franco Burgersdijk, *Idea oeconomicae et politicae doctrinae*, 2d ed. (Leiden: H. de Vogel, 1644); ed. G. Hornius: *Idea politica cum annotationibus Georgi Horni*, 2d ed. (Leiden: Felix Lopez de Haro), 1668.

Imperium *Oecumenicum* (the Empire of the World). An essential attribute of this universal government—and the only one discussed by Burgersdijk— is religious peace:

The instruments of this religious peace are twofold: the conversion of the infidels, whereby Paganism, Judaism and Mohammedanism will come to an end; and the reconciliation of the believers (as we call all those who have been baptised and recognise Christ as God and Redeemer). The Roman Catholics and the Evangelicals can be easily reconciled if only this pretended first bishop or *vicariatus* of Christ be dismissed, and if, secondly, instead of the Council of Trent the Word of God be established as norm and judge in Religion.[19]

Since Lutheran and Calvinist Protestants only disagree on "obscure matters," which neither really understand, the only thing required to bring about *Imperium Oecumenicum* is that the kings from the south of the German Empire agree with the Prince-Electors to banish all mutual invectives and religious partisanship. "The Universal religion is, thus, the Christian one." The most interesting element of this diatribe is what is not said, or said only implicitly. A universal Christian religion, by implication, cannot be allowed to suffer from intertribal conflicts among the Reformed communities themselves. Both Burgersdijk's church politics and his conception of politics at large aimed at conciliation and consensus. The "obscurities," such as those about predestination, which had been a source of such conflict only a few years previously, must be subordinated to the more important issues of Christian reconciliation. Moreover, it is the duty of sovereigns to put an end to such conflicts.

Burgersdijk's strictures on the Pope follow the arguments against collateralism: there cannot be two authorities in religious affairs. The sovereign alone wields the sword, although he should always seek the advice of the ministers, and religious differences should be respected.[20] The sovereign may have religious convictions different from those of his subjects, something which does not prevent him from being a legitimate prince, let alone make him a tyrant. Consciences should not be forced. Blasphemers, perjurers, impostors, and demagogures, however, should be contained, insofar as they intend to seduce others and destroy the peace of the church.

Toleration in religion is complemented by consensus in politics. Burgersdijk endorsed the order of mixed government for the United Provinces, as in accordance with the freedom and the interests of the citizens.[21] Tolerance and consensus—unity in diversity—can be guaranteed only if

---

[19] Burgersdijk, *Idea oeconomicae*, 228.   [20] Ibid., 187.

[21] Ibid., 209–25: 'Superest status ex Monarchia, Aristocratia & Democratia temperatus. Hic status videtur omnium tutissimus, quia duae reliquae formae, tertiam impediunt, ne possit Remp. turbare' (218–19).

sectarian interests do not claim exclusive prerogatives in the state. Burgersdijk did not, perhaps, really believe in the efficacy of his provisions, and rightly so. Religious conflicts were to remain a feature of the Dutch Republic for the rest of its existence, as was to be expected from a federal republic that sought tolerance and consensus at the same time. The ongoing debates on religious politics continued to stress the practical dimensions of tolerance, stopping only at the final destruction of the political order and of its ability to operate effectively. Burgersdijk was right, moreover, in stressing that this balancing act required self-restraint among believers, theologians and philosophers alike, and responsible government to go with it.

The loud tone of appeasement in Burgersdijk must be heard amid the intense debate that almost tore apart the young Republic during the 1610s. Grotius, whose participation in the debates earned him a sentence of life imprisonment in 1620, had been ideologically and politically involved. He wrote several tracts in which he defended the political line taken by Johan Oldenbarneveldt, the pensionary of the States of Holland. Grotius espoused this line in the *Ordinum Hollandiae ac Westfrisiae Pietas* of 1613 and took part in the debate between the Arminian Conrad Vorstius and the Gomarist Sybrand Lubbertus in order to defend the *majestas* of the sovereign powers.[22]

Central to Grotius's argument was the ability of secular authorities to judge in religious matters. Grotius rejected the idea that the community of ordinary believers could be a better judge than the outstanding *regenten* who ruled the country.[23] He reinforced this *laudatio* of the wise and pious *regenten* by exhibiting his own competence in theology. Reviewing the history of Christianity since the earliest times, he attempted to demonstrate that the secular authorities have always executed the highest authority in religious matters. This argument was directed at King James and the theologians in England, who had been invoked by Lubbertus and his friends. According to Grotius's reading of history, political authorities have always convened, directed, and concluded church councils, because they have appointed bishops, priests, or ministers. Grotius

---

[22] Sybrandus Lubbertus, *Declaratio responsionis D. Conradi Vorstii* (Franeker: A. Radaeus, 1611).

[23] Hugo Grotius, *Ordinum Hollandiae ac Westfrisiae pietas*, ed. and trans. E. Rabbie: The Hague: E. J. Brill, 1995 (1st ed.: Leiden: Ioannes Patius, 1613), p. 7 (111): "the States of Holland ... the supreme rulers of a nation most noble from time immemorial, who have opposed a doubly unjust rule, by the Spaniards and the Romanists, with great courage and firmness. ... Outstanding nobility holds a seat in this assembly, the legitimate offspring of excellent parents, who rescued the exercise of the true religion at the risk of their lives and at the loss of their fatherland and their fortune."

suspected Lubbertus of being a Puritan since he claimed the right to convene councils and to appoint ministers for the community of believers.
He did not deny individual church members their right to private convictions. But the public church was the responsibility of the authorities,
and if they abandoned their jurisdiction in this respect, the unity of the
country would be lost.

The political leaders of Holland and therefore of the States General—
the pensionary Johan van Oldenbarnevelt, and Grotius himself—tried to
soothe the turmoil by a policy of toleration, which for various reasons
tended in practice to support one of the contending parties. The Remonstrants, whose opinions on grace and predestination were less severe than
those of their opponents, the Contraremonstrants, claimed priority in the
public church on the basis of this tolerance. With the help of Grotius and
his party, they gained control of many towns, thereby enraging their opponents still further. Many believed the *regenten* were working against the
real principles of Calvinism. An opposition coalition developed outside of
Holland, as well as in towns within Holland that had reason to mistrust
the policies of Oldenbarnevelt. In some places *regenten* were confronted
by orthodox ministers and their followers, attempting to regain their former positions within the public church; in others *regenten* and orthodox
believers made common cause against *regenten* elsewhere. Things took a
dramatic turn when Prince Maurits, the *Stadhouder*, ostentatiously visited
the Contraremonstrant church in The Hague.[24]

As the main architect and executive of the strategy of Oldenbarnevelt,
Grotius apparently combined a sincere belief in tolerance with an equally
strong belief in power politics. His fundamental conviction was that as
long as the *regenten* in the towns and the provinces retained their rightful
autonomy, a religious conflict could be prevented. Hence, all his activities were directed at increasing the power of the towns by local militia,
and that of the provinces by claiming their right to resolve the conflict
through the provincial synods. Prince Maurits replied by supporting the
Contraremonstrants and by creating a National Synod of the Reformed Church to overcome the stronghold in Holland.[25] This, together

---

[24] See H. A. Enno van Gelder, *Getemperde vrijheid. Een verhandeling over de verhouding
van kerk en staat in de Republiek der Verenigde Nederlanden en de vrijheid van menings-
uiting in zake godsdienst, drukpers en onderwijs, gedurende de 17e eeuw* (Groningen:
Wolters-Noordhoff, 1972); H. C. Rogge, *Johannes Wtenbogaert en zijn tijd*, 3 vols.
(Amsterdam: Y. Rogge, 1874–6); Jan den Tex, *Oldenbarnevelt*, 5 vols. (Haarlem: Tjeenk
Willenk, 1960–72).

[25] See A. Th. van Deursen, "Oldenbarnevelt en Maurits," in *De Hollandse jaren van Hugo
de Groot, 1583–1621*, ed. by H. Nellen and C. Ridderikhof (Amsterdam: Verloren,
1996), 55–160.

with Maurits's superior military forces, was to prove to be Grotius's undoing.

Maurits's successful *coup d'état* put a (temporary) end to the privileged position of the Arminians and forced Grotius not only to defend himself in court, but also to justify extensively his actions in writing. He was to write two books on the subject: the *Apology* of 1622 and the posthumously published *De imperio summarum potestatum circa sacra* (1647). Moreover, he made extensive notes, rediscovered and published in the nineteenth century.[26] Taken together, these writings offer a forceful picture of Grotius's conception of the existing form of government. His core argument was that the States General (manipulated by Prince Maurits) had had no right to arraign him in the first place and had thereby disregarded the rights of the States of Holland, his lawful sovereign. He claimed to be a loyal citizen of those States.

"All these events made me reflect," he wrote,

whether some advised His Excellency [Prince Maurits] to bide his time and execute his old aspirations, or in fact following the example of Philippus of Macedonia (who under pretext of the defence of religion conquered one part of Greece by the other) and of Augustus in Rome, both of whom placating the people by taking the name of captain-general and keeping the appearance of the old form of government, usurped all power; likewise it happened in Florence when the Medici simulated the defence of the common people against the rulers. I for my part have considered that the aristocratic government which has been obtained by so much expense and blood, with God's remarkable blessing, ought not to be changed into a monarchy, that although at first well governed, would probably befall worse rulers, as has been experienced in Rome and elsewhere. While I considered all changes for the worse (to the point that I advised the pensionary against the public discussion of this matter), I feared most of all a change produced by popular commotion.[27]

Grotius had played for high stakes, and he had lost. Between the security offered by the long arms of King James, and the implacability of the heretic hunters, Grotius had attempted to articulate and enforce a church order for a Protestant republic. Crucial to this model was the responsibility of the ruling elite for the proper functioning of religion in society. The combination of Erastianism and aristocratic leadership forced tolerance within the confines of the principles of republican sovereignty. As Spinoza would later point out, the only solution in an aristocracy is to let the

---

[26] Hugo Grotius, *Memorie van mijne intentien en notabele bejegeningen*, manuscript written in 1621; Ed. R. Fruin: *Verhooren en andere bescheiden betreffende het rechtsgeding van Hugo de Groot* (Utrecht: Kemink, 1871), 1–80.

[27] Grotius, *Memorie van mijne intentien*, 11–12.

regenten be the leaders of the public church, as wardens and as ministers, while tolerating other sects as private denominations outside the public realm. As Spinoza also pointed out, however, an aristocracy is a weak form of state, and its rulers live in permanent fear of the disenfranchised popular masses.[28]

The outcome of Grotius's quest for an alliance between church and state was thus the failure of classical, aristocratic republicanism. In the end it proved impossible to eradicate the "puritan" tendencies that had plagued Flanders in the sixteenth century[29] and now the northern Netherlands as well. Later two responses were attempted. The first was to articulate a theory of sovereignty that did not hinge on the civic virtues of the *regenten*.[30] This was a notion of absolute sovereignty, supported by Pauline perspectives on authority, of the kind to be found in Grotius's *De iure belli ac pacis* and in his friend Dirk Graswinckel's *De iure majestatis*.[31] The second response was to find a better understanding of the relationship between the rulers and the masses than that available in the simple Lipsian dictum that rulers have to rule and subjects have to obey.[32]

THE MORAL CONTAINMENT OF REASON OF STATE

In 1641 Corvinus edited the *De arcanis* of Clapmarius, and in a long preface he explained the *simulacra imperii seu libertatis*, the "shadows" of rule or liberty.[33] This was sufficiently popular to be reprinted in 1644. It would, however, be wrong to see this success as a clear indication of the Dutch acceptance of reason of state in full. Lipsius before him had explained *prudentia mixta* as actions to some honorable end, mixed with an element of deceit, and emphasized the well-being of the people as the honorable end of any ruler.[34] Clapmarius argued fully in this line in his

---

[28] *Tractatus Politicus* [Amsterdam, 1677], chs. 8 and 9.
[29] *Pietas*, 199 (237).   [30] Elaborating on *Pietas*, 98 (175).
[31] See Hans W. Blom, "Les réactions hollandaises à l'exécution de Charles I: 'Monarchie' et 'république' dans les Provinces-Unies après 1649," in *Monarchie et république*, ed. V. C. Zarka (Paris: Vrin, in print).
[32] See Justus Lipsius, *Politicorum libri six* (Leiden: F. Raphelengius, 1589), ch. 1.
[33] *De arcanis rerumpublicarum libri sex, illustrati a Joan. Corvinus I.C. Accessit v.d. Chr. Besoldi de eadem materia discursus, nec non Arnoldi Clapmarii et aliorum conclusiones de jure publico* (Amsterdam: L. Elzevir, 1641; 1644, 2d rev. ed.).
[34] On Lipsius in particular, see Richard Tuck, *Philosophy and Government, 1572–1651* (Cambridge: Cambridge University Press, 1993); Karl Enenkel and Chris Heesakkers, eds., *Lipsius in Leiden: Studies in the Life and Works of a Great Humanist* (Voorthuizen: Florivallis, 1997).

interpretation of Seneca's famous saying that "necessity, this great fosterer of human weakness, breaks any law."[35] Corvinus approved of the first part of the phrase and expressly embraced necessity as the protector of the human deficit, *patrocinium imbecillitatis humanae*, but was less sure about it being a legitimate ground for breaking the law. The Dutch, jealous of their fundamental laws and privileges, would never go along with the latter view, although they agreed with Clapmarius that "it is this force of necessity, this dignity, which often brings lawfulness and equity to an illicit business."[36]

Corvinus's *De arcanis* should be seen as part of a larger set of writings, which included books by both Gerard van Wassenaer and Pieter de la Court. A surprising fact about all three books on the *arcana* is that their respective authors or editors, from Joannes Corvinus to Pieter de la Court, had a shared political allegiance. Corvinus studied theology in Leiden and was a pupil of Arminius. As such he not only defended his master against his detractors, but also represented the Remonstrants at the Synod of Dordt in 1618–19. For Corvinus, as for many Remonstrants, this episode ended in exile. Not until 1632 did he establish himself as a lawyer and sometime professor in law in Amsterdam. The author of several books on law, he was highly thought of by Grotius.[37] Wassenaer (1589–1664), the Utrecht lawyer, lived with a vivid memory of the *coup d'état* of Prince Maurits. He lost his position in the Utrecht *vroedschap* after that event, never to return to his seat again. Many of his friends were important Remonstrants. His son studied under that arch-enemy of Dutch Calvinism, the Cartesian and Utrecht professor of medicine, Henricus Regius. Pieter de la Court, as a student in Leiden, was already heavily involved in the Cartesian movement. Partly through the agency of Grotius's son Pieter, he sought the protection of the States-party. He was a vehement opponent of orthodox Calvinism.

Wassenaer published *Arcana in Republics and Principalities* in which he combined Corvinus's Dutch version of reason of state with the modern

---

[35] "Necessitas magnum imbecillitatis humanae patrocinium, omnem legem frangit." This phrase was coined by Justus Lipsius in his *Politicorum libri sex* (Leiden: Plantijn, 1589), book 4, chap. 14, from M. A. Seneca (rhetor), *Declamationum Excerpta*, book 9, ch. 4.

[36] "Et tunc necessitatis ea vis est, ea dignitas, ut saepe rei non licitae jus et aequum tribuat." Cited by Meinecke, *Die Idee der Staatsräson in der neueren Geschichte* (München: Oldenbourg, 1924), 169.

[37] Grotius refers to "vetera nostra amicitia" in a letter to Corvinus (7 January 1640; *Briefwisseling*, XI, nr. 4458), while he praised his juridical talent in a letter to his son Pieter (8 July 1639; *Briefwisseling*, X, nr. 4194).

psychology of his day.[38] The result was an interesting handbook for strategies of bourgeois preferment in republics and monarchies alike. Pieter de
la Court pirated this text, when he republished it in 1660, under the different title *Politieke consideratien.*

Thus, the Dutch use of Clapmarius has a particular purpose: in revealing the hidden agenda of princes, it supports the exclusion of William III
from the office of *Stadhouder* of Holland in 1654 and explains the theoretical preconditions for a flourishing body politic. In dialogue with
Clapmarius, and hence with Tacitus and Machiavelli, these republicans
forged their weapons against Orangism. They showed the dismal consequences of the supposedly indispensable *simulacra imperii.* They sought
to achieve this end by demonstrating that only false reason of state reigns,
that *flagitia* (vice or baseness) and not true reason of state is the first principle of princely or monarchical rule. In other words, since false reason
of state promoted the private interest of the ruler to the detriment of the
public good, under princely rule it is the subject who suffers.

If Orangism was indeed their ideological target, how did the republicans expect to be able to exploit the reason-of-state tradition? The principal objective of that tradition was to demonstrate that true reason of state
is a real, and necessary, option. How can one argue successfully against
reason of state by attempting to demonstrate that history shows the
arcana to be a sure means for the defense of the public good? The more
prudent versions of the classical arguments against reason of state, such
as Lipsius's, relied heavily on demonstrating precisely the immorality of
the arcana. To admit this, however, would be to go against the grain of
realism that all these authors wished to embrace. De la Court, for one,
was happy to point out the similarity between his own description of man
as selfish and vicious and the Calvinist notion of the sinfulness of man. It
is not a complacent moral attitude they sought to deploy against reason
of state. Rather they were looking for means to demolish monarchy (that
is, Orangism) by demolishing one of its theoretical foundations (that is,
reason of state) by taking it as a limiting case.

In the context of this strategy, the importance of Corvinus is beyond
doubt. The elaborate introduction to his edition of Clapmarius constitutes
a highly significant summary of *De arcanis rerumpublicarum.* Moreover,
Corvinus sets the tone for Wassenaer. He presents his topic as an "ars
regnandi," the art of government, within the limits of trust, honesty, and

---

[38] Gerard van Wassenaer, *Bedekte Konsten in Regeringen en Heerschappien* (Utrecht: van
Zyll and van Ackersdyck, 1657).

virtue.[39] His goal is the longevity and stability of the common weal. The means to these ends are "surely not in the open and following the main route (*via regia*), but by means of hidden simulation."[40] They follow "on the one hand definitely from the argument of necessity, which rather gives than obeys the law, on the other hand even from public utility."[41] They should not, however, defy trust or social morality, "fidem sive pudorem," good faith or honor.

Although Corvinus summarizes the contents of *De arcanis* quite faithfully, on certain points he offers his own arguments on theoretical and practical origins. Appropriately for a jurist, Corvinus endorses Clapmarius's foundation of the arcana in the *imperii & majestatis jura*. If the latter are in peril, the former should be used. For Corvinus the application of the arcana has essentially to do with the redress of the process of decay of the state. The doctrine of Clapmarius provides the reader with an analysis or diagnosis of the *morbi Reipublicae*. The "Prince of the Peripatetici" (Aristotle), says Corvinus, claimed that diagnosing an illness amounted to identifying its cure. In the same vein, knowing the causes of the decay of states is to know how to remedy it. Therefore, in Corvinus's opinion, Aristotle, who was hostile to the arcana and considered them to be more fraud than simple false prudence, regarded their use as appropriate in totally disturbed states "where one cannot follow the right procedure, except at the risk of public injury."[42] Corvinus advises the reader to judge whether this argument is in agreement with Aristotle. The implication is that the doctrine of arcana is there to be used against *flagitia* that threaten the state performed by any of the parties of the body politic: the prince, the aristocrats, or the people. In particular the people are to be feared, but wisely Corvinus did not endorse the negative qualification by Clapmarius (chap. V, §19) of leaders who are prepared to mobilize an easily excitable mob.

The peace talks in Münster, Westphalia (1646–7), provided a further opportunity to develop this "bourgeois reason of state." Bringing the war with Spain to a close had been difficult, not only on the Spanish side,

---

[39] "Habet tamen ars simulandi suos limites; fidem, honestatem, virtutem; quos qui egreditur, nae vafri & nefarii hominis potius, quam politici nomen videtur," Corvinus, *Arcanis*, Introduction, 2–3.

[40] "non aperta quidem et via regia, sed per tacta simulacra," Ibid., 1.

[41] "tum quidem ex argumenta necessitatis, quae legem potius dat quam accipit ... tum etiam publicae utilitatis," Ibid., 26.

[42] "[Aristoteles] occultorum usum minus probat. Calliditatem iis inesse potius existimat, quam veram prudentiam plane perperam," arcana to be used in very disturbed states where "non possis recta incedere via, nisi cum damno publico," Ibid., f2v.

but also in the Republic. Local interests (privateering from Zeeland) and factional interests supported the general distrust of a world without war. Hence the talks were accompanied by a noticeable outpouring of pamphlets arguing for and against the cessation of hostilities. Not surprisingly, reason of state was prominent in these arguments. "Princes," wrote the author of the 1646 tract *Hollandsche Sybille*,

> vow a solemn pledge to their subjects to protect their preservation, good and wellbeing, with all the force, wit, and prudence. This is an iron tie that cannot be disturbed or broken by another or a paper tie. "Necessity breaks laws," said Sybille. It would be better not to conclude treaties, but necessity often obliges a prince to make them. The same necessity, however, sometimes forces him to maintain them, and sometimes to break them. As long as the foundation and the cause lasts on which the alliance was entered, so long will its maintenance last.[43]

Although in many of the Peace Talks tracts we find this awareness of the amorality of international politics—do not "the big fish always eat the small"[44]—the critical role that the Dutch Republic should play in Europe is stressed. "Nevertheless, nothing is more useful for the preservation of general peace," continued the author of the *Hollandsche Sybille*,

> than the existence of republics, which can be the intermediaries and mediators between the ambitious designs of kings and their favourites.... In Italy this duty was often taken care of by Venice, which always prudentially kept the balance between the powerful crowns, while never permitting either one or the other to prevail. The Republic of the United Provinces likewise seems to have been elected by God with the intention of preserving the political balance, to be mediators, and to maintain equality and the equilibrium.[45]

In 1650 the internal use of this Dutch version of reason of state was directed against the prince of Orange. After the prince's attempt at Amsterdam, a pamphleteer wrote, "I see now that you Hollanders butcher the children, while they are given puppets to play with; you enjoy and adorn yourself with the name of Free Hollanders, while your States are forced by a young governor."[46] This hyperbolic sentence combines a reference to both reason-of-state writing and actual Dutch politics. The "shadows" of freedom are the illusions by which cynical princes rule;

---

[43] *Hollandsche Sybille* (Amsterdam: Roelof Heyndrickz, 1646), 13.
[44] *Den on-geveynsden Nederlantschen Patriot met den argh-listigen geveynsden Franschman t'samen-sprekende op het stuck van den ghesloten vrede tussechen Spagnien ende de Vereenighde Neder-landen* (Alckmaer: Jan Claesz, 1647), 4.
[45] *Hollandsche Sybille*, 28.
[46] *Hollants praatjen tusschen vier personen, een Gelderman, een Hollander, een Vries, en een Brabander. Aangaande de souverainiteyt van Syn Hoogheyt, en tot justificatie van de Ed. Mog. Heeren Staten van Hollandt, en de Achtbare Heeren Burgemeesters en Regeerders der Stadt Amsterdam. Het eerste deel.* (Antwerpen: Jeronimus Verdussen, 1650), B^v.

they merely give the people "puppets to play." Prince William II, the "young governor," is by implication presented as such a prince.

Clapmarius and Corvinus had maintained that the simulacra could not change political relations, since the latter are founded on the *iura imperii* alone. Yet Wassenaer discussed the theory from the point of view of "the art and ways to achieve political office and status." He emphasizes the role of fortune and gives a realist analysis of politics in his dissection of the passions. He stresses the importance of prudence as the middle way between obstinacy and subservience. Politeness and civility, prognostic reasoning and artful skill, patience, humility, courage, and experience are the prerequisites of successful political behavior. In order efficaciously to control his emotions, the politician should cultivate the virtues of magnanimity, strength, and caution.[47] "But *necessity*," he wrote,

should be understood above anything else, and we should try to overcome, in every way available, with power and force, whatever opposes us, and cannot be avoided, in the pursuit of our intentions; but first we should consider the value and importance of the end we are aiming at, and that forces upon us this necessity, and we should compare its outcome with the labour and costs we will have to suffer in order to obtain the necessary means. Because if the losses are greater than the advantages that we can expect, it would be better to attempt something else. One has (also) to consider whether there are different means that lead to this end. From these one should choose first the most secure, then the most easy, and lastly the less indecent. Since necessity has no law, and the end is honest, the means used to obtain an honest end will be overlooked and excused, although they may not have been very honest.[48]

Gerard van Wassenaer's "bourgeois courtier" tries to understand his own and others' passions, prepares for the adversity of fortune, is cautious about his reputation, aims at moderation, but most of all calculates his chances to further his own interests. Although Wassenaer agreed with Clapmarius in his criticism of Machiavelli (chap. V, §1), who is said to have believed that "princes should sin as much as possible," he is rather elusive about the justification of ends. Wassenaer is convinced that people are more prone to indignation and outrage than they are to doing good. In effect, Wassenaer is saying here that there is no objective definition of the good. Violent passions are to be subdued because of their socially

---

[47] *Hollandsche Sybille*, 168: "Furthermore, to arrange our movements [of the soul] in good order, there is caution, of which the foremost effect is to take away all causes and circumstances that could produce in us intemperate movements, since it is easier to cast these off, than once introduced to command them; next we survey all good and bad things that in the pursuit of a matter can possibly happen." As is evident from this quotation, the Dutch neo-stoic does not shun from introducing Aristotelian elements as well.

[48] Ibid., 190–1.

adverse consequences only, moderation is to be the rule, risk-aversion is to be considered the wisest option in this uncertain world. Wassenaer refers his readers, if they want to understand the good, to "the common sentiment" (*'t gemeen gevoelen*) instead of to the "teachers of wisdom."

Pieter de la Court's contribution to the discourse of republicanism must be understood against this background. Adorned with a repertoire of Tacitean learning, his works attempted to provide a realistic moral psychology as the basis for an objective definition of the good. Since he is best known for the one book that was translated into English and French, the *Aanwysing* (1669), a revised edition of the *Interest van Holland*, there is a tendency to regard de la Court as primarily a student of international relations. These publications went under the name of John de Witt, and they were widely regarded as the theoretical foundation of de Witt's and accordingly of Dutch foreign policy. Because of this it is easy to overlook the fact that the reason-of-state literature became a very powerful argument in the republican debates in the middle of the seventeenth century. The literature aimed at some sort of reintroduction of "the people" into the workings of the body politic.

THE CULMINATION OF THE REPUBLICAN DEBATE

The core of Pieter de la Court's thought is thus embedded within a particular realist view of politics entrenched in Dutch political debate. In his well-known claim

the interest of every country consists in the well-being of its rulers and subjects together, and it is dependent on a good form of government, and therefore that is the foundation on which the well-being of the commonwealth is built; so one has to understand, that a good form of government is not where the well- or ill-being of the subjects depends on the virtue or vice of the rulers, but (and this should be noted) where the well- and ill-being of the rulers, by necessity follows from, or depends on, the well- or ill-being of the subjects.[49]

Interest is well-being, as yet undefined, but structurally conditioned by the interconnection, or interdependence, of the interests of rulers and subjects. But what safeguards these interests? In effect, nothing. Fundamentally, interests are a species of passions, but not all passions can qualify as interests: they must conform to the formula of interdependence of the well-being of citizens and rulers alike.

[49] *Aanwysing*, 2.

These attempts to articulate a republican theory in terms of self-interest did not, of course, go uncontested. Most of the arguments directed against the *Interest of Holland* are all too familiar. Some, however, did attempt to meet de la Court on his own ground. The anonymous author of *Den herstelden Prins (The Prince Restored)* set out to prove that a *Stadhouder* is in the interest of the United Provinces, mainly because the same self-interest, the desire for respect and reputation, that drives the *regenten* to contribute to the welfare of the state operates also for the *Stadhouder*. Just as *regenten* are recruited from well-established families, so, too, are the *Stadhouders*. There is no disagreement here over human nature. In the well-ordered republic of the United Provinces, so de la Court argues, there are ample means to keep the *Stadhouder* within his legitimate bounds. And thus he is an outstanding instrument to develop the role of the Republic as the balancer of power within the new Europe.

Spinoza took much the same line. Contracts between states, he argued, "will remain in force as long as [their] basis—namely, the consideration of danger or advantage—persists."[50] For a ruler "cannot keep whatever promise he sees likely to be detrimental to his country without violating his pledge to his subjects, a pledge by which he is most firmly bound, and whose fulfilment usually involves the most solemn pledges."[51] The big fishes still eat the little ones, but they do so now by natural right.[52] Tolerance is a matter of political convenience, as it was for de la Court. "So however much sovereigns are believed to possess unlimited right and to be the interpreters of law and piety," Spinoza wrote,

they will never succeed in preventing men from exercising their own particular judgment on any matter whatsoever. . . . Indeed, since they cannot so act without endangering the whole fabric of the state, we can even argue that they do not have the absolute right to do so. For we have demonstrated that the right of sovereigns is determined by their power.[53]

For those who regard Spinoza primarily as a follower of Hobbes, this might seem an unexpected move. But it is not. For Spinoza, the participant in the discussions over the state of Holland is one for whom the concept of sovereignty had ceded pride of place to the problems of the functional

---

[50] Spinoza, *Tractatus Theologico-politicus*, ed. B. S. Gregory and trans. S. Shirley (Leiden: E. J. Brill, 1989), ch. 16, 244.
[51] Ibid., 245.   [52] Ibid., 237.
[53] Ibid., 292; the proof of the identity of might and right is in chapter 16.

processes in politics.[54] In his *Tractatus Politicus*, Spinoza pursues precisely this line of argument. First of all, he tries to sort out the puzzles of the republic. As he follows de la Court in his description of the aristocratic form of government, he is very close to de la Court's argument about the government of states and *Stadhouder* in his presentation of what we would now call "constitutional monarchy." In discussing the latter, he is mainly concerned with the various councils that advise the monarch, and he endorses the opinion of de la Court that in a well-ordered state a monarch is tied by his self-interest to the well-being of the state. In this way the differences between the various forms of government are gradually erased. The essential characteristic of a well-ordered state is the coordination of the interests of the rulers and the ruled. In the Republic "men of every race and sect live in complete harmony; and before entrusting their property to some person they will want to know no more than this, whether he is rich or poor and whether he has been honest or dishonest in his dealings."[55]

EUROPEAN REPUBLICANISM AND THE REPUBLICAN IDEA OF EUROPE

The distinction between national and international politics becomes a gradual one. In particular, the private interests of citizens balance and counteract the interests of states and suggest the argument for the special position of republics in keeping the balance of power in Europe. This aspect of Dutch republicanism has been disregarded in Dutch historiography. The interpretations of Nicolette Mout, van de Klashorst, E. H. Kossmann, Haitsma Mulier, and van Gelderen are striking in their inwardness. None of them refers to the fact that the major political debates *originated* in the context of international warfare. Their entire emphasis is on faction and on the ephemeral manifestations of what this chapter claims was the core of the republican debate in the United Provinces— namely, how to articulate the aims of policies within a system that is open to the rest of Europe, commercially as well as militarily.

I have presented here an alternative republicanism, one that tried to distinguish between what divided the two factions (the position of the

---

[54] The centrality of Spinoza to Dutch political thought can best be seen from the fact that his *political* views were hardly contested. He was evidently suspected of being a partisan of John de Witt. But criticism was directed against his theological position. In other words, Spinoza underestimated, just as Grotius had done half a century earlier, the wrath of the theologians when outsiders and laymen meddle in their pristine science.

[55] Ibid., 298.

prince of Orange) and what united them (an interest-based conception of politics). This latter aspect, as it was developed over the seventeenth century, made possible a "commercial" republicanism and linked welfarism and international peace. Dutch republicanism contributed to an idea of Europe that focused on the wealth of nations and the continuity of exchange or commerce beyond the nation-state.

The fear for peace that Grotius said in 1607 was conducive to the loss of civic (that is, martial) spirit and to the rise of faction had been replaced, in the course of the seventeenth century, by an equally principled quest for peace as the necessary condition for the well-being of the people. In this way Dutch republicanism diverged from that of its European counterparts. But its program was raised to an international level by other means.

In 1720 a book attributed to "B.M." was published in London with the title *Free Thoughts on Religions, the Church and National Happiness*.[56] In every respect this was a republican tract, very much like the ones we have been discussing. Its Dutch origin is evident from its discussion of religion and the role of the church and from its laudatory account of William of Orange's role in establishing liberty and good government in England. In other respects as well, the text has a strongly Dutch flavor. "My aim," declares the author, "is to make men penetrate their own consciences, and, by searching without flattery into their true motives, learn to know themselves." This objective he then applies to politics.

I have often heard well-meaning people say, that would every body be honest, ours is the best constitution in the world. But this is no encomium, where every body will be honest and do their duty all government are good alike. That is the best constitution which provides against the worst contingencies, that is armed against knavery, treachery, deceit, and all the wicked wiles of human cunning and preserves itself firm and unshaken, though most men should prove knaves. It is with a national constitution, as it is with that of men's bodies: that which can bear most fatigues without being disorder'd and last the longest in health is the best.[57]

The author goes on to claim that "a very considerable part of the sovereignty remains virtually in the people." For that reason "a prince of wisdom and penetration, considering that he has almost every subject to fear, and none he can really trust, should for his own sake be willing to desist from this right of absolute sway, and share the supreme power

---

[56] Bernard Mandeville, *Free Thoughts on Religion, the Church and National Happiness* (London: T. Jauncy, 1720).
[57] Ibid., 297.

with his people."[58] Indeed, "whoever would be happy should endeavour to be wise.... There is no better way of curing groundless jealousy and pannick fears, than by daring to examine and boldly look into the face of things."[59] On these grounds, it is wrong to expect virtue from either statesmen or courtiers, and it will always be better to rely upon laws and legislation as curbs to human behavior than on "all the virtues ministers can be possess'd of." Discussion of the moral qualities of a statesman becomes merely a partisan affair. "A whole set of statesmen of different tempers and capacities, virtues and vices are extoll'd to the skies in one company, in another they are damn'd to the pit of hell, and as often as these great men change sides, so often shall those companies change their language."[60] High politics is always unlike what ordinary people imagine it to be:

He who knows how courtiers throw their own faults upon others; their artifices in spreading reports; the fastening of slander; the mines they dig for one another's destruction; the deep craft of their intrigues; and all the other machinations in practice among them, will have but little faith in what is rumour'd about publick ministers.[61]

From what has been said, it might be apparent that the author of *Free Thoughts on Religions, the Church and National Happiness* was Bernard Mandeville. By 1720 he had come a long way from his youthful involvement with factional conflict, which in the early 1690s had forced him to flee his native Rotterdam and settle in London.[62] As a critic of English "grumbling," he achieved a notoriety he would probably never have attained if the *regenten* of Rotterdam had exercised some of the public virtue that Mandeville later came to realize he should never have expected of them. In England, "in the midst of so much ease, and greater plenty than any empire, state or kingdom now enjoys," Mandeville applied essentially Dutch republican principles to the explanation of man and society.[63] And unlike those of his great predecessor, Spinoza, Mandeville's writings would have a continuous impact on political thought throughout the eighteenth century. When later Adam Smith set out his republican program for the enhancing wealth of nations, and Jeremy Bentham argued that nature had given mankind two sovereign masters—pleasure and pain—they

[58] Ibid., 303, 307. [59] Ibid., 335.
[60] Ibid., 343. [61] Ibid., 341.
[62] See Rudolf Dekker, "Private Vices, Public Benefits Revisited: The Dutch Background of Bernard Mandeville," in *History of European Ideas* 14 (1992): 481–98.
[63] Mandeville, *Free Thoughts*, 334.

became the true heirs to this originally Dutch "commercial" republicanism. It is a program that still reverberates through all the political and economic moves toward greater European union, a union that is likely to be the only effective means of undoing the nineteenth-century fiction of national sovereignty and of making governments more responsive to the needs and demands of their citizens.[64]

Montesquieu, it would seem, had been attacking the wrong kind of republic. Quentin Skinner's "liberty before liberalism" seems to misdirect his argument in a comparable manner, although here the opposition is between classical republicanism and the new liberty apparent in seventeenth-century England.[65] Philip Pettit, on the other hand, has correctly interpreted the program of Dutch republicanism as the institutional organization of the liberty a citizen has if he is to safeguard himself against the domination of others.[66] This modern articulation of the core of Dutch republicanism, emphasizing tolerance and freedom from domination as well as the prerequisite of viable, self-sustaining institutions, might well provide the link between this early-modern "anomaly" and the future of Europe.

The Dutch Republic had mirrored itself in the reason-of-state politics of the surrounding monarchies and produced a modern, realist, bourgeois, and republican theory of politics. This new model reflected upon political thinkers like Algernon Sidney and the earl of Shaftesbury in England and Jean-Jacques Rousseau in France. At the better moments of Dutch history, the Dutch perspective asserted itself on the forum of European politics. Even today, when talk of a federalist reformation of the European Union is being heard, the seventeenth-century Republic of the Seven United Provinces is a model to look to.

---

[64] It is precisely its disregard for the place of the republican tradition in the formation of the modern European state system that makes S. F. Finer's posthumous *magnum opus* so unsatisfactory. See his *ad hominem* attack on J. G. A. Pocock, *The History of Government. I: Ancient Monarchies and Empires. II: The Intermediate Ages. III: Empires, Monarchies and the Modern State* (Oxford: Oxford University Press, 1997), 1021.

[65] Quentin Skinner, *Liberty before Liberalism* (Cambridge: Cambridge University Press, 1997).

[66] Philip Pettit, *Republicanism: A Theory of Freedom and Government* (Oxford: Oxford University Press, 1997).

5

The Napoleonic Empire and the Europe of Nations

BIANCAMARIA FONTANA

Or che regna fra le genti
La più placida armonia,
Dell'Europa sempre fia
Il destin felice appien

In 1824 the Italian musician Gioacchino Rossini, who was at the time at the height of his reputation, living in golden retirement in Paris, was commissioned to write an opera celebrating the coronation of King Charles X, the former Comte d'Artois, youngest brother of the unfortunate Louis XVI. Rossini obliged: the opera was called *Il Viaggio a Reims* (The Journey to Reims); it was performed a few times—apparently with success—in the presence of the royal family, but then, judging it unsuitable for ordinary theatrical repertoire, the author withdrew it, using the score for his popular *opera buffa Le Comte Ory*.

The plot of *Il Viaggio a Reims* is quite thin: a group of travelers of different nationalities, on their way to Reims to assist in the ceremony of the coronation, meet in the spa town of Plombières; marooned in a local auberge by a series of mishaps and unable to pursue their journey, they decide to celebrate the event on the spot with a banquet and a musical performance. Each character in the opera impersonates rather comically a national stereotype: a French countess is a fashion-mad flirt, a Spanish nobleman clicks his heels and breaks into flamencos, a German baron is called Trombonok and appears on stage with the accompaniment of a military brass band, and so on. To emphasize these cultural diversities, the score incorporates appealingly the tunes of national anthems and traditional folk songs.

The opera ends with the triumph of Harmony in the double sense of music and of the newly found peace among European nations—a peace made possible by the return of the legitimate sovereigns after the disruption caused by the French Revolution and by Napoleon's conquests.

Ironically, *Il Viaggio*—a celebration of restored European monarchies—is the work of the son of an Italian Jacobin who in 1797 had enthusiastically welcomed the troops of General Bonaparte when they occupied Pesaro on their way to "liberate" the southern regions of the peninsula. Yet in the short time of twenty-odd years that had elapsed since the planting of the liberty tree in Rossini's hometown, the whole image of Europe, of her identity and collective purpose, had undergone an unprecedented transformation.

THE ENLIGHTENMENT VIEW

The eighteenth-century reader who wished to acquire some information about the identity of the European continent, and who turned to the most prestigious reference work of Enlightenment culture, the *Encyclopédie* edited by Diderot, would find a disappointingly short and laconic account of the subject. The article "Europe" was written by that extremely prolific contributor to the *Encyclopédie*, the Chevalier de Jaucourt. After a few philological remarks on the origins of the name "Europa," Jaucourt stated simply that Europe was one of the four continents, the least important for its dimensions but the richest and most civilized:

If Europe is the smallest of the four parts of the world for its extension, it is however the most considerable for its commerce, navigation, fertility, for its enlightenment (*lumières*) and industry, for its knowledge of the arts, sciences and trades.[1]

The article stressed that European supremacy was confirmed by "the immensity of expenses, the magnitude of engagements, the number of troops" that enabled European monarchs to achieve "a high degree of power" and by Europe's contribution to the establishment of the law of nature and nations (*droit politique et droit des gens*).

This confident belief in the superiority of the European continent expressed in the *Encyclopédie* was justified in at least one respect: the concentration of resources and technology, although Europe remained second to Asia for population. In eighteenth-century opinion, however, this belief was only vaguely associated with specific geographical or demographic

---

[1] *Encyclopédie*, repr. of the 1756 ed., Stuttgart, 1966–7, 35 vols., vol. 6, 211–12.

factors, which were brought into the argument simply to illustrate the opposition between Europe and other "inferior" civilizations.[2]

Already in the *Esprit des Lois* Montesquieu had identified one important feature that set Europe geographically apart from the rest of the world and in particular from the Asian continent to which it was connected. In Asia the presence of immense plains, uninterrupted by mountains or rivers, favored the establishment of empires, since only despotic power could control such vast extensions of territory. In Europe, on the other hand, the existence of natural frontiers that limited the size of nations to a relatively small scale favored the spirit of independence, the *génie de liberté*, making the establishment of empires a difficult and precarious enterprise.[3]

In practice, however, it was not clear where the European territory actually began and ended. The frontiers of the great Western European powers did not change substantially during the eighteenth century, and the most significant expansion of the European borders was toward the East: but observers could not decide whether that space actually counted as "Europe" or not. Voltaire—like Montesquieu before him—hesitated to classify Russia as "European," and the very concept of "Eastern Europe" was only beginning to take shape.[4]

Culturally, it was generally agreed that Europe alone had a legitimate claim to the inheritance of ancient Greece and Rome (though Voltaire insisted polemically on the priority of the civilizations of the East, India and China).[5] In addition, Europe's identity had been decisively shaped by the advent of the Christian religion and by the unique fusion of Mediterranean peoples and northern tribes.

It was, again, Montesquieu's belief that the unification of the European peoples under the spiritual influence of Christianity predisposed them to moderation and humanity and militated against despotic practices.[6] These common features set Europe apart from the rest of the world. Combined with the superiority of its political and legal institutions, they ensured the existence of a shared cultural space that favored exchanges within

---

[2] Pierre Chaunu, *La civilisation de l'Europe des lumières* (Paris: Arthaud, 1971).

[3] Charles-Louis Secondat de Montesquieu, *Esprit des Lois*, in *Oeuvres complètes*, ed. Roger Caillois, 2 vols., Paris, Gallimard, vol. 2, 529 (Book XVII, ch. 6).

[4] Larry Wolff, *Inventing Eastern Europe* (Stanford: Stanford University Press, 1995).

[5] Jean-Marie Arouet de Voltaire, *Essai sur les moeurs* (1745), ed. R. Pomeau, 2 vols. (Paris: Garnier, 1963).

[6] Montesquieu, *Esprit des Lois*, cit., Book XXIV, ch. 3; see also Book XI, ch. 6, on the comparison between European and non-European judicial systems.

an enlightened community of educated aristocrats, writers, and scientists. A long-established tradition called this phenomenon the *république des lettres*. Indeed, evidence of this reality could be found in the wide circulation of books and periodicals within Ancien Régime Europe. Its geographical boundaries were displayed by the practice of the Grand Tour.

In spite of the existence of such an intellectual community, "European" did not then mean anything other than French, English, Spanish, and so on. In the collective imagination of the century, European nations were separate entitites, connected by close commercial and cultural exchanges but still divided by economic, dynastic, and territorial rivalries.

The relations of European states with one another remained necessarily competitive. Enlightened intellectuals might wish for peace and good commercial relations, deplore any form of aggressive patriotism, or disapprove of the destructive and ill-conceived military ambitions of kings; but since international relations were thought to be economically and territorially a zero-sum game, to love one's country meant necessarily to militate against the success of other nations. As Voltaire stressed, it was part of the human condition that to wish for the greatness of one's country meant to wish ill of one's neighbors. He who should not wish to see his country larger rather than smaller, richer rather than poorer, would be a citizen of the universe.[7]

REVOLUTION AND CONQUEST

What happened to this rather vague notion of Europe when the political relations within the European continent were suddenly disrupted, from 1792, by the French revolutionary wars and by France's subsequent transformation into an imperial power? When France declared war against Prussia and Austria in 1792, most people expected a desperate defense of the French national territory against overwhelming foreign armies. Twenty years later, in 1812 (the moment of greatest expansion of Napoleon's empire), France ruled directly over 44 million subjects (the population of France itself being about 28 million) to which must be added 33 to 35 million people in countries that had become

---

[7] Voltaire, *Dictionnaire Philosophique* (1764), ed. Etiemble (Paris: Garnier, 1967), article "Patrie." See also *Encyclopédie*, article "Paix"; and Istvan Hont, "The Permanent Crisis of a Divided Mankind," in John Dunn, ed., *Contemporary Crisis of the Nation State? Political Studies*, vol. XVII, 1994.

France's satellites: in all about 40 percent of the entire European population.[8]

The traumatic, if successful, experience of French conquest resulted in two different and quite incompatible notions of what the collective identity of European nations was or should be: a duplicity that can still be recognized in the ambiguity of contemporary views about the desirable role of the European Union.

The first of these notions is associated with the ambitions of the French revolutionary government and of its successors, the Thermidorian and Bonapartist regimes. Its central assumption was that if Europe was the most civilized part of the world and revolutionary France the most civilized nation in Europe, then the same historical process leading to the reform and modernization of France would create in due course a united European continent in her image.

In the highly utopian vision of Enlightenment philosophers such as Condorcet, the progress of equality within a single nation would eventually lead to the disappearance of inequality between nations and between Europe and the rest of the world. If the European monarchs of the Ancien Régime had exploited the poverty and barbarism of "savage" populations all over the world for their own commercial advantage and had fought among themselves for supremacy, the advent of free republican governments in France and America would, in time, bring to an end all military conflict within Europe and all colonial domination outside it.[9]

Clearly, Condorcet's belief that some day "the sun...[would] only shine upon free men" and Bonaparte's far more prosaic notion that "ce qui est bon pour les français est bon pour tout le monde" (what is good enough for the French is good enough for everybody) were not exactly the same thing. Yet both phrases assumed the fundamental identity of needs and expectations in human beings, regardless of their circumstances, ethnic origins, traditions, and national characters. The abolition in France of Ancien Régime institutions and their replacement with the new principles of liberty, equality, and fraternity brought about the increasing political, legal, and cultural homogeneity of those nations that came in contact with it, in the first instance the European ones.

---

[8] A. Fierro, A. Paullel-Guillard, J. Tulard, *Histoire et dictionnaire du Consulat et de l'Empire* (Paris: Robert Laffont, 1995); Andrina Stiles, *Napoleon, France and Europe* (London: Hodder & Stoughton, 1993); J. Lovie and A. Paullel-Guillard, *L'Episode Napoléonien*, vol. 2, "Aspects extérieurs," Nouvelle Histoire de la France Contemporaine, vol. 5 (Paris: Seuil, 1972).

[9] Jean-Marie Caritat de Condorcet, *Esquisse d'un tableau historique des progrès de l'esprit humain*, ed. M. and F. Hincker (Paris: Editions Sociales, 1971), "Dixième période," 253ff.

These universalistic aspirations were expressed by the National Assembly in the Declaration of Rights of 1789. The Declaration never specifically mentioned "France," but it referred to "governments" (in the plural) and to "any society" or "any political community." During the extensive debate about the Declaration, it was made clear that the document outlined "the fundamental principles which must provide the ground for all government" and that "the French people [were] the first of all peoples and a model for every nation."[10]

France's leading role, as originally understood by the National Assembly, was not to impose French rules and French standards on other nations, even less to conquer them by force. As François Furet has reminded us, moderate forces in the National Assembly initiated the war in 1792 for reasons far more connected with domestic problems than with international concerns; in principle, the Jacobins were hostile to the competitive logic that opposed European nations in the Ancien Régime political tradition.[11]

The French Constitution of 1791 stated clearly France's commitment to respect the freedom and autonomy of other peoples: "The French nation will never undertake any war with the aim of conquest and will never employ her armed forces against the freedom of any country."[12] This is why, during the revolution, annexation (in 1791 Avignon, in 1792 the Savoy, in 1793 Nice) was pursued halfheartedly, generally on the more or less spontaneous solicitation of local "patriots" rather than by direct initiative of the Assembly. The notions of "natural frontiers," of the "liberation" and "reunion" of "sister republics," filled the gap between the practice of occupation and the project of a confederacy of free states.[13]

French conquests spread farther under the Directory (Holland in 1795, northern Italy and Genoa in 1797, Switzerland in 1798). To the ideological uneasiness was added the anxiety of how to rule over peoples and

[10] Christine Fauré, ed., *Les déclarations des droits de l'homme de 1789* (Paris: Payot, 1988), 22.

[11] François Furet, "Les girondins et la guerre: les débuts de l'Assemblé législative," in F. Furet and M. Ozouf, eds., *La Gironde et les Girondins* (Paris: Payot, 1991); Paul W. Schroeder, *The Transformation of European Politics, 1763–1848* (Oxford: Clarendon Press, 1994).

[12] Montmorin to the National Assembly, 22 May 1790; later embodied in the Constitution, Titre VI: "La Nation française renonce à entreprendre aucune guerre dans la vue de faire des conquêtes et n'emploiera jamais ses forces contre la liberté d'aucun peuple" in Jacques Godechot ed., *Les constitutions de la France depuis 1789* (Paris: Flammarion, 1979), 65.

[13] See Denis Richet, "Frontières naturelles," in F. Furet and M. Ozouf, eds., *Dictionnaire critique de la Révolution française* (Paris: Flammarion, 1988).

territories that were far from homogeneous and sympathetic. The lack of global hegemonic design, the occasional character of military aggression, and the piecemeal strategy of opportunity and improvisation remained constant features of French conquest.

Naturally, both the Directory and the Consulate derived very substantial advantages from the politics of conquest, and soon these benefits became essential to their political and financial survival. Moreover, in realizing some of the cherished military and economic ambitions of the old monarchy, these governments reproduced to some extent the strategies and organizational patterns that had been designed for similar purposes (in some cases by the same people) under the Ancien Régime. In particular, the renewal of army personnel and army ranks, the development of new technologies for the artillery, the reorganization of transport and supplies, and above all the introduction of conscription to cut military expenses were projects hatched by Louis XVI's war office, but the faltering monarchy had been unable to implement them.[14]

In spite of this continuity postrevolutionary French governments could never entirely free themselves from the universalistic and, paradoxically, pacifist postures of the Jacobins. In the long run the empire became the only viable solution to these contradictions, the only formula that made it possible for Bonaparte to reconcile French supremacy with the vision of a peaceful sisterhood of European nations, a sisterhood that would come fully into being as soon as all perverse resistance and sinister opposition against it ceased. The attempts at administrative integration of the occupied territories, the imposition of the Code Napoléon, and the creation of a large bureaucratic class (which in some cases included important sections of the local élites) were all part of this design.[15]

Napoleon regarded this process of "modernization" and administrative unification as the real strength of his rule and as the self-evident proof of its historical legitimacy. In 1807 he wrote to his brother Jerôme, king of Westfalia:

The benefits of the Code Napoléon, the publicity of procedures, the establishment of juries should be the distinctive characteristics of your monarchy. And, to be honest, I trust more to their effects to extend and strengthen your power than to

---

[14] On these aspects of the reform of the French army, see Azar Gat, *The Origins of Military Thought from the Enlightenment to Clausewitz* (Oxford: Clarendon Press, 1989), 25–53. For further bibliographic references, see Biancamaria Fontana, *Politique de Laclos* (Paris: Kimé, 1996), 55–63.

[15] Stuart Woolf, *Napoleon's Integration of Europe* (London: Routledge, 1991).

the results of the greatest victories. What people would submit itself again to an arbitrary government [that is, Prussia] after having enjoyed the benefits of a wise and liberal administration?[16]

To the end of his life Napoleon remained attached to an implausible vision of his empire as a confederation in the model of ancient Greek federations or of the American Congress. During his final captivity in St. Helena, he confessed to Las Cases:

> One of my great designs was the agglomeration, the concentration of the same geographical peoples (*peuples géographiques*) which revolutions and politics had broken down. I would have liked to make of each of these peoples one and the same national body.... After this first approximate simplification, there would be more opportunities to bring everywhere unity of laws, of principles, of opinions, sentiments, views and interests. Then perhaps it would have been possible to dream for the great European family of a political model such as that of the American Congress or of the Amphictyons of Greece.[17]

It would be only too easy to question the good faith and credibility of such statements. In some cases the French occupation encountered the strenuous resistance of the local populations—a resistance that, in the case of Spain for example, could hardly be described as the product of a reactionary conspiracy. Even in those countries where the French troops were welcomed at first as liberators by the local patriots, this initial enthusiasm soon gave way to bitter disappointment when French conquest showed its true colors in the practice of systematic pillage and repression as well as in the ruthless surrendering of territories to the enemy—the "exchange" of Lombardy and Venice sanctioned by the Treaty of Campoformio that left the Venetian patriots who had supported the French at the mercy of the Austrians.

Similarly, the integration of local elites in the new French administrations all over Europe had a very limited impact and offered no real alternative to the straightforward enforcement of French interests. Yet for all its inadequacies, Napoleon's imperial adventure remained inextricably bound with the revolutionary heritage and with the universalistic tradition of the Enlightenment; it represented a novel, distinctly modern

---

[16] Napoleon to Jerôme, 15 November 1807; see also his speech to the Corps législatif of 15 February 1805: "It is my task, our task, the task of the most gentle, most enlightened, most human of peoples to remind to the civilized nations of Europe that they are part of one family and that the energies they engage in their civil conflicts are a blow to the common prosperity."
[17] Napoleon to Las Cases, 11 November 1816.

project of European hegemony, one that unsettled all traditional views about national rivalries and the balance of powers.

THE OPPOSITION TO NAPOLEON

An alternative notion of Europe to emerge from the French revolution was associated with those liberal intellectuals who, at the beginning of the nineteenth century, found themselves in opposition to Napoleon's imperial regime. Their critical response was primarily directed against the military ambitions of the French revolutionary and postrevolutionary governments. In contemplating the disastrous consequences of a prolonged European war, however, they were led to question those cosmopolitan ideals to which some leading exponents of the Enlightenment had been so ready to subscribe.

This anti-imperialist approach is well exemplified by the works of Germaine de Staël and Benjamin Constant, two writers who, though assimilated within French culture, were born in "sister republics" whose territories were threatened by the expansionistic ambitions of the French: the republics of Geneva and Bern.[18] De Staël's chateau of Coppet, near Geneva, was for several decades a cosmopolitan meeting point for exiles and political refugees as well as an important center for collective reflection on the future of European politics and culture.[19]

These critiques of the unification of Europe under French rule re-echoed themes that Montesquieu had employed to stigmatize the administrative centralism of the French monarchy: namely, uniformity was a mode of absolutism, and the suppression of local differences and regional specificities was an essential feature of despotic power. Montesquieu wrote:

The monarch, who knows each one of his provinces, can establish different laws and tolerate different practices. But the despot knows nothing, and cannot fix his attention on anything in particular; he needs a general approach (*une allure générale*); he governs through a rigid will which is the same everywhere; everything is flattened under his feet.[20]

---

[18] After the French occupation of 1798, Constant's hometown, Lausanne, was detached from the Bernese territory and became the capital of a new canton established under French "protectorate," the Vaud.

[19] See AAVV *Le Groupe de Coppet et l'Europe*, 1789–1830, 5ème Colloque de Coppet (Lausanne and Paris: Jean Touzot Libraire/Editeur, 1994); Pierre Kholer, *Madame de Staël et la Suisse* (Lausanne and Paris: Payot, 1916); *Annales Benjamin Constant* 18–19, special issue, "Les conditions de la vie culturelle et intellectuelle en Suisse Romande au temps des Lumières" (Genève: Slatkine, 1996).

[20] Montesquieu, *Esprit des lois*, cit., Book VI, ch. 1.

Although the majority of national characters in *Il Viaggio a Reims* were the product of Rossini's own imagination, one of them, the Italian poetess Corinna, was borrowed from *Corinne, ou l'Italie*, a successful novel published by de Staël in 1807. Set in contemporary Rome, the novel celebrated the importance of the Italian republican tradition as a bulwark against present decadence and tyranny: an implicit attack against the French occupation that did not escape the emperor's attention.[21]

More generally, de Staël's writings focused upon national specificities within European literature and philosophy as well as on the original contribution of Italian, Spanish, German, and English culture, which in her view were too little known and appreciated by the French public. In *De la littérature considerée dans ses rapports avec les institutions sociales* published in 1800, as in her influential work of 1810, *De l'Allemagne* (destroyed at the printer by the Napoleonic police), she returned to Montesquieu's idea of the fusion of peoples of the North and peoples of the South to show that the winning feature of European civilization was the diversity of contributions and the variety of national traditions and talents.[22] Thus, the efforts made during the revolution to impose uniform patterns of aesthetic achievements were bound to prove counterproductive. Similarly, in *Considérations sur la Révolution française* (1812–18), de Staël stigmatized Napoleon's policy of "denationalization" and claimed that Europe would free itself from despotism only on the strength of national sentiment.[23]

The vision that emerged was no longer that of a European *république des lettres* dominated by the more advanced and sophisticated French culture, but of an integrated unity that depended on a variety of traditions and local experiences to preserve political liberty as well as to promote artistic achievement.[24]

In his passionate pamphlet of 1813, *De l'esprit de conquête*, Constant traced a dramatic picture of the evils of modern imperialism. Unlike ancient tribes, which fought for need and to satisfy their heroic instincts,

---

[21] Ghislain de Diesbach, "Napoléon juge de Corinne," in *Madame de Staël* (Paris: Perrin, 1983), 373–5.

[22] On the importance of the fusion between peoples of the North and of the South in shaping the French nation, see Robert de Montlosier, *De la Monarchie française* (Paris: Gideet fils, 1814).

[23] On de Staël, see Henri Guillemin, *Madame de Staël et Napoléon* (Paris: Seuil, 1987); Simone Balayé, *Madame de Staël, Lumières et Liberté* (Paris: Klincksieck, 1979).

[24] On the transformation of republican culture in the postrevolutionary period, see Biancamaria Fontana, ed., *The Invention of the Modern Republic* (Cambridge: Cambridge University Press, 1994).

modern conquerors acted in cold blood and were motivated by greed
alone. Although ancient empires respected the diversity of the peoples
they dominated, allowing them to retain their own customs and beliefs, the
modern empire imposed an artificial uniformity of rule, administration,
law, cult, and even language. By flattening local differences, it crushed
at the same time the fundamental dignity and identity of its subjects,
depriving them of all capacity for resistance, making of them the passive instruments of its political and military ambitions. "It is somewhat
remarkable," wrote Constant

that uniformity should never have encountered greater favour than in a revolution
made in the name of the rights and liberty of men.... While patriotism exists only
by a vivid attachment to the interests, the way of life, the customs of some locality,
our so-called patriots have declared war on all of these. They have dried up this
natural source of patriotism and have sought to replace it by a fictitious passion
for an abstract being, a general idea stripped of all that can engage the imagination
and speak to the memory.[25]

To this deadly uniformity of the empire, Constant opposed the living
association of European nations, bound by mutual commercial interests
and a common need for freedom and peace. It was in vain that Bonaparte's
despotism tried to impose commercial restrictions—such as the Continental blockade—or to force countries into antagonistic positions: while in
Europe a single nation, England, remained free, despotism would never
triumph, since the close communications existing among countries would
always enable people, resources, and ideas to circulate, escaping from the
regime's destructive grasp.

FROM PARIS TO VIENNA

Constant's idealized picture of a community of peaceful, commerce-
oriented European nations united against despotism, if justified in the
context of a pamphlet written on the eve of Napoleon's defeat, concealed
the most problematic implications of his analysis. The Europe of commerce and freedom—where money fled from the constraints of national
frontiers, and individuals refused to fight for a cause they did not understand or left their country in search of a better lifestyle or more liberal
government—was no less exposed to the risks of instability than had been

---

[25] *The Spirit of Conquest*, in Biancamaria Fontana, ed., *The Political Writings of Benjamin
Constant* (Cambridge: Cambridge University Press, 1988), ch. 16, 73–4.

Bonaparte's empire, as the general economic crisis that followed the end of the French wars in 1815 was soon to show.[26]

Commerce was at least as effective as war in destroying national identities and local attachments; it turned the population of Europe into "a great mass of human beings, that...despite the different names under which they live and their different forms of social organization, are essentially homogeneous in their nature."[27] In this respect the long-term effects of the development of an international market economy went in the same direction as imperial conquest, bringing about the creation of a large, anonymous, potentially disaffected market society.

No doubt Napoleon's conquests had alerted European governments to the dangers of revolution and uncontrolled imperial ambitions. Above all, however, they proved the inadequacy of the balance-of-power system that had dominated European international politics throughout the eighteenth century. This system assumed that European powers, while pursuing their particular national interests, would achieve a kind of spontaneous equilibrium through commercial and military competition. It was now clear that this assumption was implausible and unrealistic—as utopian, in fact, as any Enlightenment ideal of universal brotherhood and world peace.

The protracted negotiations that began on the occasion of the peace of Paris in May 1814 and continued at the Congress of Vienna (between October 1814 and June 1815) reflected a new vision: European stability could no longer be left to the operation of spontaneous forces or to opportunistic dynastic alliances; it had to be constructed and closely monitored at a continental level.

Although the rhetoric of the participants to the Congress advocated the restoration of legitimate sovereigns and the return to the prerevolutionary status quo, several changes brought about by the Napoleonic wars to the configuration of European frontiers were implicitly endorsed. The Congress accepted, for example, the disappearance of a plethora of small states (the number of German principates was reduced to 38 from about 300) and promoted the creation of large buffer states to protect the

---

[26] On the economic performance of the Napoleonic regime and the 1815 crisis, see the evaluations offered by Thomas Malthus and by Constant's Scottish friend James Mackintosh. They both stress the advantages for France of Napoleon's commercial protectionism and imperialistic policy. T. R. Malthus, *The Ground of an Opinion of the Policy of Restricting the Importation of Foreign Corn* (London: 1815), footnote p. 12; and S. Hollander, "Malthus and the Post-Napoleonic Depression," *History of Political Economy*, vol. 1 (1969), 306–35; James Mackintosh, "France," *Edinburgh Review* 34 (August 1820): 1–39.

[27] *Spirit of Conquest*, ch. 2, cit., 52–3.

areas of potential conflict. Similarly, the Congress rejected the Prussian proposal for a partition of French territory: in fact, France was restored to her frontiers of 1790, thus depriving her of all conquered territories but confirming her status as a major European power. The creation of the Quadruple Alliance in November 1815 established the principle of permanent consultation and concerted agreements among the major powers to preserve stability.[28]

This unwillingness to restore the past was not confined to strategic arrangements and piecemeal solutions. It implied a profound transformation of the global vision of the European continent, a transformation for which Napoleon's imperialism, even in its defeat, must ultimately take the credit.

The Europe of the Congress of Vienna, dominated by the interests of the great powers at the expense of their subjects and satellites, little resembles de Staël's Europe of nations in which the genius of northern and southern peoples would come together in freedom and peaceful cooperation. Indeed, the tension between these two visions would recurrently surface in national conflicts throughout the nineteenth century. Yet with the settlements of the Congress of Vienna, the modern idea of Europe had reached a point of no return. From now on the European identity would no longer reside in shared traditions, in religious and cultural affinities. It had become a distinctive political reality, the privileged framework within which single nations had to find their place and a mode of coexistence.

---

[28] On the balance of powers, the French wars, and the Congress of Vienna, see Schroeder, *The Transformation of European Politics.* See also David Thompson, *Europe since Napoleon* (Harmondsworth: Penguin Books, 1957); Derek McKay and H. M. Scott, *The Rise of Great Powers, 1648–1815* (Harlow: Longman, 1983); Jeremy Black, *The Rise of European Powers, 1679–1793* (London: Edward Arnold, 1990).

6

Homo Politicus and *Homo Oeconomicus*: The European Citizen According to Max Weber

WILFRIED NIPPEL

The monumental though fragmentary work of German sociologist and economist Max Weber (1864–1920) is focused on the quest for the particularity of modern Western civilization.[1] Its vanishing point is the uniqueness of modern "rational capitalism" with its preconditions in, and repercussions on, all aspects of social life. Weber, however, did not develop a theory of the modern world; he embarked rather on its prerequisites in classical antiquity and the middle ages and on crosscultural comparisons with the great civilizations of the Oriental world. That was partly because of his scholarly education; he started his career with works on the interdependence of legal and economic structures in late medieval Italy and ancient Rome.[2] But it was also because of his growing insight that the structural preconditions that enabled the development of a capitalistic culture in the Occidental world and hampered it in the Oriental world could be adequately analyzed only from a point of view of universal history.

The more Weber developed his comparative approach, the more significant became the implications of diverse types of citizenship in the West and the absence of a notion of citizenship in the East. He had already covered certain aspects of this subject in his article "Agrarverhältnisse

---

[1] The following abbreviations are used for Weber's publications: ASAC for *The Agrarian Sociology of Ancient Civilisations*, trans. R. I. Frank (London: New Left Books, 1976) [contains the 3rd ed. of "Agrarverhältnisse im Altertum," 1909]; E&S for *Economy and Society: An Outline of Interpretive Sociology*, ed. Guenther Roth and Claus Wittich (New York: Bedminster, 1968); GARS for *Gesammelte Aufsätze zur Religionssoziologie*, 3 vols. (1920–1), reprinted (Tübingen: Mohr (Siebeck), 1988); MWG for *Max Weber Gesamtausgabe* (Tübingen: Mohr (Siebeck), 1982–); SWG for *Gesammelte Aufsätze zur Sozial- und Wirtschaftgeschichte* (1924), reprinted (Tübingen: Mohr (Siebeck), 1988); and WuG for *Wirtschaft und Gesellschaft: Grundriss der verstehenden Soziologie*, 5th ed., ed. Johannes Winckelmann (Tübingen: Mohr (Siebeck), 1976).

[2] *Zur Geschichte der Handelsgesellschaften im Mittelalter* (Stuttgart: Enke, 1889), and *Die römische Agrargeschichte in ihrer Bedeutung für das Staats- und Privatrecht* (Stuttgart: Enke, 1891) = MWG I/2, ed. by Jürgen Deininger, 1982.

129

im Altertum" for the encyclopedia *Handwörterbuch der Staatswissen-schaften*, which in its final version (1909) became a text of book length.[3] His most mature treatment, however, is the essay "Die Stadt" (The City), published posthumously in 1921 and nowadays known as part of his main work, *Wirtschaft und Gesellschaft* (Economy and Society).[4] The article is obviously incomplete; it was apparently drafted between 1911 and late 1913 or early 1914 and drew on Weber's studies on the sociology of world religions, something he had been working on since about 1910 or 1911.[5] "Die Stadt" probably originated as a special section on "nonlegitimate domination" within his discussion of the sociology of domination intended for *Wirtschaft und Gesellschaft*. But it is far from certain whether Weber would have incorporated the text exactly as it now is into this work or used at least parts of it in the context of his work on the sociology of world religions.[6]

The title "Die Stadt" is somewhat misleading. True, Weber began by attempting to provide an adequate definition of the "city." He tried out definitions based on geographical, economic, social, and legal criteria one after the other, but he came to the conclusion that, given the variety of cities all over the world, any comprehensive definition must necessarily be incomplete. In his essay Weber concentrated on the city with a distinct political-administrative status—namely, the commune consisting of a self-governing body of citizens (*die Stadt im Rechtssinne, die Gemeinde*) who enjoy some autonomy and are entitled to install a magistracy, administer a judiciary of their own, and pass bylaws. There is a certain ambiguity in this definition since Weber wanted to cover different legal types of cities: the fully autonomous ancient city-state, and the Italian city-republics as their equivalent, as well as self-governing medieval cities that (as subjects of a kingdom, principality, or the Holy Roman Empire) could make no claim to sovereignty. By using the *Gemeinde* as the key criterion, he chose the minimum definition for a self-governing urban community that could be matched by the ancient and Italian city-republics *a fortiori*. Whereas cities—fortified settlements with marketplaces—can be found all over the world, Weber's commune of urban citizens is a peculiar phenomenon that prevailed only within the culture of the Occident.

---

[3] SWG 1–288 = ASAC 35–386.
[4] *Archiv für Sozialwissenschaft und Sozialpolitik* 47 (1921): 621–722; WuG 727–814.
[5] Beginning in 1915, a series of articles by Weber on Confucianism, Hinduism, and Buddhism was published. The collection in GARS is now superseded by MWG I/19 and I/20, ed. Helwig Schmidt-Glintzer, 1989 and 1996.
[6] See my edition of "Die Stadt," MWG I/22, 5, 1999.

OCCIDENT VERSUS ORIENT

Weber had already stressed in "Agrarverhältnisse im Altertum" that this was the fundamental difference between the Occidental (Graeco-Roman) world and the Oriental world (ancient Egypt, Mesopotamia, and Israel). In that article he had described two distinct patterns of development "for all the peoples in Antiquity from the Seine to the Euphrates among whom urban centres developed."[7] The difference between them was attributed to basic geographical and ecological factors. The citizen-state as a self-organizing military body developed in the coastal civilization of the Greco-Roman world, because there the aristocracies had access to the gains made from commerce and thus could reduce the kingdom to a merely military leadership and finally get rid of it altogether. Later they had to accept the political participation of the bulk of the citizenry who, as hoplites, provided most of the military.

Priests were always mere functionaries of the community: they could claim no independent authority in political questions. In the civilizations at the banks of great rivers, the necessities of river regulation and irrigation strengthened the primordial kingdoms and nurtured the development of a centralized bureaucracy subject to a monarch with an indisputable monopoly in political, military, and economic power. The monarch could rely on the support of a privileged priesthood. On this basis there later emerged what Weber described as "the authoritarian liturgical state." In it "the state's necessities were met by a carefully contrived system of duties imposed on the state's subjects."[8] In the end this authoritarian liturgical state, especially as it had been created in Ptolemaic Egypt, came to dominate the later Roman Empire.

Weber used this scheme again in "Die Stadt" in order to stress the distinctness of developmental patterns, once the primordial state of universally similar urban centers had been abandoned. The crosscultural comparison now included the Middle Ages on the European side and India, China, and in some respects Japan on the Oriental side. The great Oriental civilizations were seen as almost invariable with respect to their main structural features from ancient to early modern times. The interdependence of irrigation systems and bureaucratic state apparatus—a version of the topic of "Oriental despotism" familiar since Montesquieu—was again mentioned with respect to the strength of the Chinese monarchy. But Weber now stressed cultural factors in order to explain why in China

---

[7] ASAC 69 = SWG 35.   [8] ASAC 74 = SWG 39f.

and India a breakthrough in this direction never took place despite certain tendencies toward city autonomy and the actual, if not legally endorsed, role of the "guilds."

In his view commune-building depends on the ability of the members to unite in a ritual community that he calls *Verbrüderung* (confraternity), a community based on artificially-created and freely-willed mutual ties, not on consanguinity. This meant that the community depended on the equal rights (in principle at least) of all its members, solidarity against nonmembers, *connubium*, and a common cult symbolically expressed in communal cult meals.[9] According to Weber's interpretation, the rigid caste system established in India after the final victory of Brahmanism prevented (particularly through its exclusion of any kind of commensality between members of different castes) the emergence of any confraternal structure.[10] In the Chinese case it was the ancestor cult that had the corresponding effect, since it bound the city-dwellers to their respective sibs, or clans, and villages of origin.

MIDDLE AGES VERSUS ANTIQUITY

The notion of *Verbrüderung* explains the fundamental difference between Occidental and Oriental city-dwellers and their different potential for commune-building; it also allows Weber to accentuate an important distinction between European Antiquity and the Middle Ages. He assumes that confraternity can be established by groups such as sibs or by individuals, but the highest intensity is achieved only in the latter case.

In pre-Christian Antiquity religion did not inhibit confraternity, but it did not provide any positive predispositions for it either. Confraternity materialized in the union of heads of sibs that originally constituted the city-state by means of *synoikismos* (the real "housing together" in an urban center or the constitution of a singular political center for hitherto separate communities). The patrician clans, however, tried to preserve their ritual exclusivity with respect to the plebeians, an exclusivity abolished only after prolonged struggles between the social orders had resulted in a more equitable relationship between citizens of all social ranks. According to Weber, the ancient city-states failed to reach the intensity of confraternity that was later achieved in the medieval commune

---

[9] E&S 1241 = WuG 744.

[10] Buddhism flourished especially in the age of the Maurya Dynasty in the third century BC; its decline and final supersession by Brahmanism took several centuries.

where burghers constituted the community by means of the *coniuratio* (an oath taken by each individual).

In the European Middle Ages confraternity possessed a positive religious basis, since all the members already belonged to the same church, as symbolized in the community of the Eucharist. (Of course, this inevitably implied the outsider-status of the Jews.) Confraternity was also the constituent element of the formation of nonprivileged citizens within the commune (the Italian *popolo*) and of the guilds (social clubs as well as economic pressure groups) and diverse kinds of religious associations.

In this context the role of Greco-Roman Antiquity is somewhat diminished. The constitutive acts of founding a commune in Antiquity (by *synoikismos*) and in the Middle Ages (by *coniuratio*) are seen as equivalents, whereas community-building within the ancient city is depicted as deficient in some respect. This is due to Weber's decision to concentrate on the act of foundation rather than analyze the different kinds of confraternities that developed out of the religious festivals of the city-state and its subdivisions.[11] And it leaves open the question of how and when the emergence of Christianity changed the social and cultural character of the cities in the Roman Empire. Weber referred (here and elsewhere) to the breakthrough in Antioch praised by St. Paul (Galatians 2) when the community of the Lord's Supper was practiced for the first time between circumcised and uncircumcised Christians. This practice implied that the Judaeo-Christians no longer considered themselves to be bound by Jewish ritual law. This event, Weber claimed, was the moment of the conception of the citizens' association, although it would not see the final light of day until the first *coniurationes* of city-dwellers in the medieval cities a thousand years later.[12] He did not enter into the complicated historical and theological questions that created numerous controversies within the early Christian community (characterized in the Antiochene case by the conduct of St. Peter who first participated in the new table-fellowship and then later withdrew from it).[13] Weber was only interested in a theme in

[11] Wilfried Nippel, "Max Weber zwischen Althistorie und Universalgeschichte: Synoikismos und Verbrüderung," in Christian Meier, ed., *Die okzidentale Stadt nach Max Weber* (München: Oldenbourg, 1994), 35–57.

[12] GARS II, 39f. = MWG I/20, 96f.

[13] For the complicated details see James D. G. Dunn, "The Incident at Antioch (Gal. 2: 11–18)," *Journal for the Study of the New Testament* 18 (1983): 3–57; E. P. Sanders, "Jewish Association with Gentiles and Galatians 2: 11–14," in R. T. Fortna and B. R. Gaventa, eds., *The Conversation Continues: Studies in Paul and John in Honor of J. Louis Martyn* (Nashville: Abingdon Press, 1990), 170–88.

which the "incident at Antioch" could be perceived retrospectively as the turning point that led to the universality of Christianity. His argument thus left a huge void between the beginning of the Christian era and the high Middle Ages, a period of a thousand years that is not discussed in any of the historical parts of Weber's work.

Instead, Weber embarked on a comparison of the structural similarities between the constitutional development in Antiquity and the Middle Ages that in each case led from a domination of patrician families to more popular regimes (which in most cases, however, were finally led by a new political elite formed by the merger of an old patriciate with the leading members of the hitherto underprivileged citizens). These processes led to the rationalization of the political system by the establishment of magistracies with restricted terms of office and clearly defined competencies, by the codification of laws, and by rules for the creation of new laws. Weber's comparison relates to the "classical" ancient city-states (Sparta, Athens, Republican Rome) and the Italian city-states. It considers *inter alia* similarities between the Roman *plebs* and the Italian *popolo*, who with their respective representatives (*tribuni plebis*, *capitani del popolo*) formed an alternative political organization that duplicated, in certain respects, the institutions of the city-government. (Weber also discussed at length the exceptional case of Venice. The Venetian patriciate maintained its political hegemony for centuries without being seriously challenged by the bulk of the population.)[14] But Weber warns that parallels between political superstructures may indicate identical economic bases. (It is also worth mentioning that Weber's comparisons always begin with the Middle Ages and that the medieval examples are described in much more detail than the ancient ones.) The fundamental difference between the ancient and the medieval city lay in the relationship between the city and its hinterland. In the ancient world both spheres constituted a political unity that implied that the peasants made up the majority of citizens. In the Middle Ages city and hinterland were two legally distinct spheres, and peasants were not entitled to citizen-rights.

In the last part of "Die Stadt" Weber returned to the question of economic rationality in Antiquity and the Middle Ages, ideas he had originally sketched out in the concluding part of "Agrarverhältnisse im

---

[14] With his comparison of popular magistrates of ancient and Renaissance times and his allusion to the "Myth of Venice," Weber followed a centuries-old tradition of political thought. See Wilfried Nippel, "Ancient and Modern Republicanism: 'Mixed Constitution' and 'Ephors'," in Biancamaria Fontana, ed., *The Invention of the Modern Republic* (Cambridge: Cambridge University Press, 1994), 6–26.

Altertum." In "Die Stadt" he makes the famous distinction between the ancient *homo politicus* and the medieval *homo oeconomicus*:

> The specifically medieval city type, the artisan inland city, was altogether economically oriented.... Whereas in Antiquity the hoplite army and its training, and thus military interests, increasingly came to constitute the pivot of all urban organisation, in the Middle Ages most burgher privileges began with the limitation of the burgher's military duties to garrison service. The economic interests of the medieval townsman lay in peaceful gain through commerce and the trade, and this was most pronouncedly so for the lower strata of the urban citizenry.... The political situation of the medieval townsman determined his path, which was that of a *homo oeconomicus*, whereas in Antiquity the polis preserved during its heyday its character as the technically most advanced military organisation. The ancient townsman was a *homo politicus*.[15]

For the purpose of this particular comparison, the medieval city was represented by the type of the artisanal inland city (*bürgerliche gewerbliche Binnenstadt*) of Europe north of the Alps. These cities were embedded in a power structure that did not allow them to play an independent military role. Consequently, they did not offer their citizens opportunities for material gain by military and political means or burden them with more than a minimum of military service. Therefore, the northern European cities stood in sharp contrast to the ancient city-republics. The Italian city-states were located between these extremes. The maritime republics of Venice and Genoa were closer to the ancient example; some of the Italian inland city-states also displayed some of the features of the ancient ones because of their ability to pursue expansionist policies. But the bulk of the citizenry (largely craftsmen) was like its northern European counterpart, overwhelmingly interested in economic policies that promoted its commercial interests.

In Antiquity the typically declassed citizen was a dispossessed farmer. In the Middle Ages he was an unemployed craftsman. This difference determined the different character of the class struggle in the two societies, as well as the direction of the cities' economic policy, which only in the Middle Ages sought to protect the interests of local producers. An ancient *demos* (which participated in the gains of an expansionist policy by colonization, booty, grain distributions, soldier's pay, and political reward) was only concerned about preserving the exclusivity of its status and not inclined to a peaceful acquisition of wealth through industry and trade.

These "warrior guilds," therefore, maintained a closed-shop with respect to citizen status. This implied, especially in the Greek case, an

---

[15] E&S 1353f. = WuG 805.

inability to build up stable empires. Citizens maintained status distinctions against metics (resident aliens), freedmen, and slaves. This meant that groups such as metics and freedmen were the only ones truly oriented toward the pursuit of peacefully acquired profit through commerce and trade. There could be no guilds in the proper sense. The creation of guilds for the first time during the Middle Ages constituted the organization of labor on the basis of formally free contract, which Weber qualified as the most productive type of labor organization in history. Thus, citizens are likely to choose economic rationality only if they have no chance to acquire material gains by military means or, to put it another way, only if they are no longer occupied by compulsory military functions. That is why the foundations for rational capitalism could be laid only in the later Middle Ages and not in Antiquity.

Missing from this thesis are two crucial test cases—namely, the cities within the Hellenistic and Roman Empires. Weber himself said that in a "unified and pacified" Mediterranean world "the ancient city became the centre of exclusively economic interests."[16] Therefore, these structures would have required a more thorough analysis beyond the statement that the bureaucratic monarchy, and the shift from coastal to continental civilization, dealt a fatal blow to any dynamic economical development. It is also a pity that Weber did not expand his argument concerning the preconditions of economic rationalization with respect to the later developments in early-modern Europe. The Netherlandish and English cities could have served as test cases. Weber stresses the exceptional status of English cities (apart from London) whose communal rights in the Middle Ages had always depended on concessions by the crown.

Since he held that the political structures of Antiquity were responsible for the limits of economical rationalization, Weber was unable to understand fully the essence of ancient politics, especially in those areas where it distracted the bulk of the citizenry from rationalized economic production. This comes out most clearly in Weber's rather gloomy and one-sided picture of Athenian democracy. The political participation of citizens (service in the political institutions and in military campaigns "of proportions which no other differentiated culture in history has ever experienced before or since") is seen as an impediment to "pacific economic acquisition based on rational and continuous economic activity." The liturgies, a mixture of compulsory duties and volunteer engagements by which wealthy citizens contributed to the financing of the fleet and of

---

[16] ASAC 358 = SWG 271.

public festivals, are viewed unfavorably by Weber, since in his opinion they subjected any accumulation of wealth to the utmost instability. The system of popular courts in which even civil trials were decided by hundreds of lay jurymen implied an "arbitrariness of justice" that "imperilled the safeguards of the formal law." As a result, "the mere continued existence of wealth is to be marvelled at, rather than the violent reversals of fortunes which occurred after every political mishap."[17] Moreover, the demands of the *polis* as a military association implied that it punished "any kind of behaviour which might endanger the military and political morals and discipline.... As a matter of principle, thus, there was no freedom of personal conduct."[18]

Weber followed a long tradition of criticism that held Graeco-Roman Antiquity responsible for cultivating the omnipotence of the state and preventing economic progress. This tradition goes back to the Scottish and French Enlightenment. It then was taken up in the French postrevolutionary debate (in reaction to the cult of Antiquity fostered by the Jacobins). In 1819 Benjamin Constant summarized and sharpened it in his famous essay on the distinction between the freedom of the ancients and that of the moderns. Finally, the tradition was developed in greater historical detail by late-nineteenth-century authors such as N. D. Fustel de Coulanges and Jacob Burckhardt.[19]

CONCLUSION

I have deliberately stressed certain lacunae of Weber's account and some of his more questionable judgments. But that should not obscure the importance of his approach. His analysis is unsurpassed with regard to the emergence of political structures, the institutionalization of magistracies acting on the basis of rules defined by the community, the establishment

---

[17] E&S 1361f = WuG 810.   [18] E&S 1360 = WuG 809.

[19] Benjamin Constant, *De la liberté des anciens comparée à celle des modernes* (Paris, 1819) [English translation in Biancamaria Fontana, ed., *Benjamin Constant: Political Writings* (Cambridge: Cambridge University Press, 1988), 307–28]; Numa Denis Fustel de Coulanges, *La cité antique* (Paris, 1864) [English translation: *The Ancient City*, Baltimore: Johns Hopkins University Press, 1980]; and Jacob Burckhardt, *Griechische Kulturgeschichte*, 4 vols., Berlin, 1898–1902). Compare on this tradition Nicole Loraux and Pierre Vidal-Naquet, "The Formation of Bourgeois Athens: An Essay on Historiography between 1750 and 1850," in Pierre Vidal-Naquet, *Politics, Ancient and Modern* (Cambridge: Polity Press, 1995), 82–140. For the increasing dissociation from the model of antiquity by the American "Founding Fathers" see Paul A. Rahe, *Republics: Ancient and Modern* (Chapel Hill: University of North Carolina Press, 1992). For further references see Wilfried Nippel, "Republik, Kleinstaat, Bürgergemeinde," in Peter Blickle, ed., *Theorien kommunaler Ordnung in Europa* (München: Oldenbourg, 1996), 225–47.

of formal rules for the administration of laws and for the passing of new laws. Indeed, his analysis opens up comparative approaches that illuminate both the similarities and the differences between the ancient and the medieval type of citizenry. The fundamental distinction between *homo politicus* and *homo oeconomicus* holds true despite all the objections that might be raised with respect to specific details. Finally, Weber's insistence on the cultural and religious foundations of citizenship cannot be overrated.[20] Again, one may object that his selective treatment of Oriental cultures (aiming, as it does, at the contrast with the Western world) reveals a certain Eurocentrism (or "Orientalism," the fashionable term). But the peculiarity of the Western tradition of personal liberty, political participation, and rule of law is not just a projection of cultural prejudice.[21] The notion of *Verbrüderung*, as an account of the process of individualization fostered by Christianity, brilliantly captures the fundamental differences between the West and the various civilizations of the Orient.[22] Anyone who wishes to come to terms with the historical dimensions of this tradition, however it may be constructed, must accept Weber's challenge.[23]

[20] Stephen Kalberg, "Cultural Foundations of Modern Citizenship," in Bryan S. Turner, ed., *Citizenship and Social Theory* (London: Sage, 1993), 91–114.

[21] R. W. Davis, ed., *The Origins of Modern Freedom in the West* (Stanford: Stanford University Press, 1995); Donald W. Treadgold, *Freedom: A History* (New York: New York University Press, 1990). The latter book is rather disappointing.

[22] See Benjamin Nelson, "On Orient and Occident in Max Weber," *Social Research* 43 (1976): 114–29.

[23] This can be seen in the works of John A. Hall, *Powers and Liberties: The Causes and Consequences of the Rise of the West* (Oxford: Blackwell, 1985) and Michael Mann, *The Sources of Social Power*, vol. 1: *A History of Power from the Beginning to A.D. 1760* (Cambridge: Cambridge University Press, 1986).

7

The European Self: Rethinking an Attitude

MICHAEL HERZFELD

Individualism has long been a stereotype of European identity. In such magisterial works as C. B. Macpherson's *The Rise of Possessive Individualism* and, in a contrastive mode, Louis Dumont's *Homo Hierarchicus*, the conventional self-view of Europeans as autonomous selves possessing discrete property and distinctive properties appears as a fundamental assumption, the bedrock on which virtually all explorations of European society and culture comfortably rest.[1] In the nineteenth century, notably in the writings of the conservative politician-pamphleteer François Guizot, that self was expanded to fill the image, not only of a nation (France), but of a far larger entity that was at once continent, idea, and culture—namely, Europe itself.[2]

That concept was powerfully exported through colonial and other extensions of the imperial European presence. An outstanding example is the celebration of "rugged individualism" in the United States, where today that notion of tough self-underscores a range of ideologies

The first version of this chapter was presented as the inaugural Distinguished Lecture in European Ethnology given at the University of Massachusetts, Amherst, Massachusetts, on November 7, 1996. I am especially grateful to Jacqueline Urla and Ralph Faulkingham for their hospitality and for the opportunity to explore one of the fundamental challenges that the current anthropological investment in the study of Europe poses both to the discipline (on which see also Talal Asad et al., "Provocations of European Ethnology," *American Anthropologist* 99 (1997): 713–30) and to the concept of Europe itself. I also greatly appreciate Nigel Rapport's critical reading of an early draft.

[1] Louis Dumont, *Homo Hierarchicus: An Essay on the Caste System* (Chicago: University of Chicago Press, 1970); C. B. Macpherson, *The Political Theory of Possessive Individualism: Hobbes to Locke* (Oxford: Clarendon Press, 1962).

[2] François Guizot, *Histoire de la civilisation en Europe: depuis la chute de l'empire romain jusqu'à la révolution française*, 6th ed. (Paris: Didier, 1859) and *L'histoire de France depuis les temps les plus reculés jusqu'en 1789*, vol. 1 (Paris: Hachette, 1872). For further discussion see Michael Herzfeld, *Anthropology through the Looking-Glass: Critical Ethnography in the Margins of Europe* (Cambridge: Cambridge University Press, 1987), 53–4, 81.

from official voluntaristic doctrines to the rantings of the far right. In Québec, as Richard Handler has shown, it underwrites the logic and appeal of Francophone nationalism.[3] In Australia its realization as a form of egalitarian "mateship" is perhaps blunter in its gendered and racial exclusivity,[4] but for that reason exemplifies and illustrates the same basic pattern. Thus exported, individualism has acquired a truly global signifi-cance: as the "common sense" of universalizing models of responsibility and rationality, it precludes alternative visions of the relationship between self and society. Like a virulently prolific lichen overwhelming the diversity of an entire ecosystem, it threatens to overwhelm the variety of conceptual and cultural logics existing in the world today.[5]

Anthropology can provide some useful ways of taking a critical step back from this stifling situation, by showing how such values become incorporated—that is, quite literally, embodied—in the practices of every-day life, reducing the space for alternative visions. It can also suggest ways in which persistent forms of localism and resistance to official dogma can subvert and refashion these dominant ideas to the point where the official ideology may emerge as a serious misrepresentation of large segments of the popular imagination.

This is a crucial point. If the nation-state is an "imagined community," grounded in an idealized notion of "national character" and the modal national self, it would be wise to ask whose imagination it is that we are discussing.[6] The vision of the nation-state promulgated by elites may not be profoundly shared by most citizens *even though they may speak of the nation using exactly the same language and imagery.*[7] I emphasize this last point because many theorists of nationalism have fallen prey to a semiotic delusion in which the appearance of a common code has been allowed to suggest the existence of a corresponding commonality of intent.[8]

---

[3] Richard Handler, *Nationalism and the Politics of Culture in Quebec* (Madison: University of Wisconsin Press, 1988).

[4] Bruce Kapferer, *Legends of People, Myths of State: Violence, Intolerance, and Political Culture in Sri Lanka and Australia* (Washington: Smithsonian Institution Press, 1988), 158–61; see also Judith Kapferer, *Being All Equal: Identity, Difference and Australian Cultural Practice* (Oxford: Berg, 1996), 231.

[5] James Ferguson, *The Anti-Politics Machine: "Development," Depoliticization, and Bureaucratic Power in Lesotho* (Cambridge: Cambridge University Press, 1990), xiii.

[6] See Benedict Anderson, *Imagined Communities: Reflections on the Origin and Spread of Nationalism* (London: Verso, 1983).

[7] See the discussion in Michael Herzfeld, *Cultural Intimacy: Social Poetics in the Nation-State* (New York: Routledge, 1997), 30–2.

[8] The problem of intentionality is especially acute for studies of nationalism. Psychological explanations do not get us very far. Thus, for example, one might read Anderson's

Even leaving aside the methodological and epistemological question of how one would ever establish empirically that uniformity of hearts and minds really existed, even at the level of collective representation there is considerable variation among groups of citizens in their interpretation of the significance, viability, and appropriate forms of nationhood. Indeed, as Anthony Cohen has suggested, the success of nationalist ideology largely depends on its ability to appeal to and encompass highly personal visions of national identity.[9]

The irony is that this is exactly what an individualistic worldview would logically entail. Perhaps all the world's nationalisms are individualistic in this sense? At the very least, we should not assume that this is an exclusively European characteristic or that it is characteristic of all Europeans. If we are to work with such psychological models as imagination, and especially if we start out with the idea that those who do the imagining are individualists, we logically must entertain the possibility of multiple—and often mutually contradictory—images and interpretations. Moreover, the point applies to a whole range of psychologistic explanations of the persistence of strong nationalistic ideologies, from Alan Dundes's attribution of national inferiority complexes to Liah Greenfield's notably less condescending but equally reductionist delineation of *ressentiment* as the crucial motivating force of nationalism.[10] If these models are allowed to stand in their undifferentiated forms, they mechanistically reproduce as universal the rhetoric of resentment that many nationalisms employ. In other words, they represent the nation as a collectivity in psychological terms: all its constituent hearts beat as one. This not only entails a loss of critical purchase; it is also implausible and obviously inaccurate.

---

argument (see note 6 above), or Liah Greenfield's invocation of *ressentiment* to explain the emergence of nationalist solidarity (*Nationalism: Five Roads to Modernity*, Cambridge, Mass.: Harvard University Press, 15–17), as more or less adequate accounts of elite projections of sentiment, but they do not explain the willingness of ordinary people to accept, or at least acquiesce in, the logic of self-sacrifice that nationalism demands at moments of extreme crisis.

9 Anthony P. Cohen, "Personal Nationalism: A Scottish View of Some Rites, Rights, and Wrongs," *American Ethnologist* 23 (1996): 802–15.

10 Greenfield, *Nationalism*. Greenfield's model might perhaps be recast in less reductionistic terms, but Dundes's neo-Freudian approach leaves little space for such reformulation; see his "Nationalistic Inferiority Complexes and the Fabrication of Fakelore: A Reconsideration of Ossian, the *Kinder- und Hausmärchen*, the *Kalevala*, and Paul Bunyan," *Journal of Folklore Research* 22 (1985): 5–18. Here the reductively psychologistic explanation of "fakelore"—a term that ignores the internal logic of participation in a "national" culture—obscures the complex dynamics of cultural hierarchy, including, ironically, its psychological aspects.

THE MENTALITY TRAP

Key to this discussion, then, is the identification of a persistent confusion in the concept of mentality between the object of our analysis—the rhetoric of national and pan-European identity—and the instrument through which we carry it out. All the models of national homogeneity are grounded in some notion of "mentality." This, again, is a concept of dubious analytic power. Especially significant for this critique is the fact that "mentality" has long been a key term of nationalistic discourse, from which it has filtered into popular usage throughout Europe.[11] Its use in scholarly discussion thus replicates the confusion between analytic instrument and object of analysis.

Individualism and mentality are both products of a particular kind of essentializing discourse. Individualism sometimes appears as programs of political philosophy—most notoriously in Margaret Thatcher's declaration that there was no such thing as society, only individuals. In Europe individualism has a long history. In the nineteenth century it was already used to separate specific kinds of regional "mentality" into more and less "European" versions. Indeed, Dora d'Istria's declaration, so pleasant to the ears of the Western-supported Greek elite, that the Greeks had escaped the "somehow communistic influence of the Slavs" finely illustrates the role of individualism in the global hierarchy of value that came into existence in the great colonial empires.[12]

The political denial of the social—Thatcher's remark illustrates this well—masks the fundamentally social nature of dogmatic forms of individualism, whether methodological or political. In fact, those who write about the social, especially in an era that emphasizes practice, are more concerned with the role of individuals in reinterpreting and refashioning the polity than are their opponents. Anthony Cohen, an early and distinguished practitioner of ethnography in European societies (in Scotland), has argued that most accounts of nationalism do not explain why people follow its prescriptions to such an impressive degree. [13] And his plea for an awareness of the self is specifically couched in terms of a critique of Thatcherism.[14]

---

[11] In Greece, for example, the concept of *noötropía* (mentality) is widely adopted as an explanation of alleged national traits and actions.

[12] Dora d'Istria, "La nationalité hellénique d'après les chants populaires," *Revue des Deux Mondes* 70 (1867): 590. See also my discussion in *Ours Once More: Folklore, Ideology, and the Making of Modern Greece* (Austin: University of Texas Press, 1982), 56–61.

[13] Cohen, "Personal Nationalism," 806–7.

[14] Anthony P. Cohen, *Self Consciousness: An Alternative Anthropology of Identity* (London: Routledge, 1994), 171–6.

In different but mutually complementary ways, Cohen and I both want to disengage the dominant tradition in social history and anthropology from the essentialism to which even its most resolutely constructivist approaches often fall prey. The problem, ironically, is most strikingly seen in the Marxist arguments of Hobsbawn and Ranger's in their edited volume *The Invention of Tradition*.[15] These authors have effectively ignored the ways in which ordinary people *recast* what their leaders tell them about their national identity. Yet perhaps this is not surprising: taking the orthodox view that ideology is a mystification always imposed from above, Hobsbawm in particular has treated people (from social bandits to the members of emergent nation-states) as dupes of imposed systems of thought, rather than as individuals capable of reworking such ideologies to their own individual *and* collective ends. That capability can be investigated only through a painstaking ethnographic as well as historical study of those involved in the process; a rare example is the late Jerome R. Mintz's subtle and revealing retrospective study of a group of peasant Anarchists who achieved a heroic notoriety in pre–Civil War Spain.[16]

It is this capacity to recast the wisdom received from "above" that Cohen, in the context of Scottish politics, calls "personal nationalism." This model extends the argument he offers in *Self Consciousness*: the sociocentrism of the Durkheimian mainstream in anthropology has subverted our awareness of the different ways in which people experience collective belonging. In his essay on personal nationalism Cohen wisely reduces the emphasis on experience in order to focus on something more accessible empirically: the pragmatic ways in which, no doubt as a result of experience in all its inevitable diversity, people recast the official images of nationalistic ideology. Their *uses* of that ideology allow them to carve out personal maneuvering space within the collective, whether a Thatcherite Tory world or an orthodox Marxist vision of the world.

It might be argued that Cohen is simply reproducing the European ideology of individualism and that he is countering Durkheimian sociocentrism

---

[15] Eric Hobsbawm and Terence Ranger, eds., *The Invention of Tradition* (Cambridge: Cambridge University Press, 1983).

[16] Jerome R. Mintz, *The Anarchists of Casas Viejas* (Chicago: University of Chicago Press, 1982). Mintz (pp. 271–6) takes issue with an earlier argument of Eric Hobsbawm's concerning the causes of the Casas Viejas uprising. His objection is essentially the same as my disagreement with the later work: Marxist-evolutionary models fail to recognize the agency and perspectives of local actors in social groups they place at an "early" point on the evolutionary scale.

with its old nemesis, methodological individualism. But that would exemplify the sort of mischief that Cohen is attacking. Methodological individualism, in political terms, is precisely the abandonment of the social that characterizes the philosophy and practice of Thatcherism. Cohen's aim is quite the reverse: to recognize the capacity of ordinary social actors to recast and reconfigure received orthodoxies. The Thatcherite agenda, as Cohen notes, was quite different. It was to destroy the very possibility of agency by emasculating the social in favor of a centralized and centralizing ideology of personal autonomy.

At the other edge of Europe, and especially during periods of relatively conservative rule, we find the same tactic in use. Greek politicians claim that provincial artisans are craftspeople who treasure their originality and so will not submit to the "oriental" love of soulless homogeneity, but that they are indeed so "oriental" in their willful refusal to standardize the products of their labor that they must be led by—predictably—these same politicians. Another and very germane version of this argument is that Greeks are wonderfully independent people who represent the true Greek (and therefore "European") love of freedom, but that these same virtues, recast as selfish atomism and familism, are the ineradicable marks of the Turkish stain on their collective character, which debars them from the right to collectivize or unionize.[17]

Cohen's argument allows us to work away from generalizations about individualism and toward a clearer sense of what cultural features such stereotypes invoke and why they might prove appealing to particular segments of a population. Who has an interest in promoting the idea that there is a distinctively European self and under what conditions? Which elements in this stereotype appear to be constant, and which are contested? How do these localized usages articulate with nationalistic and regional identity politics and ideologies, and how do individual actors deploy the rhetorics of these ideologies for more immediate practical ends? I will not try to answer all these questions here. Instead, I will sketch by example the kind of empirical research that is needed to answer them.

---

[17] See my article "It Takes One to Know One: Collective Resentment and Mutual Recognition among Greeks in Local and Global Contexts," in Richard Fardon, ed., *Counterworks: Managing the Diversity of Knowledge* (London: Routledge, 1995), 124–42; and "The Aesthetics of Individualism: Artisanship, Business, and the State in Greece" (paper presented at the annual meeting of the American Anthropological Association, Washington, D.C., 1997). The research for these papers was funded by the National Science Foundation (award # 9307421).

A VIEW FROM THE MARGINS

The "idea of Europe" has percolated through the complex populations of the European continent and is "refracted" through the prism of daily interactions.[18] The task of understanding the ways in which this has occurred can perhaps be best performed, as through a magnifying lens, in the geographical and political margins of Europe. Even in the most formal sense, European colonialism was by no means confined to non-European peoples. The British domination of Malta and Cyprus (and briefly of the Ionian Islands in Greece) attests otherwise. That pattern is reproduced—and was technically perfected—in the English domination of Scotland and Ireland; one might also wish to consider the internal dynamics of regional power in *Franquista* Spain.[19] The consequences linger on: in Cyprus, for example, as Vassos Argyrou has demonstrated, littering is a trivial but deeply pervasive activity that expresses deep discontent—discontent, that is, with the postcolonial perpetuation of elite control in ways that will be immediately familiar to Africanists and others. [20] The Soviet domination of much of Eastern and Central Europe offers another instructive example.[21] Greece exemplifies a place and a people forced to internalize the categorical obsession with separating the West from the Rest. The case of Greece illustrates the pain visited on the weak by the strong—pain passed down internally to minorities whose very existence is denied.[22]

Europeanist anthropologists today do not confine their attentions to the obviously exotic or picturesque corners of the continent. Rather they have turned the tables of exoticism on the familiar. John Borneman, for instance, has treated the family law provisions obtaining in pre-1989 East and West Berlin as the intricate kinship dynamic of two paired

---

[18] Federico Chabod, *Storia dell'idea dell'Europa* (Bari: Laterza, edition by Ernesto Sestan and Armando Saitta, 1964). See also E. E. Evans-Pritchard, *Nuer Religion* (Oxford: Clarendon Press, 1956), 117–18, 196.

[19] Jane Nadel-Klein, "Reweaving the Fringe: Localism, Tradition, and Representation in British Ethnography," *American Ethnologist* 18 (1991): 500–17. See also Isidoro Moreno Navarro, "La antropología en Andalucia: desarollo historico y estado actual de las investigaciones," *Ethnica* 1 (1971): 109–44.

[20] Vassos Argyrou, "'Keep Cyprus Clean': Littering, Pollution, and Otherness," *Cultural Anthropology* 12 (1996): 159–78.

[21] It is nevertheless important to avoid becoming entrapped in the hermetic logic of "evil empire" scenarios, which are often no less essentialist than the ideologies at which they are directed. For a sophisticated retrospective view of the Soviet sphere, see especially Katherine Verdery, "Theorizing Socialism: A Prologue to the 'Transition'," *American Ethnologist* 18 (1991): 219–439; idem, *What Was Socialism and What Comes Next?* (Princeton: Princeton University Press, 1995).

[22] Herzfeld, *Cultural Intimacy*, 77–8.

moieties.[23] Stacia Zabusky has examined the fashioning of cultural idioms of communication in the European Space Agency in the Netherlands.[24] I have applied Mary Douglas's analysis of the symbolism of pollution and taboo to bureaucratic practices throughout Europe, an argument that has been extended to the global reach of the United Nations' refugee agency, and Robert Hayden has applied this argument in detail to the horrors of "ethnic cleansing" in the former Yugoslavia.[25] Jacqueline Urla's work on "Western" phenomena—from statistics to Barbie dolls—similarly raises the question of why we fail to see ourselves as no less symbolically grounded than the people we study in supposedly exotic places.[26] Miner, in an instructive joke in the 1956 *American Anthropologist*, tackles the bizarre body purifications before the bathroom mirror of the Nacirema, who are none other than Americans spelled backwards. Among the new defamiliarizations of the West, playing with familiar images in this fashion offers an effective way of bearding exoticism in its lair as well as a useful analytic strategy. [27] The ability this strategy gives us to examine our everyday assumptions is invaluable: the anthropological analysis of European (and European-derived) societies and cultures both enriches the comparative purview of anthropology and offers a valuable corrective to the self-confirming tendencies of disciplines that for too long have been hostage to the hitherto unchallenged sway of Eurocentric perceptions.[28] As Deborah

[23] John Borneman, *Belonging in the Two Berlins: Kin, State, Nation* (Cambridge: Cambridge University Press, 1992), 3–4.

[24] Stacia E. Zabusky, *Launching Europe: An Ethnography of European Cooperation in Space Science* (Princeton: Princeton University Press, 1995).

[25] The model is provided by Mary Douglas, *Purity and Danger: An Analysis of Concepts of Pollution and Taboo* (London: Routledge and Kegan Paul, 1966). See also Michael N. Barnett, "The U.N. Security Council, Indifference, and Genocide in Rwanda," *Cultural Anthropology* 12 (1997): 551–78; Robert Hayden, "Imagined Communities and Real Victims: Self-Determination and Ethnic Cleansing in Yugoslavia," *American Ethnologist* 23 (1996): 783–801; Michael Herzfeld, *The Social Production of Indifference: Exploring the Symbolic Roots of Western Bureaucracy* (Oxford: Berg, 1992). For a comparable use of Douglas's model in an African and international setting, see Liisa Malkki, *Purity and Exile: Violence, Memory, and National Cosmology among Hutu Refugees in Tanzania* (Chicago: University of Chicago Press, 1995).

[26] Jacqueline Urla, "Cultural Politics in an Age of Statistics: Numbers, Nations, and the Making of Basque Identity," *American Ethnologist* 20 (1993): 818–42; Jacqueline Urla and Alan Swedlund, "The Anthropometry of Barbie: Unsettling Ideals of the Feminine Body in Popular Culture," in Jennifer Terry and Jacqueline Urla, eds., *Deviant Bodies: Critical Perspectives on Difference in Science and Popular Culture* (Bloomington: Indiana University Press, 1995), 278–313.

[27] Horace Miner, "Body Ritual among the Nacirema," *American Anthropologist* 58 (1956): 503–7.

[28] Some social science discourse curiously essentializes "the West" in ways that reproduce the "fundamentalisms" against which they are directed. See especially Samuel P. Huntington, *The Clash of Civilizations and the Remaking of Word Order* (New York:

Reed-Danahay has noted for Pierre Bourdieu, and as we might equally observe with respect to Louis Dumont, the conflation of all Europeans as essentially individualistic is empirically unpersuasive. It also, perversely, allows Westerners to be differentiated among themselves in distinction to all "others"—a key component of nineteenth-century arguments for their own superiority.[29]

The advantage of working in Greece, or in other less "mainstream" European sites, is that this defamiliarizing tension between "being European" and "being other than European" is already in place—indeed, is a staple of everyday conversation and media attention.[30] One constant challenge to easy assumptions lies in the apparent lack of fit between Greece *quâ* the Europeans' spiritual cradle and Greece *quâ* the orientalized "bad child" of the European Union.[31]

It is important to understand what such examples can tell us. First, and foremost, they are not about typicality, a statistical concept that implies the possibility of essentialist definitions. Typicality is fine fodder for tourist advertising—typical Italian style, Greek hospitality, and the like—but it makes for poor analysis when the object is to probe *beyond* stereotypes, or to ask who *uses* the stereotypes, for what purposes, and under what circumstances. Greek notions of selfhood are no more "typical" of Europe than the swashbuckling Cretan sheep thieves with whom I have worked are typical of Greece. Recourse to extreme (or, indeed, marginal) cases allows us to argue *a fortiori* that the more diffuse instances of related values and forms of action provide some commonality throughout the larger area. Moreover, the salience of these extreme or marginal examples may be locally recognized, as when Greek nationalists uphold the swashbuckling freebootery of the *kleftes* (thieves)—the historic heroes of the national struggle for independence—as redolent of the "national" passion for freedom; or when the same Greek nationalists claim to be the last true individualists.

Simon and Schuster, 1995). For a discussion of "occidentalism" as a global phenomenon, see James G. Carrier, ed., *Occidentalism: Images of the West* (Oxford: Clarendon Press, 1995). For a thoughtful disquisition on some of the implications of existing essentialisms, see Fernando Coronil, "Beyond Occidentalism: Toward Nonimperial Geohistorical Categories," *Cultural Anthropology* 11 (1996): 51–87.

[29] Deborah Reed-Danahay, "The Kabyle and the French: Occidentalism in Bourdieu's Theory of Practice," in Carrier, ed., *Occidentalism*, 61–84.

[30] Michael Herzfeld, "Productive Discomfort: Anthropological Fieldwork and the Dislocation of Etiquette," in Marjorie Garber, Rebecca L. Walkowitz, and Paul B. Franklin, eds., *Field Work: Sites in Literary and Cultural Studies* (New York: Routledge, 1996), 41–51.

[31] This is fundamentally the argument I developed in *Anthropology through the Looking-Glass*.

It is no coincidence, and indeed represents a classic illustration of the self-confirming properties of hegemony, that such glorifications of rebellion act to confirm outsiders' judgment of the Greeks as unreliable. In the same way the most ardent advocates of the "individualism" of the market economy are the quickest to condemn the Greeks for their uncooperative stance toward European Union regulation, and the most fervid nationalists are the quickest to claim, at one and the same time, that minority or marginal populations are the purest representatives of the majoritarian nation—even as they accuse these groups of forming a treacherous fifth column or of betraying the ideals of national pride. The authorities are heirs to a dilemma born of their own emergence from a liberation struggle. The mantle of past insubordination sits uneasily on the shoulders of those who must now wield power. It is in this context that the yoking of a "European mentality" with models of individualism and the love of freedom becomes both an urgent task and a highly problematic one for the more authoritarian of European leaderships.

For all these reasons, we must view claims about the existence of a peculiarly European selfhood with deep skepticism. Occidentalism may be a reaction to orientalism, but it often serves the same ends; it is the other side of the same coin.[32] Analytically, we must shift the focus away from a putative European character or mentality and toward the uses to which such claims are made and contested by local actors.[33] This is a tactic that satisfies both the logical argument against confusing the object with the instrument of study and the anthropological insistence on examining elites and subalterns within a common framework of comparison.

CONTESTING THE CLAIMS OF RATIONALISM

Closely associated with the view that Europeans were individualists is an intellectualist rendition of the same argument—namely, that, unlike "natives," Europeans think for themselves and thus have exclusive claims on rationality.[34] One rendition of this view is that European thought is literal, whereas that of all other human beings is "merely" metaphorical. Despite the widespread recognition of the metaphorical basis of scientific and other forms of reasoning, initiated by Giambattista Vico in the mid-eighteenth century and elaborated by thinkers from Max Black

---

[32] See James G. Carrier, "Introduction," in *Occidentalism*, esp. 1–6.

[33] This position is consistent with both "practice theory" in contemporary anthropology and sociology and concepts of "use" (or "action") in the study of language.

[34] There is an implicit homology in this kind of thinking: that "they are to us as passivity is to activity." Such binary discourses have long underwritten colonial and neocolonialist enterprises; for a discussion, see my *Anthropology through the Looking-Glass*, 82–9.

in the 1960s to the more recent analyses of George Lakoff and Mark Johnson, the equation of literalness with European industrial rationality persists.[35]

Yet it has also been attacked at its very roots, in a remarkable reexamination of the ancient roots through which European rationalism usually seeks legitimation. The Classicist G. E. R. Lloyd critically addresses the concept of *mentalité* in European thought. He suggests that the distinction between a rational European "us" and a "prelogical," alien "them" (which reached its apogee in the writings of Lucien Lévy-Bruhl) has its origins in the litigious practices of the ancient Athenian marketplace. There, in a fashion not unfamiliar in an election year in modern industrial democracies, contestants called their own arguments literal and dismissed those of their opponents as mere metaphor.[36]

The genius of Lloyd's insight is that it shows historically how ideas can take on the force of logical abstraction even though—or perhaps because—they are grounded in the social environments that their exponents seek to govern. We live in a world in which our own forebears have shaped relations of power that invest the contingent with the force of eternal verity. Those who resist are often silenced. I find it revealing that in Bertrand Russell's magisterial *History of Western Philosophy*, a work whose hero is surely René Descartes, Descartes's gadfly Giambattista Vico does not even rate an entry in the index.[37]

The Cartesian agenda was adopted as the touchstone of differentiation between colonizing Europeans and colonized "natives." Moreover, as a motivating and shaping force in the construction of the colonial *habitus*, it reinforced the self-fulfilling properties of this stereotypical division. Paul Rabinow has shown how the march of colonial building in French Morocco adopted Cartesian principles of town planning in contrast to the "native" mode of architecture. He has also pointed out the engagement of social theorists of the *Année sociologique* school in this program—a salutary warning of the ever-lurking risk of cooptation.[38] Note that these theorists were founders of the sociocentric tradition that Cohen attacks in his formulation of "personal nationalism."

---

[35] Max Black, *Models and Metaphors: Studies in Language and Philosophy* (Ithaca: Cornell University Press, 1962); George Lakoff and Mark Johnson, *Metaphors We Live By* (Chicago: University of Chicago Press, 1980).

[36] Lucien Lévy-Bruhl, *Les fonctions mentales dans les sociétés inférieures* (Paris: F. Alcan, 1910); G. E. R. Lloyd, *Demystifying Mentalities* (Cambridge: Cambridge University Press, 1990).

[37] Bertrand Russell, *History of Western Philosophy* (New York: Simon and Schuster, 1945).

[38] Paul Rabinow, *French Modern: Norms and Forms of the Social Environment* (Cambridge, Mass.: MIT Press, 1989).

THE EVERYDAY USE OF "NATIONAL CHARACTER"

"National character" permits nationalisms to ignore or suppress any evidence of internal differentiation. It is perhaps not so much a "myth," as Julio Caro Baroja has called it, as a device that serves the homogenizing imperatives of nation-state policy.[39] Indeed, when one hears Greeks declaiming that all Greeks are freedom-lovers, that all Greeks are masters of their own destiny, and that all Greeks are hospitable, one might well think the official discourse had utterly permeated their hearts and minds.

As discourse—the external code—it has certainly been successful. Listening to such declarations, however, one often hears other—equally sweeping—kinds of generic assertions that do not sit comfortably with the official rhetoric: that all Greeks are unreliable, tempestuous, quick to anger, underhanded and deceitful, full of low cunning (poniri), and unwilling to submit to law and order. Indeed, such stereotypes have sometimes been coopted by the authorities. For example, the military régime of 1967–74 declared that the rebellious character of the Greeks deserved a strong disciplinary hand, a sentiment echoed by its supporters in their everyday speech. This was perhaps the closest that any Greek government came to an open admission of traits thought best kept confined within the national "domestic space." The regime even prohibited the smashing of plates at the feet of dancers because, it was said, this was both dangerous and a disgraceful vision of the Greek self before the scandalized eyes of foreigners.

Unflattering self-stereotypes do not tell us very much about what Greeks are really like, any more than do positive characterizations voiced by the authorities (or by ordinary civilians to foreigners they do not know intimately). But they do tell us something very important: the basis of sociability among Greeks may be contrary to official ideas, yet essential to national cohesion. "What is said in the house should not be said in the public place," goes the old saw, but what is said in the house provides the day-to-day sense of commonality necessary to national viability and, at the same time, a resource for conceptualizing opposition to those who happen to be in power. This relativity of access, at many different levels (nation, region, village, kin group), demarcates insiders from outsiders; and it is here that questions of essentialized, collective "character" become important as resources in the defense of those same boundaries.[40]

---

[39] Julio Caro Baroja, El mito del caractér nacional: meditaciones a contrapelo (Madrid: Seminarios y Ediciones, 1970).
[40] Herzfeld, Cultural Intimacy, 28.

The idea of "national character," like that of *mentalité*, is part of the prevailing vocabulary of everyday nationalism in most European countries (and for that reason is directly comparable to phenomena reported from many non-European sources). The idea had a long history in American anthropology as well (witness the work of Ruth Benedict on Japan, to take only the most famous example). The habit of pontificating about whole populations as though they moved and thought as one— *The Nuer*, for example—is not confined to the study of so-called exotic peoples.[41] It is just as prevalent in the study of *The Italians, The Greeks*, and so forth: these are the actual titles of widely read books. It is also part of the language of official nationalism.[42]

Cohen's exploration of *personal* nationalism provides a welcome and provocative opportunity to free ourselves from an analytic strategy that properly belongs to the official discourses we study. As he notes, a structural approach "renders ... individuals as *merely* members of ... collectivities, and in so doing, posits a qualitative difference between *them* and *us*: they are satisfactorily generalizable; we are preciously individualistic." There is a remarkable irony in the fact that it is a Europeanist who arrives at this conclusion on the basis, in part, of accounts of *European* nationalism, a point that I think reinforces Cohen's argument. He continues: "We have been complicit in the colonization, massification, or anonymization of the human subject." Recognizing the role of the individual cross-culturally is "a step toward liberating ourselves from such a superior and narrow field of vision."[43] There are risks in such an approach, to be sure, not the least of which is that of backsliding into a solipsistic *methodological* individualism or some degree of psychological reductionism. But Cohen is right to suggest that at the very least we can learn something from a nationalism, articulate about its intended relationship with individual needs and desires, that in turn is expressed in a variety of ways by a variety of informants.

---

[41] E. E. Evans-Pritchard, *The Nuer: A Description of the Modes of Livelihood and Political Institutions of a Nilotic People* (Oxford: Clarendon Press, 1940). For quite varied critiques of this usage, see especially James Clifford, "On Ethnographic Authority," *Representations* 2 (Spring 1983): 118–46; Johannes Fabian, *Time and the Other: How Anthropology Makes its Object* (New York: Columbia University Press, 1983); Richard Handler, "On Dialogue and Destructive Analysis: Problems in Narrating Nationalism and Ethnicity," *Journal of Anthropological Research* 41 (1985): 171–82.

[42] See, for example, Luigi Barzini, *The Italians*, 1st American ed. (New York: Atheneum, 1964) and H.D.F. Kitto, *The Greeks* (London: Penguin Books, 1951). Kitto's book is exclusively about ancient Greeks. See also A. R. Burn, *The Modern Greeks* (London: J. T. Nelson, 1944). Note the significantly different title of Burn's book, written by a classical historian: unless otherwise advised, readers should always assume that Greeks are ancient!

[43] Cohen, "Personal Nationalism," 2.

The apparent contradiction between individualism and the nation-state teleology that demands conformism in matters of identity can be resolved in at least three ways. First, state representations of individualism are undeniably social prescriptions.[44] Second, the anthropological convention that opposed state structures to segmentary polities is misleading, in that nation-states are administratively and conceptually arranged in hierarchically ranked tiers of mutually opposed subunits; the convention itself is an example of segmentary logic (pitting "them" against "us") at the broadest level of differentiation. Third, the reification of culture as a national possession renders it immediately analogous to land, which is always divisible as private property even though "territorial integrity" justifies its defense in times of war. The literature of many European (and other) countries is replete with stirring tales of homes and fields, privately owned, providing the very basis of the emotional appeal that inspired citizens to acts of patriotic heroism.[45]

The representation of culture as a kind of property requires further elaboration. Here, following the lead of Richard Handler's perceptive treatment of Québecois nationalism, we can usefully turn to Macpherson's notion of "possessive individualism."[46] Handler's argument is in effect that the concept of a person individuated by the possession of property provided a model for the collective self of the nation. That self owns—or "has"—land. Above all, however, it "has culture." The progressive reification of culture, in a move that places nationalism and anthropology on parallel trajectories, thus makes the heritage—in Québec, the *patrimoine*—an object of proprietary defense. It is surely no coincidence that, in the aftermath of the collapse of Soviet hegemony, numerous nationalisms—all eager to enjoy the new pleasures of untrammeled self-expression—seized on various mutant forms of cultural anthropology as their primary source of scholarly legitimation, much as their predecessors had turned to folklore.

But this new possession often turns out to be a surprisingly unmanageable thing. Owning a national culture meant that one could find in it all the virtues that had created the new nation-state: heroism, a love of

---

[44] As is, for example, official teleology. See Shaun Kingsley Malarney, "The Limits of 'State Functionalism' and the Reconstruction of Funerary Ritual in Contemporary Northern Vietnam," *American Ethnologist* 23 (1996): 540–60.

[45] See Michael Herzfeld, *Portrait of a Greek Imagination: An Ethnographic Biography of Andreas Nenedakis* (Chicago: University of Chicago Press, 1997), 84.

[46] Handler, *Nationalism and the Politics of Culture*; Macpherson, *Political Theory of Possessive Individualism*.

independence, a stubborn resistance to authority. All these are richly celebrated in poetry, opera, and visual art. They are also part of the historical indoctrination of every schoolchild. But there a paradox arises, one that reproduces in mythopoeic terms the paradox underlying the genesis of the nation-state. As Edmund Leach pointed out, the human race arose from the incestuous union of Adam and Eve, but thenceforward it was committed to strict rules against incurring such pollution ever again.[47] Similarly, nation-states are created out of a miscegenation the repetition of which must be debarred by the logic of national purity. The list is extensive: France, offspring of Germanic Franks and Celtic Gauls; England, crossroads of Saxons and Normans (to name but a few); Greece, where the constant infusion of Saracen ancestry became the subject of a "national epic" created out of a set of songs and medieval manuscripts virtually at the behest of nationalistic scholars, and where the most hotly denied cultural affinities seem to furnish the most intimate images of "typical" Greek culture.[48] Italy, more subject to localist sentiment than many countries, openly paraded the paradox in d'Azeglio's often-quoted dictum: "Now that Italy has been made, we need to make the Italians."

These parentages, moreover, seem to be reproduced as politics in a tense marriage of order and disorder in which the side of disorder always remains a potent presence. The Greek revolution was carried forward by *kleftes*, whose contempt for authority provides a model for a continuing disrespect for the national government, successor to the Turks in the popular imagination; many of the *kleftes* were speakers of Koutsovlach, Turkish, and other languages that today mark minority identities that the bearers of official policy refuse to acknowledge.[49] Robin Hood's standing remains so great in England that a decision by a group of Thatcherite Nottingham promoters to have him unfrocked as the town's official symbol drew howls of outrage from local residents and the national media.[50] Americans' image of themselves as rebels who humiliated the tax-levying English at the Boston Tea Party is reenacted in every confrontation with the Internal Revenue Service—an everyday "social drama" that

---

[47] E. R. Leach, "Lévi-Strauss in the Garden of Eden: An Examination of Some Recent Developments in the Analysis of Myth," in E. N. Hayes and T. Hayes, eds., *Claude Levi-Strauss: The Anthropologist as Hero* (Cambridge, Mass.: MIT Press, 1970), 47–60.

[48] See Greenfield, *Nationalism*, 91–4; Herzfeld, *Ours Once More*, 120.

[49] Herzfeld, *Ours Once More*, 58–74.

[50] See especially Andre Pierce, "Sheriff of Nottingham Banishes Robin at Last," *The Times* (London), March 26, 1996, Home News; Martin Wainwright, "Nottingham Sheriff Springs to Robin's Aid," *Manchester Guardian Weekly*, March 31, 1996, UK News, 11.

perversely provides some of the experiential, as opposed to discursive, basis for the sense of national identity among a people of explicitly heterogeneous origins (*e pluribus unum*).[51]

The case of Robin Hood is quite revealing in this respect. The Nottingham Partnership, a civic and corporate association, decided in March 1996 that Robin Hood was the wrong symbol for a city devoted to attracting investment and trade on a large scale. The counterattack was led, ironically, by the current Sheriff of Nottingham, heir to the mantle of opposition to Robin in medieval times but at this point a respected Labour Party councillor. The struggle reveals how tenacious the ideology of antiauthoritarianism could be on both sides: the Thatcherites invoked individualistic prowess, while their opponents held high the banner of local autonomy and "social conscience"—a clear invocation of individualistic ideals to refute the Tories' rejection of the very idea of the social.

In this debate we see that the common ground of the two mutually opposed political camps is indeed some notion of individualism. The debate parallels an old battle within the social sciences, that between a Durkheimian sociocentrism and a much more atomistic idiom usually described as "methodological individualism." This has important implications as we follow Cohen's argument about nationalism. Cohen wants us to consider what nationalism means for those who must carry its standard—what it means for them as people, rather than as ciphers to an impersonal cultural account. This is not so much a retreat to psychology as a recognition that nationalism can work only by persuading its adherents to map their sense of an individuated self onto the collective—to accept (whether they "believe" it or not) that their very individuation is what renders their collective identity special.[52]

Such paradoxes abound because nation-states that grew out of acts of rebellion must find ways of legitimizing their newfound authority. This is not a peculiarly European phenomenon; indeed, it has been largely forgotten in the West, a fact that marks the successful completion of the process. Some Western media representations of new Third World nations as inherently unstable occlude the familiarity to Europeans of precisely this pattern: rebellion is not easily routinized as everyday bureaucratic

---

[51] On social dramas, see Victor Turner, *Dramas, Fields, and Metaphors: Symbolic Action in Human Society* (Ithaca: Cornell University Press, 1974); on their reproduction in everyday life, see Herzfeld, *Cultural Intimacy*, 143.

[52] For anthropologists, belief is not an appropriate category of analysis here. The issue is one of adherence to social convention (a social fact) rather than what people actually think (a psychological one).

procedure. Yet this is what must happen if a nationalist revolution is to consolidate its success.

Moreover, the idea that the members of European nations are collectively more individualistic than other peoples is contradicted at base. The Greeks, asked to perform the role of aboriginal Europeans, were nonetheless forced to do so in a passive way in obedience to the dictates of Great Power politics and philology. Everything that seemed most familiar in their everyday lives was represented by the national elite as "foreign" to the duly essentialized Hellenic character, and as such debarred to ordinary Greeks through authoritarian schooling and an aggressive cultural program sustained by successive central governments.[53] This vision of Greek society has proved durable and pervasive, even among those who have been generally critical of the Western-imposed model of Hellenism. Thus, for example, Martin Bernal—whose *Black Athena* infuriated many in the Greek elite precisely because it suggested that "their" culture had not been autochthonously generated in ancient times—neglects to describe the impact of this same ideology on the Greeks of today, an impact that is perfectly reproduced by the hostile reception of his book! By neglecting to tackle the modern Greeks' predicament head-on, Bernal inadvertently reinforces their persistent marginality to the project of investing "Europe" with a classical pedigree.[54] It leaves them the passive victims of a history made for them by more powerful forces.

Yet their response to those attempts was to try to take control of their own history. They read the "resurrection of Hellas" that began in 1821 as a clarion call to irredentism in blatant defiance of the Great Powers: hence the "Great Idea" that led them to attempt the disastrous adventure in Asia Minor in 1920–2. Their self-assertion arose, not, I suggest, because of some European quintessence that predetermined their actions, but because their leaders were bluff and practical souls who thought they saw the main chance—and (at least in the person of the folklorist Nikolaos Politis) understood what a drag on their ambitions the persistent and orientalist charge of fatalism would be: his and his colleagues patriotic reworkings of vernacular texts were hardly devoid of agency and represented an attempt to take charge of a history stolen from the Greeks, so

---

[53] Thus the "Hellenic" model, a largely foreign-derived idealization of ancient culture, came to predominate in official discourse (and to some extent in everyday perceptions) over the "Romeic." Comprised of familiar cultural items, the "Romeic" model was regarded as "foreign" because it was both "Roman" (an allusion to the status of Byzantium as the capital of the eastern Roman empire) and, more seriously, "Turkish." See Herzfeld, *Ours Once More*, and *Anthropology through the Looking-Glass*.

[54] Martin Bernal, *Black Athena: The Afroasiatic Roots of Classical Civilization*, vol. 1 (New Brunswick: Rutgers University Press, 1987).

they had deduced from the master narrative of Western philosophy, by the Western powers themselves.[55] While the Greek leaders saw this development as a claim on European identity, it provides the historical backdrop against which they learned to suppress *internal* self-assertion by local and minority populations by insisting on the illegality of rebellion but also of minoritarian politics.[56] In other words, the "European" individualism and love of freedom entailed in the genesis of the nation-state became "oriental" or "Turkish" whenever it appeared as subsequent rebellion, cultural or political, from within. To the extent that the Greek leadership could assume a "European" mantle, it could also deny the European claims of those who dared disobey its dictates at home.

But there is another side to this proactive stance. Because it entails standing up to those who would dub the Greeks as fatalists, thereby disproving the charge, it entails actions—from the recasting of folklore to uncooperative acts in international councils—that serve to confirm the *negative* aspects of this Greek individualism for those who wish to force the country into compliance. At the height of the Macedonian crisis, an article in the Athens daily *Eleftherotipía* demanded an end to such self-confirming hegemony: "Since, dear 'friends' and 'allies,' the greatest newspapers of England, the U.S.A., but also of France and Germany have used *ad nauseam* negative adjectives to dub our tactic on the Skopje issue as 'unjustified' (!), very often calling our policy by the Greek-derived words *paranoic, hysteric, myopic*, we reply to you that when you discover and incorporate into the vocabulary of your languages words that render the sense of the Greek words *paranoic, hysteric*, and *myopic*, then you will be able to understand even our 'curious sensitivity' on the matter of the name of Skopje."[57] As a proactive response to international bullying, this may have made fine copy at home. But it is because Greece is a country

---

[55] Handler, *Nationalism*. The folklorists evidently saw their interventions in the content of texts as a reassertion of agency in the face of Western overlordship. By adhering to the classicizing conventions of the "protectorate" powers, however, they found themselves caught in the usual traps of hegemony. If they failed to adhere to this line, they were condemned as unpatriotic or un-European.

[56] See Adamantia Pollis, "Greek National Identity: Religious Minorities, Rights, and European Norms, *Journal of Modern Greek Studies* 10 (1992): 171–95; Stephanos Stavros, "The Legal Status of Minorities in Greece Today: The Adequacy of their Protection in the Light of Current Human Rights Perceptions," *Journal of Modern Greek Studies* 13 (1995): 1–32.

[57] Sakis Lefas, "I Skopianí, i etéri mas, ki i istoría mas," *Eleftherotipía*, March 2, 1994, 46. This is an example of what A. J. B. Wace and M. S. Thompson called "political philology." See Wace and Thompson, *The Nomads of the Balkans* (London: Methuen, 1914), 9. See also Michael Herzfeld, "Political Philology: Everyday Consequences of Grandiose Grammars," *Anthropological Linguistics* 39 (1997): 351–75.

taught by tutelary powers (the "allies" of the article) that its ability to gain and keep international respect depends on its success in reproducing the ancient glories, etymology and all. In that larger international context, however, the article also appears to confirm the stereotype of the Greeks as unreasoning chauvinists who operate out of a *ressentiment* much like the "complex" attributed by Dundes to the nationalistic folklorists. It thereby illustrates perfectly the operation of hegemony at the most international level. For, outside Greece, who would take such an argument seriously?

THE GREEK ATOMIST INDIVIDUALIST: A PARADIGMATIC CASE

Greece dramatically embodies the tensions of European identity. At once the spiritual ancestor and the orientalized client-state of the modern European powers, it is both the idealized central source and the contested border of Europe itself. As such, it reproduces a pattern of core-periphery relations at the international level that are perhaps more easily observed in the lower level relationship between a nation-state and its border regions. In the estimation of its self-appointed protectors, Greece is both the guardian of a glorious tradition and beyond the pale of modernity. That this is something of a caricature of the prevailing situation—one that is perpetuated to some extent by those segments of the elite that identify their political interests with Western political and cultural power—should not blind us to the painful, lived reality of this paradox for the Greeks of today.

Ideals of selfhood are subject to wildly divergent kinds of evaluation. Exemplifying the range of possibilities, the concept of *eghoïsmós*, commonly glossed as "self-regard," is a semantic doublet, capable of conveying both admiration for a supposedly European love of freedom and personal autonomy and contempt for the supposedly oriental characteristics of boastfulness, atomism, and intractability.[58] The concept of *eghoïsmós* is enshrined in the national mythology: after independence, the successors to the newly heroized *kleftes* were excoriated by the newly installed Greek authorities as foreign bandits who had nothing to do with their glorious precursors. This is not an uncommon pattern when liberation struggles consolidate their bureaucratic and territorial authority. The salience of the Greek case lies in the implications of a peculiar kind of selfhood—one

---

[58] Probably the best account of *eghoïsmós*, "self-regard," remains that of J. K. Campbell, *Honour, Family, and Patronage: A Study of Institutions and Moral Values in a Greek Mountain Community* (Oxford: Clarendon Press, 1964).

that historically represented the idealized nation but in the context of the routines of bureaucratic statehood must be excluded from it.

Eghoïsmós is not a stable concept even in rural communities. For some villagers, especially for wealthier farmers, it is a destructive force; for others, notably for shepherds still engaged in competitive forms of masculine self-aggrandizement (such as reciprocal theft), it is a virtue—and one they can now, with the smattering of education they have received from the state, turn against the state by reminding its officers that the heroes of the struggle for freedom were themselves "thieves." Some Greek shepherds also buy into a larger rhetoric by deriding some politicians as "Turks," either explicitly or otherwise. One could hardly wish for a clearer demonstration of the ways in which official ideology can be coopted for causes quite contrary to the intentions of the state bureaucracy.[59]

But the exaltation of *eghoïsmós* as a positive virtue does not stop with these marginal shepherds. Not only do some farmers seem to engage in actions that seem dictated more by *eghoïsmós* than by any values of cooperation, but businesspeople, academics, and officials of every kind act in comparable ways. It is here that the analytic tactic I suggested earlier in this chapter becomes especially useful: to use the unfamiliar patterns discerned in relatively remote rural communities heuristically as a way of identifying modulations of the same values in social contexts in which these patterns are more discrete or diffuse. James Faubion has done just that. He uses a Weberian gloss of "sovereignty" to explain the persistence of *eghoïsmós* in modern Athenian literary circles—precisely, that is, in the spaces where, as he argues, a distinctively Greek modernity is being forged.[60]

That Faubion's effort was not appreciated by most Athenian intellectuals may be a measure of its perspicacity.[61] It may well be the case that they felt that their sovereignty was actually impugned by its being linked to the values reported by ethnographers from the countryside rather than to those of the cosmopolitan centers of Europe. Yet it is hard not to recognize in accounts of academic, parliamentary, and business disputes some of the same rhetorical devices, and much of the same concern with individual

---

[59] In a Cretan highland village just before the 1981 elections, a villager who supported the soon-to-be-victorious socialists told me that the people had already had "400 years" of the conservatives—a clear allusion to the Turks and reminiscent of the bitter jibe of Greece's first president, Capodistrias, at the uncooperative wealthy landowners as "Christian Turks."

[60] See James Faubion, *Modern Greek Lessons: A Primer in Historical Constructivism* (Princeton: Princeton University Press, 1993), 122–38.

[61] V. Pesmazoglou, "Me kremmídhia, parakaló," *To Víma*, November 6, 1994, B 6.

reputation, that one meets among shepherds and farmers. The ideology that views the countryside as the repository of the national quintessence, representative as it is of a larger pattern of West European romanticism,[62] does not happily face the key consequence of that pedigree: Greek modernity may in some respects be radically different from the very models in Western Europe with which its advocates most eagerly claim kinship.

In one sense the *eghoïsmós* of the rural population is a form of conformity. As the driving force of social contest, it can be—and often is—assimilated to a capitalist ethos of competition.[63] Competition differentiates individuals only insofar as it lures them with the promise of distinction; the fact that they are competing to acquire a commonly esteemed advantage belies the distinctiveness of their respective motives. And the modernist claim to despise such games, which we might expect to be unique to the modern sphere as Anthony Giddens has described it, or indeed as some ethnographers have found for its historical emergence (for example, Jane Collier for Andalusia), has its roots in the contemptuous pride of rural actors.[64] While the urban Greek intellectual may today dispose of much greater ranges of choice and self-determination, there is nevertheless an identifiable continuity with modes of action more dramatically described in the ethnographies of rural society. Indeed, Renée Hirschon has made the extremely important point that the social and symbolic organization of domestic space—the physical *habitus*, as it were—shows this continuity clearly. In more recent work she has also shown how the transmission of agonistic modes of action is much the same among urbanites as among rural dwellers.[65] That perception is consistent with the persistence of ideas about causation and responsibility, in forms distinctive to the Greek society, within that most modernist of projects, the national bureaucracy.[66]

---

[62] See, variously, Malcolm Chapman, *The Gaelic Vision in Scottish Culture* (London: Croom Helm, 1978); George L. Mosse, *Nationalism and Sexuality: Respectability and Abnormal Sexuality in Modern Europe* (New York: Howard Fertig, 1985); Nadel-Klein, "Reweaving the Fringe"; Raymond Williams, *The Country and the City* (London: Chatto and Windus, 1973).

[63] In a mountain village on Crete, I was told that *eghoïsmós* produced beneficial effects when it led to competitive commercial success, as in the extraordinary proliferation of coffeehouses.

[64] Anthony Giddens, *Modernity and Self-identity: Self and Society in the Late Modern Age* (Stanford: Stanford University Press, 1991); Jane Fishburne Collier, *From Duty to Desire: Remaking Families in a Spanish Village* (Princeton: Princeton University Press, 1997).

[65] Renée Hirschon, *Heirs of the Greek Catastrophe: The Social Life of Asia Minor Refugees in Piraeus* (Oxford: Clarendon Press, 1989); "Greek Adults' Play, or, How to Train for Caution," *Journal of Modern Greek Studies* 10 (1992): 35–56.

[66] See my *Social Production of Indifference*, esp. 122–3.

None of this is to propose a deterministic model of culture, but simply to argue that when people insist on the distinctiveness of their cultural idioms, they may do so for better reasons than their reading of global cultural hierarchy would lead them to want to admit. When, for example, the most sophisticated Athenians continue to follow normative naming practices—especially that of naming the first son for his father's father—they commonly invoke the superficially uncomplicated explanation of "tradition"—a "justification" that is nevertheless extremely familiar from village practice.[67] Urban elite parents may be able to exercise more direct control over the choice of names than can their peasant counterparts, who must often yield the choice to a powerful baptismal sponsor. Indeed, they may be able to follow "traditional" prescriptions more closely than the peasants ever could. But this claim of traditionality is by no means a simple matter at all, and it is closely bound up with issues of selfhood.

When I originally submitted a study of Greek naming practices to an onomastics journal, it was rejected on the basis of a brief report written by, I was informed, a native-born Greek. The latter contemptuously dismissed my analysis of the regularity of name transmission, and my discussion of the idea that name replication implied the "resurrection" (*anstasi*) of antecedent eponyms, as "just a custom" and therefore not worthy of scholarly dissection.[68] Such "corrections" of foreigners' interpretations are a common experience. They often represent metropolitan resistance to outsiders' having what some urbanites consider an unseemly depth of knowledge of the rural culture.[69] But I think more than a simple defense of "cultural intimacy" was intended in the case of the names article. Rather, this was also a rejection of the idea that rural notions of the self were significant in themselves, let alone when they occurred among sophisticates. To understand why, we must briefly examine the further ramifications of the naming system.

These have to do with two features, which, in order to underscore their mutual relevance we can call material *property* and spiritual *properties*.

---

[67] See Juliet du Boulay, *Portrait of a Greek Mountain Village* (Oxford: Clarendon Press, 1974), in which we find the expression *étsi to vríkame* ("that's how we found it") invoked by villagers to account for customs they may have feared—although she does not raise this issue—it might strike the visiting anthropologist as primitive or otherwise undesirable.

[68] This paper was eventually published as "When Exceptions Define the Rules: Greek Baptismal Names and the Negotiation of Identity," *Journal of Anthropological Research* 38 (1982): 288–302.

[69] On one occasion I was criticized for my Greek by a Greek-born copy editor in the United States who failed to realize that the texts in question were in Cretan dialect.

In the article in question, building on the work of Margaret Kenna and others,[70] I tried to demonstrate a systematic covariation between the rules of name transmission and those of property inheritance in several parts of Greece. I found that even the exceptional cases could largely be explained in terms of the cosmology underlying this correspondence: the "resurrection" of a persona, enshrined in a name, is an act of reciprocity, and one that creates a close spiritual connection between namesake and recipient. Bernard Vernier, in an exhaustive study of ethnopsychology, inheritance, and the rules of naming on the Dodecanesian island of Karpathos, has shown that personal *properties* are also construed as following the same logic, so that psychological and physical features are thought to be bilineally distributed in the same way as personal names and property.[71] At first glance it would appear that this is a system in which heredity, marked by the transmission of the personal name and the property associated with it, is locally considered to predetermine absolutely the personality of the individual. Such a system would afford little play to anything like free will—a key component of the individualism envisaged by the ideologues of pan-European identity.

Sometimes we do encounter creative reworkings of the basic principles of name transmission, usually in connection with unusual arrangements for the transfer of property or with the manipulation of powerful patrons' desire to perpetuate names from their own families. This suggests that the ostensible rigidity of such a system permits a good deal of rearranging of social relations, because it allows skilled actors to invoke general norms in justification of specific exceptions. Although on Karpathos the range of rearrangements may be more restricted than it is elsewhere, this lesser flexibility does not necessarily correspond to the "facts on the ground." We need only think of English-speaking parents arguing about which of them their newborn baby "takes after" to realize that attributions of this kind, invocations of natural resemblance that they are, are actually grounded in social and cultural criteria. Iconicity—the semiotic relationship whereby a sign's meaning derives from its supposed resemblance to its referent—is, of necessity, always culturally contingent.[72] Much is at stake in attributions of genetic resemblance: property, the perpetuation of a line, political alliances.

---

[70] Margaret E. Kenna, "Houses, Fields, and Graves: Property and Ritual Obligation on a Greek Island," *Ethnology* 15 (1976): 21–34.

[71] Bernard Vernier, *La genèse sociale des sentiments: aînés et cadets dans l'île grecque de Karpathos* (Paris: Éditions de l'École des Hautes Études en Sciences Sociales, 1991).

[72] See my extended discussion in *Cultural Intimacy*, 56–73.

Moreover, iconicity is the basis of Anderson's model of the imagined community.[73] The members of this entity are presumed to be *all alike*. This does not sit well with our usual ideas of individualism; but ideologues of European and national identity, notably François Guizot, got around that difficulty by arguing, in effect, that what made Europeans all alike was their shared capacity for being different.[74]

Resemblance is relative in precisely this segmentary sense. This has interesting consequences for the European claim to a uniquely individualistic character, refracted through the various subunits of nation, region, community, and kin group. For just as a normative system of naming poses challenges to individual uniqueness—in the Greek system an act of commemoration ("resurrection") becomes, over several generations, a means of deindividuation—so the tensions between being a nation and being European involve arguments about distinctiveness: can Danes produce *féta* and *oúzo*, or should the Americans be permitted to label their sparkling wines "Champagne"? Can the European Union prevent the Greeks from eating their beloved *kokorétsi* (stuffed and roasted tripe) in the name of some collective desire to avert mad cow disease, or does this Turkish-named delicacy (from Turkish *kokoreç*) suddenly provide the means of self-disaggregation from the homogenous culture allegedly propounded by the bureaucrats in Brussels and exemplified by their attempts to regularize the shape of bananas and cucumbers for the purposes of control?[75]

One might well suspect so: the much-maligned Turkish strain in Greek culture becomes a means of asserting difference, but always at the price of ridicule (not to speak of charges of anti-Hellenism!). For similar reasons, we should not be surprised when the libertarian Adam Smith Institute complains about the regulation from Brussels of condoms and cucumbers as "threatening to swamp the European ideal." Too bad that it was the Portuguese love of carrot jam that led the commissioners to classify carrots as a fruit; it was not the commissioners' job, thought the critics, to impose one nation's standards on all the others.[76]

---

[73] Ibid., 27–9.

[74] This line of argument is not uniquely European, but ideologues like Guizot elaborated it to an unusual degree of specificity in nineteenth-century Western Europe.

[75] On the *kokorétsi* story, see "Gutsy Greeks Fight to Save Delicacy," *The Herald* (Glasgow), September 12, 1997, 14.

[76] On the European Union's attempts to control the size and shape of bananas, see William Miller, *Boston Globe*, September 22, 1994, 19. He reports that under the new rules a banana must "not be 'abnormally curved' "). The article also reports earlier attempts to ban the curved cucumber and to classify carrots as fruit. British Foreign Secretary Douglas

The desire for distinctiveness, touted as a European ideal long before the days of Guizot, exposes the segmentary logic underlying the ideology of European unity. Especially in Greece and Britain, the haunts respectively of kleftes and merrie men, the battle is explicitly about who defines that distinctiveness. For what Bourdieu says about distinction as the hallmark of class can be argued, *a fortiori*, for the hierarchy of cultures now conjoined in a single administrative system: just as people place great significance in symbols to which only a select few have access, nations lay claim to the exclusive authorship and possession of whatever passes globally for "high" culture.[77]

Thus, the very possibility of distinctiveness is logically entailed in a collective identity: a finite pool of names closes the circle against "foreign" intrusions but constrains the degree of individuation possible, while the demands of "resurrection" as well as the exigencies of practical politics (such as the need to flatter a baptismal sponsor) both enable and constrain the short-term possibilities of individuation and identification. Implicit in these arrangements for naming are ideas about whether the selfhood implied by *eghoïsmós* is European, Greek, regional, local, or personal. At one extreme is a Cretan village with strict naming rules but a parallel system of nicknames that become generalized as clan ("patrigroup") markers through time. There the height of *eghoïsmós* consists in adopting with pride the unflattering nickname that others have conferred, while making it clear that it will allow one to become the eponymous ancestor of a named subclan—a true snatching of pride from the jaws of humiliation and, as such, an excellent illustration of how a skilled social actor can turn social structure to personal advantage.[78] In a quieter vein, the inventiveness sometimes shown by urban sophisticates of both sexes in generating new diminutives for their own and others' personal names again speaks to the ever-negotiable tension between having a Greek name and being oneself. At the other extreme, the ways in which Greeks approach national territorial issues such as the "Macedonian question" (official policy has been to deny the name of Macedonia to a neighboring state and to a

---

Hurd provides explanations in "Hurd Highlights Myths and Lunacies of Brussels," *The Herald* (Glasgow), November 7, 1992, 7. The excerpt from the Adam Smith Institute report, authored by Timothy Evans and Russell Lewis, appears in Andrew Griffiths, "Cucumber Threat by Supernannies," *The Daily Telegraph*, May 5, 1993, 21.

[77] Pierre Bourdieu, *Distinction: A Social Critique of the Judgement of Taste*, trans. Richard Nice (Cambridge, Mass.: Harvard University Press, 1984).

[78] For an example of this, see Michael Herzfeld, *The Poetics of Manhood: Contest and Identity in a Cretan Mountain Village* (Princeton: Princeton University Press, 1985), 234.

Slavic-speaking minority within Greece's borders) is locally interpreted through the filter of the naming system, providing ample opportunities for the exercise of "personal nationalism" in Cohen's sense.[79]

PREDICAMENTS OF THE PICTURESQUE: VARIEGATIONS OF A EUROPEAN SELFHOOD

Thus far I have examined a *structural* relationship between self and society. I have suggested that it exhibits a high degree of internal flexibility. But that flexibility is not well described by simply reducing it to the level of individualism permitted by an otherwise determining social conformity. We do not thereby satisfactorily answer the questions of how such ideologies are actually maintained, how they interact with the new circumstances of class and globalization, or how they are inculcated at the level of daily action. To answer these questions, I turn to a somewhat different line of argument.

This approach is perhaps best exemplified by the idea of "crafting selves" described by Dorinne Kondo in her study of Japanese artisans and their self-fashioning.[80] Kondo shows that the artisans see in the products of their labor models of their idealized collective selves (although the point is rather submerged in her account). Among Greek (especially Cretan) artisans, I have found an immediate formal analog: differentiation among artifacts reproduces individualism among artisans. The political leadership both hails this as an expression of the European quintessence and excoriates it as resistance to modernity. The artisans, for their part, both boast of their disgust with "homogenization" and self-critically lament the difficulty of achieving "standardization," a term that acquires negative reverberations only in the soundbox of intellectual debate, whence it returns to everyday speech and further complicates the picture.

Such questions are not usefully addressed in terms of "resistance," except in the sense that acts of resistance may confirm the marginalization of those who engage in them and claim them as evidence of moral purity (which, in the European context, is often equated with political weakness).[81] As Debbora Battaglia has rightly insisted, self-making—which

---

[79] See David E. Sutton, "Local Names, Foreign Claims: Family Inheritance and National Heritage on a Greek Island," *American Ethnologist* 24 (1997): 415–37.

[80] Dorinne K. Kondo, *Crafting Selves: Power, Gender, and Discourses of Identity in a Japanese Workplace* (Chicago: University of Chicago Press, 1990).

[81] This must be understood contextually: moral purity is claimed as a compensation for political marginality. This is the process that Edwin Ardener identified as "englobing" (that is, of the politically stronger by the politically weaker); see his "The Problem Revisited," in Shirley Ardener, ed., *Perceiving Women* (London: J. M. Dent, 1975), 19–27.

often engages rhetorics of individuation and collectivity in ways for which we are ill-prepared by the standard rhetoric of Eurocentrism—is far more than the liberated residue of a structural ideology; it is inescapably caught up in the inevitable inequalities of social existence.[82] Thus, resistance to standardization, or reluctance to embrace it, may serve a rhetoric of picturesque European traditionalism and a refusal to submit to the rule of bureaucracy; by that very token, it ensures the marginalization of "old-fashioned" artisans.

Obviously, there are differences in *kinds* of artisanal labor that produce differences of emphasis in the evaluation of its products. Standardization is more desirable in the building trade; the picturesque may more legitimately appear in the personal touch in the output of, say, a goldsmith. But even the latter requires a disciplined body; as one exasperated Cretan goldsmith told me, lamenting the difficulty of finding apprentices who were willing to spend long hours at the workbench doing repetitive mechanical tasks: "It requires a lot of backside!" Discipline here is intended to provide reliability. The essence of artisanal labor is that its products are reliable, yet also individuated and distinctive. The long hours of apprenticeship serve to routinize this linkage of forms of labor with idioms of selfhood.

Following on Kondo's analysis, we can now begin to sketch a relationship between the kind of material objects that artisanal labor produces and the kind of selfhood that these express. But note where this argument has led us. We are not talking about a self individuated beyond the pale of social relations, or a self that has so transcended its social context as to be independent of it. Quite to the contrary, this is a self that can be recognized only by virtue of its disciplined attention to the skills that permit a modest but confident range of a variation—modest because extreme deviations from the norm would look like sheer indiscipline; confident because artisans, who once made artifacts for experienced users, are today forced into the role of experts for the benefit of tourists.

For tradition is in fact a modernist invention. By the same token, what we might call "picturesque individualism" is the invention of a particular kind of modernism: the aggressive personal autonomy first described in detail for Greece by J. K. Campbell about the rough-hewn Sarakatsan shepherds of northern Greece and recast as the in-your-face pose of extreme autonomy that one meets in Athenian taxi-drivers and

---

[82] Debbora Battaglia, "Problematizing the Self: A Thematic Introduction," in Debbora Battaglia, ed., *Rhetorics of Self-Making* (Berkeley: University of California Press, 1995), 1–15.

intellectuals.[83] This is, to be sure, unequivocally a stereotype of such people. It is, however, their own self-stereotype. It is what leads Cretan men to force me to accept their hospitality without reciprocation, on the grounds that this "is what we Cretans do"; like all stereotypes, it is by no means universally accepted or enacted, but it is above all *recognizable*. This is truly "picturesque individualism," the modernist rendering of personal sovereignty as a "tradition."

What is especially interesting about this notion of the rewritten traditional self is that it takes on dramatic overtones borrowed from the language imprecisely glossed as "honor and shame." The Greek term usually translated as "honor" can more accurately be defined as the capacity to live up to people's expectations of someone in accordance with that person's current social status. This is a highly conformist notion, but its visibility is always contingent on a measure of aggressive nonconformism—a deformation of convention that becomes what James Boon has aptly called an "exaggeration of culture."[84]

Crete enjoyed a period of artisanal corporatism under Ottoman rule, but that corporatism collapsed with the establishment of the welfare state in Greece. Few Cretans are still artisans, and those who are cannot legally employ artisans without incurring punitive compulsory insurance charges. Deeply discontented with this restriction and aware that the present-day state discourages them from organizing corporately, Cretans commonly break the law in order to get cheap labor. Neither they nor their apprentices would easily recognize themselves in, for example, the historian James R. Farr's description of artisans in seventeenth-century France. These artisans, claims Farr, evinced a deep concern with matters of honor in consequence of their desire for order, itself a product of pre-Revolutionary corporatism. [85]

If there were a direct correlation between the touchiness of honor and the collective will to maintain the security of a corporatist polity, one would expect the extreme concern with such matters found in Crete not to have survived the collapse—far from recent—of artisanal corporatism. Farr remarks, "There was a strong connection between moral and physical order in artisan mentality."[86] But what, precisely, is an "artisan

[83] See Campbell, *Honour, Family, and Patronage*; Faubion, *Modern Greek Lessons*.
[84] James A. Boon, *Other Tribes, Other Scribes: Symbolic Anthropology in the Comparative Study of Cultures, Histories, Religions, and Texts* (Cambridge: Cambridge University Press, 1982).
[85] James R. Farr, *Hands of Honor: Artisans and their World in Dijon, 1550–1650* (Ithaca: Cornell University Press, 1988).
[86] Farr, *Hands of Honor*, 195.

mentality"? Is this another exoticizing device, relegating the pre-Revolutionary French working classes to something analogous to Lévy-Bruhl's "prelogical mentality"? Is the concern with honor a sign of some collective inability to distinguish between symbolic and literal forms of truth, as we might infer by applying Lloyd's reading of the *mentalité* concept?

Once we recognize that almost everything that has been classed as "honor" has less to do with adherence to a structural code than with meeting expectations, we can see that the whole game of reputation politics is a matter of social calculation and strategy. The strategy that leads social actors to capitalize on "tradition" is in that sense continuous with what it mimics, for what we call honor is a calculating claim to lineage, to a past, to history. If today the expectations one must meet are manufactured through media representation, that suggests that "tradition" plays the role once accorded by anthropologists, in rural contexts in southern Europe, to honor. Tradition is the collective representation of an expected conformity. In the European context its lack of homogeneity can be read as the sign of a "European" individualism and as the mark of backwardness.

But such self-stereotyping is not uniform throughout Europe. Post-Soviet Muscovites, for example, classify themselves as "collective people."[87] Unless one wishes to view such pronouncements as proof of the older stereotypes—that Slavs are collectivist and therefore not really European[88]—they should alert us to the dangers of conflation, much as do differences in local usages so often lumped together as "honor." In both instances circularity leads to preemptive arguments that ill serve the goals of analysis.

One important difficulty with historical attempts to explain collective values, as Farr attempts to do for the seventeenth-century artisans, is that such reconstructions most commonly are made in the absence of much knowledge of the ways in which the objects artisans created were locally understood as models of the self. Even in social anthropology, scholars have begun to pay serious attention only recently to the crafting of subjectivities and the crafting of objects. If the artisans in Farr's account were really so subject to the ideological dictates of the corporatist polity, were the products of their labors similarly functional and uniform? Were they perceived to be so? And what notions of artisanal (but also of literary)

---

[87] I owe this information to Melissa C. Caldwell (Program in Social Studies, Harvard University).

[88] These sentiments, already noted in the work of Dora d'Istria, appear to have animated Finnish dislike of the Russians. See William A. Wilson, *Folklore and Nationalism in Modern Finland* (Bloomington: Indiana University Press, 1976), 132–3.

originality and license were in the ascendant at that time and in that place?

To address those questions, I briefly mention Susan Terrio's remarkable work on French *chocolatiers*. Terrio describes how she arrived for a tasting filled with fear of revealing her lack of expertise. She quickly realized that she would not, indeed *could* not, admit to liking the sweeter chocolates. Informed that the tasting was an "apprenticeship," she found herself swept into a new process of creating national culture by educating the entire population into conformity with comprehensive models of how things should taste. She suggests that the imperative for this massive inculcation—which is about social representations of taste rather than about a psychological preference—came from the threats posed to French autonomy by incorporation in the European Union: "Attempts to forge Europeanness in the name of a universal culture were especially problematic given the existence of a notion of French culture also defined as universal and embodied in French cultural achievements from literature to cuisine."[89] The threat posed by Belgian chocolates led the French manufacturers of hand-crafted chocolates to accent their "Aztec" origins, using exoticism to describe their *product* in complementarity with the "traditional" (or domestically exotic) aspect of its *production*.

Here is the logic of segmentation in full force, etched in the dark bitter chocolate that the new French cultural logic demands. Universality itself becomes a remarkable fissile property—just like the Divine Being of the Nuer, refracted through all the divisions of the body politic: my universality is better than yours, because my chocolate is better than yours—much as Guizot had argued over a century earlier that the French were the most European of all because they were the most internally differentiated.[90] Possessive individualism *is* sovereignty.

French *chocolatiers* have been able to insert their cause in the larger cultural hierarchies of taste that dominate world markets. The Cretan artisans have been less lucky. Their alleged individualism allows them to claim a "European" tradition, but their supposedly traditional products have not achieved the popular appeal that perhaps may be possible only in a country confident of its own modernity—a place where, as Michael Thompson has argued, garbage becomes valuable and feeds an entire

---

[89] Susan J. Terrio, "Crafting Grand Cru Chocolates in Contemporary France," *American Anthropologist* 98 (1996): 67–79.
[90] Ibid., 77.

industry in nostalgia.[91] Greek artisans do not occupy the same role in Greek national self-imagination that their French counterparts do in France. In Greece many artisans produce cheap and obvious copies of older artifacts, an outcome derided as kitsch. These artisans are legally marginalized, their quarrelsome selfhood both a stick with which the local elite continually beats them and an emblem of the whole nation's standing among the European powers. In France artisans represent an idealized past that is still glorious, their products an expression of the values a conservative national government holds dear. In Greece the few remaining artisans, strike some sophisticates as an affront to the modernity of which most authorities are not yet confident.

FROM ARTISANAL MODELS TO MODEL SELVES: TOWARD THE HISTORY OF AN IDEA

I have dwelt on the role of artisans in European self-fashioning in part because they have come to signify the quintessential European combination of artistic invention and confident conformity. Although this assumption of a modernist traditionality works to the great benefit of those who inhabit the powerful core countries, it becomes a device of self-marginalization at the weaker periphery. The proud French individualist—the hero of Guizot's imagination—becomes, in his Greek counterpart, a quarrelsome egotist, a slavish imitator, or an incompetent amateur, and above all an "oriental" incapable of factory standards. Thus, the relationship of craft to stereotype also becomes an index of sometimes painful political differences within the presumed unity of Europe.

But are these really different people? And are they so very different from the post-Soviet "collectivists" of Moscow? The answer is an important prolegomenon, I suggest, to thinking about orientalist fantasies about alleged Indian or Chinese or Middle Eastern notions about selfhood, the value of human life, and so on. For just as Nadel-Klein has suggested that intra-European (and even intranational) patterns of domination provided the template for global colonialism,[92] so too the intra-European creation of a hierarchy of selfhoods may have furnished a model for these orientalist illusions—and a critical review of the discourse about individualism

---

[91] Michael Thompson, *Rubbish Theory: The Creation and Destruction of Value* (Oxford: Oxford University Press, 1979).
[92] Nadel-Klein, "Reweaving the Fringe," 502–4.

and sociocentrism within Europe may help us to understand much more fully how European colonizers learned to articulate that discourse with more directly coercive means of turning subjectivity into subjection.

My story ends at this point, in some necessary degree of confusion. For it is clear that the idea of a distinctive European selfhood is a mirage. The idea of a uniform "European self" is considerably less promising than that of a single European currency. Yet the goal of creating a truly pan-European subjectivity dies hard: much everyday ideological labor goes into suppressing the presence of disagreement and difference, as in the European Space Agency.[93] While this certainly has practical implications as well—it would be hard to run such an agency without at least the semblance of cooperation—it is clear that ideas of a common European subjectivity with common goals have political durability of an impressive order.

The idea of a typically European individualism confuses the discourse with its subject matter. That discourses of individuality are widespread in Europe, and that they share a considerable range of rhetorical guises, seems incontrovertible. But the tensions that pit individualist against collectivist sentiment are not confined to Europe, and even there, as Battaglia sagely notes, we sometimes find that the binary opposition between them is a misleading rhetoric. In her edited volume on the making of selves, all the authors construct their arguments around, or in reaction to, a purported "Western" model of the individualistic self. But this, again, says much more about the Western provenance of the authors and their received theories than it does about any inevitable linkage of "the West" with "individualism"—beyond, that is, the ideological discourse through which, in a rich array of variegated interpretations, political leaders in Europe have decreed that such a linkage existed.

Thus, the ultimate irony is that the European ideology of individualism is necessarily a conformist concept, grounded in the relationship between property ownership and selfhood. Of late it seems to have figured less prominently in the discourse of European integration. Perhaps, indeed, as the European program of political unification lurches ahead, the entire issue of individualism will seem less important than the conformity of cucumbers. But that, too, would be an ignominious end for the enormous volume of intellectual labor that has sustained it as dogma for over two centuries.

---

[93] Zabusky, *Launching Europe*, 20–6.

8

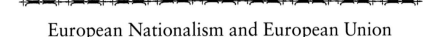

European Nationalism and European Union

ARIANE CHEBEL D'APPOLLONIA

At first sight the concept of a "European nationalism" would seem to be meaningless. At the very least it evokes either an empty abstraction or an impossible dilemma. Nationalism, after all, is tied to the nation (and vice versa), and although Europe is composed of nation-states, the European Union is presented as being an antinational construction, a-national at best, sometimes even as supranational. During the 1950s, the European founding fathers presented the European Coal and Steel Community (ECSC) and then the European Economic Community (EEC) precisely as a means to suppress the oppressive and warlike nationalism that had plunged Europe into two internecine wars in less than a century. This theme created a confusion between nationalism and the idea of the nation, between nationalism and state sovereignty.

Today, however, European unification is no longer considered to be a step forward, nor for many people even a real necessity. The debate over the Maastricht Treaty has made things worse. On one side, the supporters of the treaty have turned most mentions of the national idea into diabolical references to a dark historical past, since these were the main arguments employed by the treaty's opponents. "Consolidating European unification is a modern way of limiting the damaging propensity of nations to become nationalist" was a recurring motto proclaimed in the name of a so-called European identity. On the other side, "national nationalism" (that is, the usual defensive nationalism of the nation based on a selfish love of a specific country) was celebrated as the last barrier protecting national identity against a diabolical supranational European Union. This anti-Maastricht rhetoric resulted in a highly questionable equation: "Building Europe means destroying nations." The first of these attitudes is based on a false sacralization of Europe. The second, on a false sacralization of the nation.

In order to understand the various meanings of European nationalism, one must recognize that there is no necessary contradiction between
European ideals and national identities, between European unification
and national nationalism. Far from it. European identity must reside
in the concrete and symbolic realities created by centuries of history.
Furthermore, the affirmation of national identities—which should be distinguished from narrow and aggressive nationalism—can even act as a
democratic counterweight to a European Union that is not, or is not yet,
an entity possessed of a totemic transcendence to which national realities,
feelings, and symbols must be sacrificed.

A second preliminary objection must be clarified. It is unclear whether,
as is generally believed, the nation created nationalism or, as Ernest Gellner
has suggested, nationalism, in fact, created nations.[1] Neither account,
however, is immediately relevant to a discussion of the situation within
the European Union as it is currently constituted. In the first place the
nations that now make up the Union have not always been nationalist
during Europe's long history; in the second nationalism has often been
expressed within frameworks that were both larger and smaller than that
of the nation itself. In other words, it is difficult to analyze nationalism
apart from the idea of nation and national territory. "Afro-Asianism"
and "Arabism" are, for instance, examples of transnational nationalisms
that, in these cases, have sought to unite the disparate nations of the
developing world. (The same, of course, is true of the European colonial empires that preceded them; they represent but one of the possible
versions of European nationalism.) Inversely, the present resurgence of
national-populism (in the East as in the West), the emergence of multiple
forms of communitarianism stemming from a hodgepodge of ethnic or
religious solidarities, and the relative successes of separatist regionalisms
(Northern Italy, the Basque Country, Corsica, and so on) represent just
as many examples of infranational nationalisms.

European nationalism can be defined through an ideological and historical analysis of the evolution of the nation-states within the present
European Union on one side and with reference to the past and present
aspirations for a postnational Europe on the other side. A clear and significant parallel exists between European cosmopolitanism in the eighteenth and nineteenth centuries and aspirations that underlie the creation
of the European Union. From the Enlightenment to the Second World
War, European nationalism had two meanings: a romantic conception

---

[1] Ernest Gellner, *Nations and Nationalism* (Oxford: Basil Blackwell, 1992).

of a new united Europe that would bypass the modern nation-state by limiting state sovereignty, and an ideological tool used to create or legitimate new nation-states. The first of these, which rested on the heritage of European cosmopolitanism, may be called "antinational European nationalism." The second, which appeared after and in reaction to the European order imposed in 1815 at the Congress of Vienna and then in 1919 at the Congress of Versailles, may be defined as a "pro-national European nationalism." Both gave birth to today's Europeanism, which can be understood either as the continuity of the eternal dream of a European federation or as a more modest attempt to make the European states collaborate more closely. Both, however, gave birth to anti-Europeanism, the present form of the old anticosmopolitanism. In both cases the historicity of the nation-state and of its national state control is strikingly apparent.

FROM EUROPEAN COSMOPOLITANISM TO ANTINATIONAL EUROPEAN NATIONALISM

History reminds us that nations emerged slowly. It took many decades, many wars and revolutions for them to take shape. We must keep in mind this historicity, grounded, as it is, in ethnic-cultural references and symbols, in order to refuse them any sacralization. Furthermore, the idea of "nation" is politically neutral and could easily be adapted to any available political regime. It appeared in parliamentary monarchies, authoritarian empires, and in republics of various types. One of the reasons for the failure of the 1848 revolutions was that all the nationalists—Italians, Germans, Hungarians, Czechs—were divided into conservatives, liberals, and republicans. In other words, the nation itself was politically neutral.

Beginning in the eighteenth century, however, national sentiments became more and more exclusive with the emergence of narrow nationalisms based on an increasingly closed conception of the nation. A process of antagonistic identification allowed European nations to define themselves against each other: the proliferation of mutual exclusion stereotypes (the Anglo-Saxon "Krauts," the French "Boches") was a proof of the gradual construction of national consciousness. Even the universalistic philosophers of the Enlightenment talked about the spirit of nations largely in terms of stereotypes. For Rousseau, the English had "the prejudices of pride" and the French "the prejudices of vanity." A. W. Schlegel compared unfavorably the French to the "good German, honest, loyal, solid, precise and profound."[2] Here was the embryo of the coming conflicts between aggressive nationalisms that have divided Europe since the nineteenth century. Here also was the beginning of the grand strategies for a unified Europe based on closer, more enduring cosmopolitan projects.

Cosmopolitanism was fueled by a rising feeling of European unity as well as by a European superiority complex toward non-European populations. The closed conception of the nation, illustrated by Johann Gottfried Herder and Johann Gottlieb Fichte, for instance, was rejected by many writers and philosophers throughout Europe, but for two very distinct reasons.[3] For some, the nation-state was too recent a creation to possess any effective reality, or it was conducive only to conflict. European cosmopolitanism, by contrast, was rooted in a long tradition from Antiquity to the Renaissance, which had included such figures as Erasmus and Leonardo da Vinci, and which drew upon the Christian ideal of universal peace. For others, the narrow conception of the nation seemed to lead only to an aggressive nationalism that had been the prime cause of most of the wars of the modern era.

Consequently, the reinforcement of national nationalism gave rise to the first expression of European nationalism. As Europe was divided into aggressive nation-states, there was a convergence between the idea of "Europe" and the condemnation of national nationalism. This European nationalism took three successive forms. Firstly, from the Enlightenment to 1848, it proclaimed that the nation was just a step toward a larger totality, humanity. The universe contained Europe, which contained nations without any hierarchy. For Rousseau, in his *Considérations sur le gouvernement de Pologne,* there "are no more French, German, Spanish, even Englishmen whatever one says, there are only Europeans. They all have the same tastes, the same passions, the same habits." As Iselin declared, "Real patriotism is only an emanation of the pure love of humanity."[4] To these antinational European nationalists, there was a concentric order of allegiances, from the family to the nation, from the nation to Europe, from Europe to the universe. There was also no contradiction between Europeanism and national sentiments when these sentiments were not exclusive. For Montesquieu, "Matters are such in

---

[2] Quoted in Paul Hazard, *La pensée européenne au XVIIIè siècle* (Paris: Fayard, 1963).

[3] Johann Gottfried Herder, *Lettres sur le progrès de l'humanité* (1793–1797) and *Idées sur la philosophie de l'humanité* (1784–1791); Johann Gottlieb Fichte, *Discours à la nation allemande* (1808).

[4] Iselin quoted by Hazard, *La pensée.*

Europe that all states need each other. Europe is a state made up of several provinces."[5]

This first expression of European nationalism was determined by a conviction of the superiority of the European over the non-European areas of the world. Even before Europe entered the final, and most expansive phase of its overseas expansion, most Europeans held their continent to be well above the others. For Voltaire, in *Le siècle de Louis XV*, Europe was one "great republic divided into several states, all with common religious bases, all with the same legal and political principles unknown in other parts of the world."[6] Intellectual supremacy, military power, economic development, and commercial prosperity marked Europe as a homogeneous whole and gave it a unity far beyond national divisions. Until the First World War, European nationalism was mixed with Eurocentrism. European universalism was paradoxically founded on the particularism of the continent: it was precisely because European culture was unique that it could claim to be also universal.

This claim to universalism equally marked various pacifist projects, as illustrated by Kant's *Perpetual Peace*, written in 1795. For Kant, the European idea was linked to pacifism (with the proposal of a disarmament plan), to the respect for morality, and to the application of rights as the emanation of Reason. In proposing the creation of a general confederation of the European states as an essential step toward the construction of a "world republic," Kant was, of course, consciously participating in a discussion that had been going on for centuries. It was started during the Renaissance by the Spanish humanist Juan Luis Vives, continued by Hugo Grotius, and hugely extended during the eighteenth century by, among others, William Penn in *Present and Future Peace of Europe* (1693), Charles Irénée de Saint Pierre (*Projet pour rendre la paix perpétuelle en Europe, Projet pour rendre la paix perpétuelle entre souverains chrétiens*, written between 1713 and 1717), and Jeremy Bentham with his *Plan for an Universal and Perpetual Peace* (1786–9).[7]

Even before the "people's spring" of 1848, European nationalism was characterized by two basic characteristics: the will to protect Europe against itself by establishing a federation, and the ambition to protect European interests and European supremacy against non-European

---

[5] Montesquieu, *De l'Esprit des lois* (Geneva, 1748), book XI, where he analyzes the characteristics of the federal republic.
[6] Voltaire, *Le siècle de Louis XIV* (1756), Cap. XXXIX.
[7] In 1761 Rousseau published an abridged version of Saint Pierre's *Projet*, and in 1782 he wrote his *Jugement sur la paix perpétuelle*.

enemies. The fact that neither project was ever realized should not lead to the conclusion that Kant and others were merely Utopians. Far from it. Some of Kant's critics, and Kant himself, insisted that his cosmopolitanism did not derive from an exaggerated concern for the human race as such, but from the importance he attributed to right (*Recht*) law, to the pragmatic recognition of the advantages of a peaceful alliance that could be achieved only with the consent of the people. In other words, Europe was an ideal-type that would be achieved in future time.

From 1848 to 1939, European nationalism assumed its second form with the antinational theme of the "United States of Europe." Derived from the currents of opinion that opposed the new European order imposed in 1815, the various projects for the United States aimed to limit the bellicose effects of state nationalisms and to combat the specter of the decline of Europe. Unlike the proponents of Kant's "Cosmopolitan Right" (*ius cosmopoliticum*), it was essentially the fear of seeing Europe lose its dominant position that motivated the followers of European nationalism. Defended by Victor Hugo and Richard Cobden, the two principal figures at the Congress of Peace organized in 1849 in Paris, the project of the United States of Europe was a response more to the conscious desire to adapt the European states to the demands of a new international environment than to an innate desire to unify them. This was why the free-exchange economists of the time supported the idea. Hugo evoked the "markets opening themselves to commerce," these new "battlefields," in his famous speech of 1849. "The day will come," he declared, "when you France, you Russia, you England, and you Germany, when all you nations of the continent, without losing distinctive qualities or your individual glories, will bind yourself tightly together into a single superior entity, and you will come to constitute a European fraternity, as absolutely as Brittany, Burgundy and Alsace are now bound together with France."[8]

For certain intellectuals and economists, the state was an outmoded political and economic entity, and nationalism an obsolete expression of old narrow-minded beliefs. The success of the Zollverein, then of German and Italian unification, confirmed these convictions, which were defended at the third International Congress in Rome in 1891 and at the 1900 Congress of the Free School of Political Sciences. On this last occasion, the participants proved themselves ardent propagators of European

---

[8] Victor Hugo, *Douze discours* (Paris, 1850). See *Oeuvres complètes: Actes et Paroles* (Paris: Hetzel, 1882).

nationalism by insisting that Europe was being threatened by the rise of new countries (including the United States of America): "clients of Europe which have become its rivals."

This belief in an external menace became a certitude during the interwar period, during which European nationalism became as virulent as it was inefficient, and all the more antinational since it was the nationalisms of the nation-states that had unleashed the Great War. On the political level, the United States of Europe was revived by Richard Coudenhove-Kalergi and his Pan-European Movement. On the economic level, the desire to bypass the narrow parameters of the existing nation-states led to several attempts at commercial and customs unions, including the European Customs Union created in 1925. The Spaniard Ortega y Gasset perfectly summed up the content of the European nationalism of this time: "each nation which was at one time a large open space, has become a province.... All nationalisms are at an impasse.... Only the decision to build a great nation with the continental populations will resuscitate the pulse of Europe. It was historical realism which taught me to understand that the unity of Europe as a society is not an ideal but a fact of a very ancient everyday life."[9]

Confronted by the threat of Bolshevism, on the one hand, and by the economic power of the United States, on the other, the Pan-European Movement became a lobby incorporating eminent politicians in what constituted a veritable regional organization. Provided with a council composed of delegates from its member states, an assembly of delegates from the national parliaments, and a Court of Justice, this organization was supposed to remedy the crisis in European civilization. To allay the fears of the antifederalists, Coudenhove-Kalergi and Aristide Briand assured them that nothing, in Coudenhove-Kalergi's words, would "touch the common sovereignty of the nations who were a part of such an association."[10] Juridically speaking, such a plan was completely incoherent. But from the point of view that interests us, pan-Europeanism was clearly the expression of a European nationalism of self-defense at a time when the seeming menace of internal and external enemies made European unity a necessity, although one that was as yet unobtainable.

"Unite or die": the formula returned in force after the Second World War. The disasters provoked by the new conflict, the division of the world

---

[9] José Ortega y Gasset, *La rebelión de las masas* (first published in 1926).
[10] Richard Coudenhove-Kalergi, *J'ai choisi l'Europe* (Paris: Plon, 1952), 176. See also Fondation Archives européennes, *Le plan Briand d'union fédérale européenne* (Genève, 1992).

into two blocs, and the loss of most of the European colonial empires motivated the speeches of the Founding Fathers of Europe. Whether unionists or federalists, these Founding Fathers personified the third expression of European nationalism: a mixture of pacifism, of reaffirmed faith in market mechanisms, of commercial ambitions, and of nostalgia for past glories justifying the ambition for future glories. On this last point Winston Churchill's famous speech in Zurich in 1946 is explicit: "if the European countries succeeded in uniting, their 300 to 400 million inhabitants would know, by the fruit of their common heritage, a prosperity, a glory, a happiness that no boundary, no border could contain. . . . We must construct such a thing as the United States of Europe."[11] This declaration can be compared to the definition of the nation given by Ernest Renan in 1882: "the common possession of a rich legacy of memories" which must be brought to fruition, "that is the social capital upon which a national idea can be established."[12] It is therefore during the postwar years that European nationalism has borrowed most from the national mystique by defining itself according to the same criteria as the nation-state: historical memory-building, a common identity and culture for all of the entities grouped within the bounds of a given territory, and political and economic objectives destined to ensure general prosperity and to defend the global interests of its participants.

The rediscovery or the total and/or partial recomposition of an historic past justifies certain references to a common identity and culture. If, as Jean-Baptiste Duroselle maintained in *L'Europe: Histoire de ses peuples*, "history has created a real Europe," there can be no such thing as a European history of Europe.[13] In other words, European history is just a juxtaposition of national histories. But, if the facts are not European, the interpretations are.

Wars have always played a fundamental role in the composition of the national identity. For the French the battle of Valmy in 1792 is the foundational act on which the mystique of the modern Republic is founded. The Founding Fathers of the European Union adopted the same mechanism of symbolic identification. Only in this case it is not the memories of glorious victory on which the new "nation" is founded but rather the desire to escape from a conflict that for all those involved has been, in one way

---

[11] Churchill, quoted by Elisabeth du Réau, *L'idée d'Europe au XXè siècle* (Bruxelles: Complexe, 1996), 133–4.

[12] Ernest Renan, "Qu'est-ce qu'une nation?" Conférence à la Sorbonne, 11 Mars 1882, in *Oeuvres Complètes*, tome 1 (Paris: 1947), 887–906.

[13] Jean-Baptiste Duroselle, *L'Europe: Histoire de ses peuples* (Paris: Perrin, 1990), 24ff.

or another, a form of defeat. The basic paradox of European nationalism is that it is fed by the memory of events that divided and bloodied, rather than united, Europe. In the eyes of the European nationalists, it is of little consequence that these wars were experienced differently by the different European nations, that they were the supreme manifestation of opposing interests.

The wars themselves were a dividing factor; the interpretation of the wars by the Europeanists, however, has become a supremely unifying factor. To this must be added the theme of a common enemy, an indispensable ingredient for any antinationalism. Beginning in the 1950s, this common enemy was the Soviet presence in Europe. The Founding Fathers therefore presented their initiatives as so many steps in a crusade for the defense of the Western world. On the cultural level, too, the differences between the peoples of Europe disappeared from the speeches of the Europeanists. In 1949, at the end of the Lausanne Conference, Denis de Rougemont, soul of the European Center of Culture, declared: "for what ends do we desire these cultural means and this teaching of a common European conscience? Europe has always been open to the entire world. Right or wrong, by idealism or by ignorance, by virtue of its faith or by its imperialist views, it has always perceived its civilisation as an ensemble of universal values."[14] Since the cosmopolitanism of the Enlightenment, the discourse has hardly varied.

Next, European nationalism gave itself a clearly defined territory, the Cold War having temporarily settled the eternal question of Europe's eastern borders. In this geographic or, more precisely, geo-political framework, European nationalism justified its position by arguing the expected advantages of unification, for present and future generations. On a par with national nationalism, European nationalism has always included a good dose of messianism. In 1948 the participants at the Hague congress parted company by pledging "to support with all their might the men and the governments who are working for this measure of public good, a supreme chance for peace and guarantee of a great future for this generation and for those to come." Even today the champions of the Maastricht Treaty justify their position in the name of a reconstructed past and an idealized future.

Similarly, the defensive conception of European nationalism has hardly changed since the end of the nineteenth century. The discourse of the

---

[14] Denis de Rougemont, *Oeuvres complètes*, 3 vols., *Ecrits sur l'Europe*, vol. 1: *1948–1961* (Paris: Editions de la Différence, 1994), 85.

Count of Saint-Simon on the need to establish a large economic and commercial space is still a topical question. He was one of the first, after the collapse of the Napoleonic empire, to understand that it was only through unity that the various states of Europe could prevent Europe from losing its global supremacy. Furthermore, he fully grasped the importance of the industrial revolution and the impact it would eventually have upon the nations of the Old World. In order to meet the need to unite economically, while still preserving the sovereignty of the individual European states, he presented a proposal in 1814 at the Congress of Vienna. Written in collaboration with Augustin Thierry, it was entitled *Réorganisation de la société européenne, ou de la nécessité et des moyens de rassembler les peuples d'Europe en un seul corps politique en conservant à chacun sa nationalité* (The reorganization of European society, or the need and the means to unite the peoples of Europe in a single political body while still preserving their individual nationalities). Saint-Simon's arguments were "modern": the problem he outlined is still a pressing one—the relationship between the economical and the political in the construction of Europe. This he described as the outcome of a necessary evolution that would at once protect Europe from itself and save it from decline. Thus he praised a collaboration between the member states on a number of specific projects such as railways, central European banks, and an increase in the commerce of free exchange—to paraphrase the Schuman declaration of 1950. Finally, in the image of the nationalist historiographers, the partisans of European nationalism have always had a tendency to reconstruct the history of their doctrine, and of the achievements to which it has led, as a rectilinear trajectory in order to justify the theory of a linear evolution over the centuries of the European idea.

FROM EUROPEAN COSMOPOLITANISM TO PRO-NATIONAL EUROPEAN NATIONALISM

A second type of European nationalism, rather than opposing European construction and national interests, proclaimed that Europe was the best way to protect the national interests of old and new nations. This nationalism, which appeared after the new European order imposed in 1815, is based on the evolution of nationalism from a narrow to a broadened form. Europe is no longer conceived as the sum of the nation-states of which it is constituted, united, in a more or less supranational structure, according to the ambitions of the various governments involved. It is perceived instead as a means to bypass national governments by giving a voice to the populations that make up the nation-states and by ensuring the protection of national identities outside the strict framework of the state. In other words, this second model dissociates state sovereignty from popular sovereignty, national identity from state sovereignty. Europe is conceived as serving the national interest of all its members. Antinational European nationalism thus led to a European construction from the top. Pro-national European nationalism implied a unification from the bottom.

In recent history this second model has taken two forms. Before 1945 it was the Europe of peoples opposed to the Europe of princes, the Europe of nationalities opposed to the Europe of realpolitik. Since the 1950s, pro-national European nationalism has fed infranational claims: the Europe of regions is presented as a counterweight to the federative logic of the European Union and as an antidote to the widely perceived supranational technocratic tendencies of the Union. It is the Europe of the "heartlands" against the Europe of the Eurocrats.

This form of pro-national European nationalism was particularly powerful at the end of the eighteenth century and throughout the nineteenth century in those regions of Europe that were struggling to emancipate themselves from the older imperial structures, Ottoman Turkey in the East and the Austro-Hungarian monarchy in the West. For Rhigas Velestinlis, the principal Greek and Albanian nationalist of the period, some kind of united Europe or Balkan federation seemed to be the only way to secure national independence. In Velestinlis's *Thouros*, a hymn celebrating independence that was greatly influenced by French philosophers, European unification was conceived as the only vehicle for achieving an independent Greek homeland.[15] Similarly, Teofan Noli, leader of the short-lived Albanian democratic government in 1924, created a Pan-Albanian federation (Vatra) for the same objective.

In Italy Giuseppe Mazzini provided the best example of a romantic pro-national European nationalism. From his *Young Italy* in 1831 to his *Young Europe* in 1834, he pursued the same goal: to build Europe in order to build Italy and vice versa. His conception of the resurgence (*risorgimento*) of Italy was a mixture of Jacobin-inspired liberalism, religiosity ("God and the People"), and universalism. His nationalism, however, was

---

[15] Rhigas Velestinlis lived from 1757 to 1798. While he was secretary to the hospodar de Valachia, he became an enthusiast for the French Revolution and wrote a national anthem modeled on the *Marseillaise*. Some years later, after he had settled in Vienna, he participated in the diffusion of the Declaration of the Rights of Man in the Balkans. After an abortive attempt to return to his native country, he was arrested by the Austrian police and then handed over to the Pasha of Belgrade who executed him.

very far from being xenophobic. Convinced that the people could win the free exercise of their sovereignty only by making state and nationality coincide, Mazzini proposed a "Holy Alliance of Nations" to combat the Holy Alliance concluded in 1815 and the concert of nations orchestrated by Metternich. For him, humanity was not a cosmopolitan world split into immutable nation-states but a whole, created by God, that united all peoples in the awareness of a common origin and a common future. In 1834 he published the program for his *Young Europe* according to which free national associations signed "an act of brotherhood, a declaration of principle constituting the universal moral law and referring to the principles of Liberty, Equality and Progress." In his essay of 1860, *The Duties of Man,* he described Europe as the means to achieve a superior political order.

Mazzini's pro-national European nationalism was also founded on an antigovernmental inter-European dynamic and on a democratic conception of the nation-state. His thinking sums up perfectly the desire to promote a people's Europe instead of a Europe of monarchs. The whole of humanity, he argued, had now been called upon to restructure itself into a federalist system of unitary nations under the aegis of republicanism. The republic was, for him, the only form of government that was legitimate and logical, and thus compatible with both morality and nationality. It was at once the mark of national identity and of the universality of a body of citizens united in a federal system of individual nations. As such, the republic was the sole form of government capable of reconciling national sentiment and European unity. Promoter of an International League of Peoples in April 1847, Mazzini personified the Europe of the "people's spring" of 1848 with its blend of internationalism, Europeanism, and messianic nationalism.[16] After the failure of the revolution of 1868, he tried to materialize his ideals with the notion of a universal republican alliance in September 1866.

The double patriotic and Europeanist inspiration of Mazzini reflects the three ambiguities inherent in pro-national European nationalism. First, the bond between the unitary nationalist vocation and the idea of the spontaneous solidarity of populations has never resisted the ravages of the aggressive nationalism of nation-states. Second, while opposed to the conservative theories more or less based on the notion of an unchanging natural order, Mazzinian thinking integrated a strong dose of organistic

---

[16] Giuseppe Mazzini, "Le programme de la Jeune Europe," in R. Benichi and M. Nouchi, *Le livre de l'Europe* (Paris: Stock, 1990).

convictions. Evidence for this lies in his scheme for a territorial redivision of the European States, a project that owed more to Fichte or to David Frederic Strauss than it did to Ernest Renan. Mazzini proposed the creation of fourteen groups divided according to history, tradition, geography, and language. This new European map would have equitably repartitioned the whole of the continent between the great Graeco-Roman, Germanic, and Slavic families. Third, just as antinational European nationalism utilizes the same criteria for defining Europe as for defining the nation, while at the same time claiming to bypass the latter, Mazzini's pro-national European nationalism remains confined to the strict logic of the national framework. In short, Mazzini was conflating Italy with Europe.

What was good for Italy, however, was not necessarily applicable to Europe as a whole. Furthermore, Mazzini was prevented from becoming a prophet in his own country since the Risorgimento was carried out from the top by a process of governmental centralization and not according to the rights of the peoples to govern themselves. The resisters to unification by a Piedmontese monarchy were numerous, particularly in the South. As the federalist Carlo Cattaneo argued in his *Gli stati uniti d'Italia,* "Sicily and Naples are not regions, but states." And from 1848 until 1870, in particular with the uprising in Palermo in 1866, the unification was constantly threatened by the "Southern Question," as in one way or another it has continued to be ever since. At the time of the defeat of Adoua in 1896, Ferdinando Martino, the minister of public instruction, commented: *"Fatta l'Italia, bisogna fare gli Italiani"* (We have made Italy, now we must make the Italians)—a phrase echoed by many of Europe's present observers: *we have made Europe, now we must make the Europeans.*[17]

Nonetheless, Mazzini was one of the first to emphasize the necessity of transnational solidarities to establish European unity, whether under a supranational or intergovernmental form. For the Italian patriot, the republican ideal was, as it had been for Kant, the only possible transnational bond between the European peoples. The European federalist system that he envisioned would have allowed the republican conquests that had occurred in France and Italy to be extended to the whole of the continent. After the failure of the revolution of 1848, Mazzini turned to the possibility of a workers' international union on a European scale as another form of opposition to an exclusively narrow national framework. The European

---

[17] See J. C. Lescure, "Faire les Italiens," in *L'Europe des nationalismes aux nations* (Paris: Sedes, 1996), 2:9.

dimension of this project, rivaled then ruined by the creation of the First International, was more important than the protection it offered to the interests of the worker. Other representatives of the European left similarly refused to fashion European construction after the state model (the goal of pro-national European nationalism being precisely the defense of national interests against the omnipotence of governments that were detested because of their policies). Those left-leaning Europeans proposed various federalist plans that would comply with two fundamental criteria: the guarantee of the exercise of a democratic citizenship and a real control over state power by a series of counter powers, with Europe considered as a "intermediary organism." For Joseph Proudhon, author of *The Federative Principle* (1863), Europe should be a "confederation of confederations" respecting individual interests in a national collectivity and national interests in a European collectivity. The self-government of the basic groups was doubled by a federal structure ensuring the coordination of the whole. The sharing of power on all levels ensured the respect of pluralism despite the propensities of states to unification or annexation. In 1872 in *Federalism, Socialism and Antitheology,* the anarchist Mikhail Bakunin proposed the creation of a United States of Europe far removed from that envisioned by Victor Hugo or Richard Cobden. For Bakunin, the question was not one of obtaining the agreement of states in order for them to cooperate economically and politically. It was rather a question of suppressing unitary states for the good of nations, of replacing the existing hierarchical organization with a federation of free individuals.

Proudhon and Bakunin had only a limited influence on the construction of Europe. One should not conclude, however, that their plans were buried under the weight of history. Both imagined the emergence of a European social organism, similar to the one currently being discussed within the European Union. Both accented the need to respect the pluralism at the heart of European unity and the need for the people's support in the vast project of European unity. Finally, both considered the problem of minorities—whether cultural, religious, or even social—in a Europe that would be homogeneous while still ensuring the free expression of diversity.

To these projects should be added the efforts of the Austro-Marxists after the fall of the Austro-Hungarian monarchy. They began to rethink the relationship of state and citizenship. For Karl Renner, European nationalism was the only force capable of protecting the liberty of individuals and the autonomy of nations. He even suggested dissociating nationality from territorial limits in order to make it a personal attribute, in the image of religious allegiance: each person would have the right to choose his or her national affiliation, and the nations thus constituted would possess their own legislation, budget, and administration. The coherence of the whole would be ensured at the European level, with constant care to favor participation by citizens and their free expression of the desire for community and national identity.[18]

In the Europe redrawn by the various treaties that concluded the First World War, the directors of the new states proved to be the most receptive to the projects of European unification in order to protect the interests, the very existence even, of their "national constructions." According to polls conducted between June and August of 1930, the general attitude toward Aristide Briand's European Union plan was one of refusal, with the exception of such recent creations as Yugoslavia and Czechoslovakia. Although they were somewhat older creations, Greece and Bulgaria also approved the plan because they saw in Europe a means to limit the influence of the great powers, the same powers that had amputated a part of Bulgaria and had prevented Greece from achieving the Megale Idea.

In the aftermath of the Second World War, pro-national European nationalism thus expressed itself in two ways. First, it was expressed through the intermediary of various community actions, the most recent being the creation, under the Maastricht Treaty, of a "citizenship of the Union." Second, it was expressed by the partisans of transnational solidarities, and even more so by the defenders of intranational autonomist forces. The common link between these forms of European nationalism was the desire to reinforce the intermediary actions between state and individual, between the individual and market, between the centralization of econo-political power and the necessary adaptation to the logistics of globalization. They also shared the rejection of a narrow nationalism.

The demand for a citizen's Europe reflects the conditions of the exercise of citizenship outside of the limits of the nation-state according to a double ideological heritage: (1) a broadly liberal consensus that views citizenship as a means to control executive powers, as much national as European, and (2) the progressive current that since the eighteenth century has pleaded in favor of the defense of particular interests for the

---

[18] The chancellor and then president of the Austrian Republic (1945), Karl Renner, belonged to the reforming wing of the Social-Democrat Party. Before the war he and Otto Bauer edited the journal *Der Kampf*. His basic ideas are set out in *La fonction sociale du droit* (1904).

common good. These two traditions are reactivated today by the debate on the "democratic deficit" of the European Union.

The latest variation of pro-national European nationalism is the attempt to bypass the nation-state from the bottom, that is to say, from the regions. The argument is simple: the nation-state is becoming outmoded, its historicity leading it to a rapid obsolescence after the European and worldwide developments brought about by globalization. The construction of Europe could accelerate this process by redefining new territorial boundaries. Furthermore, according to its adherents, the resurgence of regional identities would favor greater democratic expression, by permitting more direct participation by citizens (local referendum theory) and a better understanding of national and infranational diversities.

The Maastricht Treaty thus took a decisive step toward the recognition of infranational autonomist aspirations in creating a Regional Committee. This move was preceded by an initiative on the part of the Council of Europe. Having long supported the creation of cooperative transnational organizations, the Council in 1985 initiated the Assembly of European Regions. The opening of economic representation offices in Brussels by certain regions, such as Catalonia and Languedoc-Roussillon, also illustrates this evolution toward an increasingly active role for subnational entities on transregional bases. One example is the cooperation institutionalized between the members of the European Quadrige (Bade Wurtemburg, Lombardy, the Rhone-Alps region, and Catalonia) created in 1988. This process is still too recent to assess an eventual outcome. Will it lead, as the Council has always hoped, to the emergence of new infranational solidarities united at a supranational level? Or will it result in the further narrowing of European space in the name of tribal regionalism, which will further complicate a decision-making process already made cumbersome by the addition of a supplementary level of bureaucracy?

THE PREDICAMENT OF EUROPEAN NATIONALISM TODAY

The two forms of European nationalism presented here are by no means mutually exclusive. They may coexist within the same Europeanist movement, party, or policy. Their common denominator lies in a reexamination of the bond between state and nation. This bond, formed slowly over the course of history, seems to be unraveling.

Nation-states cannot make full use of their powers as long as politics, including the politics of European elections, continues to be perceived within an essentially narrow national framework—despite the operation of the economy at a worldwide level.[19] Furthermore, the ability of the nation-state to adapt itself to new modes of governance is again being questioned. This brings us back to the question of citizen participation.

The state has not always existed, and it does not have to be the only form of political expression that can legitimate control over all political, economic, and social regulatory functions. If state sovereignty is limited *de facto* by the effects of globalization, what purpose is there in defending it? Such is the essential predicament of European nationalism today. This raises a delicate question: what could replace the nation-state if the European Union is but the sum of nation-states?

The main problem is not the future of state sovereignty but the defense of democracy within the European Union and within its member states. The persistent debate between unionists and federalists should be a thing of the past. It belongs to a historical phase in the construction of Europe but is overdetermined by its own history. Outside the political structure of the Union as it is currently constituted, the traditional meaning of national sovereignty has been largely obliterated, even if the constitutional texts of the member states still pay lip service to its continuing existence. Often confused with the sovereignty of the state, national sovereignty saw its field of application reduced as the Union's rights were increased. It is therefore useless to continue to insist that national sovereignty is incarnated by the state in the international arena and by the people within the limits of the nation.

One solution, perhaps, would be to rethink and to revitalize popular sovereignty on a European scale in order to balance declining state sovereignty and to maintain democratic participation within a postnational framework. For the European Union to become a social reality, objectively and emotionally, a *real* social European body must emerge, duly represented by a Parliament with wide legislative powers. The present confusion about nationality and citizenship precludes this. History reminds us that the two notions have more often been dissociated than associated.

Derived from the Latin *natio*, the term "nationality" did not originally designate a state grouping of any sort. It was used merely to indicate the provenance of individuals. By the eighteenth century, however, as a consequence of the creation and consolidation of the modern nation-state, a

---

[19] It is necessary to relate the concept of "modernity" to what is now called "globalization." Fernand Braudel rightly pointed out that economic space has always overlapped political space even in the early-modern world. The correspondence between national political structures and national economic structures was not properly established until the seventeenth and eighteenth centuries, and they have never coincided completely. Fernand Braudel, *Grammaire des civilisations* (Paris: Flammarion, 1993).

semantic shift had taken place, and the word acquired most of its modern meanings. The *Encyclopédie* defined "nation" as "a considerable number of people who inhabit a certain extent of territory, enclosed within specific limits and bound by a single government." Since the nineteenth century, "nation" has come to describe two complementary elements: first, the infrastructure of a community (political, juridical, and above all emotional) united by a common history and a shared set of values and, second, allegiance to a state authority that rules over the territory on which the inhabitants of that nation reside.

The most economical definition of "citizenship" is the rights derived from, and the civic duties owed to, any given political community. (Of course, the content of these rights and duties has constantly varied over time.) A citizen was not merely a member of a community; he or she also possessed the right—and the obligation—to participate in the life of the *Res Publica*. By the end of the nineteenth century, the relationship between nationality and citizenship had been inverted: nationality conditioned citizenship. Only in the twentieth century, with the progressive enlargement of the franchise, did all the members of the democratic nations acquire the full status of citizenship. (Women, in France, for instance were not given the vote until 1944.)

Today the classical shape of the nation-state is changing. Why not, therefore, try to define the characteristics of a postnational citizenship? As Jürgen Habermas has pointed out, "if democratic citizenship doesn't necessarily root itself in a national identity of the people, notwithstanding a plurality of cultural forms, it requires nevertheless a socialisation of individuals in a common political culture."[20] To be acceptable, this common political culture cannot be associated with one national cultural model. For its part, the successful emergence of a common European political culture would suppose the existence of three conditions.

The first condition is the replacement of merely national politics by means of a cultural program whose purpose would be to generate a new form of allegiance, independent of the present nation-state structure. This would necessarily involve the rewriting of most national histories as they are currently conceived. The European Union should cease to be represented as the outcome of some teleological development toward a democratic consensus. It is instead the creation of an act of will and therefore should be, in Ernest Renan's phrase, "a daily plebiscite" in order to

---

[20] Jürgen Habermas, "Citizenship and National Identity: Some Reflections on the Future Europe," *Praxis Internationale* 12 (1) (April 1992): 1–19.

provide a substitute for that emotional dimension whose absence is one of the causes of the famous "democratic deficit."

Second, the European Union must make itself more accessible, and a great deal more intelligible, to its members, most of whom at present have very little idea of what it is and how it is constituted. Conversely, however, a postnational European citizenship makes no sense so long as there exists a clear distinction between nationality and citizenship. At present the concept of a European people is highly unstable. Moreover, according to Article 8 of the Maastricht Treaty, one can be a European citizen only if one is also a citizen of the country in which one resides. The constitutional innovation brought about by the treaty is a real one, but it is also unbalanced because the rules of access to citizenship vary from country to country. It is not possible to define the reciprocity of the rights of *Europeans* while each country has its own conception of what "European nationality" and "European citizens" mean. At present, despite the ever-increasing power of the various European institutions, a European "state" in the classical sense of the term does not exist. It remains an open question whether a right without a state can create a postnational citizenship.

Third, the current confusion between sovereignty and identity must be resolved. Inherited, for the most part, from the struggle for national emancipation, this confusion tends to obscure the distinction between cultural identity and political power. Yet if a postnational Europe is to exist, it must be generally accepted that culturally different national communities can exist within the same political community. What is required if this is to become a reality is one political frame of reference, but *several* allegiances to different cultural orders.

European nationalism faces another difficulty as well. The de-Sovietization of Eastern Europe has raised a number of elementary questions. What is it to be "European"? Where now are Europe's frontiers? European history is more than the history of European unity. The instrumentalization of memory in the countries of Eastern European has provoked a "return of history." Every ethnic, religious, social, and political group claims a specific identity within a national identity that is necessarily plural and therefore conflictual.

Beyond the political and economic problems created by the possible enlargement of the European Union lies the necessity of creating strong European symbols, strong enough to transcend self-regarding local identities. Since the eighteenth century, political nationalism has used culture and cultural symbols to legitimate institutions and governments. Today, however, European nationalism is very far from its symbols. Apart from a flag, a hymn, and a few festivals that occur only intermittently, the European Union offers little that can inspire collective enthusiasm. It takes longer to accept a symbol than a Brussels regulation, if it is accepted at all. But it is the only way to ground a real European identity and, perhaps, to limit the upsurge of aggressive national nationalisms. The European Union must become a visual and compelling identity. It needs myths as strong as those that sustain the individual nations of which it is composed. As Condorcet observed, "Citizens are not born; they are created through instruction."[21] *Homo Europeanus* is still waiting to be made.

[21] Quoted by Catherine Withol de Wenden, *La Citoyenneté européenne* (Paris: Presses de Sciences of Po, 1997), 88.

9

From the Ironies of Identity to the
Identities of Irony

LUISA PASSERINI

> Europe, Europe as you watch me
> descend helpless and lost into one of my
> Frail myths among the hordes of beasts,
> I am a son of yours in flight who has no
> Enemy other than his own sadness.
>
> Vittorio Sereni, *Diario d'Algeria*
> August 1942

When this poem was written, Europe was in the midst of a civil war between "hordes of beasts" (the Fascists) on one side and the anti-Fascists on the other, and its fate depended on the outcome of this conflict. The idea of a united Europe had been seized upon by both the Nazis and the Fascists in the period between the two wars, as well as during the war itself. Two examples of this are the Convegno Volta, a conference on Europe organized in 1932 under the auspices of the Fascist regime in Rome and the projects presented by Goebbels and Von Ribbentrop in 1942–3 for a "new Europe" to be united under Nazi dominion.[1] Those who resisted the various types of Fascism and claimed to be "sons" of Europe could count on only a "frail myth"—if I may be allowed to extend Sereni's metaphor—and this myth projected a possible Europe and possible Europeanness into a completely uncertain future. At that time the sense of belonging to Europe was more of a wager than a reference to a given reality.

An earlier version of this essay was published as the introduction to the anthology *Identità culturale europea: idee, sentimenti, relazioni* (Firenze: La Nuova Italia, 1998). Poems quoted in the text have been taken from *Poeti italiani del secondo Novecento 1945–1955*, edited by Maurizio Cucchi and Stefano Giovanardi (Milano: Mondadori, 1996). The author thanks Nicki Owtram of the Language Centre at the European University Institute in Florence for translating the poems into English.

[1] Walter Lipgens, *Documents on the History of European Integration*, vol. 1: *Continental Plans for European Union, 1939–1945* (Berlin–New York: Walter de Gruyter, 1985).

The tradition of a united Europe was centuries old, but the First World War had reduced it to ashes. The many attempts to revive it between the two wars included Richard Coudenhove-Kalergi's Pan-Europe of 1923 and the proposal for a United States of Europe made to the League of Nations by Aristide Briand.[2] These efforts were accompanied by a wide debate on the possibility of turning Europe into an autonomous cultural and political subject, an alternative to the choice between the United States and the Soviet Union or, for others, between the United States and Nazi Germany. The Second World War dashed once again any hopes for this tradition of a united Europe, but it contemporaneously gave rise to a new wave of Europeanism. Taking the patrimony of debates on federalism in Great Britain at the end of the thirties in organizations such as the Federal Union,[3] anti-Fascists imprisoned on the island of Ventotene drafted the *Manifesto*, which proposed the idea of a European federation. This was in the summer of 1941, exactly one year before the poem by Sereni was composed. The *Manifesto di Ventotene*, as it became known, with its stress on democracy and equality, reminds us of the legacy of ideas that emerged during the European resistance.

In this chapter three levels of discussion will be identified: (1) the concrete procedure of the unification of Europe, (2) the different ideas and ideologies regarding a united Europe, and (3) European cultural identity. The link between the idea of a united Europe and the institutional reality of the European Union has at times been underrated, as if the latter was simply the result of member states' calculations to maintain their wealth and security. Perry Anderson, however, has claimed that current European construction is inexplicable if the federalist vision of Jean Monnet and his small group of technocrats is not taken into account. Anderson has also observed that ideas did indeed play a role in the history of European integration. They were the result of the political and intellectual elites, not of the popular masses. European public opinion began to emerge as unanimous for the first time only after the collapse of the Soviet system, thus apparently demonstrating approval for some degree of opening toward the Eastern bloc. All the same, this opinion has been expressed by the media, above all the press, rather than by the wider public or the electorate. The problem of the different levels therefore intersects with

---

[2] Carl Hamilton Pegg, *Evolution of the European Idea, 1914–1932* (Chapel Hill–London: University of North Carolina Press, 1983); and Sergio Pistone, ed., *L'idea dell'unificazione europea dalla prima alla seconda guerra mondiale* (Torino: Fondazione Luigi Einaudi, 1975).

[3] Andres Bosco, *The Federal Idea*, vol. 1: *The History of Federalism from the Enlightenment to 1945* (London–New York: Lothian Foundation Press, 1991).

that of a potential European public sphere, where institutions, ideas, and ways of feeling can exist in various and connected ways.[4]

THE IDEA OF EUROPE AND EUROPEAN IDENTITY

The construction of a united Europe began during the postwar period and proceeded in stages from the founding of the European Economic Community in 1957, to the election of the first European Parliament with universal suffrage in 1979,[5] to the Maastricht Treaty in 1992. This construction was accompanied by an increasing feeling of uncertainty over just what it was that represented European particularity in the cultural field and what it meant to be European. The great histories of the idea of Europe, and the collections of documents and examples of the past published in the twenty years following the Second World War, reflect a much less problematic attitude toward the idea of a European specificity than during the decades following this.[6] It was during the sixties that "European identity" began to be posed as a problem, together with the debate on "identity"—a term little used until the fifties. It began to be used more frequently as a result of the new social, cultural, ethnic, and regional movements.

As Robert Picht has written, identity can be compared to health: one becomes aware of its disturbing elements only through the confrontation with transformations that throw into doubt its presumed normality.[7] When human beings feel unrooted, they try to reassure themselves by identifying enemies and dangers and by declaring their loyalty to collective organisms. Frequently, then, these identifications are of a regressive nature and express the need for self-protection against the unknown. Indeed, I believe the growing debate about European "identity" and the use of the term in appropriate and inappropriate contexts (many texts with

[4] Perry Anderson, "Under the Sign of the Interim," *London Review of Books*, vol. 18, no. 1, 4 January 1966; and "The Europe to Come," *London Review of Books*, vol. 18, no. 2, 25 January 1966.

[5] Edmondo Paolini, *L'idea di Europa: Nascita e sviluppi* (Firenze: La Nuova Italia, 1979); and idem, *La realtà Europa: dai trattati di Roma alla Federazione europea* (Roma: Edime, 1983).

[6] See Carlo Curcio, *Europa. Storia di un'idea* (Firenze: Vallecchi, 1958); Federico Chabod, *Storia dell'idea d'Europa* (Bari: Laterza, 1961); Jean-Baptiste Duroselle, *L'idée d'Europe dans l'histoire* (Paris: Denoel, 1965); and Bernard Voyenne, *Histoire de l'idée européenne* (Paris: Payot, 1964). See also Denis de Rougemont, *Vingt-huit siècles d'Europe* (Paris: Payot, 1961).

[7] Robert Picht, *Disturbed Identities: Social and Cultural Mutations in Contemporary Europe*, in Soledad Garcia, ed., *European Identity and the Search for Legitimacy* (London: Pinter, 1993), 81–94.

the term in their title fail to offer any sustained discussion of it) are a sign of uncertainty and discomfort on the one hand and regressive operations to protect old values on the other.

In 1973 the European Community (as the Union was called when it was composed of only nine members) issued a *Declaration on European Identity* that was approved in Copenhagen. It represented an attempt to define a European specificity despite the unavoidable contradictions of Eurocentrism. The *Declaration* was based "on the principles of the unity of the Nine," on their "responsibilities with regard to the rest of the world," and on the "dynamic nature of the construction of Europe."[8] Admitting a diversity of cultures, the *Declaration* answered the "basic necessity to ensure the survival of the civilisation which [the Nine] have in common." The identity of Europe, according to this document, should be based on a common heritage: identical attitudes toward life, converging on the creation of a society responding to the needs of individuals; the principles of representative democracy, the rule of the law, social justice, and respect for human rights. At this point, an "essential part" of Europe's supposed identity was represented by a common market based on a customs union, established institutions, as well as policies and machinery for cooperation.

The first sections of the *Declaration* repeated presuppositions that were already familiar and acceptable in the main. The rest of it established a hierarchy of relations with the rest of the world. The first aim was to intensify ties with those European countries with whom friendly and cooperative relations already existed. Then came the aim of maintaining and strengthening the historic links with the Mediterranean and African countries and with the Middle East. The "close ties" with the United States—a country that shared the values and aspirations of a common heritage—were held to be "mutually beneficial." They should be preserved "on the basis of equality and in a spirit of friendship." With Japan and Canada "close cooperation and constructive dialogue" were foreseen; with the Union of Soviet Socialist Republics (USSR) and the countries forming the Eastern bloc, a policy of détente; with China, "exchanges in various fields"; with other Asian countries, the extension of already existing commercial relations; with Latin America, and in particular with several countries in the same area, an increase in "friendly" relations. As for "the less favoured nations," the Nine declared the

---

[8] *Declaration on European Identity*, in *Bulletin EC* 12 (1973): 118–22.

"importance of the struggle against under-development" through trade and financial aid. The last point announced that the European identity "will evolve as a function of the dynamic of the construction of a united Europe."

The competitive and hierarchical nature of the *Declaration* has been criticized on the grounds that in it relations with the rest of the world are organized according to a descending scale from "equality and friendship" to "aid." Other criticisms concern the concept of identity and its legitimizing use in this context.[9] The potentially flattening as well as normative character of the concept of "identity" has sometimes led to a preference for the terms "identification" or "subjectivity."[10] Here I will use the term "identity" in order to participate in the debate around this term. Thus its use will be critical and deconstructive, and I will attempt to avoid all references to identity as a simple function or product of the European Union or as a base that is instrumental for its legitimation.

The Declaration on European Identity highlights dangers implicit in attaching the notion of European identity to the idea (and the reality) of a united Europe. Connections between the two clearly do exist, but each remains relatively independent of the other. The theme of a united Europe is in force in the political, social, economic, and cultural fields, while identity refers to a field that is at the same time wider and narrower. Identity moves from everyday life in its material and emotional aspects to "high" and "low" cultural forms of the elites and the masses. The advantage of keeping separate the identity and the idea of Europe—one of the main themes of this chapter—is that in this way the discourse on European identity can keep its distance from political projects and their realization. The tension that derives from this allows a reciprocal critical attention between such discourse and such projects.

A similar distance must be maintained between the historical forms of European identity and forms that are possible for the future. Attempts to found the future forms on cultural characteristics that are already given cannot but give rise to a sense of unease over the resulting appropriation, or the incongruity of the past with respect to the present. The central example of this is the identification of Europe with modernity and progress,

---

[9] Lutz Niethammer, *Konjunkturen und Konkurrenzen kollektiver Identitaet*, in *Philosophische Fakultaet Antrittsvorlesungen I* (Jena: Friedrich Schiller Universitaet, 1967), 169–215.

[10] Homi Bhabha, "The Third Space," in Jonathan Rutherford, ed., *Identity: Community, Culture, Difference* (London: Lawrence & Wishart, 1990), 207–21; and Luisa Passerini, *Storia e soggettività* (Firenze: La Nuova Italia, 1988).

an equation at least as old as the Enlightenment. Europe, however, is no longer at the center or the vanguard of modernity.[11] This identification has, therefore, lost its meaning.

In reaction to the loss of old identifications, the trend has been not to search for one single value capable of organizing an entire cultural universe, but to choose a way by which to accumulate various specificities. One example of this is an interesting attempt in Denmark at the beginning of the sixties to analyze "European ideas"—a long list of concepts including modern science, Christianity, human rights, evolution, imperialism, the subconscious, youth revolt, and so on.[12] Or consider the list of adjectives used by Richard Hoggart and Douglas Johnson to connote the European continent: "fragile, restless, contradictory, inconsistent."[13] To what other continents could they not also apply? The problem is that comparisons in which a clear definition of the second term is missing have always been a characteristic of Eurocentrism. Definitions of identity based on such conceptions run the risk of reproducing rhetorical formulae that are either empty or suspect.

Even "European ideology," defined by Norberto Bobbio as centered on the government of liberty, the antithesis of which was for centuries "Oriental Despotism," has worn out in the second half of this century.[14] So has a sense of guilt linked to the experiences of totalitarianism and decolonialization. One can only agree with Bronislaw Geremek when he rejects claims, based on the presupposition that totalitarian systems would be a total negation of the European tradition, that the Nazi system and the Gulag archipelago flagrantly contradict the spirit and sentiment of Europe.[15] On the contrary, "the dialectics of the Enlightenment" typical of the European tradition should be accepted, which includes the contemporaneous development of terror and emancipation, and therefore a central role in the European memory should be assigned to the Shoah and other processes of persecution and emargination. However, a collective memory of all this presents itself today as a difficult and dangerous battlefield in which opposing identities may well arise.

---

[11] Göran Therborn, "Modernità sociale in Europa (1950–1993)," in *Storia d'Europa*, vol. 1: *L'Europa oggi* (Torino: Einaudi, 1993), 461–613.

[12] Erik Lund, Pihl Morgens, and Johannes Slok, eds., *A History of European Ideas* (London: Hurst & Co., 1962).

[13] Richard Hoggart and Douglas Johnson, *An Idea of Europe* (London: Chatto, 1987).

[14] Norberts Bobbio "Grandezza e decadenza dell'ideologia europea," in *Lettera internazionale* 3 (1986): 1–5.

[15] Bronislaw Geremek, "L'Europa e la sua memoria," in *L'Ateneo*, XIII, 2 (1967), 2–19 and Idem, *Le radici comuni dell'Europa* (Milano: Il Saggiatore, 1991).

It is no coincidence that, in order to emerge from the aporiae of European identity, a pattern of insistence on a characterization that seems to pertain more to formality than to content has continued to develop: that of so-called European multiplicity. The tradition of Europe as a *unitas multiplex* is a long one. Take, for example, Diderot. Under the entry for *Législateur* in the *Encyclopédie*, he wrote on the diversity of European governments—republics and monarchies—that gave rise to a wide range of sentiments and customs. Diderot believed that as a result of such diversity in Europe, wars would always occur ("il y aura toujours des guerres en Europe"). Recently, the theme of the diversity of Europe has been reopened in connection with historical phenomena such as the fall of the Soviet regime, the accompanying explosions of nationalisms and regionalisms, the growing number of member states in the European Union, and the new waves of migrants from the East and the South. The diversity theme has reappeared in the context of an intercultural understanding and has lent itself to new interpretations.

The very title of Hans-Georg Gadamer's 1985 essay *Die Vielfalt Europas* (The Diversity of Europe) confirms the thesis that Europe has always been characterized by such linguistic variety as to oblige it to undertake the hard task of learning coexistence. According to Gadamer, the cultural destiny of Europe was formed through the distinction and dialectics between various areas of human creativity, in particular between philosophy and science. Science lay at the base of a coherent European identity. The situation in China was very different: None of the great masters there could be called a poet rather than a thinker or a theologian rather than a knower.[16] The general objective outlined by Gadamer was "to experience the other and the others, as the other of our self, in order to participate with one another."[17] Today that objective and the intermediate one of developing the heritage of regions and single groups and their ways of life in order to oppose the tendency toward leveling out are important. Yet the statement that the "spiritual unity" of Europe is "already a reality as well as a duty," where the terms "reality" and "duty" seem to be placed on the same level, is unacceptable.[18] The concrete existence of a spiritual unity has been clamorously belied by the historical events of the twentieth century. Moreover, this kind of claim goes against modern

---

[16] Hans-Georg Gadamer, "The Diversity of Europe: Inheritance and Future," in *Hans-Georg Gadamer on Education, Poetry, and History: Applied Hermeneutics* (Albany: State University of New York Press, 1992), 225.

[17] Ibid., 238.

[18] Hans-Georg Gadamer, *L'eredità dell'Europa* (Torino: Einaudi, 1991).

sensitivity. If we want to avoid all risks of essentialism, spiritual unity neither can nor should be taken for granted; it can only be understood and undertaken as a duty, mainly in regard to the future and always with a critical approach to the forms that have preceded it.

Gadamer's elegant formulation succeeds, however, in avoiding the triumphalism, almost the self-satisfaction, that less shrewd versions of European multiplicity exhibit. One version of this, exemplified by Paul Hazard's *La crise de la conscience européenne* (The European Mind),[19] is the definition of the European as a "multiform and evolutive personality" determined by an ideal, a definition connected to the concept of the European conscience as an incessant search for happiness and truth.[20] Another case is that of the interpretation of the "unity and multiplicity of Europe" offered by Cees Noteboom in *Come si diventa europei?* (How does one become a European?), a reference not only to the polyphonous chorus of European languages and the resulting polyhedral experience of learning them, but also to a hybrid lifestyle that derives from spending the winter in Amsterdam and Berlin and the summer in Spain.[21] No longer is it possible to share this facile optimism about such privileged experiences, even if they do follow experiences of oppression and positions of resistance. In reality, such statements simply reflect a nostalgia for the ease with which it was possible to travel in Europe without a passport before the First World War. One only has to think of the experience of migrants, whose migrations have been undertaken for reasons of political or economic necessity, for the multiplicity of languages to take on quite another meaning.

Ursula Hirschmann, one of the founders of the European Federalist Movement at the beginning of the forties and the founder of the group known as *Femmes pour l'Europe* in 1970, focused her attention on this experience. In a political meeting she suddenly understood why it was so much easier for her to be "European" than for the others: "I had to speak, and I realised that I could not do so in even one language." She had lost, as it were, her German mother tongue, which had become "flat and unflexible" as a result of living abroad for so long, while Italian, the language in which her children had been brought up, felt foreign to her. After likening herself to a Jewish friend in the sense that he was a "wandering European," Hirschmann concluded with a declaration of the "Europeanization of the rootless." "We *deracinés* of Europe, who 'have crossed the borders more often than we have changed our shoes' (Brecht),

[19] Paul Hazard, *La crise de la conscience européenne 1680–1715* (Paris: Fayard, 1961).
[20] Philippe Moreau Defarges, *L'Europe et son identité dans le monde* (Paris: S.T.H., 1983).
[21] Cees Noteboom, *Come si diventa europei?* (Milano: Linea d'ombra, 1994), 15.

have nothing to lose," she writes, "than our chains in a federalist Europe, and so it is that we are federalists."[22] The multiplicity of languages in Europe is expressed here in terms of suffering and alienation, of rootlessness and loss that have been the lot of many in the European history of the twentieth century. A list of these people would include Jews, women, immigrants from within and beyond Europe, refugees, the dispersed, and the "uncultured." This partial list of "others," historically present in Europe in a subordinate and conflictual position, suggests that a break is necessary: a gesture of radical discontinuity needs to be made before one can make a credible claim that the diversity of the European continent is valuable.

As a result, the problem of European identity accepts the solution offered by the formula of *multiple identity* only as a first approximation. In reference to Europeanness, Anthony Smith, among others, notes that the number and extension of currently possible cultural identities have increased.[23] Identities based on gender and generation remain vital, and even those based on class and religion continue to be influential. In addition, professional, civic, and ethnic identities have proliferated, attracting increasingly large groups from all over the world. While national identification is still frequently the political and cultural norm that transcends and organizes other loyalties, human beings maintain a multiplicity of belongings that tend to push the national one into the background. In regard to this central problem, the concept of "multiple identity" limits itself to underlining the quality of tolerance and to expressing possibilities. It remains, however, conceptually undifferentiated and undefined, as does its correlate, multiculturalism. Both terms, and the concepts to which they refer, lack a sufficiently explicit description of the power disparity between the subjects and the forms of subjectivity that they denote.

Given this situation, it is not surprising that the notion of a truly contemporary European identity is occasionally denied; according to some, no sentiment of European identity is in line with the modernization of continental affairs—a view seemingly confirmed by the fact that Europe is only marginally present in school curricula.[24] According to others, the European consciousness—however defined or justified—is none other that a form of group partiality, a kind of nationalism on a vast scale that includes some and excludes others, thereby negating every authentic

---

[22] Ursula Hirschmann, *Noi senza patria* (Bologna: il Mulino, 1993), 21–2.

[23] Anthony Douglas Smith, "National Identity and the Idea of European Unity," in *International Affairs* 68 (1992): 55–76.

[24] Sven Papcke, "Who Needs European Identity and What Could It Be?" in Brian Nelson, David Roberts, and Walter Veit, eds., *The Idea of Europe* (Oxford: Berg, 1992), 61–74.

universalism.[25] These negative opinions are often based on the impossibility of developing a European identity with the same level of emotional impact as that made by national identities. Yet, as Hartmut Kaeeble and Gian Enrico Rusconi have reminded us in two different ways, this is not the real problem.[26]

EUROPE AND ITS OTHERS

Signatures are not enough
appeals are of no use
to rid us of our smooth guilt;
the intellectual is guilty, for centuries Europe
with its principles has been guilty, the missionary
who preaches resignation is guilty, the state
which preaches segregation is guilty, the army
which crushes to be obedient is guilty.
Racial hatred plunges down onto us once more.

Nelo Risi, *Dentro la sostanza*, 1965

These lines and the date on which they were published—in the middle of a decade characterized by anti-imperialist struggles worldwide—reflect a distancing from Eurocentric attitudes that has continued well beyond this period, even if in ways that are sometimes blunted and submerged. Indeed, this distancing may be one of the main impediments to developing a concept that can advance a positive proposal for a European identity. Eurocentric attitudes continue to exist more or less implicitly, however. Although they were rejected, they were never discussed or analyzed in any great detail. Above all, their rejection was a reaction to the criticism that came from beyond—that is, from those who had been designated as "others" by the Eurocentric subject: "what characterised the experience of the Europeans was also the experience of its victims."[27]

On the cultural level the victims were often made such in the course of processes of assimilation that at the same time privileged and recompensed them, thus rendering the use of the term "victim" incongruous at first sight. Indeed, the "Other" was often to be found within Europe itself.

[25] Nico Wilterdink, *An Examination of European and National Identity*, "Archives européennes de sociologie," XXXIV, 1 (1993), 119–36. See also Ariane Chebel d'Appollonia's chapter in this volume.

[26] Gian Enrico Rusconi, "Cittadinanza e costituzione," in Luisa Passerini, ed., *Identità culturale europea*, 133–53; and Hartmut Kaeeble, "Periodizzazione e tipologia," in ibid., 29–46.

[27] Jack Goody, "La cultura europea nel secolo XX," in *Storia d'Europa*, vol. 1: *L'Europa oggi* (Torino: Einaudi, 1993), 815.

In order to understand the process of Europeanization from this viewpoint—as a leveling down of other cultures to the Western one—it is useful to read the criticism, drafted in Moscow in 1909–10 and published in Sofia in 1920, that Trubeckoj made of Eurocentric attitudes. Only by means of a "negative orientation" such as the kind that he proposed, which tends "to place the reader in front of a void,"[28] can a process that today would be called deconstructionist be initiated, as the initial premise for a process of subsequent construction whose direction cannot be prefigured except by its protagonists. Even for Trubeckoj, the essay in which both egocentricism and eccentrism (the placing of the center beyond oneself, in this case into Western Europe) were rejected formed only the first part of a trilogy—unfinished on account of his premature death.

The controversy over the eastern border of Europe goes back centuries, but the formula "from the Atlantic to the Urals" still has not lost its attraction. As the process that began in 1989 of dismantling the Soviet empire and reunifying the two Germanies and potentially Europe suggests, federative events to date have been based on Western Europe alone. This has made the question of what it means to be "European" even more difficult to answer. The war in the former Yugoslavia tragically illustrates the possibility and reality of inter-European conflicts of all dimensions. All this accentuates the need for distance between the European construction on the one hand and identity as a dimension of culture and subjectivization on the other. What kind of Europeanness is capable of embracing both the West and the East (including Russia) in cultural terms? This question should be explored immediately. Similarly, there exists no immediate obstacle to suggestions as to how best to integrate scattered items and common experiences without, at the same time, negating the discontinuity of the continent (as has been shown visually by the beautiful atlas of Central and Eastern Europe by Michel Foucher).[29]

For many years forms of European identity were built up through contrasts, such as "Orientalism" versus "Occidentalism."[30] Europe's "Other" varied from an image of Asia, to an image of Africa, to an image of America—or of peoples of these continents. Europeans' ambivalence

[28] Nikolai Trubeckoj, *L'Europa e l'umanità* (Torino: Einaudi, 1982). In these essays both egocentricism and eccentrism (the placing of the center beyond oneself, in this case into Western Europe) were rejected. The essays formed the first part of a trilogy that remained unfinished because of the author's premature death.

[29] Michel Foucher, ed., *Fragments d'Europe: Atlas de l'europe médiane et orientale* (Paris: Fayard, 1993).

[30] Richard J. Mayne, *The Europeans: Who Are We?* (London: Weidenfeld & Nicolson, 1972).

toward these others manifested itself in two different but indivisible relations. One is the area of concrete relations (political, military, socio-
economic, and missionary) with non-European peoples through colonial
expansion. The other is the area of the imagination, which created images deriving not from observation or experience but from psychological
drives.[31] The Other was therefore both the primitive, considered as a
holder of positive values with which to rejuvenate a corrupt civilization
and a touchstone for the level of progress reached by Europe, and the
savage to be exploited, converted, and "civilized." The very translation
of customs and attitudes of others into the languages of Europe—with
their own metaphors, stylistic characteristics, and forms of inertia—was
a way of assimilation that took place through the accounts of travelers,
missionaries, and anthropologists.[32]

The figure of the Other was projected onto the country that overtook
Europe on the road to modernity and progress—the United States. This
projection was so strong that it created in Europe persistent trends of anti-
Americanism.[33] In reality, these trends are often ways to claim *ex negativo*
forms of European identity or to express the crisis in which the very idea
of Europe now found itself. It is for this reason that the concept of "the
West," which includes Europe and North America and particularly the
United States, is ambiguous and conflictual. For this reason it deserves further investigation in order to clarify the aporiae and contradictions that
historically have been at the base of the European identity. One part of
the "negative" patrimony constituted by the European representations of
Others can be reversed and translated so as to endow with value the processes of cultural interaction and remind us that an implicit Europeanness
can frequently become conscious—especially for the strata of the population that are less or not at all intellectual—only through the experience
of migration or travel to other continents.

The contributions made by "subaltern studies," in particular the
emphasis placed on the positionality of any scientific view, are essential to understand the relationship between Europe and its Others.[34]
It would also seem useful to make use of the discourse on critical

---

31 Ernest Henri Philippe Baudet, *Paradise on Earth: Some Thoughts on European Images
of Non-European Man* (Westport, Conn.: Greenwood Press, 1965).
32 Talal Asad and J. Dixon, "Translating Europe's Others," in *Europe and Its Others*, vol. 1
(Colchester: University of Essex, 1984).
33 See Michela Nacci, *L'antiamericanismo in Italia negli anni trenta* (Torino: Bollati Bor-
inghieri, 1986); and idem, *La barbarie del comfort. Il modello di vista americano nella
cultura francese del '900* (Milano: Guerini, 1996).
34 Gavatri C. Spivak, "Can the Subaltern Speak?" in Nelson Cary and Larry Crossberg,
eds., *Marxism and the Interpretation of Culture* (Urbana: University of Illinois Press,
1988), 271–313.

ethnocentricism proposed by Ernesto De Martino in Italy. For De Martino, "European centrism"—inasmuch as it has always made reference to a privileged relation with the divine—has excluded "confrontation between human beings" and has compromised "the fight against the dispersion of peoples." In contrast, the unification of peoples and cultures presents itself as a concrete duty and a task that we must fulfill, not as a plan pre-established by God or materialism, for any history is constantly at risk of losing any kind of sense without the active intervention of human beings. The onset of this task is based on a twofold presupposition. First, one cannot help being ethnocentric. Second, one can make critical use of Western interpretative categories by going beyond "the scandal of reciprocal incomprehension, the extreme scarcity of common memories," and by accepting the sentiment of "guilt and remorse towards the 'separated brother'." The objective is "therefore neither a dogmatic Eurocentricism nor an unrelated cultural relativism" but "a critical European centrism" aimed at founding a new solidarity in human relations on our planet.[35]

While I agree entirely with De Martino's idea that in this undertaking "it is not a question of eliminating the West but of questioning it deeply, and of becoming aware of the limits of its humanism, which to date has been corporative," I also believe that it is no longer possible (as it probably was at the beginning of the sixties) to give back to the West "its compromised hegemonic power."[36] De Martino's proposal, however, must be corrected in the sense that the loss of the role that Europe held as "center" must be fully admitted to the benefit of the search for its cultural specificities and without any pretensions of superiority. What is left as ethnocentric is the point of view of the individual and her story, connoted by belonging to a certain gender, generation, and social and geographical collocation.[37]

This approach stakes out a perspective for cultural identity that locates the Other within the subject,[38] and it links identity with alterity. The break with the expectation of the superiority of one's own tradition is accompanied by the assertion of one's heritage and the possibility of correcting this assertion through the reciprocity of intercultural exchanges. For example, the value of peace—mediated by the consideration of other

[35] Ernesto De Martino, *La fine del mondo: contributo all'analisi delle apocalissi culturali* (Torino: Einaudi, 1977), 393.

[36] Ibid., 352.

[37] Luisa Passerini, *Europe in Love, Love in Europe: Aspects of Cultural History in 1930s Britain* (London: Tauris, 1998).

[38] Romano Màdera, *L'Alchimia ribelle* (Bari: Palomar, 1997).

world cultures and by European minorities—can be integrated into the European tradition, which has been mainly warlike, sparing only the wars of the critical spirit and claiming from our past only the arms of criticism while rejecting the criticism done through arms. From this perspective European cultural identity would be able to take a step forward toward the world and make a commitment for the unification of humanity, although no longer in the guise of a counterposition or a hegemony. Such a step would act as a reversal of most of European history and as a duty to be undertaken toward the future.

From this view, the proposals for Europe and its institutions to act as intermediaries between local, regional, national, and global levels make sense. It also becomes meaningful to situate the cultural dimension of the European project between national or local revivals and cultural aspirations of a global dimension.[39] This kind of position renders obsolete the old debate between pan-Europeans and anti-Europeans (today the latter are often dressed up as Eurosceptics) and proposes a solution to the twofold need to render justice to universalistic aspirations and to find cultural roots.[40]

BEING EUROPEAN

Milan has sunsets of red gold.
One viewpoint just like another
were the vegetable gardens of the suburbs
after the large houses of the "Umanitaria."
Between hedges of sambuco and some small doorways
made of tin and broken shutters
the smell of a coffee factory
together with the distant sound of the foundries.
Because of that rust which reigned invisible
because of that sun which set larger
in Piedmont in France who knows where
it felt as though I was in Europe;
my mother knew very well
that I wouldn't be staying with her for much longer
and yet she smiled
against a background of dahlias and clustered violets.

Luciano Erba, *L'ippopotamo*, 1989

---

[39] Smith, "National Identity."
[40] Jacques Lenoble, "Penser l'identité et la démocratie en Europe," in Jacques Lenoble and Nicole Dewandre, eds., *L'Europe au soir du siècle* (Paris: Editions Esprit, 1992), 293–315.

From the viewpoint of the history of mentalities and attitudes, few peoples have held themselves to be at the center of a European specificity; most peoples have experienced and continue to experience Europe as something to which they belong, but where they also feel they represent something separate. This was true for many years of Great Britain,[41] but also of Portugal and Spain, and certainly of Greece.[42] European identity has long included hierarchies and exclusions—a "Europe-Europe" and a "lesser Europe."[43] Although in the last few decades the conviction that the center and the periphery are now everywhere has become stronger, for many the sense of not forming a full part of Europe is still marked. This sensation can be linked to the difficulties of participating in the European Union, a participation that is rendered problematic by, for example, monetary unification. It is not, however, only a matter of a reaction to material problems: there is also, and not only in Italy, the attribution of an ideal and normative value to Europe, as though taking an active part in it meant freeing oneself from weaknesses, public vices, and national ills.

In Italy great political and idealistic value has always been attributed to the Europeanness of the country and its culture, although in a dreamlike way, as in the poem just cited.[44] Today there is still—or perhaps it has simply resurfaced—a utopian coloring linked to the idea of entering Europe or "keeping pace with Europe" or managing to "catch the European train," some of the many metaphors in the debate on the constitution of forms of collaboration between the countries of the Union. Thus, a hope has been expressed. It has spread throughout daily life and into the opinions of the public at large. This hope may irritate the Eurosceptics, but it stimulates cultural historians.

That Europe catalyzes strong hopes, including hopes for "the introduction of the private into the political" and the integration of a female politics with equal rights on the same footing as male politics,[45] should not be seen as a political program capable of being acted upon

---

41 See Passerini, *Europe in Love, Love in Europe.*
42 See Michael Herzfeld's chapter in this volume and Herzfeld, *Cultural Intimacy: Social Poetics in the Nation-State* (New York–London: Routledge, 1997). With reference to the comment about Portugal and Spain, see Eduardo Lourenço, *L'Europe introuvable: jalons pour une mythologie européenne* (Paris: Métailié, 1991); Francisco Lucas Pires, *O qué é Europa* (Lisboa: Diffusao Cultural, 1992); and Luis Diez del Corral, *El rapto de Europa* (Madrid: Revista de Occidente, 1954).
43 Lourenço, *L'Europe introuvable*, 73.
44 Sergio Pistone, ed., *L'Italia e l'unità europea dalle premesse storiche all'elezione del parlamento europeo* (Torino: Loescher, 1982).
45 Karin Hausen, "Individuo-società-Stato: la questione femminile," 615–34, in *Storia d'Europa*, vol. 1: *L'Europa oggi* (Torino: Einaudi, 1993), 643.

immediately, but rather as a cultural condition revealing the potential of a united Europe, which can then diversify and move in different directions. The results may well depend on the kind of cultural commitment made by intellectuals, teachers, and cultural operators. There can be no doubt, for example, that pedagogic activity with regard to Europe in forms that include its emotional and relational aspects is virtually nonexistent in schools. However, the question of what to teach about Europe and its possible cultural identity is now being raised in secondary schools.[46]

In conclusion, I shall return to the discourse on European cultural identity, assuming that we have now moved sufficiently toward that "other heading" (to use the title of an essay by Derrida on the theme of identity). "Europe," claims Derrida, "has always recognised itself as a cape of headland."[47] The first "heading" was Europe itself, what Nietzsche, in *Beyond Good and Evil*, called that "small prominent peninsula which wishes at all costs to represent itself as 'mankind's progress' with respect to Asia." Moving to the other heading, therefore, could mean renouncing the claim to being the vanguard of progress and center of knowledge, and accepting that one's position can be found only on the other side.

In relation to this, Derrida's criticism of Valéry is extremely significant. Valéry had expressed what we might call the Eurocentric paradox: "our special quality (sometimes our ridicule, but often our finest claim or title) is to believe and to feel that we are universal—by which I mean: *men of universality*.... Notice the paradox: to specialise in the sense of the universal."[48] Derrida's response implies that "to be men of universality" cannot be the exclusive right of the Europeans, and he highlights the choice that even today divides the European conscience: to accept foreigners by assimilating them or to accept their otherness.

Derrida ends by accepting something of the multiple identity: "I am not, nor do I feel, European *in every part*, that is, European through and through." He continues, "my cultural identity—that in the name of which I speak—is not only European, it is not identical to itself.... I feel European *among other things*.... [I]t is up to the others, and up to me *among them*, to decide."[49] Multiplicity has here acquired a twofold

---

[46] Margaret Shennan, *Teaching about Europe* (London: Cassell, 1991).

[47] Jacques Derrida, *The Other Heading: Reflections on Today's Europe* (Bloomington and Indianapolis: Indiana University Press, 1992), 20. This is a translation of *L'Autre Cap* (Paris: Les Editions de Minuit, 1991). In French *cap* may mean a heading, in the sense of direction, or a headland or promontory.

[48] Derrida, *The Other Heading*, 74.   [49] Ibid., 82–3.

meaning. Firstly, in regard to European identity, belonging to the continent is not only not interpreted as being dominant, that is to say, it is not the value that hierarchically organizes a whole set of other values (as used to be the case, for instance, with the value of work in the phenomenology of oral and written autobiographies). Secondly, identity can include within the category of European the fact of being born in Africa, being male and of Jewish origin, as well as belonging to a certain generation and social class. This will hold, however, only if these definitions are not thrown together higgledy-piggledy in an exaltation of undifferentiated multiplicity—being European *among other things*—but instead lead to being *among the others* and to taking on roles that have traditionally been assigned to those who for many years represented the Other, such as Jews, women, and immigrants, and therefore siding with those who are *today* cast in the role of representing the Other.

Framing this perception in terms of the feminist tradition, Rosi Braidotti has written that European identity has always been "a notion fraught with contradictions" and has "never been *One*." Indeed, "its alleged unity was at best a poor fiction."[50] She believes that it has forged its position during the course of history as the center, not only of the world economy but also of thought, knowledge, and science. At the symbolic and discursive level, this implies that "others" are peripheral and underrated. At the roots of Braidotti's feeling of "Europeanness" is "not the triumphant assumption of a sovereign identity but rather the disenchanting experience of disidentifying myself with sovereignty all together." The Europe to which she feels she belongs is the place of possible forms of resistance to the systematic devaluation of the Other and to the destructive conflicts to which this leads. "To be European today" is an expression typical of both Ursula Hirschmann and Braidotti. For Braidotti it means positioning herself within the historical contradictions of a European identity and experiencing "the political need to turn them into spaces of critical resistance to hegemonic identities of all kinds."[51] Despite the fact that the subject of feminist nomadism falls into the trap of triumphalism when she exalts "the joyful nomadic force," the position that Braidotti proposes—of resistance to our past—is a primary stage in the criticism of the European cultural heritage.

According to Agnes Heller, although it may be true that Europeans are old, Europe is itself still young given that "a European culture as such has

---

[50] Rosi Braidotti, *Nomadic Subjects: Embodiment and Sexual Difference in Contemporary Feminist Theory* (New York: Columbia University Press, 1994), 9–10.

[51] Ibid., 8.

never existed but it could develop in the future."[52] This projection toward the future is a constant in the approach proposed in this chapter, and it is from this point of view that I now draw a conclusion. Situated between positions that either completely negate the possibility of a European identity and those that formalize it within a community already possessed of values and attitudes, and expressive of a single European spirit, this chapter has attempted to describe forms of identity that are problematic, critical, and linked to a "nonsovereign" subject.[53] Such forms are not based on exclusion or on a contrast with others, but recognize differences within ourselves, our worlds, and the world. This presupposes maintaining the tension between knowledge and practice, politics and culture, ideas and emotions, as well as searching incessantly for their links. In addition, it means being aware of the foundational character of intersubjectivity as a horizon for new identities, and a readiness to welcome the "new-born" (in the Arendtian sense) from future generations, as well as "foreigners"—in the many senses of the term—without losing a sense of one's self and the direction of one's own itinerary.

The title of this chapter refers to two kinds of detachment. The first is necessary in order to recognize the aporiae, nemesis, and tricks that the fate of Europe has played on the identities linked with it. The second is indispensable to capture the tension between the self and the self, and between the self and the other—both inside and outside us. This last point reminds us of the links between identities and masks (*personae*). To act one or more parts on a stage composed of concentric circles—the city, the country, Europe, the world—cannot be separated from an attitude that is ironic, at least in part, toward the performance and one's role within it. To express the hope that these futures will be identities of irony means hoping that they will be strong enough to oscillate, move, and change and that they will be able to avoid the need to base themselves on rigidity and exclusion—as did those created in times of economic scarcity and cultural contraposition. It also means hoping that they will always allow irony to be shown both toward themselves and toward the illusions of grandeur and the hegemonic expectations of the old subject.

---

[52] Agnes Heller, "Europe: An Epilogue," in Brian Nelson, David Roberts, and Walter Veit, eds., *The Idea of Europe* (Oxford: Berg, 1992), 25.
[53] Bhabha, "The Third Space."

10

Muslims and European Identity: Can Europe Represent Islam?

TALAL ASAD

> Simultaneously, and despite the parochialism of the governments at
> home, a sort of international solidarity was slowly evolving in the
> colonies. . . . Out of interest if not out of good will, an embryonic European
> understanding had at last been found in Africa. We could hate one another
> in Europe, but we felt that, between two neighboring colonies, the interest
> in common was as great as between two white men meeting in the desert.
>
> Count Carlo Sforza, *Europe and Europeans*, 1936

Muslims are present in Europe and yet absent from it. The problem of
understanding Islam in Europe is primarily, so I claim, a matter of understanding how "Europe" is conceptualized by Europeans. Europe (and
the nation-states of which it is constituted) is ideologically constructed in
such a way that Muslim immigrants cannot be satisfactorily represented
in it. I argue that they are included within and excluded from Europe at
one and the same time in a special way.

I take it for granted that in Europe today Muslims are often misrep-
resented in the media and discriminated against by non-Muslims.[1] More
interesting for my present argument is the anxiety expressed by the majority of West Europeans about the presence of Muslim communities and
Islamic traditions within the borders of Europe. (In France, for example,
a 1992 poll showed that two-thirds of the population feared the presence
of Islam in that country.[2]) It is not merely that the full incorporation of
Muslims into European society is thought to be especially hard for people

Michael Blim, William Connolly, Vincent Crapanzano, Heiko Henkel, Aseel Sawalha, David
Scott, and Gerry Sider commented on this essay at various points. I am grateful to them.

[1] See J. Wrench and J. Solomos, eds., *Racism and Migration in Western Europe* (Oxford:
Berg, 1993), esp. the excellent contribution by S. Castles.

[2] See A. Hargreaves, *Immigration, Race and Ethnicity in Contemporary France* (London:
Routledge, 1995), 119.

who have been brought up in an alien culture. It is their attachment to Islam that many believe commits Muslims to values that are an affront to the modern Western form of life.

Admittedly, there is no shortage of voices that respond to such anxieties with characteristic liberal optimism.[3] They speak of the diverse linguistic and ethnic origins of Muslim immigrants, and of the considerable variation in individual attachments to old traditions. There is little to fear from most immigrants—liberals say—and much more from the consequences of the higher unemployment and greater prejudice to which they are subjected. Muslims in Europe can be assimilated into Western society. Liberals maintain that it is only the extreme right for whom the presence of Muslims and Islam in Europe represents a potential cultural disaster, and that right-wing xenophobia is rooted in the romantic nativism it espouses, and consequently in its rejection of the West's universalist principles. In this, as in other matters, liberals stand for tolerance and an open society.

All these claims may be true, but the liberal position is more layered than one might suppose. To begin with, the Islamic disregard of "the principle of secular republicanism" (as symbolized by the *affaire du foulard*), and the Islamic attack against "the principle of freedom of speech" (as exemplified in the Rushdie affair) have angered liberals and the left no less than the extreme right. These events within Europe have been read as all of a piece with the Islamist resort to civil violence in North Africa and West Asia, and they have led even liberals to ask with growing skepticism whether the Islamic tradition (as distinct from its human carriers) can find a legitimate place in a modern Western society.

But I begin elsewhere. I focus not on liberal opposition to right-wing intolerance or dismay at the closedmindedness of immigrants but with a larger question. How can contemporary European practices and discourses represent a culturally diverse society of which Muslim migrants (Pakistanis in Britain, Turks in Germany, North Africans in France) are now part? To answer this question I shall first address another: How is Europe represented by those who define themselves as authentic Europeans?

The general preoccupation in the social sciences with the idea of *identity* dates from after the Second World War. It marks a new sense of

---

[3] Many of these voices are found in recent collections: B. Lewis and D. Schnapper, eds., *Muslims in Europe* (London: Pinter, 1994); S. Z. Abedin and Z. Sardar, eds., *Muslim Minorities in the West* (London: Grey Seal, 1995); G. Nonneman, T. Niblock, and B. Szajkowski, eds., *Muslim Communities in the New Europe* (London: Ithaca Press, 1996).

the word, highlighting the individual's social locations and psychological crises in an increasingly uncertain world.[4] "This is my name," we now declare. "I need you to recognize me by that name." More than ever before identity depends on the other's *recognition* of the self. Previously, the more common meaning of *identity* was "sameness," as in the statement that all Muslims do not have "identical interests," and attributively, as in "identity card." In Europe the newer twist on the sense of the word is almost certainly more recent than in America. Perhaps in both places the discourse of *identity* indicates not the rediscovery of ethnic loyalties so much as the undermining of old certainties. The site of that discourse is suppressed fear. The idea of European identity, I say, is not merely a matter of how legal rights and obligations can be reformulated. Nor is it simply a matter of how a more inclusive name can be made to claim loyalties that are attached to national or local ones. It concerns *exclusions* and the desire that those excluded recognize what is included in the name one has chosen for onself. The discourse of European identity is a symptom of anxieties about non-Europeans.

MUSLIMS AND THE IDEA OF EUROPE

What kind of identity, then, does Europe represent to Europeans? An empirical response would base itself on comprehensive research into literature, popular media, parliamentary debates, and local interviews. My primary interest, however, is in analyzing the logic of a discourse rather than in tracing its empirical spread. So I begin with a partial answer to the question. Consider this anecdote as reported in the 1992 *Time* magazine cover story on Turkey's attempt to become a member of the European Community:

However it may be expressed, there is a feeling in Western Europe, rarely stated explicitly, that Muslims whose roots lie in Asia do not belong in the Western family, some of whose members spent centuries trying to drive the Turks out of a Europe they threatened to overwhelm. Turkish membership "would dilute the E.C.'s Europeanness," says one German diplomat.[5]

---

[4] Philip Gleason points out that the first edition of the *International Encyclopedia of the Social Sciences*, published in 1930–5, carried no entry under the term "identity," and that one appeared only in the 1968 edition. See "Identifying Identity: A Semantic History," *The Journal of American History*, vol. 69, no. 4 (1983): 910–31.
[5] "Across the Great Divide," *Time*, October 19, 1992, 31.

Clearly, neither the genocide practiced by the Nazi state nor its attempt
to overwhelm Europe have led to feelings in Western Europe that would
cast doubt on where Germany belongs. I do not make this statement
in a polemical spirit. On the contrary, I affirm that given the idea of
Europe that exists, such violence cannot dilute Germany's Europeanness.
Violence is—among other things—a complicated moral language. Far
from being threatened by internal violence, European solidarity is strengthened by it.

Let me explain: Tony Judt powerfully argues that the idea of Europe
stands as a convenient suppressor of collective memories of the widespread
collaboration with Nazi crimes in East and West alike, as well as of mass
brutalities and civil cruelties for which all states were directly or indirectly
responsible.[6] His account has nothing to say, however, about violence per-
petrated in this period by Europeans outside Europe—in colonial Africa,
say, or in the Middle East. No mention is made even of Algeria, which
was, after all, an internal Department of France. I stress that my comment here is not moralistic but descriptive. It has to do with how the
conceptual boundaries of moral and legal solidarity are actually traced.
I do not object to Judt's leaving colonial violence out of his discussion.
I merely point to what he thinks is important. I indicate that his discussion
of collective culpability is limited in precisely the way that the "myth of
Europe" defines the extent of its own solidarity. "The myth of Europe"
does not simply suppress the collective memories of violence within
Europe; the resurrection of those memories strengthens that myth. Moral
failure is considered particularly shameful in this case because Europeans
try to cover up their past cruelties in Europe to *other Europeans* instead of
confronting that fact fully. The Turkish assault against Europe has quite
a different salience.

Historically, it was not Europe that the Turks threatened but Christendom. Europe was not then distinct from Christendom. "For diplomats
and men of affairs, writes Denys Hay,

the intrusion of the Turk was a fact which could not be ignored and the practical
acceptance of a Moslem state into the field of diplomacy might well have produced
an early rejection of Christendom in the field of international relations....The
language of diplomacy maintained the established terminology: "the common
enemy, the Christian republic, the Christian world, the provinces of Christendom"
are found in the phraseology of a large number of sixteenth- and early seventeenth-
century treaties. A similar attitude is to be found in the treatises of the international

---

[6] Tony Judt, "The Past is Another Country: Myth and Memory in Postwar Europe,"
Daedalus, vol. 121, no. 4 (1992).

lawyers down to, and even beyond, Grotius. If the Turk was not different under natural law, he was certainly different under divine law: the Turk was not far short of a "natural enemy" of Christians.[7]

In the contemporary European suspicion of Turkey, Christian history, enshrined in the tradition of international law, is being reinvoked in secular language as the foundation of an ancient identity.

Consider another example: the 1995 interview with Tadeusz Mazowiecki on the subject of his principled resignation as the U.N. representative of human rights in the Balkans. At one point the interviewers, Bernard Osser and Patrick Saint-Exupéry, pose the following question: "You are Polish and Christian. Is it strange to hear yourself defending Bosnians, many of whom are Muslims?" Some readers might wonder how it is that two French intellectuals, heirs to the secular Enlightenment, can formulate such a question in Europe today. But of course the aim of this leading question is to elicit the plea for tolerance that the interviewers know will be forthcoming. So I find it more significant that Mazowiecki expresses no surprise at the question itself. Instead, he responds as expected by urging tolerance. He assures his interviewers that the war in Bosnia is not a religious one and that Bosnian Muslims are not a danger to Europe. "It bodes ill for us," he warns, "if, at the end of the twentieth century, Europe is still incapable of coexistence with a Muslim community."[8]

Mazowiecki's assumption (accepted without comment by his French interlocutors) is that Bosnian Muslims may be *in* Europe but are not *of* it. Even though they may not have migrated to Europe from Asia (indeed, they are not racially distinguishable from other whites in Europe), and even though they may have adjusted to secular political institutions (insofar as this can be said of Balkan societies),[9] they cannot claim a Europeanness—as the inhabitants of Christian Europe can. It is precisely because Muslims are external to the essence of Europe that "coexistence" can be envisaged between "us" and "them."

---

[7] Denys Hay, *Europe: The Emergence of an Idea* (Edinburgh: Edinburgh University Press, 1957), 113–14.

[8] B. Osser and P. de Saint-Exupéry, "The U.N.'s Failure: An Interview with Tadeusz Mazowiecki," *The New York Review of Books*, vol. 42, no. 14, September 21, 1995.

[9] "In its historical practice," writes François Thual, "Caucasian, Balkan, Greek, and Slav Orthodox Christianity has never known secularism based on the separation of Church and State." ("Dans le monde orthodox, la religion sacralise la nation, et la nation protège la religion," *Le Monde*, January 20, 1998, 13.) It is a little known fact—and one very rarely publicized—that the Greek constitution is proclaimed in the name of the Holy Trinity, and that it affirms that "the dominant religion in Greece is that of the Eastern Orthodox Church of Christ."

For both liberals and the extreme right the representation of "Europe" takes the form of a narrative, one of whose effects is to exclude Islam. I do not mean by this that both sides are equally hostile toward Muslims living in Europe.[10] Nor do I assume that Muslim immigrants are in no way responsible for their practical predicament. I mean only that for liberals no less than for the extreme right, the narrative of Europe points to the idea of an unchangeable essence.

ISLAM AND THE NARRATIVE OF EUROPE

Europe, we often read, is not merely a continent but a civilization. The word "civilization" is no longer as fashionable in the West as it was at the turn of the nineteenth century, but it appears to be returning. Some, like Michael Wintle, still object that the term "civilization" should not be applied to Europe, while insisting that there is something that Europeans share:

> To talk in terms of a quintessential or single European culture, civilization, or iden-
> tity leads quickly to unsustainable generalization, and to all manner of heady and
> evidently false claims for one's own continent. Nonetheless, if the triumphalism
> can be left to one side there is a long history of shared influences and experiences,
> a heritage, which has not touched all parts of Europe or all Europeans equally,
> and which is therefore hard and perhaps dangerous to define in single sentences
> or even paragraphs, but which is felt and experienced in varying ways and degrees
> by *those whose home is Europe*, and which is recognized—whether approvingly
> or disapprovingly—by many from outside.[11]

The key influences on European experience, Wintle continues, are the Roman Empire, Christianity, the Enlightenment, and industrialization. It is because these historical moments have not influenced Muslim

---

[10] The hostility of secular liberals, however, is often difficult to distinguish from that of the extreme right. In France, for example, a headmaster suspended three Muslim school-girls in September 1989 for wearing head scarves on the grounds that they were in contravention of French laws of *laïcité*. Later the headmaster's suspension order was overturned by France's education minister. The response that followed was remarkable. A group of leading intellectuals, including Régis Debray and Alain Finkelkraut, com-pared the minister's decision to the 1938 appeasement of Nazi Germany at Munich: "by implication," observes Hargreaves, "the Islamic bridgehead established by the three girls in Creil now represented a comparable threat to the future well-being of France." The form in which the issue was publicly represented helped the extreme right-wing Front National Party to win a sweeping by-election victory near Paris, an event that in turn contributed to the adjustment of government policy on immigration. See Hargreaves, *Immigration*, 125–6.

[11] Michael Wintle, "Cultural Identity in Europe: Shared Experience," in M. Wintle, ed., *Culture and Identity in Europe* (Aldershot: Avebury, 1996), 13 (emphasis added).

immigrants' experience that *they are not those whose home is Europe.*
These moments are precisely what others have designated "European
civilization."

Raymond Williams notes that the word "civilization" is used today in
three senses: (1) a single universal development (as in "human civilization"); (2) the collective character of a people or a period that is different
from and incommensurable with others (as in "the civilization of the renaissance in Italy"); and (3) the culture of a particular population, which
is rankable as higher or lower than another, and perhaps also capable
of further development.[12] Although Williams does not say so, the three
senses together articulate the essence of "European civilization": it aspires to a universal (because "human") status, it claims to be distinctive
(it defines modernity), and it is (at least in terms of quantifiable criteria)
undoubtedly the most advanced. Taken together these senses require a
narrative definition of "Europe."

The two journalistic examples I cited earlier both assume a historical definition of Europe as a civilization. But they do so in ways that
are largely implicit. Hugh Trevor-Roper's *The Rise of Christian Europe*
is one of many academic texts that expresses the essence of European
identity explicitly by means of a historical narrative.[13] Trevor-Roper's
book is interesting because it defines European civilization—and therefore
European identity—as a narrative, or at least as the beginning of one
whose proper ending is already familiar. Like other texts with which it
may be compared, it presents a twofold notion of history: the history of
"the idea of Europe" and of "European history."[14] It also has an interesting historical location. It appeared in 1965, when British decolonization
was more or less complete and when the flood of non-European immigrants from the former colonies was stemmed by legislation passed—
amidst charges of betrayal of its principles—by the Labour government.
At the time a new role for Britain in its postimperial phase was being
vigorously debated in all sections of the political spectrum. The option
of "joining Europe" politically was an important part of that debate.

---

[12] Raymond Williams, *Key Words* (London: Fontana (Collins), 1983).
[13] Hugh Trevor-Roper, The *Rise of Christian Europe*, 2d ed. (London: Thames and Hudson,
1965). Described by a *Times Literary Supplement* reviewer as "one of the most brilliant
works of historiography to be published in England in this century," it has been reprinted
numerous times, most recently in 1989.
[14] For example, Hay, *Europe*; J.-B. Duroselle, *L'idée d'Europe dans l'histoire* (Paris:
Denoel, 1963); R.H. Foerster, *Europa: Geschichte einer politischen Idee* (Munich:
Nymphenburger, 1967); K. Wilson and J. Van der Dussen, eds., *The History of the
Idea of Europe* (London: Routledge, 1995).

When Trevor-Roper speaks of "European history," he does not mean narratives about the inhabitants of the European continent, which is why there is nothing in his book about Byzantium and Eastern Europe, or about North-Western Europe (other than brief references to the Vikings' destructiveness), or about Jews (other than as victims), or about Muslim Spain (other than as an intrusive presence). "European history" is the narration of an identity many still derive from "European (or Western) civilization"—a narrative that seeks to represent homogeneous space and linear time.

What is the essence of that civilizational identity? Trevor-Roper reminds his readers that most of its ideas and many of its techniques entered European civilization from outside. The things that belong to European civilization, therefore, are those that were taken up and creatively worked on by Europe. Productive elaboration becomes an essential characteristic of Europe as a civilization. This view makes sense, I would suggest, in the context of a particular Enlightenment theory about property first propounded by John Locke. Locke argued that a person's right to property comes from the mixing of labor with the common things of this world. "God gave the world to men in common, but since He gave it them for their benefit and the greatest conveniencies of life they were capable to draw from it, it cannot be supposed He meant it should always remain common and uncultivated. He gave it to the use of the industrious and rational (*and labor was to be his title to it*); not to the fancy or covetousness of the quarrelsome and contentious."[15] Applied to whole peoples, property was "European" to the extent that Europeans appropriated, cultivated, and then lawfully passed it on to generations of Europeans as their own inheritance.

"European history" thus becomes a history of continuously productive actions defining as well as defined by Law. Property is central to that story, not only in the sense familiar to political economy and jurisprudence, but in the sense of the particular character, nature, or essence of a person or thing. It is a story that can be narrated in terms of improvement and accumulation in which the industrial revolution is merely one central moment. According to this conception, "European civilization" is the sum of properties, all those material and moral acts that define European identity.

---

[15] John Locke, *Two Treatises of Civil Government* (London: J. M. Dent & Sons, 1924), book II, chapter V, paragraph 34 (emphasis added).

It follows from this view of Europe that real Europeans acquire their individual identities from the character of their civilization. Without that civilizational essence, individuals living within Europe are unstable and ambiguous. That is why not all inhabitants of the European continent are "really" or "fully" European. Russians are clearly marginal. Until just after World War II, European Jews were marginal too, but since that break the emerging discourse of a "Judeo-Christian tradition" has signaled a new integration of their status into Europe.[16] Completely external to "European history" is medieval Spain. Although Spain is now defined geographically as part of Europe, Arab Spain from the seventh to the fourteenth centuries is seen as being outside "Europe," in spite of the numerous intimate connections and exchanges in the Iberian Peninsula during that period between Muslims, Christians, and Jews.

There is a problem for any historian constructing a categorical boundary for "European civilization" because the populations designated by the label "Islam" are, in great measure, the cultural heirs of the Hellenic world—the very world in which "Europe" claims to have its roots. "Islamic civilization" must therefore be denied a vital link to the properties that define so much of what is essential to "Europe" if a civilizational difference is to be postulated between them. There appear to be two moves by which this is done. First, by denying that it has an essence of its own, "Islam" can be represented as a *carrier civilization* that helped to bring important elements into Europe from outside, material and intellectual elements that were only contingently connected to Islam.[17] Then, paradoxically, this carrier civilization is attributed an essence: an ingrained hostility to all non-Muslims. That attribution constitutes Islam as Europe's primary alter. This alleged antagonism to Christians then becomes crucial to the formation of European identity. In this, as in other historical narratives of Europe, this oppositional role gives "Islam" a quasi-civilizational identity.[18] One aspect of the identity of Islamic civilization is that it represents an early attempt to destroy Europe's civilization from outside; another is that it signifies the corrupting moral

---

[16] Of course, anti-Semitism has not disappeared in Europe. But no one who aspires to respectability can now afford to be known publicly as an anti-Semite.

[17] "The Arabs themselves ... *had little of their own to offer.* ... But as carriers, their services to Europe were enormous." Trevor-Roper, *The Rise of Christian Europe*, 141.

[18] In Trevor-Roper's picturesque language: "Out of this union [of ecclesiastical and feudal power] would come, in due time, the combined spiritual and material counter-attack of the enslaved West against its Moslem exploiters: the Crusades." Ibid., 100.

environment that Europe must continuously struggle to overcome from within.[19]

This construction of civilizational difference is not exclusive in any simple sense. The de-essentialization of Islam is paradigmatic for all thinking about the assimilation of non-European peoples to European civilization. The idea that people's historical experience is inessential to them, that it can be shed at will, makes it possible to argue more strongly for the Enlightenment's claim to universality: Muslims, as members of the abstract category "humans," can be assimilated or (as some recent theorists have put it) "translated" into a global ("European") civilization once they have divested themselves of what many of them regard (mistakenly) as essential to themselves. The belief that human beings can be separated from their histories and traditions makes it possible to urge a Europeanization of the Islamic world. And by the same logic it underlies the belief that the *assimilation* to Europe's civilization of Muslim immigrants, who are for good or for ill already in European states, is necessary and desirable.

The motive of "European history" in this representation is the story of Europe's active power to reconstruct the world (within Europe and beyond) in its own Faustian image.[20] Europe's colonial past is not merely an epoch of overseas power that is now decisively over. It is the beginning of an irreversible global transformation that remains an intrinsic part of "European experience" and is part of the reason that Europe has become what it is today. It is not possible for Europe to be represented without evoking this history, the way in which its active power has continually constructed its own exclusive boundary—and transgressed it.

THE SHIFTING BORDERS OF MODERN EUROPE

It is often conceded that several peoples and cultures inhabit the European continent, but it is also believed that there is a single history that articulates European civilization and therefore European identity. The official

---

[19] Hence Trevor-Roper's account of the European Crusaders who established a principality in Jerusalem from the end of the eleventh century to the end of the twelfth: "The Christian kingdom of Jerusalem continued for less than a century. The Christian virtues, such as they were, evaporated in the East. The Christian dynasties ran out.... [T]he sons—or rather the successors, for there was a dearth of sons—settled down to a life of luxurious co-existence in which feudal bonds were rotted and oriental tastes indulged." Ibid., 104. By "Christian" Trevor-Roper refers, of course, only to those who originated in "Europe," because the Middle East at the time was largely inhabited by indigenous Christians who were central contributors to "Islamic civilization."

[20] On Europe's "Faustian" identity, see Agnes Heller, "Europe: An Epilogue?" in B. Nelson, D. Roberts, and W. Veit, eds., *The Idea of Europe: Problems of National and Transnational Identity* (Oxford: Berg, 1992).

European Union slogan expresses this thought as "unity in diversity." But determining the boundaries of that unity continues to be an urgent problem for anyone concerned with the civilizational basis of the E.U. Perry Anderson has noted some of the difficulties about boundaries encountered in recent discourse:

Since the late Eighties, publicists and politicians in Hungary, the Czech lands, Poland and more recently Slovenia and even Croatia have set out to persuade the world that these countries belong to Central Europe that has a natural affinity to Western Europe, and is fundamentally distinct from Eastern Europe. The geographical stretching involved in these definitions can be extreme. Vilnius is described by Czeslaw Milosz, for example, as a Central European city. But if Poland—let alone Lithuania—is really in the center of Europe, what is the east? Logically, one would imagine, the answer must be Russia. But since many of the same writers—Milan Kundera is another example—deny that Russia has ever belonged to European civilization at all, we are left with the conundrum of a space proclaiming itself center and border at the same time.[21]

Anderson's witty account highlights the illogicality of recent definitions of Europe. Yet it is precisely the politics of civilizational identity that is at work in the discourse of Europe's extent. For Poles, Czechs, and Hungarians it is a matter not only of participating in the European Common Market, but of distancing themselves from a socialist history. Where Europe's borders are to be drawn is also a matter of representing what European civilization is. These borders involve more than a confused geography. They reflect a history whose unconfused purpose is to separate Europe from alien times ("communism," "Islam") as well as from alien places ("Islam," "Russia").

J. G. A. Pocock has spelt out another aspect of this politics of civilization: "'Europe'—both with and without the North America whose addition turns it from 'Europe' into 'Western Civilization'—is once again an empire in the sense of a civilized and stabilized zone which must decide whether to extend or refuse its political power over violent cultures along its borders but not within its system."[22] In Pocock's separation between a "civilized culture" and "violent cultures," we sense that Europe's borders at once protect and threaten its unity, define its authority, and engage with external powers that have entered its domain. The "inside" cannot contain the "outside," violent cultures cannot inhabit a civil one, Europe cannot contain non-Europe. And yet Europe must try to contain, subdue, or incorporate what lies beyond it and what consequently comes to be

---

[21] P. Anderson, "The Europe to Come," *London Review of Books*, January 25, 1996.
[22] J. G. A. Pocock, "Deconstructing Europe," *London Review of Books*, December 19, 1991.

within it. European capitalism and European strategic interests cannot be confined to the European continent.

The representation of Europe's borders is, of course, symbolic. But the signs and symbols have a history. Like the borders of its constituent states, the European Union's boundaries are inscribed in treaties according to the conventions of international law—the cumulative result of earlier narratives of Europe. The status of individual borders as well as the very institution of international law that regulates today's worldwide society of nation-states have been constituted by narratives of Europe. Adam Watson summarizes the story:

> The expansion of Europe was neither uniform nor systematic. It occurred over several centuries, for a number of reasons, and assumed many different forms. Chronologically we can distinguish in retrospect four main phases. First came the medieval crusades into Iberia and round the Baltic. The second phase covered three centuries of competitive maritime exploration and expansion and the parallel evolution of a European international society. Thirdly in the nineteenth century the industrial revolution enabled the European Concert to encompass the entire globe and to administer most of it. Lastly in our own century the tide of European dominion ebbed, and was replaced by a world-wide society based on the European model but in which Europeans now play only a modest role.[23]

What this story misses is that Europe did not simply expand overseas; it made itself through that expansion. This story also underestimates the role that Europeans—especially those who inhabit the United States— still play in regulating "world-wide society," a role that is by no means "modest." The borders of political Europe have varied not only over time, but also according to the European model governing global relations.

Can Muslims be represented in Europe? As members of states that form part of what Watson and others call European international society, Muslims have, of course, long been represented (and regulated) in it. But representing Muslims in European liberal democracies is a different matter. It raises a question that does not apply to the international system: how can a European state represent its "minorities"?

EUROPEAN LIBERAL DEMOCRACY AND MINORITY REPRESENTATION

So far I have explored the idea that Islam is excluded from representations of Europe and the narratives through which the representations

---

[23] Adam Watson, "European International Society and its Expansion," in H. Bull and A. Watson, eds., *The Expansion of International Society* (Oxford: Clarendon Press, 1985), 32.

are constituted. I now approach the question from another angle: are there possibilities of representing Muslim minorities in modern European states?

The ideology of political representation in liberal democracies makes it difficult if not impossible to represent Muslims as Muslims. Why? Because in theory the citizens who constitute a democratic state belong to a class that is defined only by what is common to all its members and its members only. What is common is the abstract equality of individual citizens to one another. Marie Swabey has stated the issue succinctly:

> The notion of equality central to democracy is clearly a logical and mathematical conception.... [O]nce equality is admitted, the notions of number, per capita enumeration, and determination by the greater number are not far to seek.... Citizens are to be taken as so many equivalent units and issues are to be decided by the summation of them.... Once we conceive the whole (the state) as composed of parts (the citizens) which are formally distinct but without relevant qualitative differences, we are applying the notion in its essentials. Involved here is the assumption not only that the whole is authoritative over any of its parts, but that what there is *more of* has *ipso facto* greater weight than that which differs from it merely by being less. In the democratic state this idea is expressed as the postulate that the opinion of the people as a whole, or of the greater part of them, is authoritative over that of any lesser group.[24]

It follows, Swabey goes on, that the opinion of a majority "is more likely to represent approximately the opinion of the whole body than any other part." In this conception representative government is assimilated to the notion of an outcome that is statistically representative of "the whole body" of citizens. The same principle applies to segments of "the whole (the state)" according to which representatives of geographically demarcated constituencies represent aggregates of individual voters. It is no accident that the statistical concept of representativeness emerged in close connection with the construction of the welfare state (a process that began toward the end of the nineteenth century) and the centralization of national statistics. Both in the history of statistical thinking and in the evolution of democratic politics, these developments were especially important—demography, social security legislation, market research, and national election polls.

In principle, therefore, nothing should distinguish Muslims from non-Muslims as citizens of a European democratic state other than their fewer number. But a "minority" is not a purely quantitative concept of the kind stipulated by Swabey, not an outcome of probability theory applied to

---

[24] Marie Collins Swabey, *The Theory of the Democratic State* (Cambridge, Mass.: Harvard University Press, 1939), 18–20 (emphasis in original).

determine the opinion of a corporate body—"the people as a whole."
The concept of minority arises from a specific Christian history: from
the dissolution of the bond that was formed immediately after the Reformation between the established church and the early modern state. *This*
notion of minority sits uncomfortably with the Enlightenment concept of
the abstract citizen.

The post-Reformation doctrine that it was the state's business to secure
religious uniformity within the polity—or at least to exclude Dissenters
from important rights—was crucial to the formation of the early-modern
state. By contrast, the secular Enlightenment theory that the political
community consists of an abstract collection of equal citizens was propounded as a criticism of the religious inequality characterizing the absolutist state. The most famous document embodying that theory was the
"Declaration of the Rights of Man and the Citizen." The theory was criticized almost from the moment it was first stated—notably by Edmund
Burke for the license it gave to destructive passions and by Karl Marx for
disguising bourgeois self-interest. However, the decisive movements that
helped to break the alliance of church and state seem to have been religious rather than secular—Tractarianism in England and Ultramontanism
in France and Europe generally. The arguments they deployed most effectively were strictly theological and were aimed at securing the freedom of
Christ's church from the constraints of an earthly power.[25] An important
consequence of abandoning the total union of church and state was the
eventual emergence of "minority rights" as a central theme of national
politics. Members of minorities became at once equal to all other citizens,
members of the body politic ("the people as a whole"), and unequal to
the majority in requiring special protection.

The political inclusion of minorities has meant the acceptance of groups
formed by specific (often conflicting) historical narratives, and the embodied memories, feelings, desires that the narratives have helped to shape.
The rights that minorities claim include the right to maintain and perpetuate themselves as groups. "Minority rights" are not derivable from
general theories of citizenship: minority status is connected to membership in a specific *historical* group not in the abstract class of citizens. In
that sense minorities are no different from majorities, also a historically
constituted group. The fact that they are usually smaller in number is
an accidental feature. Minorities may be numerically much larger than

---

[25] Joseph Heim, "The Demise of the Confessional State and the Rise of the Idea of a Legitimate Minority," in J. W. Chapman and A. Wertheimer, eds., *Majorities and Minorities*
(New York: New York University Press, 1990).

the body of equal citizens from whom they are excluded. In the British empire vast numbers of colonial subjects were ruled by a democratic state of citizens far smaller in number through a variety of constitutional devices.[26] Minorities are defined as minorities in structures of dominant power.

Take the case of France. Religious Muslims who reside in France are similar to the Christian (and post-Christian) inhabitants of that country in this regard: each group has constituted itself *as a group* through its own narratives. These narratives, and the practices they authorize, help to define what is essential to each group. To insist in this context that Muslim groups must not be defined in terms they regard as essential to themselves is in effect to demand that they can and should shed the narratives and practices they take to be necessary to their lives as Muslims. The crucial difference between the "majority" and the "minorities" is, of course, that the majority effectively claims the French state as its national state. In other words, to the extent that "France" embodies the Jacobin narrative, it essentially represents the Christian and post-Christian citizens who are constituted by it.

Thus Jean-Marie Le Pen's insistence in the early eighties on the right of the majority ("the French in France") to protect its distinctive character against the influence of minority difference is not only an extension of the left slogan "the right to difference." It is a claim that the majority's right to be French "in their own country" precludes the right of minorities to equal treatment in this regard. "We not only have the right but the duty to defend our national personality," Le Pen declares, "and we too have our right to be different."[27] Given the existence of a French national personality of which the Jacobin republic is claimed to be the embodiment, and given that the majority is its representative, Le Pen can argue that only those immigrants able and willing to join them (thereby ceasing to

---

[26] "Colonies, protectorates, mandates, intervention treaties, and similar forms of dependence make it possible today for a democracy to govern a heterogeneous population without making them citizens, making them dependent upon a democratic state, and at the same time held apart from the state. This is the political and constitutional meaning of the nice formula 'the colonies are foreign in public law, but domestic in international law'." Carl Schmitt, *The Crisis of Parliamentary Democracy* (1926; trans. ed., Cambridge, Mass.: MIT Press, 1985), 10.

[27] "Nous croyons que la France est notre patrie, que les Français y ont des devoirs mais aussi des droits supérieurs à tous autres, et que nous avons non seulement le droit mais le devoir de défendre notre personnalité nationale et nous aussi notre droit à la différence." *Le Monde*, 21 September 1982, cited in part, and in English translation, by Miriam Feldblum, "Re-Visions of Citizenship: The Politics of Nation and Immigration in France, 1981–1989," Ph.D. diss., Yale University, 1991, 48. My translation of the original is slightly different from Feldblum's.

belong to a minority) have the right to remain in France as French citizens. It follows that the "inassimilable" ones (North African Muslims)
should be encouraged to leave when their labor is no longer required by
France. This may be an intolerant position but it is not illogical.[28] To be
a French citizen is to reflect, as an individual, the collective personality
that was founded in the French Revolution and embodied in the laws
and conventional practices of the French Republic, and that is recounted
in its national story. Although that personality may not be regarded as
eternal and unchangeable, it represents a precondition of French citizenship. As even liberals concede, the individual citizen cannot make with
the state any contract he or she chooses independently of that personality.
In brief, the narratives that define "being French" and the practices they
authorize cannot be regarded as inessential. *French citizens cannot be
de-essentialized.* This view, shared by the Left, Center, and Right, rejects
the notion that the citizen is identical only with himself or herself, that
he or she therefore essentially represents an abstract quantity that can be
separated from his or her social identity, added up and then divided into
groups that have only numerical value. It should not be surprising that
Le Pen has been able to push the greater part of the majority toward endorsing reforms of the Nationality Code in the direction demanded by the
extreme right.[29] The very existence of the French Jacobin narrative permits the extreme right to occupy the ideological center in contemporary
French immigration politics.

Liberals are generally dismayed at the resurgence of the Right, but the
notion of primordial intolerance will not explain it. Many critics have
observed that part of the problem resides in the identification of national
boundaries with those of the state. Some of them have sought a solution
in the radical claim that all boundaries are indeterminate and ambiguous.
William Connolly has recently theorized the matter more perceptively.
He asks, pointedly, "whether it is possible to prize the indispensabil-
ity of boundaries to social life while resisting overdetermined drives to
overcode a particular set." He goes on to question the assumption that
"the boundaries of a state must correspond to those of a nation, both of

---

[28] Feldblum, in "Re-Visions," argues that the immigration politics of the extreme right are
better described as "nativist" than as "racist," because the latter term does not explain
why many of the nonracist left also share certain crucial elements of the same position.
While Feldblum's study as a whole is valuable for understanding developments in recent French ideas of national identity, she does not discuss the contradictions inherent
in liberal ideas of citizenship. Her use of the pejorative term "nativism" to denote pop-
ulist denunciation of "foreign influences" deflects her from an adequate consideration of
liberal forms of exclusivism.

[29] See Hargreaves, *Immigration*, 169–76.

these to a final site of citizen political allegiance, and all three of those to the parameters of a democratic ethos."[30]

The problem of representing Islam in European liberal democracies cannot be addressed adequately unless such questioning is taken seriously. With America especially in mind, Connolly urges a shift in the prevalent idea of pluralism "from a majority nation presiding over numerous minorities in a democratic state to a democratic state of multiple minorities contending and collaborating with a general ethos of forbearance and critical responsiveness."[31] The decentered pluralism he advocates in place of liberal doctrines of multiculturalism requires a continuous readiness to deconstruct historical narratives constituting identities and their boundaries (which, he argues, have a tendency to become sacralized and fundamentalized) in order to "open up space through which *care* is cultivated for the abundance of life."[32]

To what extent and how often historical narratives that constitute identities can be deconstructed remains a difficult question. Thus I have been arguing, on the one hand, that Europe's historical narrative of itself needs to be questioned and, on the other, that the historical narratives produced by so-called "minorities" need to be respected. This apparent inconsistency is dictated partly by my concern that time and place should be made for weaker groups within spaces and times commanded by a dominant one. Muslims in Europe, I have implied, should be able to find institutional representation as a minority in a democratic state where there are only minorities. For where there are only minorities the possibilities of forging alliances between them will be greater than in a state with a majority presiding over several competing minorities.

My comments also reflect an unresolved tension: how can respect for individual "identities" be ensured *and* conditions be fostered that nurture collective "ways of life"? The latter concern is not merely a matter of "recognition"—of the demand that one should be able to name oneself and be confirmed by others as the bearer of that name, and thereby have one's anxieties allayed. It is also a matter of embodied memories and practices that are articulated by traditions, and of political institutions through which these traditions can be fully represented. (The constituency represented does not have to be geographically continuous.) Our attention needs to be directed not so much at how identities are negotiated and recognized (for example, through exploratory and constructive dialogue,

---

[30] W. E. Connolly, "Pluralism, Multiculturalism and the Nation-State: Rethinking the Connections," *Journal of Political Ideologies*, vol. 1, no. 1 (1996), 58 (emphasis in original).
[31] Ibid., 61. [32] Ibid., 70 (emphasis in original).

as Charles Taylor has advocated).[33] Rather, the focus should be on what
it takes to live particular ways of life continuously, cooperatively, and
unself-consciously.

John Milbank's arguments for decentering are different from
Connolly's, and they are linked to a specifically medieval historical experience. His contrast between what he calls "enlightenment simple space"
and "gothic complex space" has implications for a Europe of nation-
states: "complex space has a certain natural, ontological priority; simple
space remains by comparison merely an abstracting, idealizing project. . . .
This is the case because there is no such thing as absolute non-interference;
no action can be perfectly self-contained, but always impinges upon other
people, so that spaces will always in some degree 'complexly' overlap, jurisdictions always in some measure be competing, loyalties remain
(perhaps benignly) divided."[34] The sovereign state cannot (never could)
contain all the practices, relations, and loyalties of its citizens.

The idea of complex space, in contrast to the discourse of a border-
less world, is in my view a fruitful way of thinking about the intersecting
boundaries and heterogeneous activities of individuals as well as of groups
related to traditions. But we need to think also of complex time: of how
embodied practices are rooted in multiple traditions, each drawing on
temporalities that connect present and future, and of how each tradition cultivates a distinctive experience of the present and privileges some
desires over others.

The scope for "national politics" with its exclusive boundaries is reduced in complex space and time—though not simply in favor of supranational or subnational structures. The question is not simply one of
devolution or of regional integration, the question now being debated
in the European Union, but of how to allow for more complicated patterns of territory, authority, and time. The scope of national politics is
already reduced in part for the well-known reason that the forces of global
capitalism often undermine attempts to manage the national economy—
although this is truer of some national economies than of others. It is
reduced also because networks that straddle national boundaries mobilize variable populations for diverse enterprises. This latter needs to be
explicitly accommodated.

[33] See Charles Taylor, *Multiculturalism and "The Politics of Recognition"* (Princeton, N.J.:
Princeton University Press, 1992).
[34] J. Milbank, "Against the Resignations of the Age," in F. P. McHugh and S. M. Natale,
eds., *Things Old and New: Catholic Social Teaching Revisited* (New York: University
Press of America, 1993), 19.

But there is something else: because the temporalities of many tradition-rooted practices (that is, the time each embodied practice requires to complete and to perfect itself, the past into which it reaches and which it reenacts and thereby extends) cannot be translated into the homogeneous time of national politics, scope for the latter is further reduced. The body's memories, feelings, and desires necessarily escape the rational/instrumental ambitions of such politics. (This is not properly understood by those well-wishing critics who urge Asian immigrants to abandon their traditions, to regard some of their collective memories and desires as not essentially their own, and to embrace instead the more modern conception of self-determination underlying the European nation-state in which they now live.[35]) For many Muslim minorities (though by no means all), being Muslim is more than simply belonging to an individual faith whose private integrity needs to be publicly respected by the force of law—and more, certainly, than a social identity to be guaranteed by the nation-state. It is being able to live as part of a collective way of life that exists beside others in mutual tolerance. The question for them is: what kind of political conditions can be developed in Europe in which *everyone* lives as a minority among minorities?

I conclude with another question because decisive answers on this matter are difficult to secure. If Europe cannot be articulated in terms of complex space and time, which allow for multiple ways of life and not merely multiple identities to flourish, it may be fated to be no more than the common market of an imperial civilization,[36] always anxious about (Muslim) exiles within its gates and (Muslim) barbarians beyond. In such an embattled modern space—a space of abundant consumer choice and optional life-styles—is it possible for Muslims to be represented as Muslims?

---

[35] See Homi Bhabha, *New Statesman and Society*, March 3, 1989: "where once we could believe in the comforts and continuities of Tradition, today we must face the responsibilities of cultural Translation." This was written in a spirit of friendly advice to Muslim immigrants in Britain during the Rushdie affair. Yet how innocent is the assumption that Muslim "Tradition" carries no responsibilities, and that "cultural Translation" to a British lifestyle in Britain is without any comforts?

[36] "Europe is again an empire concerned for the security of its *limites*—the new barbarians being those populations who do not achieve the sophistication without which the global market has little for them and less need of them." Pocock, "Deconstructing Europe." There is, of course, a periodic need for barbarian labor.

11

The Long Road to Unity: The Contribution of Law to the Process of European Integration since 1945

PHILIP RUTTLEY

The formation of Europe—and of the European Communities and the Union that lie at the heart of the continent's political life—has largely been expressed in legal terms.[1] In the space of more than fifty years, the antagonists of two savage world wars have so far merged their economies and some of their legal systems that any further conflict between the major European states is now almost unthinkable. It has instead become increasingly likely that, within the next few decades, full-scale economic, monetary, and political union will take place between the fifteen Member States of the European Union.[2]

If, however, one had asked any of the leading European figures about their vision for Europe at various critical periods of the postwar era, one would have received rather different answers, largely conditioned by the wider geopolitical scene. It cannot, therefore, be said that there was a linear path from the rubble of 1945 to the vision of a federal United States of Europe that is emerging. Almost from the beginning the reassertion of national independence and sovereignty polarized states with a "federalist" vision of a United States or Confederation of Europe and those with an "intergovernmental" vision of a concert of states acting together in their mutual self-interest rather than as part of a wider union. This tension is far from resolved. Indeed, the price of keeping the European Union

Although all errors and omissions are my own, I gratefully acknowledge the generous support and advice of His Hon. Judge Nicholas Forwood of the EC Court of First Instance and of my colleagues Dominic Spenser Underhill, Kate Learoyd, and Christian Charlesworth who read the original manuscript.

[1] I have attempted to describe the state of EU law as of December 1, 1998.

[2] For historical surveys see Charles Zorgbibe, *Histoire de la Construction Européenne* (Paris: PUF, 1993); Marie-Thérèse Bitsch, *Histoire de la Construction Européenne de 1945 à nos Jours* (Paris: Editions Complexe, 1996); and Elizabeth du Réau, *L'Idée d'Europe au XXe Siècle* (Paris: Editions Complexe, 1996).

together has been the institutionalization of these divisions into the very architecture of the two Treaties on European Union of Maastricht (1992) and Amsterdam (1997).

FROM THE TREATY OF PARIS TO THE TREATY OF AMSTERDAM: THE UNIFICATION OF EUROPE THROUGH THE EC TREATIES

The treaties on European Union have produced an inchoate mixture of shared competence between the Union and the Member States, the enshrinement of the concept of "subsidiarity," and the increased use of opt-out clauses permitting an à la carte approach to common European policies. Nevertheless, the ideal of an "ever closer union of the peoples of Europe" has served as the fundamental inspiration for much of the development of the European Communities.[3] Sometimes overtly federalist sentiments were expressed, as in the immediate postwar period in response to outside military and political threats (for example, the Soviet threat during the Cold War). At other times such sentiments appear to have been kept judiciously in the background (as during the antifederalist ascendancy of the Thatcher administration in the United Kingdom in the mid-1980s). More recently, outspokenly federalist sentiments have come to the fore again. In 1998 German chancellor Gerhard Schroeder openly advocated a fully fledged United Europe, and his foreign minister, Joschka Fischer, described the creation of a single European state as "the decisive task of our time."[4]

In the immediate aftermath of the German surrender of May 1945, there was an upsurge of enthusiasm for a unified Europe to replace, once and for all, the destructive nationalist ideologies that for so long had torn

[3] Article 2, EC Treaty. The nomenclature of the various European Community treaties is liable to confuse the uninitiated. The original three Communities were each created by a separate treaty: the European Coal and Steel Community (ECSC) was established by the 1951 Treaty of Paris; the European Economic Community (EEC) was established by the 1957 Treaty of Rome; and the European Atomic Energy Community (EURATOM) was established by the Second Treaty of Rome of 1957. The 1965 Merger Treaty unified all the Community Institutions common to the three Communities to create a single Council, Commission, and Parliament. "EC Treaty" refers to the EEC Treaty as expanded by later treaties such as the Maastricht Treaty on European Union of 1992. The Maastricht Treaty created the European Union, a political union separate from the European Communities (which create economic integration through the implementation of common policies). Thus it is more accurate to speak of *EC law* when discussing the rules in the EC Treaty or tax harmonization or the removal of customs barriers. *EU law* refers to the legal obligations created by the Maastricht Treaty, such as the mechanisms for arriving at common positions on foreign policy or judicial cooperation.

[4] *The Times*, November 27, 1998.

the old continent apart. Before the Stalinist takeover of much of Eastern Europe in 1948, many advocated a grand vision of a United States of Europe. Most vocal among them was Winston Churchill, who used his unrivaled moral authority to make such a proposal in Zürich on September 19, 1946.[5] The start of the Cold War, and the consciousness of their distinct national identities on the part of France and the United Kingdom, quickly replaced this enthusiasm for pan-European unification with a more hard-headed sense of national interest. Nevertheless, the very real threat of invasion or war by Soviet Russia (in 1948 during the Berlin airlift, in 1952 during the riots in East Berlin, in 1956 during the Hungarian uprising, and in 1968 during the Czechoslovak crisis), as well as the economic rivalry of the United States and Japan, led to a realization that some form of unity for the democratic countries of Europe was necessary.

Paradoxically perhaps, the Socialist-led United Kingdom of 1945, as the main victorious Western European power, held aloof from the moves toward European integration. While Churchill used his immense prestige to advocate a federalist union of Europe, the United Kingdom considered that its long-term interests lay with its Empire and the British Commonwealth. This proved to be a colossal geopolitical mistake. The British Empire was quickly swept away by a tide of nationalism in the Third World, leaving Britain isolated on the sidelines of European integration for two decades until the United Kingdom finally joined the European Economic Community in 1973.

By contrast, France correctly perceived that its long-term strategic interests lay primarily in the European continent. France led the process of integration with the political field largely free of serious competition, since Germany and Italy could hardly take a lead in the immediate postwar period, while Belgium, Luxembourg, and the Netherlands could not match French economic and military power. This period of French hegemony over the process of European integration during its formative stages had a fundamental consequence for the future shape of European institutions: during the crucial formative stages, the European Community was ideologically led by France, with its very individual tradition of government and conception of civil administration. Not surprisingly, the resulting institutional structure of the three European Communities described in footnote 3 is essentially French in character. To Anglo-Saxon eyes, the executive power of the European Commission and the judicial activism of the European Court of Justice are incompatible with traditions of separation of powers and noninterventionist judiciaries. The internal *modus*

---

[5] See du Réau, *L'Idée d'Europe*, 166.

operandi of the Commission, and the types of legislative acts that the Community Institutions can adopt, are again strongly French in character. The Commission is divided in "Directorates-General" with their officials organized in divisions along the model of the French civil service. The "motor language" of the Community was and remains French, with official documents first drafted in that language and then translated in the other official languages. The European Court of Justice is essentially French in its character and procedure. An impersonal court, it produces anonymous judgments with no dissenting minority opinion being recorded. The Court is even assisted in its deliberation by a legal expert, the Advocate General, whose nearest equivalent is the "Commissaire au Gouvernment" of the French administrative law system.

As noted earlier, the fundamental political and legal structure of the European Communities is French in character, with subtle and far-reaching consequences for the vision of Europe that has conditioned the imagination of political leaders. This character has led to tension when the European Communities have expanded to include new Member States of different legal and administrative traditions. Such tension was particularly acute in the United Kingdom and in Denmark. Their adoption of *communautaire* ways has been particularly troubled, but a Romano-Gallic, as opposed to Anglo-Saxon, legal tradition has largely prevailed, giving the European Union a subtly different character than it would have had if the United Kingdom had participated in the initial formative stages of the European Coal and Steel Community Treaty or the Messina Conference of 1995 (which led to the creation of the EEC and EURATOM).

The centripetal forces of ever-increasing cooperation led to the desire for more centralization and more fusion of the powers of the EC states. The Single European Act of 1987 strengthened integration in certain areas to create an "Internal Market" (as opposed to the looser "Common Market"). Federalist sentiments then resurfaced quickly. These unifying ambitions led to the Maastricht Treaty of 1992, vigorously opposed by the United Kingdom and Denmark. Their governments were adamantly against the idea of a federal union.

The collapse of the Soviet Union in the early 1990s has led to a wholly novel geopolitical situation. The competing ideological blocks of capitalism and communism have now been replaced by a world where the United States is the unrivaled single superpower with three strong regional rivals—the European Union, China, and Russia. The discredited Marxist ideology has been replaced, virtually worldwide, by an acceptance of liberal capitalism. This has led to two far-reaching consequences, both of which profoundly affected the future shape of the European Union: the creation in 1994 of the World Trade Organization (WTO) and the collapse of Soviet rule in Eastern Europe and the former Union of Soviet Socialist Republics (USSR). Faced with these two developments the European Community felt increased pressures toward some form of federal or even confederal union. This was most clearly manifested during the intergovernmental conference that led to the Treaty of Amsterdam of 1997 with its thinly disguised federalist ideology. As has been acutely observed, "the European Community signifies very different things to different people and constitutes a political forum in which competing and even conflicting aims and goals are mediated and negotiated."[6]

The historical process of European integration through the successive EC Treaties conveniently divides into five distinct phases. The first phase, from 1945 to 1955, saw the creation of the "prototype" for all the later European Communities—the European Coal and Steel Community established by the Treaty of Paris of 1951 for a period of 50 years. The first phase also saw the abortive negotiations concerning the European Defense Community and the European Political Community. The second phase, from 1955 to 1968, saw the creation of the EURATOM and the EEC, both by the Treaties of Rome in 1957. The third phase, from 1965 to 1987, was a period of dynamic integration and severe institutional and political clashes between the Member States and the supranational centralized Community Institutions, which began to flex their political and legislative muscles. The European Communities expanded from six Member States to twelve. The fourth phase, from 1987 to 1992, saw the next leap forward toward greater economic and political integration, through the vast legislative program of harmonizing legislation of the 1987 Single European Act. The fifth phase, from 1992 to the present day, saw Europe at the crossroads. After the Treaties of Maastricht (1992) and Amsterdam (1997), the 15 European states now stand on the threshold of federal union. This is creating the strains and tensions that currently bedevil European politics. Each of these five phases will be discussed in detail.

The First Phase, 1945–1955

To a significant measure, the success of European "unification"—a far more accurate term than the word "integration"—is the work of the European Court of Justice and the far-sighted federalist politicians—

---

[6] Paul Craig and Gráinne de Burca, *EU Law: Text, Cases and Materials*, 2d ed. (Oxford: Oxford University Press, 1998).

Robert Schuman, Jean Monnet, Paul-Henri Spaak, Jacques Delors—who have led Europe through its critical stages.

The experience of administrating the Marshall Plan gained through the Organization for European Economic Cooperation (OEEC), created in 1948, was a useful prototype of intergovernmental coordination.[7] Other factors increasing the "habit" of cooperation between European states were the 1948 Treaty of Brussels between the United Kingdom, Belgium, Luxembourg, and the Netherlands; the North Atlantic Treaty Organization (NATO) of 1949; and the Western European Union Treaty of 1954. These were largely political alliances, but attempts also were made at genuine economic interstate cooperation. In 1944, while the Second World War was drawing to a close, the Netherlands, Belgium, and Luxembourg agreed to create a far-reaching economic integration program under the "Benelux" Treaty, including a customs union between the three signatories. As we have seen, however, the postwar Labor administration in Britain systematically rejected closer union with Europe. Various reasons of principle lay behind this: a desire not to turn Britain's back on the Commonwealth that had supported it through two world wars; the belief that what remained of the British Empire would allow it to stand aside from its continental partners; a fundamental concern that national sovereignty should be preserved and not transferred to supranational institutions beyond the control of the British electorate.[8]

In 1948 a "congress for Europe" was gathered at the Hague to negotiate an acceptable form of continent-wide cooperation. Because of British objections, the result was the creation of a rather truncated organism, called the Council of Europe, which provided for a Committee of Ministers (meeting every six months) and a Parliamentary Assembly (with limited powers to make recommendations to the Council of Ministers). The Council's main activities since its creation in 1949 have been in the spheres of cultural, scientific, and economic cooperation but most prominently of all in the European Convention on Human Rights of 1953. This Convention created a Commission and a Court dealing with human rights guaranteed by the Convention (among them the right of fair trial and the

---

[7] The OEEC developed into the Organization for Economic Cooperation and Development (OECD), whose membership expanded to include the United States, Canada, and Japan.

[8] Britain was not alone in holding such sentiments. At the Havana conference in 1948, the United States effectively vetoed the creation of the proposed International Trade Organization on the grounds that its powers would undermine the national sovereignty of the United States; it would take until 1994 for a similar institution, the World Trade Organization, to be created. (Nationalistic sentiments are still being expressed about the WTO on Capitol Hill.)

right of free expression and of holding private property without undue interference from the state).[9] Its original signatories included the states currently in the European Community, plus Switzerland and Turkey.

Since Britain refused to agree to further European unification, other European states decided to embark on an interstate integration without the United Kingdom. Behind these moves toward unity was the theory that the root cause of war in Europe was the economic rivalry of Germany and France. The federalist French politician Jean Monnet proposed the bold plan of merging the coal and steel production of France and Germany, particularly in the heavily industrialized border areas of the Ruhr and the Saar rivers, which have been fought over since the 1870s. Robert Schuman, the French foreign minister, strongly supported this plan. He proposed a wholly novel European Coal and Steel Community. The ECSC was not a mere intergovernmental forum. It entailed the creation of a supranational High Authority with wide regulatory powers, a Council with legislative powers, a political representative Assembly; and a supervisory European Court of Justice. This was a giant step toward European unification: for the first time the European states had created a supranational entity whose independent *sui juris* and *sui generis* institutions had the power to bind the ECSC's constituent states.[10]

The ECSC Treaty of Paris was signed in 1951 by France, Germany, Italy, Luxembourg, Belgium, and the Netherlands. The clear intention of the ECSC was to act as a prototype for wider European integration; the treaty was not merely about fusing coal and steel production.[11]

Not all attempts at unification could be thwarted by sensitivities over national sovereignty when the United Kingdom saw its vital interests threatened. France could be equally intransigent. The heightening tensions of the Cold War raised the difficult question of the rearmament of Germany. The United States advocated that this process should be conducted within NATO. France proposed instead a European Defense

[9] For surveys see P. Van Dijk and G. J. H. Van Hoof, *Theory and Practice of the European Convention on Human Rights*, 2d ed. (Deventer: Kluwer, 1990) and Louis-Edmond Pettiti, Emmanuel Decaux, and Pierre-Henri Imbert, *La Convention Européenne des Droits de l'Homme* (Paris: Economica, 1995).

[10] It is an interesting anecdotal fact that the foreign ministers of France, Italy, and Germany at the time of the ECSC negotiations all spoke German as their first language. (The French foreign affairs minister was originally from Alsace-Lorraine and the Italian from the Alto-Adige.) This factor apparently greatly assisted them in building mutual trust and understanding.

[11] See F. Duchene, *Jean Monnet: The First Statesman of Europe* (New York: Norton, 1994), 239 (with quotes from Monnet's comments from 1952).

Community (EDC) with a European army, joint institutions, and a common budget. This proposal in 1950 led to the signing of the EDC Treaty by the six ECSC states in 1952.

The following year a draft statute for a European Political Community was proposed as a complement to the EDC. It set out a detailed federal program, including joint institutions and a coordinated foreign policy. However, a combination of nationalist and Communist deputies in the French National Assembly defeated the proposals in 1954, and both the EDC and EPC were abandoned.

The Second Phase, 1955–1968

Although the process of European unification had suffered significant setbacks through the opposition of Britain and France at various moments, the idea of a European union strengthened markedly in the second phase. A conference of the six ECSC foreign ministers was held in Messina, Italy, in 1955; Britain declined to take part. Under the chairmanship of the Belgian prime minister, Paul-Henri Spaak, a wide-ranging proposal for a European Economic Community and a European Atomic Energy Community was produced. The rationale of the EEC was to create a trading bloc, with a customs union and the removal of barriers to internal trade (such as the free movement of people, goods, services, and capital). This "Common Market" would harmonize the national economic, fiscal, and social policies of the six participating states.

Accordingly, the six ECSC states, under the Treaty of Rome of 1957, established a far-reaching and radical European Economic Community. The EEC Treaty covered most forms of economic activity (except the defense industry), harmonized taxation, removed internal customs barriers, and established common rules for economic activity (for example, competition, free movement, and rights of establishment).

To implement "common policies" designated to create this Common Market, the EEC established an institutional structure based on the ECSC model. Thus, legislative authority was vested in a Council (where Member States are represented); executive power was conferred on a Commission; a political representative assembly was established (the European Parliament); and constitutional control over the legality of the acts of EEC institutions was given to the European Court of Justice.

These four institutions are supranational institutions with powers derived from the constitutive Treaty of Rome of 1957. A long line of cases from the European Court of Justice has established the doctrine of the supremacy of community law over conflicting national law.[12] To the extent that legal competence to act in a particular way has been transferred to the Community by the Member States, the EEC states no longer have the right to act unilaterally or independently.[13]

The EEC, like its precursor, the ECSC, has international legal personality.[14] Therefore, the EEC can enter into diplomatic and treaty relations in much the same manner as a conventional sovereign state.[15] The rationale for the EURATOM was, of course, different from that for the ECSC and the EEC. In essence, the six states recognized their inability (individually) to match the investment and technological strength of the United States or of the USSR in the field of nuclear energy. Consequently, their best option was to fuse their individual strengths in a common enterprise, the EURATOM. The EURATOM Treaty reproduced the same institutional pattern as its sister Communities: a Council, Commission, Assembly, and Court of Justice.

In 1965 a Merger Treaty was concluded between the six states in order to merge the institutions created by the ECSC, the EEC, and the EURATOM into a common Council Commission, Parliament, and Court.[16] Henceforth, therefore, the Commission became a single Commission with powers under all three constitutive EC Treaties in the spheres covered by their provisions.

The European Economic Community Treaty, in its original form, was a wide-ranging economic and political cooperation treaty. Its aim was to increase the prosperity of the citizens of the EEC states:

The Community shall have as its task, by establishing a common market and an economic and monetary union and by implementing the common policies or activities referred to in Articles 3 and 3a, to promote throughout the Community a harmonious and balanced development of economic activities, sustainable and non-inflationary growth respecting the environment, a high degree of convergence

---

[12] See Case 26/62, *Van Gend en Loos* v. *Netherlands Tax Administration* (1963), European Court Reports; Case 6/64, *Costa* v. *Enel* (1964), ECR 585; Case 106/77, *National Finance Administration* v. *Simmenthal* (1978), ECR 629; and Case C-213/89 *R* v. *Secretary of State for Transport, ex parte Factortame Ltd and Others* (1990), ECR I-2433. For a general survey, see T. C. Hartley, *The Foundations of European Community Law*, 4th ed. (Oxford: Clarendon Press, 1994), chap. 7.

[13] Case 22/70, *Commission* v. *Council* (1971) ECR.

[14] Article 210, EC Treaty; Article 6, ECSC Treaty; and Article 184, EURATOM Treaty.

[15] See Ian Brownlee, *Principles of Public International Law*, 4th ed. (Oxford: Clarendon Press, 1994), chap. 30; and I. Macleod, I. D. Hendry, and Stephen Hyett, *The External Relations of the European Communities* (Oxford: Clarendon Press, 1996), chap. 2.

[16] The Merger Treaty of 1965 was repealed and then repeated without any substantive changes by Article 9 of the 1997 Treaty of Amsterdam.

of economic performance, a high level of employment and of social protection, the raising of the standard of living and quality of life, and economic and social cohesion and solidarity among Member States.[17]

To achieve this, the EEC Treaty authorizes the pursuit of several "common policies," such as the Common Agricultural Policy, the Common Transport Policy, the Common Customs Union, and the Common Commercial Policy (for external trade). To achieve these objectives, the Community Institutions, such as the Commission, are conferred legislative powers and executive authority in the form of Regulations, Directives, and Decisions. *Regulations* are directly applicable laws that automatically become part of the national domestic laws of the Member States and operate in much the same way as an act of Parliament in the United Kingdom or an act of Congress. *Directives* define objectives for the Member States. They must be achieved by a certain date. Each Member State can use its discretion concerning the legislative means to achieve the objective. Finally, *Decisions* are addressed to individual Member States.[18]

To facilitate the achievement of the Common Market, the fathers of the EEC Treaty were conscious of the need to break down the many overt and hidden barriers to unity such as customs duties, differing professional or technical standards, residence permits, and administrative registration requirements. The EEC Treaty therefore created four fundamental freedoms: the freedom for citizens to move between states (Articles 48–51); the freedom to establish oneself in another state (Articles 52–58); the freedom to provide services in another state but one's own (Articles 59–66); and the free movement of capital (Articles 62–73). Later treaties, described in subsequent parts of this chapter, considerably expanded the scope of the Treaty of Rome.[19]

The Third Phase, 1965–1987

Dynamic growth and dramatic internal clashes characterized the third decade of European Unification. These difficulties came out of France's nationalist ambitions under General Charles de Gaulle; the enlargement of the Community in 1973 and 1980 to absorb the United Kingdom, Denmark, Ireland, Greece, Spain, and Portugal, thus fundamentally

---

[17] Article 2, EC Treaty.
[18] See Article 249 (formerly Article 189), EC Treaty; and Article 161, EURATOM Treaty. The ECSC Treaty enumerates two types of binding acts: binding "decisions" and "recommendations," which operate like EEC directives (see Article 14, ECSC Treaty).
[19] Examples include the Single European Act 1987, the Maastricht Treaty of 1992, and the Treaty of Amsterdam of 1997.

altering the political and social composition of the Union; and the political and institutional lethargy of the 1980s, when the European Communities seemed to have run out of steam.

The conflicts between Gaullist France and its five EEC partners erupted in a full-scale crisis in 1965 when the transitional provisions of the original EEC Treaty expired. This led to the move from unanimous voting in the Council to qualified majority voting. The Commission at that moment made a fiscal proposal to the Council of Ministers that the Community should raise its own funds from direct taxation on agriculture and external trade tariffs, rather than relying on funds contributed by Member States.

Attacking the "federalist logic" of the Commission's proposals, de Gaulle attempted to persuade his partners in the Council of Members but without success. As a result, France boycotted Council meetings by means of an "empty-chair" policy for a full seven months from June 1965 to January 1966, until a compromise was eventually reached. This compromise, known as the "Luxembourg Accords," effectively gave France the victory it was seeking. Where the vital interest of a Member State (or those interests it considered to be vital) were at stake, voting in the Council would be by unanimity (thus giving individual states a veto power). Ordinary matters were to be decided on the basis of qualified majority voting. The Luxembourg Accords significantly shifted power back to the Member States and away from the centralized institutions of the Community, particularly the Commission.

While the Community was facing difficulties internally, it began to acquire an increasingly strong personality externally, and gradually began to express itself with a single voice. Thus, it negotiated as a block of contracting nations during the 1967 Round of GATT (General Agreement on Tariffs and Trade) negotiations and, in 1963, successfully concluded a far-reaching trade and development aid agreement with 18 African states at Yaoundé. This agreement would subsequently become the prototype of a whole service of aid and trade agreements between the European Community and its former colonies in Africa, Asia, and the Pacific, known as the Lomé Conventions (after the capital of Togo where they were signed).[20]

However, not all Western European states agreed with the "EC six" that an integrationist model was appropriate. Seven states—the United Kingdom, Sweden, Denmark, Switzerland, Austria, Norway, and Portugal—created the European Free Trade Association (EFTA), which

---

[20] The Lomé I, II, III, and IV agreements are examples. See Macleod, Hendry, and Hyett, *External Relations*, 380ff.

sought to provide a large measure of reciprocal trade liberalization but fell short of creating supranational institutions with legislative powers, such as the European Community. Broadly, the EFTA Treaty of 1960 provided for the elimination of customs barriers and of quantitative restrictions for industrial products. Various reasons inspired adherence to the EFTA: traditional neutrality in the case of Sweden and Switzerland or resistance to the dilution of national sovereignty in the case of the United Kingdom. The seven EFTA countries were geographically and commercially very diverse, and one has the impression of a *faute de mieux* economic treaty. Later Iceland and Finland joined the EFTA, lending it at least a greater Scandinavian coherence.

Thus, by the early 1960s the Western European nations were grouped into two trading blocks: the original six EC states making the Common Market and the seven EFTA states. The only states of any size that remained isolated for one reason or another were Greece, Spain, and Turkey.

By 1961 the United Kingdom began to reconsider its global strategy that relied on ties with the Commonwealth and the Empire. The sweeping independence movement in the developing world led to the final disintegration of nearly all of what remained of the British Empire. While maintaining close ties with its former colonies, such as India, Britain recognized that the most promising focus for its exports was the massive common trading area emerging on its very borders. Britain accordingly applied for EEC membership in 1961 only to be vetoed by de Gaulle, and then once again on Britain's second application in 1967. After de Gaulle fell from power following the events of May 1968, the road became clear for an expanded membership of the EEC, with Britain, Ireland, Norway, and Denmark applying for membership. Certain other European states (such as Greece, Portugal, and Spain) could not be considered for EEC membership since their military regimes precluded adherence to the fundamental norms of EEC membership.

The tensions that constantly underlie membership in the European Union—national sovereignty and independence versus fused sovereignty and the increase of collective power—emerged strongly at this time. Norway's electorate rejected membership in a referendum in 1973. The United Kingdom had to undergo a national referendum in 1975 to confirm the electorate's approval of its EC membership.

When the United Kingdom, Ireland, and Denmark became Member States on January 1, 1973, the six became the nine. After the fall of its military regime, Greece became the tenth Member State in 1980. Portugal and Spain followed in 1986 once they, too, had become parliamentary democracies.

Intergovernmental cooperation deepened during the 1970s. The 1970 Davignon Report (commissioned after the 1969 Hague Summit) proposed quarterly meetings of the foreign affairs ministers of the six Member States; this was later institutionalized in the European Political Cooperation scheme of 1973, giving the EEC states a mechanism for achieving a common voice in those international organizations where all Member States were members (for example, the Organization for Economic Cooperation and Development). Then in 1974 the European Council was established to give a regular forum for holding summits. The drawback to this form of "summitry" was, of course, that it weakened the unification process in favor of continued individual comportment by Member States. Parliamentary supervision was also weakened. Intergovernmentalism now dominated at the expense of more integrative forces.

This negative trend was largely the result of the Luxembourg Accords, by which the French won the right from Member States to block or retard new policies. Under the original EEC Treaty scheme, the Commission was to have the role of formulating policy and of proposing new laws to the Council. As Piet Dankert, a leading Commissioner of the time, has observed:

The Council of Ministers, which was originally intended to be a community body, has now become largely an intergovernmental institution thanks to the famous Luxembourg Agreement, which under French pressure, put an end to the majority decisions which the Council was supposed to take according to the [EEC] Treaty on proposals submitted by the European Commission. This [new voting rule as a result of the Luxembourg Accord] that decisions could only be taken unanimously had the effect of gradually transforming the Commission into a kind of secretariat for the Council which carefully checked its proposals with national officials before deciding whether or not to submit them. This in turn has a negative effect on the European Parliament which can only reach for power, under the Treaty, via the Commission.[21]

There were, however, forces working in the other directions; the system of the Community's own resources (a strong federalist element) and the related extension of the European Parliament's budgetary powers and in 1979, the direct election of that Parliament.[22]

---

[21] This was written before the co-decision procedure between the Council and the Parliament and the Parliamentary consultation procedures introduced in the legislative architecture of the European Community by the Treaty of Maastricht in 1992.

[22] Piet Dankert, "The EC—Past, Present and Future," in *The EC—Past, Present and Future*, ed. L. Tsoukalis (Oxford: Blackwell, 1983), 7.

The result of heightened intergovernmentalism was political stagnation. States freely exercised their Luxembourg Accord right to veto new initiatives.

With no clear political direction for the European Communities in the mid-1970s and early 1980s, various proposals were made to strengthen integration. Most noteworthy were the Tindermans Report of 1974, the Report of the "Three Wise Men," the European Parliament's draft "Treaty on European Vision," and the Genscher-Colombo Plan of 1983. None of these was ever acted upon—clear evidence of the unresolved tensions between national sovereignty and closer European integration.

The Tindermans Report (produced by Belgian Prime Minister Leo Tindermans) was commissioned by the 1974 Paris Summit to make proposals for the Community's future. The Tindermans Report was radical. It proposed moving away from intergovernmentalism by strengthening the Commission and the European Parliament, the latter to be elected by universal suffrage. The report also proposed reforming the Council and suggested further measures toward monetary integration and citizenship rights. In addition, it advocated developing social and regional policy.

The so-called Committee of "Three Wise Men" was established after the 1978 Brussels summit. Its mandate was to consider means of achieving greater political integration. Like the Tindermans Report, the Committee favored strengthening the role of the Commission and lessening the effects of intergovernmentalism. The Committee recommended qualified majority voting in the Council (providing that certain measures could be adopted by the Council only if they achieved a certain percentage of votes).[23]

The Genscher-Colombo Plan, the brainchild of the German and Italian foreign ministers at the time, advocated institutional reform, budgetary reform, and an expansion of the areas where the Community had exclusive competence to act at the expense of the Member States. Although no action was taken, the Council did consider the Genscher-Colombo Plan, and it issued a Declaration on European Union in 1983.[24]

Pressure built to find a way out of the political stagnation that was beginning to bring into question the raison d'être of the European Community. In 1979 direct elections to the European Parliament were held. Although the turnout, which averaged 62 percent, was low, the election of a representative assembly (albeit with limited powers) in all nine EEC Member States was a symbolic step forward.

[23] See Bulletin EC-11-1978: 1.5.2.   [24] See Bulletin EC-6-1983: 1.6.1.

The European Parliament is the most federalist of the Community Institutions. This is perhaps not surprising since the rationale for its powers and activities is, by definition, supranational and contrary to the continued role of the national assemblies of the Member States. In 1984, on the basis of a report compiled by the leading Italian federalist member of the European Parliament (MEP), Alberto Spinelli, the European Parliament overwhelmingly approved a Draft Treaty on European Union. This document proposed radical reform: a stronger Community, a Council that shared its legislative and budgetary powers with the European Parliament, and greater use of qualified majority voting on Council decisions.

No action was taken on the basis of the draft treaty, but the Fontainebleau Council Summit of 1984 knew that action was needed if the European Community was to emerge from stagnation. The result was the formation of two committees: the Adonnino Committee to examine the question of furthering European identity and a "people's Europe" and the Dooge Committee on political reform. This led to the landmark meeting in 1985 of the ten Member States in Milan. A majority voted to convene an intergovernmental conference to discuss an amendment to the original Treaty of Rome.[25]

The Fourth Phase: The Single European Act of 1987

Given the opposition of certain Member States (in particular the United Kingdom) to any further transfer of political sovereignty to the Community, the "integrationists" chose the subtle maneuver of concentrating on the more economic aspects of integration. Their aim was to increase the drive toward economic, monetary, and fiscal integration that a "core" Internal Market would bring, rather than propose controversial schemes for greater political cooperation. Lord Cockfield, then a Commissioner, produced a "white paper" in 1985 proposing to remove a whole series of internal trade barriers by December 31, 1992.[26] This would create an Internal Market described by the (amended) EEC Treaty as follows:

The internal market shall comprise an area without internal frontiers in which the free movement of goods, persons, services and capital is ensured.[27]

---

[25] The objections of Greece, Denmark, and the United Kingdom were overridden by their fellow members of the European Community.

[26] COM (85) 310. (COM is the standard way of referring to EC Commission documents.)

[27] Article 18, EC Treaty (formerly Article 8A).

It is no accident that the White Paper proposed not to achieve the Internal Market through Regulations (which are, as I noted earlier, primary and legally binding forms of EC legislation). Instead, the Internal Market was to be created by means of over 200 Directives, the form of legal act that allowed the greatest legislative freedom to Member States. The chief architect for the revival of European integration was Jacques Delors, the former President of the Commission. He skillfully exploited divisions between the Member States to achieve his objectives. The United Kingdom and Denmark were the two most reluctant integrationists among EC states. It is in no small measure due to Delors that momentum toward unification regained speed after 1987 and led to the Treaty on European Union of Maastricht (1992) and the Treaty of Amsterdam of 1997.

The Single European Act of 1987 (SEA) introduced sweeping institutional changes. The mechanism for achieving joint international positions was given treaty status by the creation of the European Political Cooperation.[28] The decision-making process of the Community was changed with the introduction of a "cooperation procedure" whereby the Parliament was to be consulted prior to the adoption of new legislation by the European Community. The Parliament was also given a power of veto on both the accession of new Member States and the conclusion of association agreements with states outside the community. In addition, qualified majority voting was introduced in the Council in many areas previously reserved for unanimous voting.

"Exclusive Community competence"—that is to say, reserving for exclusive action by the Community and prohibiting the right of Member States to act individually—was extended to many areas hitherto reserved for the national governments: cooperation in economic and monetary union, social policy, economic and social cohesion, research and technological development, and environmental policy.

In effect, the SEA changed EC politics. It broke the hegemony exercised by the Council (that is, the Member States), and the purely European institutions, which could afford to go beyond narrow national interests, began to set the agenda. By concentrating on economic and fiscal integration, and by avoiding an ambitious political program, it succeeded in being all things to all Europeans: the antifederalists considered it a sound (if rather technocratic) set of proposals that had the virtue of leaving sovereignty relatively intact; the federalists, perhaps sensing that

[28] Title III of the SEA, which does not form part of the EC Treaty.

institutional and political reforms would inevitably emerge from the
achievement of the internal market, bided their time. The Single European
Act thus succeeded in performing the remarkable political feat of reconciling two opposing strands of European ideology at a critical stage of the
Community's history. One commentator has perceptively written:

> Unlike all earlier attempts and proposals to revive the Community, the 1992
> White Paper, although innovative in its conception of achieving a Europe without
> frontiers, was entirely functional. Critically, it eschewed any grandiose institu-
> tional schemes. These were to come as an inevitable result once the programme
> of internal market Directives to be achieved by 31 December 1992 was in place.
> Because of this technocratic approach, the White Paper apparently appealed to
> those with different and often opposing ideological conceptions of the future of
> Europe. To some it represented the realisation of the old dream of a true common
> market-place which, because of this inevitable connection between the social and
> the economic in modern political economies, would ultimately yield the much
> vaunted "ever closer union of the peoples of Europe" [envisaged by Article 2
> of the EC Treaty]. To others, it offered a vision of the European dream finally
> lashed down to the marketplace, and importantly, a market unencumbered by the
> excessive regulation that had built up in the individual Member States.[29]

A fundamental area of European unification is financial, fiscal, and monetary policy. It lies at the very heart of functional national sovereignty.
Therefore, the proposals for greater Community centralization in these
areas predictably generated the loudest debate.

   With relative ease the original six Member States agreed on the principle of eventual monetary union.[30] This was achieved as far back as
1969. They also agreed that the Community should be funded from its
own sources of tax revenue rather than from financial contributions by the
Member States.[31] The Budgetary Treaty and the Own-Resources Decision
of 1970 had an important "federalist" element: they made the Community
financially independent from its "parent" Member States. Contributing
to the "federalist current" was the new role given to the Parliament: to
it was transferred the Council's powers of adopting the Community budget. The Parliament lost little time in flexing its political muscles by using this effective right of veto over the Community budget.[32] To oversee

---

[29] J. Weiler, "The Transformation of Europe," *Yale Law Journal* 100 (1991): 2457–8.
[30] See the report of the committee headed by Werner (Luxembourg's prime minister) in
Bulletin EC-11-1979. See also the Council Resolution of 1971 on the achievement of
monetary union in successive stages (*EC Official Journal* 1971, C28/1).
[31] Its own sources were agricultural levies, customs duties levied at the Community's external borders on products of non-EC origin, and 1 percent of the Value Added Tax (VAT)
levied by the EC Member States.
[32] See Hartley, *The Foundations of European Community Law*, chap. 1.

Community revenue and expenditure, a Court of Auditors was set up and required to report at the end of each financial year.[33] Progress toward more substantial monetary integration had to wait a decade: ten years later the nine Member States established a European Monetary System, with a mechanism for mutually defending the value of national currencies, the Exchange Rate Mechanism.[34] More symbolically, the Member States also agreed on a joint unit of monetary account, the European Currency Unit (ECU), calculated daily based on a basket of EC currencies.

The Fifth Phase: The Maastricht Treaty on European Union of 1992 and the Treaty of Amsterdam of 1997

The 1987 SEA proved to be a catalyst for greater integration. The European Council decided that political and economic integration should be pursued by holding an Intergovernmental Conference (IGC) to discuss further steps on European Monetary Union and political integration. The IGC negotiations led to the drafting of a new treaty in 1991. This became the landmark "Treaty on European Union" signed at Maastricht in February 1992. After much public debate, a narrow majority accepted the treaty in France, the United Kingdom, Denmark (where it required two national referenda), and Germany (where a constitutional challenge was defeated in the Federal Supreme Court). The Maastricht Treaty finally came into force in November 1993.

The European Community had grown to twelve Member States by 1992, and by 1995 (when the Amsterdam Treaty negotiations started), to fifteen Member States. This Community of states was utterly different from the original "core" (six countries) that had created the ECSC, EEC, and EURATOM Treaties. The Union now included countries, not only with a wide variety of cultures (Scandinavians, North Europeans, Mediterraneans), but with an equally wide range of economic strengths (Portugal compared with Sweden, Greece compared with Germany). But fundamental political differences still divided the fifteen Member States as to what form European "Union" should take: federalist, confederalist, or intergovernmental.

---

[33] See David O'Keefe, "The Court of Auditors," in *Institutional Dynamics of European Integration*, ed. D. Curtin and T. Henkels (Deventer: Kluwer, 1994); and I. Harden, F. While, and K. Donnelly, "The Court of Auditors and Financial Control and Accountability in the European Community," *European Public Law* 1 (1995): 599.

[34] Bulletin EC-12–1978, a Council Resolution strengthened by an Agreement between the national central banks of the Member States.

It is perhaps not surprising that the Maastricht Treaty provided for another intergovernmental conference four years hence to examine "to what extent the policies and forms of co-operation introduced by this Treaty may need to be revised."[35] This second IGC led to the Treaty of Amsterdam of 1997, which has not really solved these fundamental differences.

The Treaty of Amsterdam amended the Maastricht Treaty on European Union by adding a principle of open government.[36] Decisions within the EU are to be taken "as openly as possible" and as closely as possible by the citizens of the Union. The Treaty of Amsterdam also expanded the objectives of the Union to include the promotion of a high level of employment and the creation of an area of "freedom, security and justice."[37] In addition, the Treaty declares that the Union is founded on respect for human rights, democracy, and the rule of law. Respect for human rights, particularly those enshrined in the European Convention on Human Rights (ECHR) are made central to the Union. New applicant states must commit themselves to respect these rights.[38] The Treaty makes observance of the ECHR legally actionable against defaulting states or Community Institutions.[39] If the Council finds a state to be in a "serious and persistent breach" of these obligations,[40] the Council may suspend the infringing state's voting rights (without affecting its obligations).[41] An earlier proposal allowed for the expulsion of a defaulting state, but this was rejected as too radical.

Political realism has demanded that the signatories to the Maastricht and Amsterdam Treaties accept fundamental political differences and adopt a variegated approach. The Member States are being allowed to opt out of certain common policies, and certain programs are being implemented only by those states that have the means or the level of development to do so. This is the price being paid for keeping the Union together. It does, however, lead to incoherence and to a slowing (although not an outright denial) of the process of unification. It also throws into question the notion that the principle of an "ever closer union among the peoples of Europe" means an integrative process flowing in only one

---

[35] Article N.2 and B, Maastricht Treaty.
[36] Article 1 (formerly Article A of the Maastricht Treaty).
[37] Article 2 (formerly Article B of the Maastricht Treaty).
[38] Article 49, Treaty of European Union of Maastricht of 1992 (TEU).
[39] Articles 6 and 46 of the TEU.   [40] Under Article 6 of the TEU.
[41] See also the new Article 309 of the revised EC Treaty, which empowers the Council, where action has been taken under Article 6 of the TEU, to suspend other Treaty rights of a defaulting state, voting rights being suspended automatically.

(federalist) direction.[42] Some have seen this as potentially damaging to the raison d'être of the EC. As one critic has written,

It must be said, at the heart of all this chaos and fragmentation, the unique *sui generis* nature of the European Community, its true world-historical significance, is being destroyed. The whole future and credibility of the Communities, as a cohesive legal unit which confers rights on individuals and which enters into their national legal systems as an integral part of those systems, [are] at stake.[43]

The Treaty of Amsterdam is remarkable for self-consciously emphasizing the civil rights foundations of the Union.[44] This is partly in response to persistent (and in the main justified) criticism of the secrecy and bureaucratic style of government practiced by EC institutions. However, it is also significant at the deeper and more complex level of self-identity. The Treaty of Amsterdam makes it unambiguously clear that the European Union is to be based on a political structure that is democratic and participatory.

The history of European integration since 1945 has been dominated, as we have seen, by two currents: a strong vision of European federalism relying on supranational institutions, and a determination to preserve national identity and sovereignty expressing itself in a preference for intergovernmentalism. These conflicting tensions were not buried at Maastricht. Instead, they were enshrined and institutionalized, creating a rather confusing mixture of supranationalism and intergovernmentalism.

To help create the European Union, the Maastricht Treaty envisaged three pillars. The first was the European Community itself—that is to say, the obligations, rights, and common activities contained in the EC Treaties. The second and third Pillars fell outside the scope of the EC Treaties altogether: interstate cooperation on a "common foreign and security policy" (CFSP); and "justice and home affairs" (JHA).[45]

"Through the implementation of a common foreign and security policy including the eventual forming of a common defence policy," the European Union hoped to achieve an international identity. The European Council was to define "common positions" and the Member States were to ensure that their individual foreign policies conformed to them. The

---

[42] Article 2, EC Treaty.
[43] Dierdre Curtin, "The Constitutional Structure of the Union: A Europe of Bits and Pieces," *Common Market Law Review* 17 (1993): 67.
[44] Treaty of Amsterdam amending the Treaty of European Union, the treaties establishing the European Communities and certain related acts (1997).
[45] Article J.1 and J.11; Article K.1 to K.9

European Council then established "guidelines" on which the Council of Ministers could decide on "joint action."

The Parliament was to be consulted by the EU presidency "on the main aspects and the basic choice" of the CFSP, with Parliament having the right to question the Council, to make recommendations, and to hold an annual debate on the CFSP's and the JHA's progress. In addition, the Commission was to be "fully acquainted" with CFSP and JHA activities.

The Justice and Home Affairs Pillar was established to develop close cooperation between Member States on these eponymous issues. It focused on policy issues such as the legal status of non-EC nationals and immigration and asylum rights. In addition, it stressed law enforcement. Cooperation was developed on international crime. Also there was to be judicial, customs, and police cooperation, including a police information sharing system, the European Police Office (EUROPOL).

The JHA Pillar of the Maastricht Treaty was formally incorporated into the main body of the EC Treaty in the Amsterdam Treaty. Finally, a new title to the EC Treaty was added, covering the free movement of persons (including visas, asylum, immigration, and judicial cooperation in civil matters).[46] Significantly, and in keeping with the à la carte approach that emerged in the 1990s, the United Kingdom and Ireland have adopted opt-out possibilities as regards the JHA title.

To remedy some of the institutional criticisms of the Maastricht JHA, the Treaty of Amsterdam created a Pillar of the Community on Police and Judicial Cooperation.[47] In essence, critics of the JHA had pointed out that many of its areas of forms (immigration, asylum, or border controls) affected fundamental rights and overlapped with other common policies, such as the free movement of persons.[48] It was desirable to allow the European Court of Justice judicial control and the input of the Parliament in the formulation of new legislation in this sphere.

The Treaty of Amsterdam has created a new phase of cooperation on issues such as freedom, security, and justice through the development of "common actions" in the fields of police cooperation, judicial cooperation in criminal matters, and the prevention of, and fight against, racism and xenophobia. It targets terrorism, drug trafficking, arms smuggling, trade in persons, offences against children, corruption, and fraud. These problems are to be combated through closer cooperation between the customs, police, and other authorities of the Member States (assisted

[46] Articles 61–69, EC Treaty (formerly Article 73$_{(i)}$–73$_{(q)}$ EC).
[47] Pillar 3, Title VI.
[48] Under Article 48 et seq., EC Treaty (now Articles 39 et seq.).

by EUROPOL). There is to be closer cooperation between judicial authorities and other relevant authorities of the Member States, and certain criminal laws in Member States are to be approximated. Practically, such cooperative action is to take the form of detection, information sharing, and training, as promoted by the Council through EUROPOL. Judicial cooperation will make its contribution by facilitating proceedings and the enforcement of decisions, by assisting extradition and addressing the issues of compatibility of rules and conflicts of jurisdiction, and by establishing minimum rules on substantive criminal laws and penalties in selected fields.

On the initiative either of the Commission or of the Member States, the Council can adopt "common positions" (defining community policy) or "framework decisions" on harmonization (although these have no direct effect), "decisions" on matters other than harmonization, and conventions (to be adopted by Member States under their domestic constitutional provisions).[49] A limited amount of judicial review is envisaged.[50] The European Court of Justice, however, cannot review the legality or proportionality of "operations carried out by the police or other law enforcement services of a Member State or the exercise of the responsibilities incumbent upon Member States with regard to the maintenance of law and order and the safeguarding of internal security."

The changes brought about by the Treaty of Amsterdam are, therefore, limited when compared to Maastricht. However, new "common policies" have been added that will eventually have an impact on the citizens of Europe.

The Community now has express legislative powers to act against discrimination on grounds of sex, race, ethnic origin, religion, belief, disability, age, or sexual orientation.[51] New legislative powers address employment crises.[52] These are not "primary" legal instruments but rather common measures and initiatives designed to support or complement national employment policies. (Article 127 of the Treaty of Amsterdam expressly records the importance of respecting the material competence of Member States in this sphere.) The Treaty of Amsterdam does, however, provide for a new Employment Committee, and the Council now has the power (drawn from conclusions of the European Council) to make Recommendations to Member States after it has examined their policies in the

---

[49] Article 34, Treaty of Amsterdam.
[50] Basically, it is envisaged when the Member State in question has accepted ECJ jurisdiction in the matter. See Article 35, Treaty of Amsterdam.
[51] Article 13, EC Treaty.   [52] Articles 125–30, EC Treaty.

light of guidelines.[53] The Council also can adopt "incentive measures" to support the policies of Member States and to encourage cooperation between them. Finally, the Treaty of Amsterdam gives the Council the power to enact standard-setting measures in the area of public health policy. However, it also stresses the need to "fully respect the responsibility of the Member States for the organisation and delivery of health services and medical care."

Conclusion

The process of European integration, as witnessed by the successive EC Treaties from 1951 to 1997, has not followed a linear path. To some extent, the twists and turns reflect geopolitical reality. During the Cold War, the natural response to the Soviet threat was a drive toward the creation of tightly knit economic union. Later, as pressure from the Union of Soviet Socialist Republics receded and European nations withdrew from their colonial empires, the European Community acted as a centrifugal force bringing Western European nations together in an expanded union. Differing traditions of government and perceptions of national identity then led to tensions between federalists and nationalists.

With the collapse of the Soviet Union, the European states began to reassert their national identities more strongly. The result is reflected in the Maastricht Treaty through an inchoate mixture of integration and respect for national sovereignty and an *à la carte* menu of opt-out clauses that somehow seeks to keep the existing Union together while at the same time broadly moving toward the eventual integration of all the peoples of Europe as envisioned by the original Founding Fathers in the early 1950s.

What is undeniable, and should not be underestimated, is the strength of the European ideal. A wide spectrum of political forces—socialist, democratic, liberal—can support this ideal. Yet it is the consciousness that Europeans have a common heritage and a common culture, that there exists a "European" way, that inspires the various intergovernmental conferences where the fifteen Member States (and ten applicant states) meet.

THE DYNAMIC ROLE OF THE COMMUNITY INSTITUTIONS

The European Community's legal system has produced one of the most adventurous—some would say interventionist—courts of any regional

---

[53] Under Article 249, EC Treaty (formerly Article 189 EC), the Council can adopt "mandatory" Regulations, Directives, and Decisions as well as "persuasive" but not binding Recommendations and Opinions.

system. Indeed, the European Court of Justice has behaved very much like the U.S. Supreme Court; it has set its individual stamp on the shape of the emerging European Union. Repeatedly, it has nudged forward the process of European unification by landmark judgments. In doing so, the ECJ has been guided by a certain vision of European unification and, to the extent that ECJ judges have expressed themselves publicly, with a strong "federalist" flavor.

As a "constitutional court," the European Court of Justice has a wide and varied jurisdiction.[54] It adjudicates on disputes between Community Institutions (for example, when the Parliament complains that the Council has not consulted it properly or under the codecision procedure); between the citizens of the Union and the Community Institutions and Member States over their implementation of EC law; and between Member States and Community Institutions (for example, when Member States challenge the *vires* of a provision of Community legislation).

Three examples will suffice to describe the ECJ's role in nudging forward Community integration with its own collegiate vision of Europe. The first example will be an analysis of how the Court has enhanced the Parliament's role in the legislative process. The second example will be taken from the ECJ's role in the development of the doctrine of exclusive Community competence by which sovereignty is transferred from the Member States to the centralized Community Institutions. The third and final example will be the ECJ's development of the doctrine of "direct effect," whereby citizens have a right to enforce Treaty articles and other forms of Community law against defaulting or recalcitrant Member States to force them to give their citizens the individual rights intended to be conferred by the provision of EC law in question.

Before the Treaties of Maastricht (1992) and Amsterdam (1997), the Parliament was an unhappy hybrid of representative assembly and consultative body. It had little active involvement in EC lawmaking, and this was thought to be a crucial gap in its nature. However, the Parliament astutely made use of certain ambiguities in the text of the EC Treaty to enlarge its role. Accordingly, the Parliament, as a distinct Community Institution, began to use its legal powers to challenge the legal validity of the acts of other Community Institutions, such as the Council. In doing so, it forced the ECJ to intervene in the constitutional architecture of the European Communities.

---

[54] The discussion here will be limited to the European Court of Justice *sensu stricto*. No substantive analysis will be made of the EC Court of First Instance, created in 1989, with jurisdiction largely limited to review European Community acts in the spheres of competition, external trade, and staff disputes.

First, the Parliament began legal actions in the European Court of Justice to force meaningful consultations on the formulation of EC legislation. Consultation was provided for in the EC Treaty, but its precise boundaries were not defined (for example, the consequence of lack of proper consultation of the Parliament on the lawfulness of laws adopted by the Council). The opportunity came when certain isoglucose manufacturers sought to challenge a measure made under the Common Agricultural Policy. They contended the measure was constitutionally invalid for lack of proper consultation of the Parliament on the part of the Council.[55] Although the Council had consulted the Parliament, internal disagreement within the relevant Parliamentary Committee resulted in a failure to deliver a Parliamentary opinion on time. Therefore, the Council went ahead and adopted the contested Regulation.

The Parliament sought the leave of the European Court of Justice to intervene in the proceedings as an interested third party, against the firm opposition of some Member States (who, being so-called "privileged applicants," have an automatic right to take part in an ECJ proceeding). Under Article 173(1) of the EC Treaty,[56] the Council and the Commission were expressly identified as Community Institutions with an automatic right to take part in any ECJ proceeding. The question was whether the European Parliament was implicitly part of that privileged list, as a fellow Community Institution to the Council or Commission. An answer in the affirmative would dramatically enhance the power of the Parliament in ways clearly not intended by the negotiators of the original EC Treaty. The ECJ firmly and decisively ruled in favor of the Parliament's right to intervene:

The first paragraph of [Article 173][57] provides that all the institutions of the Community have the right to intervene. It is not possible to restrict the exercise of that right by one of them without adversely affecting its institutional position as intended by the Treaty and in particular Article 4(1).[58]

The consultation provided for in the third subparagraph of Article 173,[59] as in other similar provisions of the Treaty, is the means which allows the Parliament to play an actual part in the legislative process of the Community. Such power represents an essential factor in the institutional balance intended by the Treaty.

---

[55] In the dispute over Parliamentary consultation in isoglucose legislation, the Council went ahead and legislated without waiting for the Parliament to deliver its opinion: see Case 138/79, *Roquette Frères v. Council* (1980), ECR 3333; and Case 139/79, *Maizena v. Council* (1980), ECR 3393.

[56] Now Article 230, EC Treaty.   [57] Now Article 230, EC Treaty.
[58] Formerly Article 7, EC Treaty.   [59] Now Article 230, EC Treaty.

Although limited, it reflects at Community level that fundamental democratic principle that the peoples should take part in the exercise of power through the intermediary of a representative assembly. Due consultation of the Parliament in the cases provided for by the Treaty therefore constitutes an essential formality, disregard of which means that the measure concerned is void.[60]

Since this landmark case in 1980, the Court has developed the Parliament's institutional standing by allowing it to join the category of Community Institutions expressly cited in the Treaty as institutions whose actions can be annulled by legal challenge.[61] Thus, Green Party activists could challenge the Parliament's acts that have a bearing on EC environmental policy.[62] More recently, the ECJ appears to have fought shy of further expansion of the Parliament's legislative role, perhaps in the belief that the Parliament's powers had increased enough and that expansion of the Parliament's functions should be left to those who would draft future EC treaties. In 1990 the ECJ ruled that the Parliament's right to bring an action to annul a Community measure operates only when its prerogatives (that is, its right to be consulted) have been infringed in the adoption of the contested measures.[63] The ECJ expressly recognized the existence of a gap in the Treaties but would not arrogate to itself the right to amend the Treaties by judicial activism:

The absence in the Treaties of any provisions giving the Parliament the right to bring an action for annulment may institute a procedural gap, but it cannot prevail over the fundamental interest in the maintenance of and observance of the institutional balance laid down in the Treaties establishing the European Communities.[64]

The Doctrine of Exclusive Community Competence

In the Community's structure the relationship between the Member States and the EC Institutions is problematic. The Member States and the Institutions have their powers. Whereas those of the Member States are derived from the sovereignty of the constituent nations, those of the Community

---

[60] Case 138/79, *Roquette Frères v. Council* (1980), ECR 3333 at paragraphs 19 and 37; Case 139/79, *Maizena v. Council* (1980), ECR 3393. The ECJ has since ruled that, in certain circumstances, a failure by the Parliament to produce an opinion does not block the Council's right to legislate. See Case C-65/93, *European Parliament v. Council* (1995), ECR I-643.

[61] Under Article 230 of the EC Treaty (formerly Article 173 EC), the acts of the Council and the Commission are expressly subject to annulment.

[62] Case 294/83, *Parti Ecologiste "Les Verts" v. European Parliament* (1986), ECR 1339.

[63] Case 302/87, *European Parliament v. Council* (1988), ECR 5616 (the so-called "comitology" case). See also Case C-70/88, *European Parliament v. Council* (1990), ECR I-2041.

[64] Ibid., paragraph 26.

have been conferred by the Treaties. The problem is particularly acute in the sphere of external trade policy. Articles 131–135 of the EC Treaty[65] have established a "common commercial policy" to create a single trading face to the outside world. Although the EC has international legal personality, and thus possesses the powers to act on the international stage consistent with the need to make these powers function effectively under public international law, in practice the exercise of these powers would clash with the desire of Member States to continue acting on the international stage as independent sovereign nations in the traditional way.[66] Thus, when it comes to an agreement between, say, rubber-producing nations and rubber-importing nations to regulate trade in this commodity, who should negotiate: the Member States, the Community, or both?

In the 1970s and 1980s, when Community integration was at its highest because of the intergovermentalism that prevailed, the Commission started a series of constitutional test cases to obtain a definition of the boundaries of Community treaty-making competence from the ECJ. Again the ECJ intervened decisively and controversially in favor of a federalist direction.

The first test case concerned an agreement between several Member States and Switzerland, a non-EC state, on road transport. The Commission challenged the *vires* of the European Road Transport Agreement (ERTA) on the grounds that such unilateral action on the part of the Member States concerned was contrary to the exclusive competence of the Community: in other words, the Community rather than the Member States should have negotiated the agreement with Switzerland. Although the ECJ upheld the validity of the ERTA, it gave the Commission an important victory of principle by declaring that the Council and the Commission should have agreed on an appropriate method of cooperation to ensure the optimum defense of Community interests.

The Commission went on to pursue this theme in test cases against the Council.[67] The Council then established the doctrine of exclusive community competence: whenever the Council adopts a common position, either expressly or by implication, in the sphere of foreign policy, it enjoys exclusive community competence in the matter, preventing unilateral action by Member States.

---

[65] Formerly Articles 110–116 EC.

[66] On the European Community's international legal community, see Article 210, EC Treaty. See also the UN Reparations for Injuries Case, 1948, International Court of Justice, Report 186.

[67] See Hartley, *The Foundations of European Community Law*, chap. 6; and Macleod, Hendry, and Hyett, *The External Relations of the European Communities*, 56 et seq.

The doctrine is a logical one, preventing carefully negotiated common positions from being undermined by the subsequent actions of individual Member States. But the ECJ went even further and subsequently ruled that the Community enjoyed internal competence as well.[68] This meant that the Member States automatically lost their right of individual action externally. Most radically of all, the ECJ ruled that the loss of power could occur whether or not the Community had acted internally in the field in question.[69] In this way the ECJ went beyond its earlier doctrine that Member States retained a sort of transitional competence in the period before the Community acted in common.[70]

By the end of the 1970s, the ECJ had radically expanded the power of the European Community in external relations, allowing it to express a more coherent voice in the international sphere. Since then, however, the Member States have successfully fought a rearguard action, and the ECJ has developed the doctrine of "mixed competence," whereby agreements dealing with issues covered partially by the [Treaties] were to be concluded by *both* the Community and the Member States in their respective spheres of competence.[71] An example is the World Trade Organization agreements that emerged from the Uruguay Round in 1994, including a new General Agreement on Tariffs and Trade.[72] This compromise solution—shared competence between the Member States and the Community—neatly symbolized the state of European integration in the mid-1990s.

The Treaty of Amsterdam in 1997 attempted to formalize this position.[73] The Commission now plays the main negotiating role in external relations; the Council concludes an external agreement subject to the Commission's recommendation and after consulting the Parliament. The Member States, of course, retain their competence when there is no exclusive Community competence.

---

[68] The European Community would enjoy internal competence if the Treaty created a common policy in, say, the field of environmental safeguards.

[69] Opinion 1/76, regarding the Draft Agreement for a Laying Up Fund for Inland Waterway Vessels (1977), ECR 741.

[70] Cases 3,4 and 6/76, Cornelius Kramer and others (1976), ECR 1279.

[71] See David O'Keefe and Henry G. Schermers, *Mixed Agreements* (Deventer: Kluwer, 1983).

[72] See Opinion 1/94 regarding the WTO agreement (1994), ECR I-5267. For the effect of the WTO within the domestic legal system of the EC, see Philip Ruttley "The Direct Effect of the WTO Agreements in EC Law," in Philip Ruttley, Iain Mac Vay, and Carol George, eds., *The WTO and International Trade Regulation* (London: Cameron, May 1998), 130.

[73] Article 300(1), EC Treaty.

Private Enforcement of the Treaties against Member States

The ECJ showed its independence and willingness to promote European integration when it developed the doctrine of "direct effect" in the 1960s. At that stage the original six Member States had arrived at the end of the first "transitional" period, and certain laws had to be harmonized on a community level. Most lawyers and constitutional theorists at that time would have considered the ECSC, EEC, and EURATOM Treaties to be conventional international agreements between states. Their effects on the citizens of the participating states would be determined by the domestic law of the Member State in question. Either the Treaties would be automatically incorporated into the domestic laws of the Member States, or national assemblies would pass specific laws to establish the extent to which the "foreign" Treaties penetrated into the domestic legal sphere—as in the "monist" constitutional approach of the Netherlands and the United Kingdom. Greece took the constitutional approach: it automatically incorporates international treaties to which Greece is a party into national law, giving them superior validity to national law in certain cases of conflict. The United Kingdom, a dualist state, passed special legislation to permit its Courts to give effect to certain parts of the EC Treaties domestically.[74] Traditionally, therefore, citizens of states could invoke international treaties to which their state is a party to the extent permitted by their national law.

The ECJ radically changed this as regards EC law. The test case was brought as early as 1963 by a Dutch transport firm named Van Gend en Loos. It imported German goods on which the Dutch customs authorities sought to levy import duties, notwithstanding the fact that Article 12 of the EEC Treaty expressly forbade the introduction of new interstate taxes of this sort. Against the opposition of Germany, the Netherlands, and Belgium, and against dire warnings that the floodgates of vexatious litigation would be opened if the citizens of EC states were able to invoke and enforce the EEC Treaty against defaulting states, the ECJ created a new doctrine, the "direct effect" of EC law.

The ECJ ruled against the traditionalist view and held that notwithstanding the EC Treaty's silence on whether private rights were granted, the Dutch importer could successfully prevent his tax authority from acting in contradiction to the Treaty. The Court held that the EEC Treaty was for the benefit of the citizens of the EEC states, who could enforce it

---

[74] The European Communities Act of 1972, as amended. See Lawrence Collins, *European Community Law in the United Kingdom*, 4th ed. (London: Butterworths, 1990).

against defaulting or recalcitrant EC states if the provision in question was absolute and did not require Member States to perform some implementing act, or to exercise discretion as to how to incorporate the provision into their domestic legal system. Article 12 of the EEC Treaty was clearly such a provision, since it imposed a general prohibition on new customs duties as between Member States. There being no room for ambiguity or administrative discretion, the Dutch transport firm could successfully resist the Dutch customs levy.[75] What is striking is the sweeping, even visionary, language of the ECJ in its judgment:

To ascertain whether the provisions of an international treaty extend so far in their effects it is necessary to consider the spirit, the general scheme and the wording of those provisions.

The objective of the EC Treaty, which is to establish a Common Market, the functioning of which is of direct concern to interested parties in the Community, implies that this Treaty is more than an agreement which merely creates mutual obligations between the contracting states. This view is confirmed by the preamble to the Treaty which refers not only to governments but to peoples. It is also confirmed more specifically by the establishment of institutions endowed with sovereign rights, the exercise of which affects Member States and also their citizens. Furthermore,... the nationals of the states brought together in the Community are called upon to co-operate in the functioning of this Community through the intermediary of the European Parliament and the Economic and Social Committee.

The... Community constitutes a new legal order of international law for the benefit of which the states have limited their sovereign rights, albeit within limited fields, and the subject of which comprise not only Member States but also their nationals. Independently of the legislation of Member States, Community law therefore not only imposes obligations on individuals but is also intended to confer upon them rights which become part of their legal heritage. These rights arise not only where they are expressly granted by the Treaty, but also by reason of obligations which the Treaty imposes in a clearly defined way upon individuals as well as upon the Member States and upon the institutions of the Community.[76]

A leading ECJ judge was quite candid later about the activism of the Court:

It appears from these considerations that in the opinion of the Court, the Treaty has created a Community not only of States but also of peoples and persons and that therefore not only Member States but also individuals must be visualised as being subjects of Community law. This is the consequence of a democratic ideal, meaning that in the Community, as well as in a modern constitutional

---

[75] Case 26/92, *Van Gend en Loos v. Netherlands Tax Administration* (1963), ECR 1.
[76] Ibid.

State, Governments may not say any more what they are used to doing in international law: L'Etat, c'est moi. Far from it; the Community calls for participation of everybody, with the result that private individuals are not only liable to
burdens and obligations, but that they have also prerogatives and rights which
must be legally protected. It was thus a highly political idea, drawn from a perception of the constitutional system of the Community, which is at the basis of
Van Gend en Loos and which continues to inspire the whole doctrine flowing
from it.[77]

In many ways the doctrine of direct effect is an application of the principle of the supremacy of Community law over conflicting national law.
Since *Van Gend en Loos*, the doctrine of direct effect has been progressively extended to allow citizens to force states to honor their EC Treaty
obligations in many areas and to deny states the possibility of frustrating
the operation of EC law by their inaction or failure to fully implement
their Community obligations. The doctrine of direct effect now applies
to EC Treaty Articles and to secondary laws, such as Regulations and
Directives, with various conditions that need not concern us here. Since
Van Gend en Loos, the ECJ has expanded the boundaries of "direct effect" as well as the doctrine of state financial liability. EC states are now
liable to pay compensation to individuals within their jurisdiction who
have suffered economic damage as a result of their manifest and serious
failure to implement their Treaty obligations.[78]

Not every Treaty provision or legal measure taken by the EC, however,
can have such direct effect. The provision or measure in question must be
"legally perfect": that is to say, it must be unambiguous and clearly intended to benefit a definable class of individuals, it must not require any
further implementation by the Member State, and it must be unconditional. The relevant EEC Treaty provision in the *Van Gend en Loos* case,
Article 12, of the EC Treaty, states that Member States of the European
Community cannot introduce new tariff barriers between each other. This
is a clear and unambiguous EC Treaty provision, which is unconditional,

---

[77] Pierre Pescatore, "The Doctrine of 'Direct Effect': An Infant Disease of Community Law,"
in 8 European Community Law Review 155 (1983): 158.

[78] See Cases C-46 and 48/93, *Brasserie du Pêcheur SA v. Germany and R v. Secretary of State
for Transport, ex parte* Factortame Ltd and others (1996), ECR I-1029; Case C-392/93,
R v. *HM Treasury ex parte British Telecommunications plc* (1996), ECR I-1631; and Case
C-5/94, R v. *Ministry of Agriculture, Fisheries and Ford, ex parte* Headley Lomas (1996),
ECR I-2553. Case C-48/93 R v. *Secretary of State for Transport ex parte Factortame Ltd
and others (III)* (1996) ECR I-1029. Proceedings to recover damages from the United
Kingdom by Spanish fishing interests claiming to have suffered economic loss from the
implementation of the Merchant Shipping (Registration) Act of 1988 held the applicants
were not entitled to claim exemplary damages from the respondent in relation to the
breaches that were the subject of the proceedings.

and does not require any enactment of subsidiary laws to give it effect.[79]

A "direct effect" provision of an EC Treaty can be enforced "vertically" by an individual against several types of public bodies: a government ministry, public bodies that are fulfilling a public function (such as state education or trade authorities), private companies with a public service function (such as transport operators that fulfill a public function by servicing the needs of remote areas), or former state-owned companies that have been privatized but operate under a public monopoly.

The doctrine of direct effect forces Member States to observe their obligations under the EC Treaties. Individuals who are harmed by another Member State's failure to comply with EC Treaties do not have to trust their governments to take up the fight for them.[80] Nor are they forced to rely on the European Commission to use its power of enforcement against defaulting Member States or other forms of enforcement at the sovereign or international level.[81]

In the twenty-first century European integration has reached a critical phase. Now that monetary and economic union is firmly on the agenda a truly fundamental transfer of sovereignty is taking place: anything before that was mere politics.

Nearly fifty years after the first European Community was created in 1951, one can discern a unique and distinct European political and legal framework. It will, in turn, create a new European identity. In retrospect, EC law and the European Court of Justice were fundamental in shaping the new political consensus.

[79] For discussion of direct effect, see Hartley, *Foundations of European Community Law*, chap. 7; Collins, *European Community Law in the United Kingdom*, chap. 2; and Henry G. Schermers and Denis F. Waelbroeck, *Judicial Protection in the European Community*, 5th ed. (Deveneter: Kluwer, 1992), 138–54.

[80] Article 227 of the EC Treaty (formerly Article 170) allows a Member State to start proceedings against another member for failure to comply with EC law.

[81] See Articles 211 and 226, EC Treaty (formerly Article 155 and 169 EC respectively).

12

The Euro, Economic Federalism, and the Question of National Sovereignty

ELIE COHEN

For years the construction of Europe has been discussed and made by experts. Because the wider public never quite knew what was going on or what the issues at stake quite were, "Europe"—at least in most European nations—enjoyed a generally positive, if also somewhat vague, reputation. Criticism became apparent only when referenda on the various stages of the development of European unification transformed it into a public affair. It was as if a long-agreed discourse on the need for a unified Europe had effectively camouflaged the consideration of all opposing interests, as if the only acceptable Europe was one that would be realized by those who alone were competent to handle such matters, and behind closed doors.

Central to all potential objections to European integration has been and remains the question of sovereignty. And it is sovereignty that has been at the core of the debate on monetary union, since the issues at stake involve such time-hallowed functions of national states as the right to mint money, the independence of central banks and their possible subordination to an exterior central power, the loss of parliamentary prerogatives, and even the loss of a fundamental element of national identity: the national currency itself.

The first difficulty that arises from any attempt to understand the relationship between monetary union and sovereignty stems from the multiple meanings that are accorded to the latter. For the term no longer implies simply the complete and absolute authority of the sovereign body. Political sovereignty, which possesses a clear legal foundation, is often confused with policy prerogatives, particularly where they concern economic regulation that may vary over time and that can be exercised directly or by delegation, depending on specific cases. In order to achieve a better understanding of monetary sovereignty, one must separate what most analysts have attempted to keep together. Can one, for instance, integrate economies and maintain national currencies? Can one set common disciplines and leave the governing of the central banks to the discretion of national political authorities? Should monetary policy be removed from the control of national parliaments? Does it make economic sense to separate the monetary and budgetary policies of individual states? The institutional complexities are multiple, and they sometimes have unexpected effects. There exist dependent central banks that follow a strict objective of inflation control, and independent central banks (such as the American Fed) whose anti-inflationist performance was for long only mediocre. Likewise, a central bank does not lack democratic legitimacy simply because it is independent. The legitimacy conferred on such a bank by constitutional provision, a monetary government made up of representatives of the federated states, and widespread acceptance by the citizens may grant it a certain weight and credibility, even if the question of accountability remains open, as is the case of the European Central Bank.

The question we must ask is a simple one: how did the European Monetary Union (EMU) become the response to contradicting needs—technical, economic, political—and in what way does the institutional model invented for this occasion prefigure the final integration of the current nation-states into an integrated Europe? In view of the complexity of the relationship between the technical, economic, and political dimensions of this debate, I shall begin by suggesting an answer to this question and then outline why I believe it to be the correct one.

WHY THE EMU?

First of all, the EMU is a vital necessity for the construction of a large European market. It is, in fact, simply impossible to sustain a single market without a single currency. A system of fixed but adjustable parities can always skid out of control, as the experience in the summer of 1993 made abundantly clear. This point of view, however, has been hotly debated by economists. Some admit that a policy of stimulation of competition and the unification of the European interior market can be ruined by erratic currency fluctuations. Others have countered this argument by maintaining that, even over a long period of time, the parities correct the differentials of competitiveness and that over a short period the changes in monetary rates may correct the volatility of the exchange rates.

These arguments, although technically acceptable, fail to recognize the political dimension of economic integration. When countries do nearly two-thirds of their exchanges among themselves, and when almost one in three jobs in the manufacturing sector depends on foreign trade, any deregulation that translates into unemployment and bankruptcy questions the ability of Brussels to manage the integrated area. In addition, since states cannot aid the sectors in difficulty without incurring the wrath of the European competitive authority, every monetary accident is bound to have a political impact. Finally, the coverage of exchange risks that could remedy the problem are not available to small and medium enterprises and thus constitute a negation of the integration process. It was, therefore, at this very stage, that the single currency came to be regarded as the essential follow-up to the single market.

The EMU and the Single European Act of 1987 illustrate the theory of impulse imbalance. In other words, they are the technical loopholes (shortcomings) of a former institutional compromise that create the necessity for a new political advance, one that also could have been achieved through economic manipulation. The Exchange Rate Mechanism (ERM) and the free circulation of capital have created an asymmetrical situation profiting Germany. In addition, financial deregulation on a national level has generated a demand for regulation at a higher level. Balancing the deal implies an advance in European Union policy. Following the same model, the transfer of powers to the European Central Bank creates a void in political legitimacy, a void, in ideal circumstances, that would be filled by political union. The necessity for a public European redistributive power has, therefore, become irresistible since in a homogeneous economic space, the adaptation to exogenous shocks cannot be realized in real terms. However, European public opinion will not accept that the adjustment must be achieved through unemployment, while, at the same time, the member states simply wash their political hands of the whole affair.

Necessity, however acute, cannot achieve the required adjustment, any more than can the European Commission's entrepreneurial political spirit. And that is the point at which functionalist explanations fall short. The centrality of the political moment leads me to my second conclusion: that the single currency is the necessary counterpoint to German reunification. From the moment that Germany became a single sovereign state, the EMU forced it to anchor itself in a process of European integration of a federal kind. In the process France was offered the opportunity to pass from a relationship of dependence to one of cooperation with a Germany that has become the leading European power.

In this event the political will of the president of the French Republic was not sufficient to bring about the political changes that were necessary, since he still had to convince his partners in the European Union of the desirability of the move. The EMU is thus the result of a convergence of strategies and of ulterior motives. To the United Kingdom, in particular, it seemed as if liberalization of capital together with financial deregulation would put an end to French "constructivism" in European affairs. It was a kind of market consecration. From this point on, the British consistently attempted to curb the process by maintaining an opt-out clause and by proposing from time to time some alternative solution (the common currency or the weighted Ecu).

The French strategy, on the other hand, has always been simple: use the EMU to win in internal influence what it lost in the framework of the ERM. The German outlook is divided. The liberalization of capital and the ERM have confirmed Germany's monetary hegemony; the EMU is thus either pointless or acceptable only at the end of a long process of real economic convergence—provided that it reproduces the German institutional model. Only the political determination to give a guarantee to France in order to hasten reunification led Hans Dietrich Genscher, Germany's secretary of foreign affairs, to ignore the opposition of the Bundesbank and to create the Maastricht compromise of 1992.

The EMU was in large part shaped by French politico-administrative elites. This was because these elites saw in it a motor for the naturalization of exterior constraint and for the limitation of the discretionary power of politicians. In reality, these elites wanted to make the decisions taken in 1983 irreversible and thereby give themselves larger and more gratifying places in the European framework. As it happened, however, the people rejected the plans of their "enlightened despots." Currency relies upon confidence, and this makes it hard to create a common currency wholly within the confines of the offices of monetary experts. The monetary crises of 1992, 1993, and 1994 were attributable less to response of defiant markets than to the reaction of a hesitant, uncertain, and ill-informed public when faced with severe economic policy decisions. As the turning point of 1983 illustrates, it was political power along with a nonindependent Central Bank that broke the inflationist mechanism by resorting to the instruments of a policy of revenues instead of the tools of monetary policy.[1]

Would it not then be economically more efficient to call upon the people in order to create a change in policy? When all is said and done, the

---

[1] Michel Aglietta "Leçons pour la Banque Centrale Européenne," in *L'Indépendance des banques centrales, Revue d'Economie Financière* 22 (Autumn 1992): 37–56.

EMU raises a fearsome question: are we witnessing a "technicizing" of a sovereign policy or the "federalizing" of all the policies of integration by way of a purely monetary device? The strategy of impulse imbalance reached its limits with the crisis in the 1990s and the awakening of public opinion. Two solutions remain open. The first implies a political process in which the democratic refounding of Europe by means of a single currency operates as the cornerstone of a new federal Europe. The second consists in treating the currency as a matter of common consent, entrusted by the sovereign nations of the Union to an ad hoc organism. This institution with a limited purpose would nonetheless find in European-wide public opinion a legitimacy based upon a transfer of confidence from friable local currencies to an enduring European one.

Next I shall attempt to explain the political arguments of the actors who negotiated the monetary section of the Maastricht Treaty even while aware of its technical limits. I then hope to show the way in which the Community's experience (the theory of impulse equilibrium) can inspire adaptations as diverse as a limited monetary union, a reinforced European Council, and even an extension of the coordination of economic policies leading ultimately to budgetary federalism. The primary goal of Maastricht was not to resolve a technical problem linked to the management of the currency in a framework of financial globalization; it was, instead, to take another step toward political integration through deployment of the device of economic constraint.

THE EMU AND THE RENUNCIATION OF SOVEREIGNTY

Among the most uncontested of the prerogatives of the sovereign is the right to mint money. This privilege is one of the foundational elements of the modern state. As a unit of account, an intermediary of exchange, and a reserve of purchasing power, a currency is the quintessential "public good." It unifies the territorial market, homogenizes prices, suppresses the costs of conversion from one currency to another. Currency being but "minted confidence," it is administered by the state, or more exactly by one of its branches: the Central Bank.[2]

"In those economies which benefit from freedom of exchange and the movement of capital," Tommaso Padoa Schioppa has observed, "the prerogative of the sovereign, formally uncontested, is in reality limited by

---

[2] Jean-Pierre Patat, *L'Europe monétaire* (Paris: La Découverte, 1990). In this book Patat describes these elementary notions with exceptional clarity.

the freedom of particular people to choose the currency with which they operate."[3]

This introduces a double limitation to monetary sovereignty. Firstly, it is the private actors (in particular the banks) that essentially create the currency. Their behavior (particularly that of business treasurers) influences most directly the stability of a currency. Secondly, in an open economy the markets arbitrate daily among currencies, compelling monetary authorities to renounce their discretionary power over rates.[4] The constitution of monetary zones is but a partial response to this loss of control by individual states. In reality, a zone is always organized around a dominant currency with prerogatives the others lack. Those others thus find themselves restricted.

Abandoning one's currency for a new one is either the recognition of the limits of monetary pluralism in a single market—in which case the state delegates a limited and specific power to an ad hoc institution—or it constitutes part of the process whereby a federation of states is created whose substance and legitimacy could be found only in approval of a federal constitution by the citizens of those states. In the first instance, the source of legitimacy remains national since jurisdiction remains an indefinable prerogative of the national state. The best proof of this is to be found in the very process by which control over any national currency is relinquished—in this instance the treaty. What one treaty does can always be undone by another, since intergovernmental coordination is not part of any constitutional process. In the second instance, the single currency and the European Central Bank, along with other institutional devices, constitute the components of a new political-institutional order. Contrary to popular opinion, one cannot go to sleep French and wake up European by means of a series of institutional shifts and the cumulative effects of reassigning public policies. There must be an act capable of manifesting the popular will.

The authority over a territory (its sovereign character, the power to do and to undo) clearly defined the limits of the modern nation-state—that is to say, the entity within which, according to Ernest Gellner, is found the identity of a people, of a territory, of a culture, of a state, and of the

---

[3] Tommaso Padoa Schioppa, "Union monétaire et concurrence des monnaies en Europe," *Commentaire* 54 (1991): 54–78.

[4] The suspicion by the French of the French currency from 1945 to 1983, and their readiness at present, as evidenced by the opinion polls, to abandon the franc for the Euro demonstrates that in France, the sacralization of the national currency is not as strong as it is in Germany.

principle of political legitimacy.[5] Is the EMU a step toward the abandonment of the nation-state and a move toward federation? Or can monetary
policy still be controlled by a delegation of powers by sovereign states to
increase collective authority over policies that are essential to economic
regulation? To answer these questions I must identify more precisely what
is at stake in monetary union and explain how and why the European
states have come to this position.

THE EMU AND THE THEORY OF IMPULSE IMBALANCE

The Europe that has been constructed so far has made extensive use of
economic means to achieve its political goals. The law and the market
operated, not as a substitute to the political will, but as the political will
in disguise. At the same time, however, monetary Europe has been the
necessary outcome of economic integration and the most obvious solution
to economic crises.

We do not have to go back to the European Union of Payments, created
in 1950, or to the European Monetary Agreement of 1955, which organized a specifically European margin of fluctuation in relation to the U.S.
dollar in the framework of Bretton Woods (0.75 percent to 1 percent), to
see that the Marjolin Report since 1962 has established monetary union as
the third step toward European unification. Following the customs union
and the common market, the Werner Report in 1970 proposed the realization by 1980 of a monetary union with "the complete and irreversible
convertibility of currencies, the elimination of margins of fluctuation of
exchange, the irrevocable setting of parity relations and the liberation of
movements of capital" throughout the whole of Europe.[6] The Werner
Report anticipated an economic union founded on the coordination of
economic policies, the harmonization of budgetary and fiscal policies,
the transfer to the Community of monetary policy as well as short-term
macroeconomic policy and medium-term programming.

The crisis began with U.S. president Richard Nixon's decision to suspend the gold convertibility of the dollar. This decision curbed the practical realization of community objectives because of the free floating of
currencies and at the same time compelled the Europeans to become

---

[5] Ernest Gellner, *Nations and Nationalism* (Oxford: Blackwell Publishers, 1983).
[6] The Werner Report, "Rapport au Conseil et à la Commission concernant la réalisation
de l'Union Economique et Monétaire dans la Communauté," *Supplément au Bulletin 11
des Communautés Européennes*, 1970.

aware of the necessity of monetary stability in an economic zone en route to integration. On March 21, 1972, the monetary snake was created. This allowed European currencies to vary within limits of plus or minus 2.25 percent. In 1978, however, it became necessary to rework the plan. On the initiative of German chancellor Helmut Schmidt and French president Valery Giscard d'Estaing, the ERM was created on December 5, 1978. A system of stable but adjustable exchange rates, the ERM was intended to evolve into full monetary union. But the second oil crisis, the adoption of divergent macroeconomic policies, and widespread monetary disorder compelled the different countries involved to turn, once again, to the discretionary handling of exchange rates—monetary policies and non-tariff obstacles to exchanges being the only devices capable of preserving the balance between national, political, and social interests.

The paralysis of the European Community during the crisis years 1974 to 1978 rendered monetary integration less urgent and less likely. The Single European Act of 1987 that revived the process of integration should have included a monetary section. But the context for the renewal of monetary construction had changed radically. In the first place, monetary policy was no longer directed only at monetary stability and the fight against inflation. Now it encompassed expansion and full employment. In the second, the realization of the enlarged market in 1992 was achieved by the freeing of all movement of capital, and especially by the financial services that constituted a powerful mechanism of financial deregulation.[7] Finally, an ever-increasing number of European countries sought monetary stability within the limits of the ERM. As a result, the German mark became the anchoring point for all the European currencies, and the German central bank the sole possessor of power in matters of monetary policy.

On January 6, 1988, the deficiencies of the European monetary code once again compelled the European states to revise it. On that occasion France's prime minister, Edouard Balladur, declared on television that "the time has come to examine the possibility of creating a European central bank which would manage a common currency." The ERM, he said, "does not really work for me. . . . [I]ts functioning is neither very egalitarian nor is it complete."[8] The leader of a party known for its coolness toward

---

[7] See Kenneth Dyson, *Elusive Union* (London and New York: Longman, 1994). He explains how the argument for the necessary liberalization of the movement of capital as a prerequisite to any discussion on the realization of monetary union allowed the English and the Germans to block French objectives of a monetary integration for a considerable time.

[8] Quoted in Pascal Riché and Charles Wypolsz, eds., *L'Union Economique et Monétaire* (Paris: Le Seuil, 1993).

Europe was calling for a decisive advance in the construction of a closer European union. Once again the institutional machine invented by Jean Monnet was set into motion.

Each advance in economic integration creates an economic and political imbalance whose victims aspire to escape "by the top"—by means, that is, of a new political strategy—and unless they are able to do so, the entire system will malfunction. A new political contract negotiated by the twelve Member States at the time establishes a new game plan. The contract is then passed to the Commission. Thanks to its monopoly on initiative, the Commission is able to give the contract technical consistency before handing it over to private actors who set in motion the European Court of Justice, which, in turn, legally unifies the European markets. With the EMU the mechanism functions according to the same design, only here the stakes are different. Since monetary union requires economic convergence, which implies control of budgetary policies and a form of redistribution among the European "regions," it cannot be achieved without political union, yet that union must be one in which the surrender of active powers does not effectively empty the democratic process of all significance. The negotiation process of the Maastricht Treaty clearly illustrates this chain of events and its limits.

In Hanover in June of 1988, "the Twelve" decided upon the formation of a committee of experts charged with reporting to the European Council on the feasibility of monetary union. One year later the Delors Report was adopted in Madrid, and the first political mediations were submitted to the Council. At this point the Council was divided between partisans of the immediate leap and partisans of what was called the "crowning strategy." According to this strategy, union would be achieved only after the full completion of macroeconomic convergence. The Guigou paper (the report of a coordinating committee created by the French president) on the problems posed by monetary union provided a veritable inventory of the instruments and institutions of monetary policy. Ornamenting it was a series of sketches for the institutional architecture that would permit the reconciliation of an efficient monetary policy with respect for national sovereignties. The latter was introduced under the notion of "subsidiarity," coupled to the Germanic theory of the separation of monetary power attributed to an independent central bank from budgetary power that would be handled by the federal chancellery.

In the autumn of 1989, however, history intervened. The Soviet Empire crumbled, and against the advice of the Bundesbank, Chancellor Helmut Kohl announced in early 1990 an economic, monetary, and social Union with East Germany for July 1990.[9] West Germany obtained support from its European partners and, most importantly, the (albeit reticent) approval of France. In return, West Germany offered a firm commitment to the accelerated realization of the EMU, even though the Bundesbank was simultaneously demanding a ten-year moratorium in order to manage the integration of East Germany. In April 1990 the stakes were raised still higher with the Kohl-Mitterrand proposal to conduct the EMU and political union at the same time.

The final negotiations began in Rome on December 15, 1990. The Bundesbank formally had no say in the matter, since negotiations were concerned with establishing a new system of exchange. Nonetheless, it insisted on ensuring that the mark was abandoned only for an equally solid monetary unit. The European Central Bank had to be an exact replica of the Bundesbank, or at least as independent and dedicated to the fight against inflation. The barter was concluded along the following lines: the sharing of monetary power was granted to "the Twelve" in exchange for allowing Germany to set the rules of the game. The famous article 107 of the Treaty states:

In the exercise of powers and in the accomplishment of the missions and duties which have been conferred by the present treaty and by the statutes of the ESBC (European System of Central Banks), neither the European Central Bank, nor any national central bank, nor any member of their decision-making bodies may solicit or accept instructions from community institutions or bodies, from administrations of the Member States, or from any other organisation. The Community institutions and bodies, as well as the administrations of Member States, commit themselves to respect this principle and will not look to influence the members of the decision-making bodies of the European Central Bank or the national central banks in the accomplishment of their missions.[10]

But what exactly is the EMU? The question is perhaps best answered in terms of its salient features. It is a process that organizes the progressive

---

[9] This is the first of the three crises that led to the abolition of the ERM. Karl Otto Poehl, then head of the Bundesbank, claimed this decision would ruin East Germany and bring about massive financial transfers from the West to the East. In the absence of a courageous fiscal policy, this could only renew inflation. His analysis proved to be perfectly correct. Chancellor Kohl was convinced that historical opportunities must be seized. The presence of Gorbachev in the Kremlin made reunification possible; from then on the German administration had to follow. The promise of the paradise of the West as a welcoming gift to the brothers from the East, and the promise made to the citizens of the West that reunification would cost them nothing, were the best means to achieve rapid reunification. To Kohl, it was obvious that the administration would follow his lead. Europe paid dearly for this strategy.

[10] *Les traités de Rome et de Maastricht* (Paris: La Documentation Française, 1992), 68.

transition from a situation marked by the diversity of national monetary systems to a common monetary system based on a single currency, the Euro, controlled by a European system of central banks whose center of influence is the European Central Bank. The EMU also is a powerful machine for economic convergence. Its essential tools are the criteria of convergence themselves and the "structural" funds. The policies designed to meet the criteria contract activity when necessary, while the funds help the poorer members of the union to expand. Finally, coupled with political union, the EMU is a means for shifting the boundaries of politics and economic strategies, both national and supranational. In this respect, however, it suffers from three basic weaknesses: it is the product of intergovernmental diplomatic agreement, which must survive highly risky periods of transition, it is at the mercy of the markets, and it is at the mercy of exogenous shocks.

THE STRATEGY OF COMPETITIVE DEFLATION INSCRIBED IN THE STONE OF INSTITUTIONS

Why, then, have the European nations, and especially the largest among them, France and Germany, committed themselves to a process that, while promising, is exposed to considerable risks? Why are these nations—their administrations, their political elites, and their trade unions—convinced that only the solutions extolled by ultra-libertarians and Friedmanian monetarists can bring about European unification? To constitutionalize maximum deficits, separate monetary and budgetary policies, confer monetary policy upon an independent central bank: these are the great principles of the EMU. Its theoretical sources are to be found in the writings of Milton Friedman, but they are hardly applied with rigor even in the United States.

In the sixties during a period of full expansion, at the initiative of the "Trilateral," a global think-tank, illustrious men and women tried hard to resolve the crisis of the western democracies. Rampant inflation was eating away at the acquisitions of growth, making covert transfers and, above all, revealing the states' incapacity to contain this movement. The established diagnosis questioned the governability of democratic market societies. In reality, the impersonal mechanisms of the market, the rigidity of salaries and prices, and the weight of social oligopoly were thought to be responsible for serious limits on the states' regulative capacity. Various solutions were considered that would have placed a check on the politicians and prohibited them from giving in to demands that might hurt the economy. Among these solutions, one enjoyed considerable popularity: prohibition of budgetary deficit by formal inscription in the constitution. But it was the separation of monetary and budgetary policies that offered a lasting solution. An independent central bank, restricted solely to the fight against inflation and not required to coordinate its actions with the actions of those in charge of the budgetary policy, would, it was believed, limit the arbitrariness of political decisions.[11] The hypothesis is now a familiar one: an independent central bank is reputed to be more credible because it is sheltered from political pressure and can thus avoid inopportune, election-timed reflation policies. Such a bank can take a long-term approach and adapt its short-term aims. A dependent central bank is compelled to change its conduct and continually revise its aims in order to meet short-term objectives. Finally, an independent central bank acts in accordance with a pre-established code instead of multiplying discretionary interventions. An independent central bank's voluntary commitment or a mandate to pursue only one goal—fighting inflation—confers upon it an uncontested credibility.

Germany's remarkable performance in the fight against inflation progressively elevated its monetary policy to the status of a model in the 1980s. The institutional factor—the Bundesbank's independence—came to be regarded as the sole explanation for Germany's stability and performance. The context for this success—the institutionalized social compromise and salary moderation—and its historical moorings—the *Ordnungspolitik*—were forgotten. After the Left took power in France in 1981, three consecutive devaluations convinced a number of administrative authorities of the excellence of the German model.

The economic administration of France, or (if one prefers) the economic decision-making community (Treasury, Bank of France, private governments of financial and industrial groups), would not have committed themselves to the EMU project if its cardinal objective since March 1983 had not been to create an institutional foundation for competitive deflation, while removing from political control the discretionary manipulation of the currency. The following statements in a 1992 issue of *Haute*

---

[11] See Robert Barro and David Gordon, "Rules, Discretion and Reputation in a Model of Monetary Policy," *Journal of Monetary Economics* (July 1983): 101–22; and Finn Kydland and Edward Prescott, "Rules Rather than Discretion: The Inconsistency of Optimal Plans," *Journal of Political Economy* 85 (June 1977). They offered a theoretical foundation for this proposal by establishing that independent central banks were more credible than governments in fighting inflation.

Finance illustrate this with clarity:

> Maastricht brings with it the assurance of an irreversible attachment of our country to the European Community, to a solid currency, to an economic policy centred on the stability of prices and the control of public deficits. The Treaty thus contributes in a decisive fashion to the reduction of uncertainties as to the future policies of each successive administration. There is no longer any alternative to the policy of a stable Franc and competitive deflation.[12]

> The value of the currency will be less at the mercy of the hazards of political life, which has often been its fate in the past.[13]

Competitive deflation thus became a form of political technology inscribed in the workings of the economy. In its initial phases this mechanism permits the naturalization of political choice in exterior economic constraints, but at cruising speed it is able to deploy its full force without recourse to political deliberation.

It is not, however, sufficient to remove from political control the discretionary manipulation of the currency. The credibility of the whole system demands the creation of a European system of central banks (ESCB). The sole and unique mission of the ESCB is to oversee the stability of the currency while combating the risks of inflation. It is even less a question of adopting the German monetary system, which gives the illusion of being merely the importation of a partial model created by an institutional system with strong internal coherence. As Michel Aglietta has observed,

> The foundation of its [the Central Bank's] independence stems from the uniqueness and the irreducible singularity of its role in the society. The confidence in the currency is none other than the popular anticipation that this role will be continually and duly assumed.[14]

But what about institutional legitimacy in a democratic society? The German monetary order, Aglietta reminds us, is based upon a principle that reconciles *de jure* and *de facto* independence; it is a *constitutional* order with a "quasi-religious" essence. This explains why the question of parliamentary control is never raised. Thus, something that could be obtained by custom, ethos, a common history, or even the traumatization of the collective conscience of the German people that followed the hyperinflation of the 1920s would now be obtained by the multiplication of "trials" and strict codification of powers and jurisdictions.

---

12 Daniel Lebègue, "Les Banques au grand large," *Haute Finance* 14 (1992).
13 Ernest Antoine Seillière in *Haute Finance* 14 (1992).
14 Aglietta, "Leçons pour la Banque Centrale Européenne," 46.

The mechanism of the convergence criteria is a masterpiece in the application of force through technical devices. At the same time it is a response to accusations of illegitimacy. None of the criteria employed, however, is persuasive for the economist. In the first place, the rules of good budgetary management will tolerate a deficit from the moment that it is inferior to the sum of investments. Criteria limiting the budgetary deficit to 3 percent of the GDP and a public debt/GDP ratio set at 60 percent are thus more severe than the codes of financial prudence require.[15] Moreover, no criteria of real economic convergence has been offered for productivity, or for employment, or for competition, or for the state of the economy as a whole. Finally, no indication has been offered as to what the central macroeconomic criteria monitored by the European Central Bank will be after the realization of the third phase. The whole technical disposition, from this point on, is analyzed as the setting, on the initiative of French and German central banks, of indicators close to the Bundesbank's implicit objectives in its management of the mark.

Five criteria have now been linked and systematized.[16] The first of these, established immediately to curb inflation, prohibits rates of inflation higher than 1.5 percent in relation to the average inflation rate of the three European countries with the lowest rates of inflation. The second criterion stated that the average nominal long-term interest rate must not exceed by more than 2 percent the rates observed in the three least inflationist countries; this means that anticipation of inflation in the long term must play a role in any final calculation. The third criterion allowed for an accelerated passage to the single currency, and for its final realization in 1999. This criterion could not be achieved unless, in addition, the exchange rate had been maintained for two years without serious tension, which means that all monetary adjustments had to be real.

As long as budgetary policy does not derive from a transfer of powers, individual states will remain in control—if, that is, there exist financial markets where the rates for financing deficits are freely fixed. In practice this is the case with the federal states, and the Union should, therefore, leave control of budgetary policy to national governments. But the haunting memory of spiraling inflation, and the leanness of the Community, mean that the financing of deficits can have a serious impact on inflation levels.

---

[15] When the criteria were set, the performance of France was twice as great: the deficit/GDP ratio was at 1.5 percent and the debt/GDP ratio was around 30 percent. This performance can be explained by the very strong growth in France from 1988 to the middle of 1990.

[16] Wiplosz and Riché, *L'union monétaire*.

The two remaining budgetary criteria are the limitation of the budgetary deficit to 3 percent of the GDP and the maintenance at less than
60 percent of the ratio of public debt to GDP. In fact, both criteria are intended to limit the possibilities for maneuver open to nation-states and to
prevent any single government unable to control public expenditure from
being tempted to turn to the monetary financing of its debt—exactly what
is happening in Germany. When the industrialists give in to unions or the
state abandons itself to lax policies, the central bank, by managing the
currency, is able to call the offending parties to order. Adjustments, however, cannot be painless: monetary revival is forbidden. The sole solution
for correcting an imbalance resides in the adaptation of the real economy
and thus in the renegotiation of the social contract.

But the authors of the Maastricht Treaty wanted to impose additional
controls on the individual states. They forbade the national treasuries
from financing themselves through privileged relations with the national
central banks. In practice, this was pointless since the treasuries had long
since abandoned such temporary solutions. Nevertheless, the measure
was retained as a token that allowed the drafters to provide a form of
legal sanction against any state that had resorted to such strategies as an
easy way out of its difficulties and might be tempted to do so again. The
measure also had the advantage of abbreviating the relations between the
monetary and budgetary policies and thereby rendering the central banks
independent.[17] Likewise, the freeing of the movement of capital makes
it impossible to recreate any form of credit limitation. On the grounds,
however, that two guarantees are better than one, when signing the treaty,
France chose not to employ this monetary facility in case of a need to
correct a budgetary disequilibrium.

Economic and monetary Europe is not, therefore, the offspring of the
European Community's will. Rather, it is the creature of a cartel of national administrative elites who, once granted political power, preferred to
naturalize the demands of structural adjustment by calling for European
constraint. The locus of this bureaucratic cartel was the Economics and
Finance Committee. In informal meetings a European monetary elite
forged a common language and achieved, with the EMU, a work of considerable political inventiveness. The denunciation of the bureaucracy in
Brussels should thus be seen as an act of political communication, as an

---

[17] See Pierre Jaillet and Christian Pfister, "Du SME à la monnaie unique," *Economie &
Statistique* 2–3 (1993): 29.

avowal by the political actors of the impossibility of reaching an agreement on monetary policy through political deliberation.

THE EMU : A STRATEGY FOR WINNING MONETARY INFLUENCE

One of the principal French arguments in favor of monetary integration and a single currency stems from France's desire to remedy the asymmetry in the European monetary system. For reasons that have to do with the influence of the German economy, its credibility, and its long-term stability, the mark became the anchor currency of the ERM. This found theoretical expression in economist Robert Mundell's "triangle of incompatibility," introduced into the vocabulary of the Community from the writings of Tommaso Padoa Schioppa.[18]

The idea is simple: in a monetary system of bilateral parities, a sole country can freely determine its monetary policy, thereby furnishing the anchoring point of the system. One cannot, as Mundell points out, simultaneously control monetary and exchange policies in a situation of free circulation of capital. Once a country such as France frees the circulation of capital and attempts to control its exchange rate, it loses all discretionary power in matters of monetary policy.[19] Inversely, Germany has seen the parity of its currency against the U.S. dollar and the yen fixed by the markets and is nevertheless in complete control of its own monetary policy. Since Germany and France are in the same monetary zone, because they are bound by the same exchange rate mechanism, and since the ensemble of currencies is determined in relation to the mark, it is the Bundesbank that sets the interest rates. All of the other countries of the European Union must adapt to these rates in order to maintain their parities in relation to the mark. They must even accept the incorporation into their interest rates of a prime corresponding to the anticipated risk of the realignment of parties—that is to say, to the deficit of credibility.

France's strategy was to ensure that the *de facto* surrender of all discretionary power in matters of monetary policy would be compensated for by an influential role in the European Central Bank and, simultaneously, to subject this role capacity to a democratic principle, "the European economic government" made up of the secretaries of economy and of

---

[18] Padoa Schioppa, "Union monétaire."
[19] The free circulation of capital became effective on July 1, 1990.

finance. Although France had hoped to secure from Germany the sacrifice of the mark and the Bundesbank, it had no desire to place any pressure on German economic administration. To do that would have been to question the underlying principles of the German monetary system, which the Europeans were, in practice, adopting in exchange for Germany's renunciation of the mark. All that now remains of this project, however, is a vague formula for the "setting of the principal orientations of the Member States' economic policy" by the heads of state and their secretaries of finance.

The fall of the Berlin Wall in 1989 suddenly rendered possible the acceleration on paper of the European project while postponing its realization. The reasons are economic dynamics, the incompatibility of the public policies pursued by France and Germany, and the German Central Bank's rejection of a strategy contrary to its fundamental charter, its sociology, and its professional culture. In the autumn of 1989, the French geo-strategic assets were brutally devalued. The crumbling of the Soviet bloc made a political alliance with France less crucial for Germany while reunification awoke in France the fantasy of an all-powerful Germany and of a drift to the East. Secretary Genscher, therefore, wanted to accord to France the possibility of an equally decisive political role in the framework of the federal Europe, then in the process of being created. The EMU, coupled with political union, should have been a relief to France, which had just witnessed the sudden reunification of Germany.

Without measuring all the implications, France relinquished its policy of autonomy and self-control for a strategy of influence. What it was unable to obtain as a nation in full control of its currency, it thought to acquire by deploying a strategy of influence at the heart of a Europe of "the Twelve" strengthened by a European Germany. For the central corps of French politico-administrative elites, Europe is as much a multiplier of force as it is a market and a vague assembly in the service of interminable discussion. A fragmented Europe has no weight in monetary or commercial matters—nor, of course, in defense and diplomatic matters. A unified Europe, on the other hand, would be the leading economic force in the world and capable of making international commercial rules. It also could undermine the power of the dollar, make the Euro into a (and possibly the) reserve currency, and ultimately form, with the United States and Japan, a world directoire, a G3. Because of the determination to make this into a reality, an agreement was reached, despite the difficulties of setting in motion such an obviously imbalanced construction as the EMU.

THE CENTRAL BANKS AGAINST THE MARKETS

The second phase of the creation of the Euro was, as we have seen, the most hazardous. A series of crises jeopardized the process of European integration. The management of these crises constitutes a useful guide to understanding the motives behind the Franco-German desire for integration.

Between July 1992 and August 1993, the ERM suffered significant destabilization, thus distancing the prospects of the EMU at the very moment that its ratification process was coming to a close. This has generally been attributed to the irrepressible force of the markets, the Anglo-Saxon conspiracy against the EMU, the lack of realism of ERM structures of parity while the economies of the member countries were still divergent, the provincialism of a Bundesbank insensitive to its European commitment, and, finally, to the political hesitations of the French Right. It would be pointless merely to enumerate all of these contributing factors. But the sequence of events after German reunification does allow us to rank them in order of importance.

To control reunification and contain nascent inflation, the Bundesbank asked Chancellor Kohl to reevaluate the mark. A reevaluated currency favors imports and complicates exports. It incites industrialists to show their rigor in internal management (salaries, prices, productive organization, and so on), which acts as a cooling agent for inflationist tensions. France, which had rightly prided itself on practicing a strategy of competitive deflation based on the German model, refused to do the same. Despite this divergence, the ERM survived, and currencies such as the peseta, the lire, and then the British pound, which were manifestly overvalued, remained or entered into the ERM.[20] While Europe was negotiating Maastricht, the anticipation of European integration by the markets' operators was so strong that they considered economic and monetary disadjustments (and even an exogenous shock as massive as the reunification) to be negligible. As Patrick Artus and Jacques Salomon have written:

The reduction of the differences between Germany's interest rates and those of its partners since 1987 has progressively led to the inversion of the credibility argument: by adhering to the exchange mechanism, a country would import credibility,

---

[20] The entry of sterling into the ERM in October of 1990 was achieved without coordination and at an unjustified level of parity. This happened even though the coordination of parity with other ERM partners is required by the Bâle-Nybourg agreements of 1987.

and all else being equal, would be permitted to reduce the cost of its deflationary adjustments.[21]

When a credible political prospect exists, governments can impose their views on the markets, even in a climate of financial deregulation and the asynchronous development of their economies. Sovereignty is not, therefore, abdicated in favor of the markets. Actually, it is imposed upon them by the political workings and coordinating mechanisms of the central banks and their national governments.

The first speculative assault on the pound in 1992 occurred after the Danish "No" and the reticent French "Yes" in their respective referenda, and after the British government had allowed wage inflation to develop. This hit a country that did not intend to join the EMU (having secured an opt-out clause) and had not practiced the necessary cooperation with Germany.[22] Beginning in September of 1992, the prospect of European integration seemed increasingly less likely, and the battle waged and won against the pound by speculators once again obliged the French and German governments to face up to their responsibilities. They then had three options: (1) escape "by the top" following the model of impulse imbalance, which implied an acceleration of the EMU timetable and the realization of a small Franco-German Euro zone with the Belgians, the Danish, and the Dutch, (2) withdraw the mark by detaching it from the ERM exchange mechanism, or (3) maintain their initial schedule for integration in the hope that the markets would not realize how distant the prospect of integration had actually become following Franco-German economic divergence.

The first of these solutions was rejected by the French government, even though it was supported by the financial administration, since France could not participate in what would have seemed to be a mark zone. The Germans equally rejected this solution because it implied a renegotiation of the Maastricht Treaty. The second solution, which had been set aside at the moment of reunification, seemed even less credible once speculation had intensified, if only because of the disintegration of the mark

---

[21] Patrick Artus and Jacques Salomon cited by Jaillet and Pfister, "Du SME à la monnaie unique."

[22] Mairi Maclean, "Le Mercredi noir et le dilemme Britannique du systeme de taux de change: coopération Européenne ou splendide isolement?" *Relations internationales et stratégiques* 11 (1993): 151–64. She tells how "Black Wednesday," which saw the pound crumble and Britain withdraw from the ERM, was preceded by repeated warnings by the Bundesbank on the unrealistic attempts at pound/deutschemark parity of 1£ = 2.95 DM. She describes how, at Bath, the proposal made by the Bundesbank for a realignment of parities was not even discussed, and how the ministers and governors present intended to accept only one policy: the lowering of German rates.

mini-zone created between the Germans and the Dutch. Consequently, the third solution imposed itself. Fed by the rise of an anti-European discourse at the core of the French Right and by the Bundesbank's reaffirmation of its constitutional prerogatives, it opened the way to speculation.

The debacle of the French Left during the 1993 legislative elections removed powerful support for a strong franc and placed the future of the ERM in the hands of a divided French government and a German Central Bank determined no longer to allow measures of questionable efficiency to be imposed upon it or upon the weakened image of a unified Europe. Efforts by the Balladur government to persuade the Bundesbank to lower its rates, and the failed attempt to pass the short-term rates below those of the Germans, actually weakened the franc. The intensity of the debate in France over the "other policy," the continuing deterioration of its employ-ment situation, and the irrationality (from the viewpoint of short-term national economic interests) of a policy of strong rates forced the French government to pressure the Bundesbank in the name of Franco-German entente. Political consensus at the heart of the French governmental ma-jority appeared impossible to achieve, however. The crisis of 1993, coming after that of 1992, illustrates the difficulties of a cooperative strategy in monetary matters in a context where Germany spoke with two voices and France maintained two discourses: one rigorous and directed toward the exterior, the other permissive and intended wholly for internal use. But "Europe" is a dynamic that creates unstable states. One cannot break this dynamic and then wonder why market actors recommence their games, for it is precisely in this dynamic that their legitimacy resides.

With the collapse of the ERM demonstrated by the adoption of large margins of fluctuation, are markets triumphing over national states that would render vain the "constructivist" efforts to create a single Euro-pean currency? Not really. Markets do not conspire. We cannot attribute a will to them even if, at a given moment, a central current of opin-ions is formed on the fate of a currency.[23] However, the central banks

---

[23] See Frédéric Lordon, "Financial Markets, Credibility, and Sovereignty," in *Revue de l'observatoire Français des Conjunctiures Economiques* 50 (1994): 103–24. According to Lordon, the operators of the Anglo-Saxon market pursue proper political objectives: keeping Europe from appearing as a decisive actor on the world stage. These ambitions are congruent with their professional objectives, since it would be more profitable to speculate on the parities of the fifteen European currencies than to operate with just one of them: the Euro. Political strategy and professional interests converge so that the market operators, in contempt of actual economic data, can make and unmake currencies, assured as they are of the effectiveness of the easily led rationality of currency speculators. Lordon's hypothesis makes sense only when the standard economic and political analysis runs aground. Political, economic, and institutional timetables with their accidents, and their telescoping delivery explanations, would seem to dispense with the need for conspiracy theories.

and the administrations can manifest a desire and then translate it into action. What has happened since Black Thursday, when the Bundesbank refused to lower rates, triggering speculation that resulted in the removal of the tight margin constituted by the ERM? The devaluation of the franc and the lowering of rates simply did not work, and even the public rebuke that the obstinate Gauls received from three leading American economists—Franco Modigliani, Paul Samuelson, and Robert Solow—did not change anything. The French authorities' desire to bring the franc to a parity with the mark as close as possible to that which prevailed before Black Thursday is the most tangible manifestation of this obstinacy.

Paradoxically, we have here an illustration, in the worst context, of how influential the state can be within the framework of a multilateral action intended to consolidate a monetary zone. The setting of secret parity objectives, the maintenance of rates at a high level and their progressive slackening, and the permanent consultation with other central banks have created a highly unpredictable situation for markets and speculators.

In May of 1996, the franc re-entered the tight margin of the ERM, thus erasing completely what had happened in the summer of 1993. In December of 1995, in Madrid, the principle of the passage to phase three was confirmed, and on January 1, 1999, the Euro officially came into existence.[24] When the markets reopened on January 4, 1999, eleven countries made the transition to the Euro without mishap. The system of parity between the various European countries in effect at the closure of the markets in 1998 became fixed. The national currencies of those countries are now fractions of the Euro.

---

[24] Until December 1995 three scenarios were imaginable. In the Big Bang scenario, the fifteen are able, in view of the Maastricht criteria, to allow a significant number of states (necessarily including France and Germany) and to negotiate a code on parities with nonqualifying countries. The Euro is adopted as the common currency, and a European Central Bank is established in Frankfurt on January 1, 1999. In the mark-CFA scenario, the absence of any real convergence of economies prohibits the realization of phase three. For political and economic reasons France agrees to link the franc and the mark in perpetuity by adopting a stable and irrevocable franc-mark parity. A European currency exists: the mark. In the stopping-of-the-clock scenario, the principal EU countries do not achieve the Maastricht criteria and decide to wait for the budgetary consolidation plans to take effect. In each case, the criteria only present an obstacle because the member states want it that way. The Treaty leaves the door open to debudgetizing operations that can mask lax budgetary policies thanks to the artifices of accounting presentation. In late 1995 the political signal was given in Madrid: the Big Bang became the scenario toward which the central banks and the financial institutions have been working since March 1996. This is the scenario that will be realized provided no unforeseeable development or catastrophe takes place before 2002.

EUROPE AFTER THE EURO

Although the Euro is now firmly established, the zones of uncertainty remain large. What policy mix will be required when the rhythms of economic growth between the different nations of Europe begin to diverge? What will be the real power of the central and national monetary agencies when all the responsibilities for control remain national? What tools will the Union possess to prohibit the less disciplined states from "free-rider" abuses? Today economists debate the criteria retained for the stability pact. They question the usefulness of coordinating economic policies in a more or less formal framework, the necessity of communitarizing prudential control, and the degree of harmonization of structural policies.[25]

The fetishization of the criteria of convergence (demonstrated concurrently by the French government's call for a "notarial application" after suggesting several widely different options and by the German government's refusal to modify its position in relation to any of the current trends) provided striking examples of the transformation of a technique into a policy. The moment the criteria were decided upon, Europe entered a phase of euphoric growth of around 4 percent, public finances improved everywhere (the deficit ratio of public administrations to GDP was at 1.5 percent in 1989), consumption was stimulated by a drop in taxes and by the effect of the wealth occasioned by the inflating of the financial bubble, and investment was particularly vigorous. The Europeans, the Americans, and the Japanese all wanted to be present before the liberalization of the market in 1993. The economists thus witnessed a surprisingly strong recovery. They had not expected it so soon after the crash of 1987. Classically, they were anticipating the continuation of the movement of growth. Nobody at the time denounced the lack of realism, or the severity of the criteria that had been devised for integrating Germany, France, and the countries of the mark zone. Italy was certainly in an objectively more difficult situation because of its deficits and its debts, but the prevailing opinion was that if it would commit itself decisively to the realization of its structural adaptation plan, Italy could be retrieved.

The first snag in this idyllic tableau resulted from Germany's decision to finance reunification by means of debt. The second occurred after France

---

[25] The exchange policy constitutes a first limitation on the effective realization of independence. It is the same for the interactions between monetary policy, lender of last resort, and prudential supervision. Prudential supervision, for example, was not included among the powers of the First European Central Bank. As Michel Aglietta notes, subsidiarity plus independence of central banks equals fragility in a deregulated universe. See Aglietta, "Leçons pour la Banque Centrale Européenne."

refused to sanction the uncoupling of the coordinated franc-mark in order to guide the transition. The third snag appeared when Britain and
Italy allowed their currencies to be re-evaluated without controlling inflation. With the recession and the debates over the ratification of the
Maastricht Treaty, technico-political consensus ended up dividing Member States and their respective political elites. For economists preoccupied
with the macroeconomic regulation of the whole, the stubbornness of
France in asking everything from the budget in order not to threaten the
franc-mark parity aggravated the employment situation and the financial
health of banks and other financial enterprises because of the excessively
rigorous character of its monetary policy. It also threatened conditions
of real convergence since the charge of the debt was bound to reduce
progressively the degrees of liberty in budgetary matters.[26]

As noted earlier, criteria technically defined to meet a specific and contingent need were inscribed in a treaty. The major political consequences
soon became evident. The cost of abandoning respect for the criteria of
convergence, even if they are not very reliable, is high. A political interpretation can always be given to any revision of technical indicators. The
obstinate desire to set up the Euro on the agreed date forced the Member States to carry out policies of convergence that objectively weakened
their economies and increased unemployment. The calamitous prospect
of a rupture of the integration process and several hasty thoughts on the
benefits of the Euro in terms of employment and activity were sufficient
to maintain the program of 1989/90 at all costs.

The question of criteria automatically posed another problem. What
discipline of management should be adopted now that monetary union has
been achieved? Formally, there was nothing that obliged the member states
to coordinate their budgetary policies. This is, at least, what "the Twelve"
had decided at the signing of the Maastricht Treaty. In practice, however,
in the name of the fight against inflation, a stability pact strictly limiting
deficits had been adopted in Dublin in 1996 and confirmed at Amsterdam
in 1997. The reason for such a decision is simple: if any one country within
an integrated monetary zone practices a lax budgetary policy, all of the
countries in that zone run the risk of inflation. The stability pact is a
budgetary policing weapon that limits authorized deficits, establishes a
system of penalties for offenders, and defines a consultation procedure

---

[26] See Jean-Paul Fitoussi, *Le débat interdit* (Paris: Arléa, 1995), which has become the
manual of the party of the "other policy." Fitoussi is one of the most vigorous critics of
the monetary orthodoxy of the Bank of France.

to evaluate the "exceptional" character of any deficit. The stability pact is not a cooperative budgetary policy, much less a community one. It is rather a quasi-automatic anti-inflationary weapon that completes the arsenal of the independent central bank.

Since then, however, the problem of how to coordinate the separate policies of the fifteen member states has become acute. Firstly, it is easy to imagine that, faced with a single authority in charge of a single currency, the fifteen budgetary authorities would have no alternative but to endorse the general objectives of the stability pact. Secondly, any country that fell victim to the shock of asymmetrical demand, instead of benefiting from the aid of a nonexistent European federal budget, would be penalized. Finally, in the absence of a responsible political authority on the European level, and faced with the powerlessness of the nation-states bound by the rules of budgetary discipline, the European Central Bank would inevitably become the scapegoat to national public opinions. Thus, if an integrated Europe does not wish to forgo all macroeconomic policies, it must invent a European policy mix. Otherwise, the actual policy of stimulation or of restriction of Europe would be the result of the unintentional sum of fifteen budgetary policies and a federal monetary policy.

For a number of economists, budgetary federalism is the logical follow-up, in an integrated economic space, to a single currency and a single market. The reasoning is simple: each country adhering to an integrated monetary zone loses *ipso facto* access to the weapons of monetary and ex-change rate policies. Any economic imbalance demands that real changes be made to that nation's policies on salaries, employment, and migration. If European migration remains limited and reallocation is unwelcome to the remaining inhabitants of the regions being abandoned, a significant federal budget may act as a stabilizer (as in the United States) through the redistribution policies that it authorizes. A European budget that represents 1.2 percent of the Community GDP cannot, however, fulfill this function.

The concrete working of the EMU allows for too many sources of uncertainty, particularly in the sharing of powers by central banks and maintained national banks. This technical difficulty is doubled by the political problem of the democratic accountability of the European Central Bank. The question of monetary sovereignty thus re-emerges. The debate centered first of all on the importance to be given to the notion of subsidiarity. Jean-Pierre Patat, in sketching out several options for the sharing of powers between national banks that are members of the ESCB and the European Central Bank, has shown the potential opportunities and risks inherent in the discourse of subsidiarity. According to Patat, nothing prohibits

> the limiting of the ESBC to the conception and the orientations of monetary policy: objective of growth of a European monetary aggregate, exchange of the Euro in relation to third party currencies, levels of interest rates and of obligatory reserves compatible with the realisation of goals. The national central banks, acting on their respective monetary markets, evaluate the liquidity of the commercial banks....[T]he intervention on the exchange market could be fractionated....[T]he national central banks would thus conserve a portion of their reserves.[27]

Although not one devoid of efficiency, a minimalist interpretation of monetary integration exists. But can such a state resist the tests of time? Can the management of systematic risk or prudential risk be decentralized? Financial crises, particularly in the summer of 1998, restated the question with renewed clarity. And can Europe continue to rely upon the Fed as the planetary banker of last resort?

With regard to the democratic accountability of the European Central Bank, two separate conceptions come face to face. For some, the centrality of monetary policy in the economic regulation of the whole implies that the central bankers should be obliged to account for, justify, and defend their policy decisions. The model that best integrates these demands is that of the Fed. This bank has, in effect, a standard of decision making that follows the level of activity and employment and not only the level of inflation. It is regularly audited by Congress, and it publishes, after only a slight delay, the transcripts of its debates in their entirety. For others, the stability of the currency, the cardinal objective of any virtuous monetary policy, implies clear objectives, indicators that are stable in their definition, and the removal of central bank decisions from all public debate. The model that best reflects this orientation is that of the Bundesbank. Before the Maastricht Treaty a simple law could modify the functioning of the Bundesbank. The institutional disposition adopted in 1992 constitutionalizes the independence of the central bank, limiting its democratic accountability to a report to the European Parliament. The 1992 outcome also renders any contradictory debate on monetary policy difficult if not impossible.

Ever since 1992 the debate over European political authority has necessarily been ambushed. Every entity—economic administration, economic pole, or economic pillar—called upon to formulate macroeconomic

---

[27] Patat, 95–6.

directives and to define a policy of exchange is immediately suspect because it carries with it the risk that it might interfere with the independent central bank. At the same time, however, and in the interest of the European Central Bank, a legitimate political authority has imposed itself. The solution was finally found with the creation of an informal group known as "Euro XI." It has neither secretariat nor defined powers. But even this minimally defined authority is contested because it excludes the countries which are, at present, out of the Euro (the United Kingdom, Sweden, Denmark, and Greece). In sum, this laborious compromise hardly differs from all of its predecessors: it is an attempt to create European Union policies out of an irreversible process that precludes any change without an explicit political decision.

There exist two interpretations of the EMU, just as there exists a single market where major sources of competitive imbalance subsist. The post-Euro Europe will be subjected to double internal and external pressure. In actual practice, the single market is going to become fully active with the introduction of the new currency: the comparability of prices, costs, and charges will be instantaneous. And the development of information technologies will accelerate the process. There is, therefore, no doubt that competitive pressure will be increased and that the social and fiscal systems will affect the localization of activities. External pressure will manifest itself through the appreciation of the Euro in relation to the dollar and the yen. In the long run a monetary zone like Europe with low demographic pressure, with an aging population, whose growth rate is weak and that has an excessive savings rate, risks seeing its currency overvalued. In either case, apart from taking a new leap toward coordination of macroeconomic policies, the internal tensions in Europe will increase, quickly jeopardizing the single currency. Today nobody is ready to imagine a substantial European federal budget, coordinated employment policies, fiscal harmonization, or a strict prohibition on fiscal, social, and regulatory dumping—in short, an advance toward a Union organization of a federative type. But European integration follows a cycle; it has its depressions and its upswings.

Today the paradox resides in the contradiction between monetary integration (all the more necessary since the single market is a success and commercial activity has become intense) and a monetary union (all the more fragile since it is founded on the automatic dispositions of economic cooperation). Following a crisis of the Euro, the most widely accepted solution is the renewal of the march toward budgetary federalism and political union. This demonstrates the extremely imbalanced character of current European construction. The European competitive crisis, the end of acquired advantages, and globalization represent a formidable challenge. Europe can rediscover its margins of maneuver only within the Union. A devaluation, to take an extreme example, of 50 percent of the Euro in a totally unified Europe whose extracommunity foreign trade represents only 10 percent of the GDP would affect the revenues of European households only slightly (by 5 percent). The simple threat of the use of the exchange rate weapon would confer upon Europe considerable power in determining the world's commercial game-rules. First, however, Europe must demonstrate that it possesses the will to operate in this way—far from likely at present.

Monetary union arrived on time in 1999 as Kohl and Mitterand had hoped. The price paid in terms of loss of growth and employment has ended up intimidating speculators and financial markets. In sum, the EMU is the coproduct of a cartel of national monetary bureaucracies and political authorities in step with the acceleration of the march of history in the East. The French and the Germans played a decisive role. The objectives of the experts, shared by the governments of the time, were to inscribe competitive deflation in the institutional workings of the state in order to shelter it from partisan political influence.[28] The independent central bank is the living proof of the success of this strategy. The war in Kosovo might have the same effect upon Europe's military future as German unification has had upon its monetary one. This has been the way that "Europe" has always progressed: by means of lengthy and obscure technical negotiations, on the one hand, and sudden political accelerations the moment that History takes over, on the other.

---

[28] A decisive advance in the realization of monetary union occurred in Verona in April 1996. A highly political affair such as the exterior value of a currency in the heart of the Europe of the "Fifteen" was placed on the road to final technicalization. In the initial conception of the EMU, the Eurofed determined monetary policy; its power was supposed to be balanced by that of the "European economic government," which reserved the privilege of setting the exterior value of the Euro and the parities with nonadmitted European currencies. In Verona, Eurofed's power to call a ministerial meeting (so as to proceed with the monetary alignments made necessary by the divergences between the Euro, hard-core currency, and currencies of the periphery) was recognized.

+>=×+ +>=×+ +>=×+ +>=×+ +>=×+ +>=×+ +>=×+ +>=×+

13

Identity Politics and European Integration: The Case of Germany

THOMAS RISSE AND
DANIELA ENGELMANN-MARTIN

"We do not want a German Europe, but a European Germany." This famous quote by the novelist Thomas Mann from the interwar period has remained the mantra of the German political elites ever since the catastrophe of World War II.[1] To be a "good German" means nowadays to be a "good European" and to wholeheartedly support European integration. To be a "good European German" also means to have finally overcome the country's militarist and nationalist past and to have learned the right lessons from history.

The political elites of the Federal Republic of Germany have thoroughly Europeanized the German national identity since the 1950s. This Europeanization of German collective identity explains to a large degree why all German governments since Konrad Adenauer was chancellor have embraced European integration—from the Treaty of Rome in 1957 to the Treaty of Amsterdam in 1997. Since the late 1950s, there has been an elite consensus in support of European integration based on a federalist model—the "United States of Europe." This federalist consensus has remained quite stable despite drastic changes in Germany's power status in Europe and the world. It is strongly linked to the Europeanized national identity, and it accounts for continued German support for European integration, even though the end of the Cold War and German unification should have challenged that elite consensus. After all, Germany was now free to choose its foreign policy orientation for the first time since 1945. Instead, the country opted for continuity.

[1] This chapter presents findings from a multiyear research project funded by the Deutsche Forschungsgemeinschaft (German Research Association): "Ideas, Institutions, and Political Culture: The Europeanization of National Identities in Cross-National Comparison." For research assistance on theoretical concepts concerning national identity, we thank Martin Marcussen. For critical comments, we thank Anthony Pagden.

Identity politics not only explains the stubborn support for European integration by all German governments from Adenauer's to Gerhard Schroder's. It also operates as a mechanism for silencing political controversies: the more that previously domestic issues become Europeanized, the less obviously contentious they become. The European Economic and Monetary Union (EMU) and the single currency are cases in point. Identity politics largely accounts for the absence of any serious political debate about the pros and cons of the Euro by the country that is among the most affected by giving up its cherished Deutsche Mark. Elite politicians, particularly former opposition leaders of the German Social Democratic Party (SPD), were effectively silenced, since objections to the Euro were seen as opposition to European integration in general and, therefore, as inconsistent with German European identity. As a result, German political elites never took advantage of the strong public majority against renouncing the Deutsche Mark.[2]

But German Europeanness is still *German* Europeanness. It comes, as do all collective understandings of "Europe," in national colors. We do not want to suggest that Germany has somehow "supranationalized" and surrendered its identity as a nation-state. German discourses on "Europe" and what it means contain distinctive features relating to particular understandings of German history and culture. In other words, German Europeanness is different from, say, French Europeanness, particularly since German understandings of the "nation" and the "state" embody different concepts and meanings than French understandings of *l'état nation*.

In this chapter we shall proceed in three stages. First, we will try to clarify the concept of national collective identity and to elucidate what identity politics can and cannot explain. Second, we will provide an overview of the evolution of German elite identities related to Europe since 1945. Third, we will discuss the question of how, and under what conditions, identity politics matters with regard to the arguments preceding the introduction of the EMU and the Euro.

The chapter is concerned with the level of political elites. Its empirical domain are discourses and controversies between and among the major German political parties. Identity politics is always about the interaction of elites and masses. But it is empirically and methodologically beyond our scope to analyze the effects of elite identity constructions on mass public opinion. It is equally impossible here to investigate how popular

---

[2] See Eurobarometer survey, October–November 1996, quoted in *The Economist*, June 7, 1997, 25.

identities have affected the collective identities of political elites. Rather, we will speculate about these questions in the conclusion.

WHAT IS "NATION-STATE IDENTITY" AND WHAT CAN IT EXPLAIN?

Before proceeding with the empirical argument, we must address three conceptual questions: What are collective identities, and how do we know them when we see them? Why do some ideas prevail over others in identity-related discourses? And finally, which causal mechanisms link collective identities to the behavior of actors?[3]

The literature on nation-building, nationalism, and national identity— these terms are sometimes used interchangeably—can be roughly categorized as follows. While almost everybody agrees by now that nations and national identities are social constructions, few agree on what this means in terms of malleability, on the one hand, and instrumental use for political purposes by elites, on the other. Concerning malleability, some authors use the notion of "national identity" in an almost primordial sense. Anthony Smith, for example, defines a nation as a "named human population sharing a historic territory, common myths and historical memories, a mass public culture, a common economy, and common legal rights and duties for all members."[4] He then argues that the community of myths and common memories on which nations are built requires something of an ethnic core based on myths of common ancestry, shared historical memories, elements of a common culture, and so on. These myths of the past are difficult to escape from, and the collective understandings on which they are based are almost frozen in time. Nationalist groups might rediscover and reinterpret them, but fundamental changes in collective national identities are almost excluded.[5] Smith is rather pessimistic concerning a collective European identity, since Europe as a nation lacks an ethnic core. From this perspective, not much in terms of Europeanization of collective identities can be expected.

---

[3] For the following, see also Martin Marcussen, Thomas Risse, Daniela Engelmann-Martin, Hans-Joachim Knopf, and Klaus Roscher, "Constructing Europe: The Evolution of French, British, and German Nation-State Identities," *Journal of European Public Policy* 6, 4 (1999): 614–33.

[4] Anthony D. Smith, *National Identity* (London: Penguin, 1991), 13–14.

[5] See also Anthony D. Smith, "Gastronomy or Geology? The Role of Nationalism in the Reconstruction of Nations," *Nations and Nationalism* 1, 1 (1995): 3–23.

At the other end of the spectrum are postmodernist arguments about collective identity constructions.[6] Identities are not much more than subject positions in political discourses. National identities are almost constantly constructed, deconstructed, and reconstructed; change rather than continuity or constraint prevails. "The hub of post-modern life strategy is not identity building, but avoidance of fixation. The overall result is fragmentation of time into episodes, each one cut from its past and from its future, each one self-enclosed and self-contained."[7] If national identities are understood in this way, the term loses its usefulness as an analytical category, and theorizing about a Europeanization of national identities becomes almost impossible.

In between these two extremes there is considerable room for conceptualizations of national identities that would seem to be more useful. Again, two broad approaches can be taken: one emphasizing the instrumentality of identity constructions in modern nation-building processes, the other focusing more on psychological and social needs for coherent systems of meanings. As to the first approach, authors such as Benedict Anderson and Ernest Gellner firmly locate the process of nation-building, including collective identity formation, in the transition from agrarian societies to modern state-building and to modernity in general.[8] One could interpret their work as a social constructivist reinterpretation of Karl W. Deutsch's earlier work on nation-building processes.[9] As Ernst Haas argues, nationalism and its inherent identity-building can be regarded as instrumental social constructions necessary to create the "imagined community" of a nation-state. He identifies this process with rationalization and modernization in a Weberian sense.[10]

If we apply this logic to the Europeanization of national identities, we would expect an elite-driven deliberate process of European identity construction to exist alongside European integration. The strong version of this argument holds that the more European integration leads to the emergence of a Euro-polity, the more nationally constructed identities would

[6] Iver B. Neumann, "Self and Other in International Relations," *European Journal of International Relations* 2, 2 (1996): 139–74.

[7] Zygmunt Bauman, "From Pilgrim to Tourist—or a Short History of Identity," in Stuart Hall and Paul du Gay, eds., *Questions of Cultural Identity* (London: Sage, 1996), 25–34.

[8] Benedict Anderson, *Imagined Communities: Reflections on the Origin and Spread of Nationalism* (London: Verso, 1991); Ernest Gellner, *Nations and Nationalism* (Ithaca, N.Y.: Cornell University Press, 1983).

[9] Karl W. Deutsch, *Nationalism and Social Communication* (Cambridge, Mass.: MIT Press, 1953); Deutsch et al., *Political Community and the North Atlantic Area* (Princeton, N.J.: Princeton University Press, 1957).

[10] Ernst B. Haas, *Nationalism, Liberalism, and Progress*, vol. 1: *The Rise and Decline of Nationalism* (Ithaca, N.Y.: Cornell University Press, 1997).

converge in a collective European identity with a common core of myths, historical memories, and visions about European order, at least among the political elites. A weak version of the same argument holds that those elites who support and actively promote European integration in line with the federalist model are also the ones most actively engaged in a deliberate attempt to construct a recognizable European identity. The degree of Europeanization of collective identities would thus be determined by support for and opposition to further integration.

A rather different picture emerges if one uses social psychology and sociological institutionalism to theorize about collective identity formation. This conceptualization focuses on the needs of social groups to give meaning to their collective selves. Social identity theory (SIT) as well as self-categorization theories provide a good starting point for clarifying the concept of "collective identity."[11] Social identities contain, first, ideas describing and categorizing an individual's membership in a social group including emotional and evaluative components. In other words, groups of individuals perceive that they have something in common on the basis of which they form an "imagined community."

Second, this commonness is accentuated by a sense of difference with regard to other communities. "We" always need "them" to distinguish ourselves and our collective identity from the "others." Individuals frequently tend to view the group with which they identify in a more positive way than they do the "out-group." This does not mean, however, that the perceived differences between the "in-group" and the "out-group" are necessarily based on value judgments and that the "other" is usually looked down at.

Third, individuals hold multiple social identities, and these social identities are context-bound. A group of Europeans might perceive themselves as fellow Europeans when dealing with Americans yet emphasize national differences when interacting mainly with each other. Moreover, only some national identity constructions are consensual; others are frequently contested. The context-boundedness of national identities also means that different components of national identities are invoked depending on the policy area in question. National identities with regard to citizenship rules might look different from national identities concerning understandings

---

[11] Dominic Abrams and Michael A. Hogg, eds., *Social Identity Theory* (London: Harvester Wheatsheaf, 1990); Penelope J. Oakes, S. Alexander Haslam, and John C. Turner, *Stereotyping and Social Reality* (Oxford: Oxford University Press, 1994); John C. Turner, *Rediscovering the Social Group: A Self-Categorization Theory* (Oxford: Oxford University Press, 1987).

of the state and political order. Because this chapter is concerned with the latter rather than with the former, we will use the term "nation-state identity" to delineate the differences from other components of national collective identities.

Fourth, nation-state identities are social identities defining social groups on the basis of mostly territorial criteria. In modern times they construct the "imagined communities" of nation-states and are closely linked to ideas about sovereignty and statehood. As a result, nation-state identities often contain visions of just political and social orders. In the case of identity constructions related to Europe, federalist visions of a "United States of Europe," of an intergovernmental confederation of nation-states, or ideas about functional market integration are examples of such concepts of political order.

Fifth, self-categorization theory argues that self/other categorizations change the more gradually the more they are incorporated in institutions, myths, and symbols, as well as in cultural understandings.[12] This would be particularly relevant for national collective identities that usually take considerable time and effort to construct and are then embedded in institutions and a country's political culture. Thus, one should assume that national collective identities are generally very compelling and subject to change only gradually.

Social psychology helps to clarify the concept of collective nation-state identity. But it is less helpful concerning the conditions under which incremental change in nation-state identities can be expected. How and under what conditions are principled ideas and identity-related concepts about Europe and European order selected, incorporated, and "frozen" in collective nation-state identities?

Two factors account for the selection of particular ideas and their incorporation in collective nation-state identities. First, instrumental and power-related interests can determine the selection of ideas. Political elites who are in the business of identity construction and manipulation can select specific ideas about European order and even try to Europeanize nationally defined identities, because it suits their instrumentally defined interests to do so. Thus, we do not claim an "identity versus interest" account that would serve only to reify both. Political elites legitimately pursue instrumentally defined interests; they want to remain and gain political power, for example. The more significant question is how

---

[12] Susan Fiske and Shelley Taylor, *Social Cognition* (New York: Random House, 1984); Oakes, Haslam, and Turner, *Stereotyping*.

nation-state identities and instrumental-power identities—"interests"—
interact with each other. Causality can run both ways. A change in instrumentally defined interests might well lead over time to identity changes.
Moreover, political elites are frequently in the business of identity construction for political reasons. In these cases the causal arrows run from
interests to identities. At the same time, however, nation-state identities
define how actors view their instrumental interests and which preferences
are regarded as possible, legitimate, and appropriate for enacting given
identities. Moreover, instrumentally defined interests might change more
frequently than nation-state identities, which are expected to be deeply
compelling for the reasons outlined above.

Second, cultural sociology and sociological institutionalism expect variation rather than convergence concerning the potential Europeanization
of nation-state identities.[13] The idea behind this argument is that identity constructions with regard to Europe and the European order are assumed to interact with given nation-state identities. Political visions and
identity constructions about "Europe" and European order influence and
are incorporated in collective nation-state identities, the more they resonate with national political cultures, with national political institutions
and the ideas about political order embedded in them. Timing as well
as substance is involved. Some nation-state identities might incorporate
"Europe" more easily than others and, thus, might change earlier. Moreover, the very content of a "European" collective identity might vary. The
outcome depends on how ideas about Europe resonate with nationally
constructed identities.

One would then expect in different national contexts different interpretations of "European" and varied definitions of Europe's "others." Political institutions and cultures as intervening factors between ideas about
Europe and national collective identities perform two tasks. First, they
incorporate specific understandings of nation-state identities that make
them resistant to change. Second, they influence actors in their efforts to
change identity constructions by distributing both ideational and material resources. Not every political actor has an equal chance to challenge
the prevailing nation-state identities. Because institutions are expressions
of certain beliefs and nation-state identities, we expect institutions to de-
marcate the range of beliefs and nation-state identities an individual exposed to these institutions can affirm. Institutions, therefore, help the

---

[13] Ronald L. Jepperson and Anne Swidler, "What Properties of Culture Should We Measure?" *Poetics* 22 (1994): 359–71; M. Rainer Lepsius, *Interessen, Ideen und Institutionen*
(Opladen: Westdeutscher Verlag, 1990).

party-political elites to construct and reconstruct nation-state identities in specific ways.

Finally, a note of caution has to be introduced concerning what the concept of collective identity can actually explain. Since national identities are broad social constructs, they can shape actors' interests and preferences but not necessarily their particular behaviors. Collective identities might account for the overall goals of actors, while the actual choices of strategies to reach these goals might be influenced by exogenous factors such as perceptions of the situation and of other actors' likely strategies. In other words, national identity constructions might explain the general orientation of German political elites toward Europe and European integration. But one should be careful about using the concept of identity to account for specific policy decisions.

GERMANY AND THE EVOLUTION OF A EUROPEAN NATION-STATE IDENTITY

The German case is one of thorough and profound reconstruction of a nation-state identity following the catastrophe of World War II. Thomas Mann's dictum about a "European Germany" quickly became the dominant tune of the postwar (West) German political elites.[14] Since the 1950s a fundamental consensus has emerged among the political elites, a consensus generally shared by the mass public, that European integration is in Germany's vital interest. Simon Bulmer calls it the "Europeanization" of German politics.[15]

Konrad Adenauer's Vision of Germany in Europe

The multilateralization of German foreign policy was initiated by Chancellor Adenauer. He regarded the integration of the German state and society in the West as the best means of overcoming Germany's past. Adenauer was a convinced Europeanist who had been active in the

---

[14] We use the term "Germany" routinely for the Federal Republic including the pre-unification period. For further details on the following, see Daniela Engelmann-Martin, "Nationale Identität im deutschen Parteiendiskurs in der Weimarer Republik sowie nach dem II. Weltkrieg (1. Untersuchungszeitraum)," manuscript (Florence: European University Institute, 1998).

[15] Simon Bulmer, *The Changing Agenda of West German Public Policy* (Aldershot: Dartmouth, 1989). See also Gunther Hellmann, "Goodbye Bismarck? The Foreign Policy of Contemporary Germany," *Mershon Review of International Studies* 40, 1 (1996): 1–39; Peter J. Katzenstein, ed., *Tamed Power: Germany in Europe* (Ithaca, N.Y.: Cornell University Press, 1997).

pro-European wing of the *Zentrum,* the Catholic predecessor party of the German Christian Democrats (CDU), during the Weimar Republic.[16]

Adenauer's thinking about Europe was heavily influenced by ideas and visions of the interwar period. The Rhinelandish *Zentrum* mixed Europeanism and Catholicism with a distinct anti-Prussian connotation. Some went so far as to suggest the creation of a Rhinelandish state within the German *Reich* that would be associated with France and thus constitute the origins of a larger European order. This vision of Europe was related to identity constructions around the concept of a Christian (that is, Catholic) Occident; the Slavic and Islamic Orient constituted "the other."[17] After 1945 the Soviet Union and communism easily replaced religiously oriented perceptions of "the other."

Adenauer's visions and identity-related ideas about Europe also originated from the transnational European movement, in particular the *Paneuropean Union* founded by Count Richard Coudenhove-Kalergi.[18] As early as 1923 Coudenhove-Kalergi argued for the creation of a United States of Europe (which would, however, exclude the United Kingdom). His ideas were less concerned with religion than with power politics, in particular the status of Western Europe among the other great powers. These ideas survived Hitler and the Nazis and prevailed within the Christian opposition movement to Hitler.[19]

After 1945 the newly founded Christian Democratic Party (CDU) immediately embraced European unification as the alternative to the nationalism of the past. As Ernst Haas put it, "in leading circles of the CDU, the triptych of self-conscious anti-Nazism, Christian values, and dedication to European unity as a means of redemption for past German sins has played a crucial ideological role."[20] The Bavarian CSU declared in 1946 in the Eichstätt Basic Program: "Europe is a supranational

---

[16] Arnulf Baring, *Außenpolitik in Adenauers Kanzlerdemokratie. Bonns Beitrag zur Europäischen Verteidigungsgemeinschaft* (München-Wien: Oldenbourg, 1969); Hans-Peter Schwarz, *Vom Reich zur Bundesrepublik. Deutschland im Widerstreit der außenpolitischen Konzeptionen in den Jahren der Besatzungsherrschaft 1945 bis 1949* (Neuwied: Luchterhand, 1966).

[17] Jürgen Bellers, "Sozialdemokratie und Konservatismus im Angesicht der Zukunft Europas," in Jürgen Bellers and Mechthild Winking, eds., *Europapolitik der Parteien. Konservatismus, Liberalismus und Sozialdemokratie im Ringen um die Zukunft Europas* (Frankfurt/M.: Lang, 1991), 3–42.

[18] Richard N. Coudenhove-Kalergi, *Pan-Europa* (1923; reprinted, Wien: Pan-Europa Verlag, 1982).

[19] Rudolf Morsey, "Vorstellungen Christlicher Demokraten innerhalb und ausserhalb des 'Dritten Reiches' über den Neuaufbau Deutschlands und Europas," in Winfried Becker and Rudolf Morsey, eds., *Christliche Demokratie in Europa. Grundlagen und Entwicklungen seit dem 19. Jahrhundert* (Köln: Boehlau, 1988), 189–212.

[20] Ernst B. Haas, *The Uniting of Europe: Political, Social, and Economic Forces, 1950–57* (Stanford, Calif.: Stanford University Press, 1958), 127.

community of life among the family of nations. We support the creation of a European confederation for the common preservation and continuation of the Christian Occidental culture." Christianity, democracy, and (later on) social market economy became the three pillars on which a collective European identity was to be based. It was sharply distinguished from the German nationalist and militarist past and from Soviet communism and Marxism, particularly during the late 1940s and early 1950s. In other words, Germany's own past as well as communism constituted "the others" in this "Christian Occidental" *(Abendland)* identity construction.

When Chancellor Adenauer came into power in 1949, he built upon and expanded these identity constructions. His construction of *Abendland*, which included the Anglo-Saxon community, was synonymous with the West, the "free world," which he saw threatened by "Asia."[21] This notion of *Abendland* versus Soviet communism also contained the construction of a central position in Europe (*Mittellage*) with the corresponding commitment to the West. From the Christian Democratic perspective, Germany "in the heart of Europe" was positioned between two power blocs with antagonistic ideologies. In order to avoid being crushed between the two blocs, the Federal Republic had to choose a side. This concept of *Abendland* left no choice other than to reject any status of neutrality and to commit oneself to the "free world."

The Christian Democratic identity construction—the politicization of "Christian Occidental culture" in contrast to the country's Nazi past and the Soviet threat—determined a new role for Germany in a European federal state: "Germany in Europe" was regarded as the future mission for the Federal Republic. Adenauer considered firmly anchoring postwar Germany in Western Europe as the best way to overcome another German *Sonderweg*. In his view West German neutrality during the Cold War was not an option, not even in exchange for reunification with East Germany. Security for Western Germany was more important than reunification, and Adenauer was convinced that this could be achieved only by anchoring the Federal Republic in the West. Interests and identity coincided, since Adenauer used his firm belief in Western institutions to regain national sovereignty for West Germany.[22]

---

[21] See, for example, Adenauer's opening speech at the Second Party Convention of the CDU in the British Zone in Recklinghausen, August 28–9, 1948, "Eine Hoffnung für Europa," in Hans-Peter Schwarz, ed., *Konrad Adenauer. Reden 1917–1967. Eine Auswahl* (Stuttgart: Deutsche Verlags–Anstalt, 1975), 124ff.

[22] Baring, *Außenpolitik*, 57; Bellers, "Sozialdemokratie, Konservatismus," 27–8.

Lack of Consensus among German Elites

But throughout the early 1950s, there was no consensus among elites on German foreign policy orientations. The main controversies at the time centered around the issue of whether German rearmament within NATO and German participation in the European Coal and Steel Community (ECSC) might hamper prospects for early reunification with Eastern Germany. Within Adenauer's own party, Jakob Kaiser, the CDU leader in Berlin and later chairman of the German trade unions, favored a neutral policy of "bridge-building" between East and West. "We need," he said, "to be a bridge between East and West, for Germany's and Europe's sake."[23] Similar concepts prevailed in Adenauer's coalition partner, the Free Democratic Party (FDP).[24] Thomas Dehler, the chairman of the party during the late 1950s, prioritized reunification over European integration. Moreover, he favored a Gaullist vision of European order—that is, a Europe of nation-states. As a result, the FDP rejected the Treaty of Rome, even though it had supported the ECSC and the European Defense Community (EDC) during the early 1950s.

The opposition to Adenauer's policies during the 1950s within his own party and within the Free Democratic Party was, however, largely insignificant. As a master of power politics, he managed effectively to silence any opposition to his foreign policy within his coalition government through a combination of sticks and carrots. His authoritarian leadership style established the primacy of the German Chancellery early on in the history of the Federal Republic's political institutions. Moreover, Adenauer was able to buy off domestic opposition to his foreign policy in exchange for concessions in important economic and social policy areas.

Adenauer's foreign policy proved to be highly successful. By 1955 the Federal Republic had essentially regained its national sovereignty and had reestablished itself among the Western democracies. It joined NATO and other Western institutions and was among the founding and leading members of the European integration process. Thus, Adenauer had created conditions by his foreign policy that were hard to oppose. At the same time he was actively involved in the construction of a postwar nation-state identity that distanced itself from the past by embracing

[23] Jakob Kaiser, quoted in Frank Pfetsch, *Die Außenpolitik der Bundesrepublik Deutschland 1949–1992: Von der Spaltung zur Wiedervereinigung* (München: UTB, 1993), 139.
[24] Sebastian J. Glatzeder, *Die Deutschlandpolitik der FDP in der Ära Adenauer* (Baden-Baden: Nomos, 1980).

Europe. Adenauer's Europe ended at the Iron Curtain, which he constructed rhetorically as the borderline between good and evil. "Europe" meant civilization, Christianity, democracy, and the market economy—in sharp contrast to the East as well as to Germany's own past.

The Social Democrats (SPD) were the main opposition party to Adenauer's policies. In its 1925 Heidelberg program, the SPD embraced the concept of a "United States of Europe" and became the first major German party to do so. When the party was forced into exile during the Nazi period, the leadership fully endorsed the notion of a democratic European federation. As in the case of the CDU, "the 'European idea' was primarily invoked as a spiritual value in the first years of the emigration. What Europe would be like after Hitler was a second-order question, though it was taken as self-evident that it would be socialist. In this period Europe was seen as an antithesis to Nazi Germany."[25] As Erich Matthias put it in 1952: "For the Social Democrats, there is no Germany without Europe, it is always Germany *and* Europe, Germany *with* Europe, Germany *in* Europe."[26] The Social Democrats constructed a connection between Germany and Europe. After the war they considered it their task to "lead Germany back to Europe."

In short, the Europeanization of German nation-state identity originated in the resistance of exiled political leaders—within both SPD and CDU—to Hitler and the Nazis. For them Europe's "other" was Nazi Germany. Europe symbolized the values of democracy, human rights, and social justice, values that had to be preserved against the Nazis. This particular identity construction then became dominant in the post–World War II Federal Republic.

From these historical memories the Social Democrats drew different conclusions than did the Christian Democrats. Conscious of not being responsible for the catastrophe of the Third Reich and convinced that the bourgeois parties had failed and were not up to the confrontation with communism, the SPD claimed to have a right to leadership and considered it self-evident that Germany and Europe would become socialist. When the SPD was refounded in 1946, its first program supported the "United States of Europe, a democratic and socialist federation of European states.

---

[25] William E. Paterson, *The SPD and European Integration* (Glasgow: Glasgow University Press, 1974), 3. See also Bellers, "Sozialdemokratie"; Rudolf Hrbek, *Die SPD—Deutschland und Europa. Die Haltung der Sozialdemokratie zum Verhältnis von Deutschland-Politik und Westintegration, 1945–1957* (Bonn: Europa Union Verlag, 1972).

[26] Matthias's emphasis. Erich Matthias, *Sozialdemokratie und Nation* (Stuttgart: Deutsche Verlags–Anstalt, 1952), 206. For the following, see ibid., 186.

[The German Social Democracy] desires a socialist Germany in a socialist Europe."[27] In other words, Europe, Germany, democracy, and socialism were conceived of as identical at the time.

It turned out, however, that postwar Germany was a divided country, and socialism did not become the guiding principle of European integration. As a result, the SPD needed to prioritize its goals. Kurt Schumacher, the SPD's leader and a survivor of Buchenwald, argued vigorously against the politics of Western integration, since it foreclosed the prospects of rapid reunification of the two Germanies. During the early 1950s, the SPD led the opposition against Adenauer's policies of integrating the Federal Republic with the West. For Schumacher, reunification became the priority. To integrate Germany into a European community required a *united* Germany first. Any other order seemed unthinkable: "German unity stands for European unity. A torn Germany would only lead to a non-unified Europe."[28]

At the same time Schumacher denounced the Council of Europe and the ECCS as "un-European," as "minimal Europe" (*Kleinsteuropa*), as conservative-clericalist and capitalist. The SPD, however, went to great pains to argue that it did not oppose European integration as such, just *this* particular version. Of course, the Social Democrats also opposed German rearmament in the context of the EDC and, later, of NATO. Their motives were not pacifist, but they emphasized reunification over German integration in Western institutions.

Two electoral defeats later (1953 and 1957), and the SPD slowly changed course. There had always been internal opposition to Schumacher's policies. Carlo Schmid, Ernst Reuter (the legendary mayor of Berlin), Willy Brandt (who later became party chairman and, in 1969, chancellor), Wilhelm Kaisen, Fritz Erler, Herbert Wehner, Helmut Schmidt (Brandt's successor as chancellor in 1974), and others always supported closer relations to the United States as well as German integration with the West. These Social Democrats were strongly influenced by the Socialist Movement for the United States of Europe founded in 1947 and by Jean Monnet's Action Committee. By the late 1950s, they had gradually taken over the party leadership.

The German Social Democrats then thoroughly reformed their domestic and foreign policy programs. Concerning the domestic realm, they came to accept the German model of welfare state capitalism, the social

---

[27] Political guidelines adopted at the Hannover Party Convention, May 1946.
[28] Schumacher's speech in Berlin, June 20, 1946, cited in Hrbek, *Die SPD, Deutschland und Europa*, 37.

market economy. With regard to foreign policy, they revisited the 1925 Heidelberg program and became staunch supporters of European integration. The changes culminated in the 1959 Godesberg program. Two years earlier the SPD had reversed its course regarding European integration: it supported the Treaty of Rome in the German parliament. The SPD's "return to Europe" went hand in hand with a complete reversal of its attitude toward the economic and social order of the Federal Republic. The SPD essentially gave up socialist principles.

A Federalist Consensus Emerges

In sum, from the late 1950s on, a federalist consensus ("United States of Europe") prevailed among the German political elites from the center-right to the center-left. Germany's nation-state identity embraced a modern Europe as part of the Western community, based on liberal democracy and a social market economy, with Europe's "other" being both Germany's past and communism. This consensus outlasted the changes in government from the CDU to the SPD in 1969 as well as the return of a CDU-led government in 1982. It also survived a major foreign policy change of West German policy toward Eastern Europe, East Germany, and the Soviet Union. When Chancellor Willy Brandt introduced *Ostpolitik* in 1969, he made it very clear that efforts at European integration were to be untouchable and had to be continued.[29] As we explain later, German unification twenty years later did not result in a reconsideration of German European policies.

The German European consensus, prompted by SPD election defeats, has remained stable despite the recent politicization of European politics. The federalist consensus has long outlasted the instrumental interests that brought it about in the first place. As mentioned earlier, it went hand in hand with a peculiar identity construction in the aftermath of World War II. Support for European integration among Germany's political elites is linked to their broad visions of the European order. It also is directly concerned with post–World War II German nation-state identity. Two aspects of the concept of "national identity" are particularly relevant in the German context: *historical memories* and the way one's own past is understood, on the one hand, and *performances and achievements*, which are claimed to serve as a model for others, on the other.

---

[29] Wolfram F. Hanrieder, *Deutschland, Europa, Amerika: Die Außenpolitik der Bundesrepublik, 1949–1994* (Paderborn: Schoeningh, 1995).

The German notion of what constitutes the "other," the non-European, has much to do with European and German *national history*. While French nationalism has always been identified with the Enlightenment and Republicanism, German nationalism came to be viewed as authoritarian, militaristic, and anti-Semitic. Germany's nationalist and militarist past constitutes the "other" in the process of "postnational" identity formation whereby *Europeanness* replaces traditional notions of nation-state identity. The new Germany has to be firmly anchored in "the West" and in Europe.

For decades European integration was regarded by German political elites as a sort of substitute for their own defeated, divided, and occupied country. Postwar Germany viewed itself mainly as a trading state. Rarely did it insist on its *national interest* because the shaming memories of extreme nationalism rendered "the language of national interest unusable."[30] Due to their problematic nation-state identity following the Holocaust and World War II, most Germans thought the aim of European unity so self-evident that they never really debated the pros and cons, only the means. The German political elite considered the establishment of a lasting European peace order as the ultimate goal of integration, "Europe" thus being tantamount to superseding nationalism. There remains a stable consensus among German parties ranging from the center-right to the center-left that the process of European unification must be irreversible. They are convinced that a unified Europe is the most effective assurance against the renaissance of nationalism, a relapse into power-political rivalries, and disastrous conflicts.

The German nation-state identity has, therefore, become thoroughly European in the sense that today a "good German" equals a "good European" supporting a united Europe. "Europe" in this identity construction stands for a stable, peaceful order capable of overcoming the continent's bloody past, for democracy and human rights (in contrast to European—and German—autocratic history), as well as for a social market economy including the welfare state (in contrast to both Soviet communism and Anglo-Saxon "laissez-faire" capitalism). "Europe" closely resembles a nation-state identity based on what Jürgen Habermas has called "constitutional patriotism."[31]

---

[30] William E. Paterson, "The German Christian Democrats," in John Gaffney, ed., *Political Parties and the European Union* (London: Routledge, 1996), 65.

[31] Jürgen Habermas, *Faktizität und Geltung. Beiträge zur Diskurstheorie des Rechts und des demokratischen Rechtsstaats* (Frankfurt/M.: Suhrkamp, 1992).

German Unification: Continuity Rather than Change

The events of the period since the end of the Cold War, the collapse of East Germany, and German unification in 1990 underscore our argument. With the unexpected end of the East-West conflict and regained German sovereignty, a broad range of foreign policy opportunities suddenly emerged. The German elites could have redefined their national interests. Instead, not much happened. Germany did not reconsider its fundamental foreign policy orientations, since Germany's commitment to European integration had long outlived the context in which it had originally emerged.[32] While the end of the Cold War and German unification certainly represented a critical juncture in German domestic politics, there was no fundamental debate about the country's foreign policy orientation, including European politics. External shocks represent critical junctures challenging given collective identities only when they are perceived as such. However, Germany was among the winners of the East-West conflict; policies toward European integration were widely considered as highly successful. So why change course?

Even though reunification apparently had no effect on West German identity constructions, one would probably expect East German elites to hold different views on European integration. Did their differing identity constructions not have an effect on previously Europeanized identities? In fact, if one looks at the utterances of East German political elites concerning Europe in the media as well as at party conventions, their views do not seem to present a major challenge to the previously consensual identities.

One potential challenge to the dominant identity constructions comes from the Party of Democratic Socialism (PDS), the successor to the former Socialist Unity Party (SED) of the GDR. The PDS is critical of the course of Germany's foreign policy in general as well as the way European policies are being conducted by the major parties. Even though the PDS claims to be "the Socialist party of the Federal Republic," and not just of a certain region or a social class, the party defines itself as *the representative for East Germans.*" The PDS "raises its voice against any social, legal or other disadvantages facing former citizens of the GDR."[33] With its rejection of the current economic system, its aim for a socialist society, and its demand

---

[32] Hellmann, "Goodbye Bismarck?"; Katzenstein, *Tamed Power.*
[33] "Mit ostdeutscher Kompetenz gegen den Euro," *Frankfurter Allgemeine Zeitung*, April 23, 1997; "Bisky: PDS ist eine linke Massenpartei. Brie: Widerstand gegen Rachepolitik," *Frankfurter Allgemeine Zeitung*, March, 14, 1994.

for the dissolution of the North Atlantic Treaty Organization (NATO) and the Western European Union (WEU), the party positions itself in opposition to the mainstream political consensus, representing the "only real alternative," "the only persistent opposition party."[34] Accordingly, the PDS was the only party to vote against the treaties of Maastricht and Amsterdam in the German Parliament and to reject the Euro for its "monetarist logic": it opposes a common currency as long as it is not linked to an increase in the level of employment and to certain social and ecological standards.[35]

Interestingly, the PDS is not opposed to "Europe" or "European integration" as such, just to *this* particular version. The PDS as "a European Socialist party" therefore "says Yes to European integration" and ultimately even to a common currency, but this consent is linked to fundamental criticism of the European Union in its current state. The party wants a change of policy regarding the EU: "Contrary to nationalist forces, for the PDS, the alternatives to the European Union and the Euro are not German hegemony and Deutsche Mark."[36] The PDS regards the EMU as a "capitalist money union" and rejects a "Europe of the Banks," but it also does not want to be identified with "Deutsche Mark nationalism."[37]

Although the PDS now regularly gains over 20 percent of the votes in *Länder* elections in East Germany, it only marginally passed the 5 percent hurdle during the last federal elections. The differing view of the East German political elite organized in the PDS does not represent a serious challenge to the mainstream identity constructions. East German Christian Democrats or Social Democrats do not challenge the dominant European identity constructions either. First, East German political elites seem to play only a minor role in this discourse since issues relating to Europe are far less visible than those relating to German unification.[38]

---

[34] "Bundesparteitag der PDS in Rostock. Vetorecht für die neuen Länder gefordert," *Süddeutsche Zeitung*, April, 6, 1998; "Wahlprogramm der Linken Liste/PDS. Für eine starke linke Opposition," *Neues Deutschland*, September 27, 1990; "PDS-Parteitag in Suhl, Ziel ist erster Einzug ins Europaparlament," *Süddeutsche Zeitung*, September 20, 1999.

[35] "Die PDS setzt 1998 auf fünf Prozent," *Die Tageszeitung*, December 17, 1997.

[36] PDS, "Alternativen 99: Europawahlprogramm. Für einen Kurswechsel in Europa," 1–2.

[37] Parteivorstand PDS, ed., "Europäische Union und linke Politik," *Hefte zur politischen Bildung*, Berlin, September 1998, 30–1.

[38] Especially East German members of the European Parliament often complain about this indifference. See "Als Zaungäste nach Europa abgeordnet. Die Erfahrungen der Ost-Beobachter, einer wirklich 'einmaligen Gruppierung', in Brüssel und Straßburg," *Frankfurter Rundschau*, September 24, 1993; "Rudolfstadt gehört ja auch dazu. Von einem Thüringer Parlamentarier in Straßburg, der auszog, den Ostdeutschen das Fürchten vor Europa zu nehmen," *Süddeutsche Zeitung*, December, 6, 1995.

East German concerns and issues related to German unity are the main topics that East German politicians usually address, and they have a higher priority and tend to supersede everything else. Statements by East German politicians on Europe in the media, just like their contributions to party conventions, are quite rare. Most East German policymakers appear to overlook, at least in their public statements, that the European Union—through its structural funds and its regulatory policies regarding state subsidies—played a major role in the German unification process.

Second, the few East Germans who do speak out on Europe, usually members of the European Parliament or rather prominent politicians, seem wholeheartedly to embrace former West German identity constructions with regard to Europe.[39] Wolfgang Thierse, leader of the Eastern SPD at the time and now speaker of the German Parliament, declared in 1990: "Our commitment to European integration, our commitment to the creation of the United States of Europe, is not merely rhetorical, but for us it symbolizes a chance for lasting stability, security and partnership in Europe."[40] "Europe" and "European integration" are almost always referred to in connection with German reunification: "Europe is our chance.... There is an indivisible link for us between German and European unification."[41]

However, East German political elites slightly differ from their West German counterparts, since they bring a stronger *Eastern* European perspective to the political discourse. They are usually firm advocates of rapid Eastern enlargement of the European Union. In view of the external frontiers of the European Union, Eastern Europe is far closer to Eastern party members who find themselves acting as "a kind of trustee for Eastern Europe" and bearing a "special responsibility" for shaping the future relationship to Eastern European countries.[42] CDU politician Lothar De Maizière reminded his party that security and stability in Europe include

---

[39] Rolf Berend, a member of the European Parliament, who cited Adenauer, at the Party Convention of the CDU in Düsseldorf 1992, proceedings, 208; "Brandenburg—mitten in Europa," in SPD Brandenburg, *Landtagswahlprogramm: Es geht um Brandenburg*, 1999, 92ff.

[40] Wolfgang Thierse's speech at the Party Convention of the SPD in Berlin, September 27–28, 1990, proceedings, 43.

[41] Contribution of Klaus Zeh at the CDU Party Convention in Düsseldorf, October 26–28, 1992, proceedings, 208; see also opening words of Markus Merkel, deputy spokesman of the GDR's Social Democrats at the Party Convention of the SPD in Berlin, December 18–20, 1989, proceedings, 93; "Wieder eine Brückenfunktion," *Frankfurter Rundschau*, September 24, 1993.

[42] "Brandenburg—mitten in Europa," 92. The first quote is from "Wieder eine Brückenfunktion." See also Merkel, proceedings of SPD Party Convention 1989, 92–94; Reinhard Schulze at the 3rd Party Convention of the CDU in Düsseldorf, October 26–28, 1992, 190; Thierse, SPD Convention speech 1990, 43.

the Soviet Union: "The vision of a common European house approaches its realization. A European consciousness supersedes the old division and a greater Europe from the Atlantic to the Urals again takes shape."[43]

In sum, the European identity constructions of the major parties have not been susceptible to change through the accession of the East German political elites. Even after unification and with more sovereignty to sacrifice for the European cause, the majority of the German political elite continued to share Chancellor Kohl's belief that only deeper political and economic union could anchor Germany firmly in the West and strengthen European institutions to ensure peace in the years ahead.[44] In the aftermath of unification, the German government accelerated rather than slowed down its support for progress in European integration. It has been argued that German initiatives for the treaty on European Union and for the EMU were part of a quid pro quo for French support for unification.[45] This is only partly correct. It is true that Chancellor Kohl proposed the treaty on political union in order to reassure his nervous neighbors that there would be no change in German Europeanness after unification. But given the federalist elite consensus, this was not a great sacrifice and was not even considered as such in German political discourse. As to the EMU, German support for monetary union was long on record before 1990, provided that the European Central Bank was autonomous and that convergence criteria would be met.[46] In other words, German support for a single currency and for a European political union was perfectly in line with long-standing attitudes toward integration and the country's European nation-state identity. It cannot simply be explained by instrumental reasons. The case of the single currency that required Germany to give up its cherished Deutsche Mark supports this argument. It also illustrates how identity politics explains specific orientations in German policies toward Europe.

[43] Speech by the leader of the GDR's Christian Democrats, Prime Minister Lothar de Maizière, at the Party Convention of the CDU in Hamburg, October 1–2, 1990, proceedings, 43.

[44] Thomas Banchoff, "German Identity and European Integration," *European Journal of International Relations* 5, 3 (1999): 259–89.

[45] Joseph M. Grieco, "The Maastricht Treaty, Economic and Monetary Union, and the Neo-Realist Research Programme," *Review of International Studies* 21, 1 (1995): 21–40; Wayne Sandholtz, "Monetary Bargains: The Treaty on EMU," in Alan W. Cafruny and Glenda G. Rosenthal, eds., *The State of the European Community: The Maastricht Debate and Beyond* (Boulder Colo.: Lynne Rienner, 1993), 125–42.

[46] David R. Cameron, "Transnational Relations and the Development of European Economic and Monetary Union," in Thomas Risse-Kappen, ed., *Bringing Transnational Relations Back In: Non-State Actors, Domestic Structures and International Institutions* (Cambridge: Cambridge University Press, 1995), 37–78.

GERMAN EUROPEANNESS AND THE SINGLE CURRENCY:
BETWEEN THE EURO AND THE DEUTSCHE MARK

It is not at all clear why a single currency was in Germany's economic or geopolitical interest, particularly after unification.[47] First, the German economy did not need a common currency, since the European Monetary System (EMS) already constituted a Deutsche Mark zone. German industry conducted its European business predominantly in Deutsche Marks; the effects of a common currency on transaction costs were, therefore, minimal. Second, why should the Germans give up the EMS as a Deutsche Mark zone controlled by the Bundesbank in favor of the Economic and Monetary Union (EMU) and a supranational European Central Bank (ECB), particularly after unification had increased German power? Third, the economic benefits of the EMU for German business were at least unclear. One could argue that the Euro increases German competitiveness on the global markets more than the Deutsche Mark ever could—provided, of course, that the Euro became as strong a currency. And even if then, European and German competitiveness on the global markets might suffer if a strong Euro was ever as overvalued as the Deutsche Mark had been at times. Nobody knew in advance. This leads to a fourth point. Even with the convergence criteria firmly enforced and the "stability pact" in place, it was uncertain whether Germany's cherished economic policies of tight money and low inflation would survive the EMU.

Finally, if the EMU and the single currency represented a "binding strategy" of the lesser European states to contain German power after unification, why did Germany agree to it? Why was it that the former German government under Chancellor Kohl remained an enthusiastic supporter of a single currency, despite all the popular misgivings? This is not to argue that the German political elites did not agree to "self-binding." Rather, the "taming of German power" through European integration had the enthusiastic support of German elites from the center-right to the center-left long before unification.[48] The underlying rationale for this support does not stem from "quasi-objective" geopolitical reasons. German acceptance of "self-binding" results from a particular collective construction

---

[47] Parts of the following were published first in Thomas Risse, "Between the Euro and the Deutsche Mark: German Identity and the European Union" (Washington, D.C.: Center for German and European Studies, Georgetown University, 1997); and in Thomas Risse, Daniela Engelmann-Martin, Hans-Joachim Knopf, and Klaus Roscher, "To Euro or Not to Euro? The EMU and Identity Politics in the European Union," *European Journal of International Relations* 5, 2 (1999): 147–87.
[48] Katzenstein, *Tamed Power.*

of historical memory, a peculiar perception of Germany's place in Europe, and, last but not least, visions of European order. German agreement to the EMU and the stubbornness with which the vast majority of the political elite supported the Euro seem strange, since Germany had more to lose from monetary union than any other country. Even more surprising was the lack of public controversy over the Euro, despite the fact that a large section of the German public rejected giving up the cherished Deutsche Mark until recently. The vast majority of the German political elite never wavered in its support for the Euro, and this consensus was only challenged by a few prominent politicians—among them Edmund Stoiber (CSU), the prime minister of Bavaria, on the right, and Gerhard Schröder (SPD) before he became chancellor in 1998 on the center-left.[49] They were joined by the more implicit opposition to the Euro voiced by the powerful German Bundesbank.[50] However, each of them framed his opposition by insisting on a strict adherence to the convergence criteria and—in the cases of Stoiber and Schröder—by an attempt to delay the third stage of the EMU. All let it be known, however, that they were in favor of European integration.

German elite attitudes toward the EMU must be understood in the framework of identity politics. Policymakers, in particular Chancellor Helmut Kohl, framed the issue of the Euro in terms of the following equation: support for the Euro equals support for European integration equals "good Europeanness" equals "good Germanness" equals overcoming the German militarist and nationalist past. In other words, Kohl managed to frame the Euro question in terms of Germany's post–World War II nation-state identity. As a result, this equation was extremely powerful, since it forced opponents of a single currency to frame their position in interest-based rather than identity-based terms and to make sure that they could not be regarded as "bad Germans"—that is, proponents of German nationalism. At the same time, however, supporters of the Euro needed to cope with another aspect of German postwar identity, "Deutsche Mark patriotism." This explains German government officials' rigid insistence on the strict fulfillment of the Maastricht convergence

---

[49] On Stoiber's position, see "Es gab einmal eine europäische Bewegung in Deutschland... das ist vorbei," *Süddeutsche Zeitung*, November 2, 1993; "Stoiber beharrt auf Kritik an EWU," *Süddeutsche Zeitung*, June 23, 1997; "Edmund Stoiber: Defender of a Decimal Point," *Financial Times*, July 7, 1997. On Gerhard Schröder's position, see for example, "Den besten Zeitpunkt suchen," *Die Zeit*, June 6, 1997.

[50] On the Bundesbank position in general, see Cameron, "Transnational Relations"; John B. Goodman, *Monetary Sovereignty: The Politics of Central Banking in Western Europe* (Ithaca, N.Y.: Cornell University Press, 1992).

criteria (to make the Euro "as strong as the Deutsche Mark"). In this case, then, the German elite consensus on European integration and the German European nation-state identity served as powerful silencing mechanisms that effectively foreclosed a public debate on the pros and cons of a single currency.

Given the federalist elite consensus, the EMU was viewed as a corner-stone of European political integration. It was supported by all major parties, despite a legitimacy crisis of a single currency in German public opinion. Since the Euro was regarded as part and parcel of this political project, supporters strongly insisted that a delay in entering the third stage in 1999 would "endanger the successes of the European integration process up to now," as Chancellor Kohl put it.[51] Former chancellor Helmut Schmidt, a Social Democrat, argued even more bluntly that "any delay means in all likelihood the ultimate abandonment of the currency union project."[52] The German political elite identified the Euro with European integration. The vast majority of the German political elite shared Chancellor Kohl's belief that only deeper political and economic union—symbolized by a single currency—could anchor Germany firmly in the West and strengthen European institutions to ensure peace in the years ahead. As Helmut Schmidt argued, "If the Euro-currency is not realized by January 1, 1999, it will most likely never again be realized. . . . This would result in the worst crisis of the European integration process—possibly its end! And Germany would be isolated—exactly the opposite of the binding which all chancellors from Adenauer to Kohl have pursued as the overarching strategic goal, in the vital German interest!"[53]

Chancellor Kohl wanted to be remembered as the one who pushed through the EMU and made a closer European Union inevitable, thus preventing a return to nationalism in Europe.[54] Kohl framed the single currency as *the* symbol of European integration, and he identified his political fate with the realization of the Euro. His unsuccessful candidacy for the chancellery in 1998 was motivated primarily by his commitment to European integration and the Euro. He labeled 1997—the year of reference for the fulfillment of the convergence criteria—as the "key year

[51] Quoted from "Huber hält Euro-Start ohne Paris für möglich," *Süddeutsche Zeitung*, July 7, 1997. See also "Biedenkopf: Euro fünf Jahre später. Waigel weist Vorstoß des sächsischen Regierungschefs zurück," *Süddeutsche Zeitung*, July 28, 1997.
[52] "Helmut Schmidt über die sechs Gründe, aus denen der Euro nicht scheitern darf—schon gar nicht an den Deutschen," *Die Zeit*, June 13, 1997.
[53] Helmut Schmidt, "Die Bundesbank—kein Staat im Staate," *Die Zeit*, November 8, 1996.
[54] See Banchoff, "German Identity."

of Europe," as *existential* for further integration. Kohl appeared to believe that if "the house of Europe" was not built then, it would not be built ten years later. He even argued that the success of the EMU was a "question of war and peace."[55] Kohl's convictions were not unique among the German political elite. It is interesting that those parts of the Green Party who supported the Euro used almost the same language as the chancellor. Foreign Minister Joschka Fischer, who was a Green Party leader in the Bundestag at the time, claimed that the only alternative to an early start of the Euro was a return to the European past of power balancing and nationalism.[56]

The strength of this elite consensus on European order and German European identity became particularly apparent when it was challenged. As argued above, even those opposed to the EMU did not dare touch the German consensus on European integration but framed their criticism in terms of asking for a delay and/or demanding a strict application of the convergence criteria. Individual politicians from the CDU/CSU coalition and the former SPD opposition had repeatedly tried to criticize the agreement that forced Germans to give up their cherished Deutsche Mark but failed to gather support even from their fellow party members.[57] When Prime Minister Stoiber criticized the Maastricht Treaty in November 1993 and called for a slowing down of European integration, he was not only condemned by the SPD and FDP in the Bundestag, but also strongly criticized by fellow Christian Democrats.[58] Kohl himself restated his party's commitment to the goal of European union in a Parliamentary address insisting that there was no alternative to European unity.

More significant, the opposition SPD had ample opportunities to challenge the consensus on the Euro during the 1994 election year when both federal and state elections were conducted in Germany. Even though most Germans opposed the single currency at the time, the SPD refrained from exploiting this sentiment for its own purpose. The consensus among the main parties regarding European unity held firm. The SPD did not want to be regarded as "anti-European."

---

[55] For the speech to the German Bundestag, see "Kohl: Bei der europäischen Währung ist Stabilität wichtiger als der Kalender," *Frankfurter Allgemeine Zeitung*, May 28, 1994.

[56] See Joschka Fischer, "Warum ich für den Euro bin. Das Jahr Europas: Im Streit um die Währungsunion geht es um den notwendigen Abschied vom klassischen Nationalstaat," *Die Zeit*, March 21, 1997.

[57] Dorothee Heisenberg, "Loud and Clear: Germany's EMU Agenda-Setting after Maastricht" (paper presented at the Tenth International Conference of Europeanists, March 14–17, 1996, Chicago).

[58] See "Es gab einmal eine europäische Bewegung in Deutschland . . . das ist vorbei."

The response by the SPD majority to occasional challenges to the EMU from within the party is also significant. Members of the party leadership at the time challenged the Euro but were defeated by the party majority. In April 1992, for example, Oskar Lafontaine, the prime minister of the Saarland who later became party chairman, tried to commit the SPD to rejecting a common European currency. He was overruled. In October 1995 then party chairman Rudolf Scharping, together with Gerhard Schröder, the prime minister of Lower Saxony, launched an attack against the EMU. They were immediately reprimanded by other SPD leaders, members of the European Parliament (EP), and the SPD youth organization that usually represents the party's left wing. When Lafontaine launched his candidacy for the SPD Party chairmanship a month later, he explicitly criticized Scharping's attitude toward the common currency as being inconsistent with the party platform. As candidate for the chancellorship, Schroder was the only voice in the party leadership to remain skeptical of the Euro, yet in early 1998 he, too, changed his position. He had originally called for a delayed entry into the third stage because of economic considerations. At the same time he made it clear that he was a "good European" by arguing that "a controlled delay would not damage Europe."[59]

It is particularly noteworthy that the German center-left largely remained silent over the EMU and that the majority of the Social Democratic elite supported it.[60] The German left blamed the record-level unemployment on the Kohl government's austerity measures, but few drew the obvious connection between those policies and Bonn's determination to meet the convergence criteria. The German trade unions refrained from criticizing the Euro, even though their constituents appeared to be the biggest losers. Despite the public's growing reluctance to give up the Deutsche Mark, a fractious debate on the Euro never occurred.

But supporters of the Euro did face significant challenges in Germany— in particular, "Deutsche Mark patriotism." This was the ultimate reason why the Euro was supposed to look very much like the Deutsche Mark and why political discourse in Germany focused on how strong a currency the Euro would become. The German government was willing to give up the previously hegemonic role of the Deutsche Mark within the EMS only if the future single currency was designed institutionally according to

---

[59] Gerhard Schröder in "Den besten Zeitpunkt suchen!"
[60] Ton Notermans, *The German Social Democrats and Monetary Union*, mimeo, ARENA, University of Oslo, May 1998.

German monetary institutions. The European Central Bank was modeled after Germany's Bundesbank.[61]

The ECB is statutorily committed to monetary stability, modest state deficits, and low inflation. The national central-bank governors on the ECB's council are expected to be independent of their governments or any other political authority. The Bundesbank insisted on the *convergency criteria* securing economic stability for member states willing to participate in the EMU. Germany even managed to commit its partners to a "stability pact" that imposed rigid central guidelines and potential fines for offenders to prevent EMU members from undermining the Euro by backsliding on economic commitments once they had joined up. Finally, the German government succeeded in bringing the European Monetary Institute and later the ECB to Frankfurt, in a further attempt to frame symbolically the ECB as the successor of the much cherished Bundesbank.

Deutsche Mark patriotism and German Europeanness constitute two significant aspects of Germany's postwar national identity. Giving up the Deutsche Mark in favor of the Euro is in accordance with the latter, but it violates the former aspect of collective identities. It is no wonder, therefore, that German elite supporters of the EMU worked hard to ensure that the institutional setup of the single currency looked extremely similar to German monetary institutions.

To the extent that there was debate in Germany on the single currency, it was largely framed in terms of German Europeanness versus Deutsche Mark patriotism. Supporters of the Euro emphasized that the single currency would be "as strong and stable" as the Deutsche Mark and that there would be virtually no difference between the two—except for the name. Critics of the EMU tried to capitalize on Deutsche Mark patriotism and suggested that the Euro would never reach the stability of the German currency. The proxy for this identity-related debate was the controversy surrounding the convergence criteria and the strictness with which they should be applied. Rigid adherence to the convergence criteria before and after the EMU became the symbolic causal mechanism by which the strong Deutsche Mark was going to be converted into an equally strong Euro.

The insistence on the convergence criteria was originally meant to reassure nervous Germans that the Euro would equal the strength and

---

[61] Goodman, *Monetary Sovereignty*; T. Notermans, "Domestic Preferences and External Constraints: The Bundesbank between Internal and External Pressures," working paper series, Center for European Studies, Harvard University, 1991; Roland Sturm, "How Independent is the Bundesbank?" *German Politics* 4, 1 (1995): 27–41.

stability of the Deutsche Mark and therefore the savings of ordinary Germans would be safe. In 1997, however, it appeared that Germany would have a hard time reaching the convergence criteria because of its sluggish economic growth and high unemployment rate. Opponents of the single currency then started using the convergence criteria as a proxy to hide their criticism of the EMU. They hammered away at popular fears that the Euro would not become as strong a currency as the Deutsche Mark. The Maastricht Treaty stipulated that the budget deficit should not exceed 3 percent of the GDP. This criterion was constructed as the benchmark for judging the future quality of the Euro.

The exaggerated emphasis on meeting the convergence criteria to the last decimal point had little to do with economic policy.[62] It reflected instead a particular reading of German history before World War II and collective memories of rising inflation and the worldwide economic crisis that helped the Nazis gain power. Again, "the other" in this part of German collective identity was the country's own past. Overcoming the German past not only meant supporting European integration but also instituting sound economic policies of low inflation and controlled budget deficits so as never again to be tempted to solve economic problems by printing money. The Deutsche Mark became the symbolic embodiment of this economic policy. Over the years the Deutsche Mark acquired a highly identity-inducing value as a powerful national symbol of Germany's prosperity and its economic miracle after World War II. Important components of the mythical story of the *Wirtschaftswunder* (Economic Miracle) at the beginning of the new Federal Republic are "social market economy," "monetary reform," and ultimately the Deutsche Mark.[63] The 1948 monetary reform with the introduction of the Deutsche Mark and the swift change from shortage of goods to consumer paradise are linked to Germans' particular understanding of a social market economy (*soziale Marktwirtschaft*), which contributed much to West Germany's self-confidence. The Deutsche Mark therefore symbolized the "rise from the ruins" of World War II.

[62] See the absurd German debate in the summer of 1997 over whether 3.0 meant "three, zero" or "three, something": "Stoiber beharrt auf Kritik an EWU," *Süddeutsche Zeitung*, June 23, 1997; "Germans Resolve Feud over Euro," *International Herald Tribune*, July 2, 1997; "Huber hält Euro-Start ohne Paris für möglich," *Süddeutsche Zeitung*, July 7, 1997; "Pressure Mounts in Bonn to Delay Emu," *Financial Times*, July 7, 1997; "Edmund Stoiber: Defender of a Decimal Point," *Financial Times*, July 7, 1997.

[63] Dieter Haselbach, "'Soziale Marktwirtschaft' als Gründungsmythos. Zur Identitätsbildung im Nachkriegsdeutschland," in Claudia Mayer-Iswandy, ed., *Zwischen Traum und Trauma—Die Nation. Transatlantische Perspektiven zur Geschichte eines Problems* (Tübingen: Stauffenburg, 1994), 256.

The irony was that the federal government was caught in its own rhetoric. Compared with its European partners, Bonn had insisted on a very rigid interpretation of the convergence criteria in order to reassure a nervous German public and to guarantee that EU members instituted the necessary austerity policies to meet the criteria. As a result, Chancellor Kohl and Finance Minister Theo Waigel reduced their own flexibility with regard to Germany meeting the criteria. When Waigel desperately tried to generate additional resources by proposing that the Bundesbank should revalue its gold reserves and transfer the revenue into Bonn's 1997 budget figures, he was immediately accused of "creative accounting" by his European partners. More important, the Bundesbank, which had only grudgingly accepted the single currency to begin with, launched a campaign against the federal government by linking up with Euroskeptics in Waigel's own Bavarian CSU. The Bundesbank won the battle, even though a re-evaluation of currency rather than gold reserves was to be accounted for in the federal budget in early 1998.[64]

In sum, German political elites, including Chancellor Kohl, who strongly supported the EMU tried to square the circle. They favored a single currency as a major step toward European political union, something they regarded as necessary to anchor a united Germany firmly in Western political and economic institutions. Moreover, the single currency would stabilize German "Europeanness" and "constitutional patriotism" at the same time. But the elites also had to deal with Deutsche Mark patriotism. Insistence on a strict application of the convergence criteria, in particular the 3 percent goal with regard to budget deficits, was meant to increase the political acceptability and legitimacy of the EMU by constructing the Euro as a Deutsche Mark with a different name. But the more rigidly the political elites interpreted the convergence criteria, the less likely it became that Germany would meet them. Delaying the entry date in a single currency was no way out, since supporters of the EMU had convinced themselves that this would have spelled the end of the single currency—and possibly of European integration as a whole. Moreover, cutting the German budget deficit increase to less than 3 percent of GDP involved deep cuts in the German welfare state. The self-inflicted strict interpretation of the Maastricht criteria challenged the famous

---

[64] See "Zentralbankrat einigt sich mit Bonn," *Süddeutsche Zeitung*, June 13, 1997. See also "Streit und Ranküne in Bonn, Paris und Brüssel: Wird der Euro verschoben?" *Die Zeit*, June 13, 1997.

German consensus on the welfare state and the "social market economy," yet another component of German national identity.

CONCLUSIONS

The German political elites thoroughly constructed a European German nation-state identity after World War II. These identity constructions originated during the interwar period and became dominant among German elites forced into exile during World War II. When the Federal Republic came into being in 1949, German nationalism had been shattered by the catastrophe of Nazi Germany. It was no longer possible to relate positively to German nationalism, since it became identified with militarism, authoritarianism, and, ultimately, the Nazis. At this critical juncture "Europe" provided the way out for the construction of a postnational identity suitable for a Federal Republic that needed to distance itself from the German past. Europe symbolized almost everything to which the new Germany aspired—the values of peace, democracy, human rights, enlightenment, modernity, and Christianity. The German SPD embraced European integration in the late 1950s, and the federalist consensus has remained stable ever since. The German European nation-state identity explains why there was not much debate about changing course after unification in 1990. Chancellor Kohl could count on the elite consensus in his conviction that united Germany would remain firmly committed to the European Union. The single currency, the Euro, became the symbol for this commitment. Stubborn German support for the EMU must be understood in this framework of identity politics. Even those who opposed the single currency framed their arguments in identity-related terms—"Deutsche Mark patriotism."

German Europeanness nevertheless contains distinctive national elements. First, Europe's "other" (against which the collective nation-state identity is being constructed) is not another region in the world, but Germany's and Europe's own past of militarism and balance of power. As a result, the new Europe is seen primarily as a stable peace order in almost Kantian terms of a "pacific federation" combining cooperation with external partners with liberal democracy internally. Second, the prevailing visions of the European order are distinctively German in the sense that German cooperative federalism serves as the primary model for the construction of Europe. The "United States of Europe" are not seen as a unitary state with a strong central government, but as a distinctively federalist order, as Joschka Fischer's speech in Berlin in May 2000 confirmed again. The model is the Bonn republic, not Paris and the Fifth Republic. In this sense, visions of European order are strongly connected and relate to the German domestic institutional setup. Thus, Germans' ideas about Europe and the European order are strongly correlated with their own domestic order.

German Europeanness also serves as an example of how political elites manipulate and instrumentalize collective nation-state identities for political purposes. Almost single-handedly, Chancellor Adenauer constructed the Federal Republic's European identity in order to justify and legitimize a foreign policy oriented toward the West. He used the German past, notions of a *Sonderweg* and of a "seesaw policy" between East and West, to denounce the political opposition to his preferred course of action. This time Germany should be firmly anchored in the West to prevent a return to the nationalist past. Since this identity construction resonated well with the widespread enthusiasm for European integration at the time, and since Adenauer's foreign and domestic policies proved highly successful, the opposition failed. When the SPD turned around after two election defeats, the German federalist consensus emerged.

Consensual identity constructions can be used for instrumental purposes. Consider the Euro. Chancellor Kohl attached his support for the single currency to the German Europeanized nation-state identity. This effectively silenced potentially strong domestic opposition. It became impossible to discuss the Euro in purely economic terms and to weigh the costs and benefits of it in a politically neutral way. The single currency was identified with the political project of European integration as a whole and, thus, with a project each "good German" had to approve. Skeptics had to demonstrate that they were "good Europeans." Only then could they criticize the Euro. "Deutsche Mark patriotism" simply was not strong enough to counter "Euro patriotism."

German Europeanness is firmly anchored in the collective nation-state identity of the German political elites. But what about the German mass public? Data on mass public opinion appear to show that the German public has supported European integration in terms of a "permissive consensus" for a long time. Cracks in the consensus occurred only recently and are probably related to the fact that European issues such as the single currency increasingly "hit home," become politicized and subject to political controversy. There is not much evidence, however, that the German public at large—East and West—strongly identifies with the European

Union.[65] This is probably the most important disjuncture between elite opinion and mass public opinion concerning the European Union. At the same time, the issue salience of European issues among the mass public is still not very high. For only a few people European policies are among the most significant themes they care about.

As a result, and given the strong elite consensus concerning European integration, dissatisfaction with European issues (including the single currency) is unlikely to translate easily from the mass public to the elite level. So far no major party has tried to instrumentalize latent anti-European feelings among the public at large. The collective identification with Europe on the elite level prevents public misgivings from becoming—at least for the time being—politically salient.

---

[65] Hans Rattinger, "Einstellungen zur europäischen Integration in der Bundesrepublik: Ein Kausalmodell," *Zeitschrift für Internationale Beziehungen* 3, 1 (1996): 45–78; Hans Rattinger, Joachim Behnke, and Christian Holst, *Außenpolitik und öffentliche Meinung in der Bundesrepublik. Ein Datenhandbuch zu Umfragen seit 1954* (Frankfurt/M.: Peter Lang, 1995).

14

Nationalisms in Spain: The Organization of *Convivencia*

ANDRÉS DE BLAS GUERRERO

If any single detail lends sense to the general theory of nationalism, it is a consciousness of the close connection between nationalist movements and ideologies within the framework of similar historical junctures and interconnected geographical and political spaces. This fact stands out even more prominently in the case of nationalisms born and developed within the limits of a single state. On a general level, Spanish nationalism has a long history with many complex precedents, as befits a society that emerged as a nation-state in the early-modern period. Since 1898, however, the course of Spanish nationalism has been inseparable from its relations with the Basque and Catalan regionalist movements that consolidated and evolved into nationalist movements after the beginning of the twentieth century. The principal political problem in Spain since the reestablishment of democracy in 1976 has been organizing *convivencia* (peaceful coexistence) among the different national consciences existing within a state immersed in the general process of European integration.

The need to observe carefully the complex relationship between the national consciences and realities of Spain has been obstructed on occasion by a reductionist vision that tends to devalue the common political nation and to emphasize Spain's privileged cultural nationalities. The rebirth of nationalism in Central and Eastern Europe has reinforced the focus of recent studies of nationalism on those manifestations of the phenomenon that originate in ethno-linguistic communities with political aspirations in conflict with the states of which they form a part. This approach runs the risk of overlooking other state-based national factors, especially those that were also influential in the emergence of the idea of the nation, and continue to carry considerable weight in the world today.

This chapter was translated from Spanish by Ben Erhlers.

At times the problem arises strictly in the definition of terms. More than one commentator has proposed reserving the concept of "nation" for those ethno-linguistic communities and using the term "patria" to describe nations with a preferential position within the state. Although this proposal could work in the abstract, it is not very feasible since the bulk of the major Western languages (English, Spanish, French, Italian, Portuguese) have not adopted this restricted use of the term "nation."

Paradoxically, Spanish nationalism has been studied considerably less on the general level than on the level of peripheral nationalisms.[1] This highly anomalous situation presents a challenge not only for the political scientist, the historian, or the practitioner of public law, but also for common sense: overall, Spanish nationalism has enjoyed a great deal of "success" (if by "success" we mean the construction and maintenance of a state over a prolonged period of time), especially in contrast to the more modest and recent political gains of the peripheral Spanish nationalisms.[2]

What are the causes of such a remarkable situation? The intellectual and academic climate proves of little use in considering the formula of

[1] On Spanish nationalism in general, see Justo Beramendi and Ramón Maiz, eds., *Los nacionalismos en la España de la II República* (Madrid: Siglo XXI, 1991); Alberto Botti, *Cielo y dinero: El nacionalcatolicismo en España* (Madrid: Alianza Universidad, 1992); Inman Fox, *La invención de España* (Madrid: Cátedra, 1997); Juan Pablo Fusi, "España, nacionalidades, *regiones,*" in Javier Tusell, Emilio Lamo, and Rafael Pardo, eds., *Entre dos siglos* (Madrid: Alianza Editorial, 1996); Guillermo Gotázar, ed., *Nación y Estado en la España liberal* (Madrid: Noesis, 1994); José Maria Jover, "Introducción," in José Maria Jover, ed., *Historia de España*, vol. 34 (Madrid: Espasa Calpe, 1981); Juan Marichal, *El secreto de España* (Madrid: Taurus, 1995); José Antonio Rocamora, *El nacionalismo ibérico* (Valladolid: Universidad de Valladolid, 1994); Andrés de Blas Guerrero, *Tradición republicana y nacionalismo español* (Madrid: Tecnos, 1991); and Andrés de Blas Guerrero, ed., *Enciclopedia del nacionalismo* (Madrid: Tecnos, 1997). See also *Studia Historica*, 1994. For a recent synthesis of state and nation building in Spain, see Luis González Antón, *España y las Españas* (Madrid: Alianza Editorial, 1997).

[2] On nationalism in Catalonia, see in particular Albert Balcells, *Catalan Nationalism: Past and Present* (London: Macmillan, 1996); Joan Benet, *Bibliografia sobre el nacionalisme català* (Barcelona: Fundació Jaume Bofill, 1974); Josep M. Colomer, *Cataluña cuestión de Estado* (Madrid: Tecnos, 1986); Horst Hina, *Castilla y Cataluña en el debate cultural* (Barcelona: Península, 1986); Isidre Molas, *Lliga Catalana* (Barcelona: Edicions 62, 1974); Jordi Solé Tura, *Catalanismo y revolución burguesa* (Madrid: Edicusa, 1970); and Eric Ucelay da Cal, *La Catalunya populista* (Barcelona: La Magrana, 1982).

On Basque nationalism, see Javier Corcuera, *Orígenes, ideología y organización del nacionalismo vasco* (Madrid: Siglo XXI, 1979); Antonio Elorza, *Ideologías del nacionalismo vasco* (San Sebastián: Haramburu, 1978); Juan Pablo Fusi, *El País Vasco. Pluralismo y nacionalidad* (Madrid: Alianza Universidad, 1984); Fernando Gracía de Cortázar y Juan Manuel Azcona, *El nacionalismo vasco: un siglo de historia* (Madrid: Tecnos, 1995); Jon Juaristi, *El bucle melancólico* (Madrid: Espasa Calpe, 1997); Juan José Solozábal, *El primer nacionalismo vasco* (Madrid: Tucar Ediciones, 1975); and Patxo Unzueta, *Los nietos de la ira* (Madrid: El País-Aguilar, 1988).

national *convivencia* that underlies Spain's current autonomous state.[3] The good intentions and bad conscience of the nationalist protests in Catalonia and the Basque country have inspired in the immediate past a pattern of general explanations that have not always recognized that the Spanish nation has never been the mere sum of its nationalities and regions—a state whose most coherent inspiration would presumably be the logic of quasi-confederation.

Among all the questions implicit in the organization of national *convivencia* in Spain, I would like to call attention to several of special relevance. First, I will briefly address the construction of the state and the nation in the Spanish case and the impact that the unification of Europe has had on both since the beginning of the twentieth century. I will then attempt to illustrate the significance of the idea of national pluralism as an indispensable prerequisite for the organization of this *convivencia*. In conclusion, I will assess the current autonomous state as a political formula capable of guaranteeing a balanced solution to the national question in Spain.

THE CONSTRUCTION OF THE SPANISH NATIONAL STATE AND THE HORIZON OF THE EUROPEAN UNION

Spanish historiographers and political scientists are now aware of the shortcomings of traditionalism, both ingenuous and politically motivated, in explaining the models for state making and nation building. The roads to modernity, as Liah Greenfeld has shown, are not reducible to a single basic design, be it French or British.[4] The peculiarities evident in the emergence of the state and the nation in Spain do not, however, constitute an exception to the panorama of Western Europe. As Charles Tilly states in his preface to *Coercion, Capital, and the European States, 990-1990*,

[3] For a survey of the Spanish autonomous state, see Juan Pablo Fusi, "El desarollo autonómico," in Javier Tusell and Alvaro Soto, eds., *Historia de la transición, 1975–1986* (Madrid: Alianza Universidad, 1996); Eduardo García de Enterría, *Estudios sobre autonomías territoriales* (Madrid: Civitas, 1985); Luis Martín Rebollo, ed., *El futuro de las autonomías territoriales* (Santander: Universidad de Cantabria, 1990); Luis Moreno, *La federalización de España* (Madrid: Siglo XXI, 1997); Francisco Peña Díez, ed., *El Estado autonómico* (Madrid: Ministerio de Administraciones Públicas, 1993); Alberto Pérez Calvo, ed., *La participación de las Comunidades Autónomas en las decisiones del Estado* (Madrid: Centro de Estudios Constitucionales, 1993); Joaquin Tornos et al., *Informe sobre las autonomías* (Madrid: Civitas, 1988); National Institute of Public Administration (INAP), *El funcionamiento del Estado autonómico* (Madrid: Ministerio de Administraciones Públicas, 1996); and *Documentación Administrativa*, 1993, nos. 232-3.
[4] Liah Greenfeld, *Nationalism: Five Roads to Modernity* (Cambridge, Mass.: Harvard University Press, 1992).

"in previous investigations I proved once and again that the Spanish experience was quite comprehensible on its own terms, although it did not conform to the generalizations developed by political scientists studying the history of England, France, and Prussia. It did not make sense to call Spain eccentric; the fault clearly lay with the generalizations, not with Spain."[5]

The long era of martial conflict with the Muslim world, present in the Iberian Peninsula since the invasion of the eighth century, culminated at the end of the fifteenth century. The Christian kingdoms born of the Reconquest would become an expression of political pluralism, but they never broke free of the influence of the idea of a unified Spain under the government of Rome or especially under the Visigothic monarchy terminated by the Muslim invasion. One of the most significant aspects of the Hispanic reunification begun in the late fifteenth century was the weight of the crown of Castile in terms of demographic potential, wealth, and territorial control. The modern Spanish state, born like other Western countries as a national state, was thus dominated by a single region at the expense of the other kingdoms and jurisdictions that constituted the union. When an alteration of demographic, economic, and social trends in favor of the periphery began at the end of the seventeenth century, the opportune political consequences for the state would not be easy to discern.

The Spanish state that emerged from the traumatic "Iron Age" of the seventeenth century experienced abnormally prolonged moments of peace in the Age of Enlightenment and a difficult assimilation of liberal politics in the nineteenth century. This was a state certain of its identity. Its status as a national state was practically beyond question. Indeed, the Spanish state was even envied on occasion by the rest of Europe.

The impact of the disturbances at the end of the nineteenth century cannot be underestimated. Political Catalan nationalism (*catalanismo*) became important during the first decade of the twentieth century, and Basque nationalism established a more modest presence over the course of the first third of this century. These movements caused centrifugal tensions in the republic, although they were in no way comparable to the social and economic tensions that ended in the tragedy of 1936. The most serious crisis of national conscience, the crisis that to a degree still afflicts us today, is that which began with the sudden interruption of our liberal

---

[5] Charles Tilly, *Coerción, capital y los estados europeos, 990–1990* (Madrid: Alianza Universidad, 1992).

tradition by Francoism. The crisis continued during the fight against his dictatorship and the process of transition to democracy.

The dictatorship of Franco attempted to terminate the nationalist and regionalist demands that had been present in Spain since the last decades of the nineteenth century. Consequently, there was a return to unifying and centralist bases of government unhindered by the limits and balances inherent in the liberal political order. The Franco regime found itself obliged to adopt this centralist option by virtue of its totalitarian, and then authoritarian, nature. The reestablishment of democracy was necessarily accompanied by various forms of territorial distribution of power. These developments were prompted as much by the pressure of peripheral nationalisms as by the prestige brought on during the 1960s and 1970s by regional economic and administrative projects designed to encourage political participation.

This pressure to reformulate the model of territorial organization of the state was complemented by the supranational integration after World War II, which had remained to a large degree at the margin under the dictatorship of Franco. Since the beginning of the twentieth century at least, the cause of European integration had been inseparable from the process of economic and social modernization and the reform of the liberal order begun in the first decades of the nineteenth century. For the majority of the opposition to the dictatorship, full integration into the European Community remained a fundamental political aspiration. Some viewed this aspiration, doubtless somewhat precipitously, as the prelude to a rapid dissolution of the national state and of the idea of the political nation, both now thrown into dispute by the processes of supranational integration and the demands of internal "devolution."

This is not the moment for a digression into this supposed process of autodissolution of the state prefigured by the new post-Hobbesian order that would develop in Spain. But we weary of the supposed imminence and inevitability of the terminal crisis of the liberal-democratic Leviathan. As Michael Mann and others have pointed out, "Eurocentricism" dominates our vision of a crisis that is not easy to determine in great powers such as the United States, Japan, and Germany, or in smaller states struggling to liberate themselves from the pre-Hobbesian stage dominant in their societies.[6] It is time to question, not only this Eurocentricism, but also the unidirectional character of certain phenomena that have been

---

[6] Michael Mann, "Nation-States in Europe and Other Continents," *Daedalus*, vol. 122, no. 3 (1993).

seen as implacably challenging the state. An example is the activity of the great multinational corporations or international organizations that, it is sometimes claimed, have actually served to guarantee the continuing existence of several state apparatus, particularly in the Third World. Neither these influences, nor the new systems of international security, nor the limitations inherent in the idea of sovereignty represent sufficient reason to speak of the immediate end of national states although these states will undoubtedly be submitted to substantial modifications and adaptations proceeding from the intensification of international relations at every level.

In the case of Spain, the lack of moderation with which this complex situation has been contemplated is most unfortunate. Nor can we ignore the vague influence of a "German syndrome" reflected in the difficulty of reconciling one segment of the Spanish people with their immediate political past. There is an obvious distance between the horror of the Holocaust and the excesses of the dictatorship of Franco. This distance, however, lessened the "discomfort with the past" manifested in a lack of loyalty to the idea of the national state. One indirect consequence of this situation has been a pronounced pro-European stance among the political elites, both state and peripheral, which merely serves to underscore the relative indifference in some quarters to the erosion of the legitimacy of the state, apparently condemned to obsolescence in a new age. In their search for long-term historical explanations, some historians have played down the importance of the events of the immediate past. In the same way, some political actors, in their determined vision of the future, have overlooked the short-term problems that will continue to plague states lacking the necessary legitimacy to carry out their functions.

PLURALISM IN THE IDEA OF THE NATION AND ITS APPLICATION TO SPAIN

The distinction between the idea of the "political" nation and the "cultural" nation, first made by Ferdinand Meinecke, has hardly ever been applied to the Spanish case, despite the rationale behind its creation and the possibilities it contains for the treatment of certain national questions from the perspective of democratic pluralism.[7] The "political" nation emerges in Europe as an ideological reference point destined to facilitate

---

[7] Ferdinand Meinecke, *Cosmopolitanism and the National State* (Princeton, N.J.: Princeton University Press, 1970); and idem, *The German Catastrophe: Reflections and Recollections* (Cambridge, Mass.: Harvard University Press, 1950).

the life of the state.[8] Far from being the consequence of a pre-existing national reality, this state is typically the *gran truchimán* (Great Interpreter) postulated by Ortega y Gasset to explain the appearance of nations.[9] The substantially political genesis of the nation is in no way exclusive to Europe. The United States, Latin America, and subsequently Africa and Asia set the stage for a pattern of nations that cannot be the result of a prior ethno-linguistic homogeneity.

The origins of this type of nation are old and can be traced to the very birth of the modern state in the form of the nation-state. Nevertheless, the question of national origins did not attain authentic importance until an advanced date. When the cohesion of the state depends upon other political and ideological means—dynastic fidelity or religious bonds surviving through the all-powerful force of tradition—the nation is an ideological construction largely without foundation. The liberal state discovered all its potential through the advantageous substitution of fallen idols. As exemplified by liberal states such as Britain, France, the United States, Germany, and Spain, national character—undoubtedly conditioned by the complex process of protonationalism—takes on a distinct meaning and an urgency to conform to the internal and external demands that bring about national mobilization. Resistance to the new liberal order, the need to proceed to the unification of the state, the exigencies of imperial enterprises, and the questioning of the state by emerging nationalist movements of a secessionist character are some of the factors that modulate the form and the intensity of this national mobilization in liberal states.

The "originality" of the nation should not be juxtaposed with the "artificiality" of the state. A nation adapts to the necessities brought about by economic, social, ideological, and political transformations, and it assumes the multiethnic character of its constituents in accordance with liberal nationalism, generating a type of nationalism that, as Eugene Kamenka has argued, is based on the citizen and not on ethnic particularism.[10] The individual, possessed of dignity and intrinsic rights, should be the subject and not the object of the nation and nationalism. Several decades ago Alfred Cobban pointed out the political consequences implicit in this type of nation, unlike the model of the organic or cultural nation.[11]

---

[8] See, in particular, Andrés de Blas Guerrero, *Nacionalismos y naciones en Europa* (Madrid: Alianza Universidad, 1994).

[9] José Ortega y Gasset, *Obras completas*, 12 vols. (Madrid: Alianza Editorial, 1983).

[10] Eugene Kamenka, ed., *Nationalism: The Nature of an Idea* (London: E. Arnold, 1976).

[11] Alfred Cobban, *Self-Determination* (Oxford: Oxford University Press, 1945).

To a certain extent, Johann von Herder served as the first great prophet of a German-based nationalist tradition that argued for a different understanding of the nation. In his view the cultural singularity of a collectivity, the "spirit of the people," is ultimately responsible for the emergence of a nation. This nation should not be constituted by historical-political factors or by the action of the state, but rather by the delimitation of territorial political organizations. The enjoyment of the state itself is considered indispensable as a guarantee of the differentiated cultural personality of the people, something that, for Herder, possesses greater value than the collectivity.[12]

One recurring problem is how to identify the causes for the sudden appearance of this second type of nation. In most cases it can be attributed to external conflicts of the kind that inspired Fichte's *Discourses to the German Nation*.[13] In other cases, however, the element that unleashes the process can be found in internal factors. Industrialism, for example, may reveal differences in wealth between territories within the state that had previously lived together in harmony. Other factors include urbanization, the impact of educating the masses, and the turmoil generated by large-scale migrations.

Even allowing for the importance of the aforementioned factors, the historian and the political scientist cannot neglect the power of ideologies and nationalist movements in constructing new communities. Several databases would doubtless be necessary for any viable quantitative study of nationalism. Even then such statistics would provide a backdrop for, rather than any strict determinant of, the new national-cultural realities. This conception of the nation will necessarily give rise to another type of nationalism, one characterized by its supra-individual foundation in addition to its taste for diversity and its inevitable enthusiasm for that which is unique to each people. The protagonist of the nation is the cultural entity, and the rights of the nation are not derived fundamentally from its citizens, but rather from the "living and eternal" organism that forms the cultural basis of the nation.

It goes without saying that Meinecke's two classes of nations, both of which echo Töennies's older distinction between the idea of "community" and "society," are ideal types rather than attempts to describe a complex reality.[14] Their usefulness, however, is beyond question for the simple

---

[12] Johann von Herder, *Obra selecta* (Madrid: Altaquara, 1982).
[13] Johann G. Fichte, *Discursos a la nación alemana* (Madrid: Editora Nacional, 1977).
[14] Ferdinand Töennies, *Community and Society* (New York: Transaction Books, 1963).

reason that "political" nations inevitably tend to project themselves into the field of cultural practice. The level of pretension to homogeneity in this area is basically a function of the level of resistance encountered by the unfolding liberal nation-state. This proof runs parallel to the fact that "cultural" nations encompass the most salient instrumental and utilitarian components of "political" nations. If we lose sight of this, we cannot understand the evolution of cultural nationalisms in the Western world into "new middle class" nationalism, so important today in some European countries and in Canada. Michael Keating's comparative study of Scotland, Quebec, and Catalonia demonstrates this point exceptionally well.[15] The usefulness of the distinction between "political" and "cultural" nationalisms lies in its ability to help us understand the plurality inherent in nations, as well as the ideological dispositions of different nationalist movements and ideologies.

In the same geographical space, different kinds of nations can coincide. The political nations of the Jacobins and the Girondins existed on the same French soil as the nation understood by E. Renan, M. Barrès, or C. Maurras, the nation of the republican and socialist tradition, the nation of the "nationalists" in the first three decades of the twentieth century, and the hypothetical cultural nationalities of the Bretons, Occitans, Corsicans, and Alsatians, all of whom have attempted in recent years to find a place within the tangled skein of European nationalities. Once the first destructive stage has been overcome, once we have abandoned the tacit or express invitation to a new and fatal "struggle of the collectivities" in which nations take the place of social classes or races, democratic politics must find a harmonizing formula for these complex communities. Cultural relativism, in which all cultural and political traditions are equivalent for the simple reason that they are "particular" and "different," may seem incompatible with this objective, but it is imperative to create mechanisms of political integration that favor shared loyalties among nations of different types that coexist in the same territory. A propitious climate for these shared loyalties can be created through the territorial distribution of power and by accepting a liberal-democratic political culture that instead of allowing itself to be dazzled by the charms of homogeneity views the call to exclusive loyalties as a return to the worst moments of a happily vanquished past. To argue in favor of the attractions of cultural pluralism and yet conclude by invoking the motto "one

---

[15] Michael Keating, *Naciones contra el estado* (Barcelona: Ariel, 1996).

people, one nation, one state" is a self-contradiction exposed long ago by the famous proponent of pluralism and scholar of nationalism, Lord Acton.

In my opinion the autonomous Spanish state, its obvious gains notwithstanding, has not fully encouraged the acceptance of a climate of national pluralism in accord with the mandates of the constitution of 1978. This situation is essentially the result of actions by peripheral nationalisms in Catalonia and the Basque country, groups immersed in a process of national construction and affirmation that has forced them to deny the Spanish national community of which they form a substantial part, both historically and today.

The response of Catalan and Basque nationalists to the idea of Spanish nationalism is not all that different from Spanish nationalists' response to peripheral nationalisms. But while Spanish democracy continues to recognize, little by little, national cultures in *convivencia* with the political nation, the peripheral nationalisms demonstrate an increasing doctrinal obstinacy—compatible at times with a remarkable flexibility in political practice. Apparently, these Catalan and Basque nationalists are convinced that their national aspirations can be achieved by means of a radical inversion of the established method of viewing the problem, and through the voluntary negation of a Spanish national community in favor of a strictly governmental interpretation of Spain. To what extent can the national government be described as an oppressor? This question frequently provides the terrain on which moderates and radicals among peripheral nationalists mark their boundaries.

This "denationalization" of Spain, which parallels certain autonomous communities' insistence on their prior status as nations, openly conflicts with the spirit of the governing constitutional framework. J. J. Solozábal, an expert on the Spanish Constitution, has examined the Spanish national state as a state of autonomies.[16] In 1931 some of those responsible for the republican constitution believed themselves to be engaged in a revolutionary process with the capacity to create a new state. The current Spanish constitution, by contrast, is the expression of the continuity of a Spanish nation that is open to *convivencia* with other eventual realities, particularly of a cultural nature.

---

[16] Juan José Solozábal, "El estado autonómico como estado nacional," *Sistema* 116 (1993).

CONCLUSION: OVERCOMING DIFFICULTIES

All the problems of legitimacy in the national liberal-democratic state cannot be attributed to the activity of peripheral nationalisms or to a process of European integration still poorly understood with regard to its consequences for the national state. Also contributing to the erosion of this state in the immediate past are three other sources: the traditional right, anarchism, and Spanish Marxism.

The first of these involves the challenge presented to the liberal democratic order by the traditional right, which with great difficulty has substituted its understanding of the state and the nation with an identification with the Altar and the Throne. It would be wise to rethink the automatic identification between Catholicism, ultraconservative thought, and Spanish nationalism over the nineteenth century and into the twentieth. This apparent identification, the phenomenon of "national Catholicism," cannot hide the fears that the far right in Spain and in other Western nations—especially France—maintained with respect to the liberal and modernizing components of the political nation, such as that created in Spain by the liberal revolution.[17] The genuine Spanish reactionaries, suspicious of any modernizing component that casts a shadow over the ideological leadership of the Catholic Church or over the supposed consubstantiality between a specific interpretation of Catholicism and the idea of Spain, distrust even Barrès and Maurras. Neither Carlism, nor wide sectors of the Spanish far right in the early twentieth century, nor the majority of the men in *Acción Española* went beyond a vague patriotism, a heightened "piety," which characterizes the legitimate defenders of the old order in the moment of confrontation with the new national reality.

This situation underwent modifications during the sharpening of social conflict under the Second Republic. At that time the "nation" came to be regarded as the last ditch defense of a threatened social order. The Franco regime co-opted the rhetoric of Spanish nationalism in its most conservative version. On the other hand, it would be a mistake to underestimate the Francoists' suspicion of the idea of the Spanish nation and its liberal roots. The dictatorship had certain permanent reference points: "Anti-Spain," the loving cultivation of the memory of the Civil War, the persistence of an image of a Spain of conquerors and conquered. These fundamental ideological positions are all manifestations of resistance to an idea of a

---

[17] Alberto Botti, *Cielo y dinero*; Raúl Morodo, *Los orígenes ideológicos del franquismo: Acción Española* (Madrid: Alianza Universidad, 1985).

national community capable of integrating its citizens in the perception of a shared present and past.

The second great negative contribution to the process now under consideration brought with it one of the most genuinely Hispanic contributions to political thought and practice in Europe and America. This was anarchism.[18] From its beginning it presented a formidable obstacle to the unification of the "divided nation." Its enmity first toward the liberal state, and subsequently toward the liberal-democratic state, proved irrevocable. Anarchists mobilized wide sectors of the working classes to deny any common political space for all Spaniards. The revolutionary utopia of libertarian communism did not survive the Civil War. The most unfortunate face of the anarchist movement, however, did. I refer to the radical individualism of Max Stirner, the diffuse influence of Nietzsche, and the early twentieth-century positions that social Darwinism brought to the door of the far right. The complex political-aesthetic position associated with anarchism contributed considerably to the problems of legitimacy of the state and the nation in Spain. The influence of this negative contribution continues to the present.

Thirdly, we must recognize the dysfunctional role of Spanish Marxism in this process. Throughout the transition, the Marxist-inspired political parties emphasized issues such as the right of self-determination and the Marxist-Leninist vision of the nation and the state—issues that could do little to help achieve a reasonable and realistic formulation of the new citizen who would emerge from beneath the repression of the dictatorship. Without neglecting the integrating potential implicit in an ideological discourse, I remain convinced that for a wide sector of the Spanish left, Marxism proved a deficient means of addressing the national-regional problem in Spain. If the Socialist Party remained indebted to Marxist-Leninist influences until 1982, the exercise of power and the assumption of clearly social-democratic positions since that time have rectified the Marxist-Leninists' vision of the national problem. This does not apply to the minority Communist Party and its electoral coalition (the *Izquierda Unida*), but these groups have been persistently confused and ambiguous on this matter.

The nationalist crisis in the Basque country and Catalonia has undermined loyalty to the re-emerging democratic state in Spain. For complex reasons, the delegitimization of Francoism was prolonged, until 1982 at

[18] J. Alvarez Junco, "La teoría polítical del anarquismo," in Fernando Vallespín, ed., *Historia de la teoría política*, vol. 4 (Madrid: Alianza Editorial, 1992).

least, by the delegitimization of the state. The boundaries have not always been clear between a dictatorial regime, a state profoundly penetrated by the logic of the dictatorship, and a nation with a long history of liberalism behind it. The updated Basque and Catalan nationalist movements have taken advantage of this ambiguity. They are intent on constructing their hegemony in the Basque country and Catalonia on fragments of legitimacy torn from the Spanish state and nation. The greater solidity and consequent self-assurance of Catalan nationalism allowed, however, the partial reconsideration of this position by the Catalan nationalist party, the CIU. The nationalism of the Basque Nationalist Party is more radical. This party is conscious of the precariousness of its political hegemony, gained in part through the exceptional circumstances created by the terrorist practices of ETA (*Euskadi y Libertad*).

Since the reestablishment of democracy in Spain and the implementation of the constitution of 1978, the obstacles to the liberal-democratic state posed by the traditional right, by anarchists, and by Spanish Marxists have finally been eliminated. The overwhelming majority of the old Spanish right has opted for the democratic political formulas expressed by parties of the center and the right of center, such as *Unión de Centro Democrático* (UCD), the *Centro Democrático y Social* (CDS), and the current *Partido Popular* (PP). The former anarchist syndicate has disappeared from our political scene, and traditional Marxism has given way to the modern social-democratic positions of the renovated *Partido Socialista Obrero Español* (PSOE). The only significant refutation of the state that remains in force today is directed against the role of the state as a nation, not against its liberal-democratic character.

In this context several commentators have inevitably argued for European integration and the convenience of forgetting the national character of the Spanish state. By this logic the state could be replaced by something like a sum of nationalities, an ambiguous "nation of nations" that vaguely recalls the hardly reassuring formula of conversion in the Austrian-Hungarian Empire on the eve of its extinction. Some believe that the forced blurring of the Spanish national conscience is the best expedient, given the importance of peripheral nationalism and the process of European integration. In Spain the problems of the legitimacy of the national liberal-democratic state have not been associated wholly with peripheral nationalism or with European integration—a process with consequences for the future of the nation-state that are still poorly understood. However, it makes better sense to think that Spanish nationalism, with distinctly liberal-democratic origins and committed both to a plural state and the cause of Europe, is better equipped to arrive at a "national accord" that would allow Spain to deal effectively with the final consolidation of the autonomous state and the complex process of building Europe.

This project would not be as difficult as it may at times appear. If one takes a dispassionate view, one can argue that there are no legitimate political motives in Spain for challenging the state: neither economic exploitation on the national level, nor particular historical injuries, nor reluctance to negotiate on the part of the government. Until the twentieth century was well under way, Spain had a well-organized democratic political system, a society conscious of the deep connections within it, and a space—much more solid in its economic, social, and cultural aspects than in its strictly political dimension—where this society could be articulated. Perhaps we ought to pay more attention to the consistently higher voter turnout in national elections than in autonomous and local elections. This suggests the "nationalization" of Spanish politics and a preference for the "locus" of the state over other public spaces. Collectively, the evidence should afford us some optimism as we face the national-region question in Spain and the process of European integration.

15

The Kantian Idea of Europe: Critical and Cosmopolitan Perspectives

JAMES TULLY

Three illustrious historians—Anthony Pagden, Biancamaria Fontana, and John Pocock —have contributed to this volume, and it is not easy to follow them. Rather than advance another survey of ideas of Europe, I would like to accept one of the ideas they present and investigate it from what aspires to be a postimperial perspective. The idea I wish to examine is of Europe as a federation of independent states, and this as a prototype for the rest of the world. It is closely associated with Immanuel Kant and Benjamin Constant. For shorthand, I will call it the Kantian or federal idea of Europe. My thesis is that a survey of the critical attitude that has developed in response to this idea over the past two hundered years will change our idea of Europe and its relation to the rest of the world, from an Eurocentric to a more cosmopolitan conception.[1]

THE KANTIAN IDEA OF EUROPE AND THE WORLD

Recall how Anthony Pagden, Biancamaria Fontana, and to some degree John Pocock presented a wide variety of ideas of Europe from various ages and went on to single out the idea associated with Kant and Constant, suggesting that it remains relevant today. This idea contains five main features. First, Europe is tending toward a federation of independent or sovereign states, each and every one of which has what Kant calls

---

[1] That is, I demur from the suggestion, advanced by many of Kant's followers, that his political philosophy *is* cosmopolitan. Kant claims only that his philosophy has a cosmopolitan "intent." See Immanuel Kant, "Idea for a Universal History with a Cosmopolitan Intent," in *Perpetual Peace and Other Essays*, ed. Ted Humphrey (Indianapolis: Hackett Publishing Company, 1983), 29–40. This I do not dispute. For a recent and unmodified claim that Kant's political and moral philosophy is cosmopolitan, see Martha C. Nussbaum, "Kant and Stoic Cosmopolitanism," *The Journal of Political Philosophy* 5, 1 (March 1997): 1–26.

a "republican" constitution: that is, the formal equality of citizens under the law, the separation of legislature and executive, and representative government.[2] Second, the federation is held together by five preliminary articles, the cosmopolitan right of universal hospitality ("the right of an alien not to be treated as an enemy on his arrival in another's country"), and commerce or "the spirit of trade."[3] In addition, as Fontana emphasizes in her chapter, Constant added the proviso that variation in local customs and ways should be tolerated within independent states.[4]

Third, the European states and their federation are the prototype for a federation of all the peoples of the world organized into identical states.[5] The rise and gradual spread of this idea of federation are, fourth, understood as the consequence of a set of historical processes and "stages" of world development, including the spread of commerce and the rule of law by European wars of imperial expansion.[6] Finally, the rise of this federal idea is understood to mark the decline of an older and incompatible idea of Europe as the center of world empires (an idea related to European imperialism associated with Napoleon or earlier concepts of European imperialism based on war, conquest, and the dispossession of Indigenous and other non-European peoples). Kant's sketch of *Perpetual Peace* in 1795 marks, as Pagden concludes, the transition from the idea of "empire" to "federation."[7] Although Kant uses his federal idea to criticize as "unjust" the imperial spread of European commerce and law-governed

[2] Immanuel Kant, "Perpetual Peace: A Philosophical Sketch," in *Perpetual Peace and Other Essays*, 107–44, 112–18. The republican constitution is the first definitive article of peace and the federation of such states is the second.

[3] Ibid., 107–11, 118–19, 125. The cosmopolitan right is the means by which commerce is offered to other nations. Immanuel Kant, *The Metaphysics of Morals*, trans. Mary Gregor (Cambridge: Cambridge University Press, 1991), 158.

[4] Benjamin Constant, "The Spirit of Conquest and Usurpation and their Relation to European Civilization," in *Political Writings*, ed. Biancamaria Fontana (Cambridge: Cambridge University Press, 1988), 73–8, 149–56. Constant realized that his defense of the variety of customs against uniformity was unpopular, and he believed that the economic and political processes of modernization would lead to uniformity in the long run.

[5] Kant, *Perpetual Peace*, 117. ("This *idea of federalism* should eventually include all nations.") See Anthony Pagden, *Lords of all the World: Ideologies of Empire in Spain, Britain, and France c.1500–c.1800* (New Haven: Yale University Press, 1995), 190. The federation can use economic power, rather than war, to force other nations to comply (125).

[6] Pagden, *Lords of all the World*, 120–5; Kant, "Idea for a Universal History," 29–40. For a recent historical survey and defense of the stages theory of historical development in Enlightenment thought, see Istvan Hont, "The Permanent Crisis of a Divided Mankind: Contemporary Crisis of the Nation State in Historical Perspective," in *Contemporary Crisis of the Nation State?* ed. John Dunn (Oxford: Basil Blackwell, 1995), 160–231.

[7] Pagden, *Lords of the all the World*, 178–200. The title of this concluding chapter is "From Empire to Federation."

colonies by warfare, Kant accepts and builds on this older imperial foundation, understood as the "will" or "mechanism" of "nature" and does not permit any resistance to it.[8]

This idea of Europe and of the world as a European federation writ large is worth serious consideration because it has played the role of something like a Kantian "regulative ideal" over the two centuries since the publication of *Perpetual Peace* in 1795. It has come to function as a more or less taken-for-granted normative standard against which many people organize and evaluate forms of political association in Europe and throughout the world. Initially, as we have seen, it gave philosophical expression to widely held assumptions about political association and historical development in eighteenth-century Europe. Across the Atlantic, James Madison, according to Nicolas Greenleaf Onuf, argued that the federation of the thirteen Euro-American states in 1787 was modeled on this "continental" idea of federation, but that the United States added an "Atlantic" element of active republican citizenship that is absent from Kant's formulation.[9] The Atlantic element is the republican or "neo-Roman" concept of freedom, which involves the civic responsibility to serve the public good through participation yet is adapted to a federal system in which citizens are represented at both the state and federal orders.[10] The United States' modification and use of the European idea served in turn as a norm for some of the non-Indigenous liberal revolutions in Latin America and, to some degree, for the federation of the four provinces of Canada in the nineteenth century.

In the early twentieth century President Woodrow Wilson's vision of decolonization, independent state building, and the League of Nations

---

[8] Kant, *Perpetual Peace*, 120–5, esp. 124. Kant explains this conservative doctrine in *The Metaphysics of Morals*, 129–33. Under no circumstances can any existing constitutional order be questioned with regard to obedience. Moreover, like many of the "stages" theorists of the eighteenth century, Kant apparently believes that legal order and peaceful relations only arise with sedentary agriculture and trade in any case, so the Indigenous peoples who hunt, fish, and herd have no laws and are "the most contrary to a civilized constitution" (*Perpetual Peace*, 122 and note).

[9] Nicolas Greenwood Onuf, *The Republican Legacy in International Thought* (New York: Cambridge University Press, 1998).

[10] For the neo-Roman or republican concept of freedom in the seventeenth and eighteenth centuries, see Quentin Skinner, *Liberty before Liberalism* (Cambridge: Cambridge University Press, 1997) and Philip Pettit, *Republicanism: A Theory of Freedom and Government* (Oxford: Clarendon: 1997). In contrast to this widespread concept of republican or neo-Roman freedom, Kant defines "freedom" as "the privilege not to obey any external laws except those to which I have been able to give my consent," yet he calls this "republican" (*Perpetual Peace*, 112 and note). It is questionable whether Madison endorses the republican concept of freedom as nondomination (independence) or the liberal concept of freedom as noninterference.

was informed by the Kantian idea. As Carl Friedrich argued in *Inevitable Peace* (1948), the idea should be seen to play a normative role in the establishment and governance of the United Nations.[11] To come full circle, Fontana and Pagden surely speak for many when they suggest that the Union of Europe in our time ought to be viewed in the light of Kant's idea of federalism. David Held sets out his model of "cosmopolitan governance" for the planet with reference to Kant's *Perpetual Peace* as his normative standard.[12]

A CRITICAL ENLIGHTENMENT ATTITUDE TOWARD THE KANTIAN IDEA OF EUROPE

Is it possible to call this idea of Europe into question and take up a critical attitude toward aspects of it and the regulative role it plays in political thought and action without denying its importance? The answer is yes. Such an attitude has developed in response to the five features of the Kantian idea over the past two hundred years. A survey of this critical attitude enables us to see the Kantian idea as a critical ideal rather than as a regulative ideal—as one form of organization of the political field among many rather than as the framework in which alternatives are evaluated. This attitude is neither anti-Enlightenment nor post-Enlightenment. It is a critical attitude that derives from the Enlightenment and finds expression, for example, in Kant's essay "What is Enlightenment?"[13] It is a test of the habitual and regulative assumptions or, more accurately, "limits" of the present, including the limits that Kant and other Enlightenment thinkers claim to have established as beyond doubt. Michel Foucault poses this critical question: "In what is given to us as universal, necessary, obligatory, what place is occupied by whatever is singular, contingent, and the product

---

[11] Carl J. Friedrich, *Inevitable Peace* (Cambridge, Mass: Harvard University Press, 1948).
[12] David Held, *Democracy and the Global Order: From the Modern State to Cosmopolitan Governance* (Stanford: Stanford University Press, 1995), 226–30.
[13] Kant, "What is Enlightenment?" in *Perpetual Peace*, 107–44. For the Enlightenment context of this essay, see James Schmidt, ed., *What is Enlightenment? Eighteenth-Century Answers and Twentieth-Century Questions* (Berkeley: University of California Press, 1996). For the interpretation of "What is Enlightenment?" as initiating a form of critical reflection on the dominant assumptions of the present, including the assumptions of the Kantian tradition of political philosophy, see Michel Foucault, "What is Critique?" and "What is Enlightenment?" in *The Politics of Truth*, ed. Sylvere Lotringer (New York: Columbia University Press & Semiotext(e), 1997), 23–82, 101–34; and James Tully, "To Think and Act Differently: Foucault's Four Reciprocal Objections to Habermas," in *Foucault contra Habermas: Two Philosophies of the Present*, ed. David Owen (New York: Sage Publications, 1998).

of arbitrary constraints?"[14] This form of critical reflection on the federal idea of Europe, therefore, is the application of Kant's critical "attitude" to one of his own ideas that has become a more or less taken-for-granted assumption of the present.

The limits of Kant's idea of Europe have been called into question by the practitioners of the Enlightenment attitude of *Sapere Aude*. Recall that his idea is presented as marking a transition in European political self-understanding from Europe as the center of world empires to the center of a cosmopolitan federation: "the creation," in Pagden's words, "of a universal federation bound by common commercial interests."[15] It was not the understanding of Kant and his like-minded contemporaries that federalism would replace the economic relations and constitutional forms spread by the wars of European imperialism and colonization but that independent states and international federalism would be built on this historical foundation.

Notwithstanding this change in European self-understanding, European imperialism did not decline and federalism did not develop (despite Kant's argument that nature "does it herself, whether or not we will it").[16] Rather, European imperialism entered into a second and heightened phase from 1800 to after World War II. "Consider," Edward Said writes,

that in 1800 Western powers claimed 55 per cent but actually held approximately 35 per cent of the earth's surface, and by 1878 the proportion was 67 per cent, a rate of increase of 83,000 square miles per year. By 1914, the annual rate had risen to an astonishing 240,000 square miles, and Europe held a grand total of roughly 85 per cent of the earth as colonies, protectorates, dependencies, dominions and commonwealths. No other associated set of colonies in history was as large, none so totally dominated, none so unequal in power to the Western metropolis.[17]

Perpetual Peace played an important role in promoting a form of postcolonial state building and international organization toward the end of this second and higher stage of imperialism. It is reasonable to question if it has not also played a role in continuing aspects of imperialism, given the context in which it was written (of the transition from one phase of imperialism to another) and the apparently uncritical stance the text takes to underlying forms of economic and constitutional imperialism. Now this is exactly the sort of historical and contextual question the

---

[14] Foucault, "What is Enlightenment?" 124–5.
[15] Pagden, *Lords of all the World*, 187.   [16] Kant, *Perpetual Peace*, 123.
[17] Edward W. Said, *Culture and Imperialism* (New York: Knopf, 1993), 8.

practitioners of the Enlightenment critical attitude, such as Said and homi k. bhabha, take up.[18] Their writings are characterized as "postimperial" and "postcolonial"—not because they believe imperialism is over but because they question the vestiges of imperialism in the received ways of thinking about and organizing politics, especially where these ways are presented as nonimperial and the imperial setting of their composition and dissemination is overlooked.

"Whether these efforts [of critique] succeed or fail is a less interesting matter than what distinguishes them, what makes them possible," writes Said, a Palestinian-American, in his classic study *Culture and Imperialism*. Referring specifically to the United States, he notes

an acute and embarrassed awareness of the all-pervasive, unavoidable imperial setting. In fact, there is no way that I know of apprehending the world from within American culture (with a whole history of exterminism and incorporation behind it), without also apprehending the imperial contest itself. This, I would say, is a cultural fact of extraordinary political as well as interpretative importance, yet it has not been recognized as such in cultural and literary theory, and is routinely circumvented or occluded in cultural discourses. To read most cultural deconstructionists, or Marxists, or new historicists is to read writers whose political horizon, whose historical location is within a society and culture deeply enmeshed in imperial domination. Yet little notice is taken of this horizon, few acknowledgements of the setting are advanced, little realization of the imperial closure is allowed for. Instead, one has the impression that interpretation of other cultures, texts and peoples ... occurs in a timeless vacuum, so forgiving and permissive as to deliver the interpretation directly into a universalism free from attachment, inhibition and interest.[19]

Of course, many aspects of the imperial setting of the Kantian idea—economic, military, geographic—have been questioned. The aspect I wish to survey is cultural, what has come to be called "cultural imperialism." Said characterizes it in the following way:

In our time, direct colonialism has largely ended; imperialism ... lingers where it has always been, in a kind of general cultural sphere as well as in specific political, ideological, economic and social practices. Neither imperialism nor colonialism is a simple act of accumulation and acquisition. Both are supported and perhaps impelled by impressive ideological formations that include notions that certain territories and people *require* and beseech domination, as well as forms of knowledge affiliated with domination.

Said then offers examples of the vocabulary of nineteenth-century imperial culture: "inferior" or "subject" races, "subordinate peoples,"

---

[18] homi k. bhabha, *The Location of Culture* (London: Routledge, 1994).
[19] Said, *Culture and Imperialism*, 56.

"dependency," "expansion," and "authority."[20] In his view many in the "so-called Western or metropolitan world, as well as their counterparts in the Third or formerly colonized world, share a sense that the era of high or classical imperialism, which...more or less formally ended with the dismantling of the great colonial structures after World War Two, has in one way or another continued to exert considerable cultural influence in the present. For all sorts of reasons, they feel a new urgency about understanding the pastness *or not* of the past, and this urgency is carried over into perceptions of the present and future."[21]

The "new urgency" to understand the imperial horizons of European texts such as *Perpetual Peace* and the cultural influence they continue to exert in the present is a critical response to a central problem raised by the struggles of decolonization after World War II and, in Eastern Europe, after 1989. These struggles and their aftermath did not unfold in accord with what Kant calls the "guarantee of perpetual peace": the tendency to republican constitutions, cosmopolitan federalism, and the acceptance of the existing economic order. Rather, they gave rise to "an acute and embarrassed awareness of the all-pervasive, unavoidable imperial setting" of these ideas and institutions.

In addition to dismantling the formal features of colonialism, the struggles of liberation aimed to overthrow a form of cultural identity that had been imposed on the colonized people by the colonizers against their democratic will and to establish practices of liberty in which they could invent and discover new identities: first through postcolonial nationalism, then by contesting the imposed dimensions of that national identity, and finally by establishing practices and institutions of liberty.[22] In *The Wretched of the Earth* (1961), Frantz Fanon was one of the first to link decolonization clearly with the struggle against the imposed cultural identity of imperialism and then against the pitfalls of national culture.[23] This struggle against cultural imperialism consists first and foremost, according

---

[20] Ibid., 9. For a very good introduction to the study of cultural imperialism, see John Tomlinson, *Cultural Imperialism: A Critical Introduction* (Baltimore: The Johns Hopkins University Press, 1991).

[21] Said, *Culture and Imperialism*, 7.

[22] For this historical sequence of decolonization, see ibid., 239–81. For the distinction between liberation and practices of liberty, see Foucault, "The Ethics of Concern for Self as a Practice of Freedom," in *Michel Foucault: Ethics, Subjectivity and Truth*, ed. Paul Rabinow (New York: The New Press, 1997), 282–3.

[23] Frantz Fanon, *The Wretched of the Earth*, trans. Constance Farrington (New York: Grove Press, 1963); note the preface by Jean-Paul Sartre. For the status of this text in the Third World as roughly equivalent to *Perpetual Peace* in the First World, see Lewis R. Gordon, T. Denean Sharpley-Whiting, and Renee T. White, eds. *Fanon: A Critical Reader* (Oxford: Basil Blackwell, 1996); and Said, *Culture and Imperialism*, 267–78.

to Fanon, in refusing to imitate precisely the sort of idea expressed in
Perpetual Peace. "Let us decide not to imitate Europe," Fanon writes.
"We today can do everything so long as we do not imitate Europe, so
long as we are not obsessed by the desire to catch up with Europe." If all
the colonized people wish is to "turn Africa into a new Europe...then
let us leave the destiny of our countries to Europeans. They will know
how to do it better than the most gifted among us."[24] The United States,
according to Fanon, provides an example of what happens when former
colonies seek to imitate Europe:

> Two centuries ago, a former European colony decided to catch up with Europe. It
> succeeded so well that the United States of America became a monster, in which
> the taints, the sickness and the inhumanity of Europe have grown to appalling
> dimensions.[25]

Rather, the task is to create "states, institutions, and societies" that do
not "draw their inspiration" from Europe or the United States. Reversing
the stages view of historical development, he concludes that if "we want
humanity to advance a step further, if we want to bring it up to a different
level than that which Europe has shown it [humanity], then we must
invent and we must make discoveries."[26]

Fanon's point seems to be that dismantling the formal ties of colonialism through struggles of liberation is a necessary but insufficient condition of liberty. If the people establish a political association modeled
on the European nation-state, these institutions and practices will impose a European cultural identity and so continue imperialism by imitation. To avoid this cultural imperialism and the devastating pathologies
associated with an imposed identity that would "linger in the general
cultural sphere," the people must establish institutions and practices of
liberty in which they can experiment with discovering and inventing new
identities.[27] By "discover" and "invent" I take it that he means that the
people should both draw on indigenous traditions, customs, and ways
and innovate with cultural borrowing and adaptation.

[24] Fanon, *The Wretched of the Earth*, 312–13.
[25] Ibid., 313.
[26] Ibid., 315. Fanon's argument here that modern Western "humanism" or the Enlightenment philosophy of "Man" serves to legitimate the violence of cultural imperialism had
a large influence in Europe as well as in the Third World. Jean-Paul Sartre emphasized
this theme in his Preface to *The Wretched of the Earth*. Michel Foucault investigated the
extent to which the Enlightenment philosophy of Man plays a role in the processes of
uniform subjectification and identity formation within Europe. See Michel Foucault, *Les
Mots et les Choses* (Paris: Editions Gallimard, 1966); idem, *Surveiller et Punir* (Paris:
Editions Gallimard, 1975); and idem, "What is Enlightenment?"
[27] Fanon, *The Wretched of the Earth*, 206–49.

On this account, then, the Kantian idea of free states and federation is not culturally neutral but is the bearer of processes of a homogenizing or assimilating European cultural identity. Constant saw it this way as well, as rendering subjects culturally undifferentiated and "uniform." On the contrary, Pagden suggests that many of the proponents of Kantian European and world federalism from Andrew Fletcher to Woodrow Wilson saw it as "culturally pluralist."[28] Those who have struggled to liberate themselves from imperialism over the past forty years have tended to agree with Constant and Fanon. They have seen their struggles not only as a means to liberate them from a formal colonial system. They also struggled for the recognition and accommodation of cultural diversity against forms of cultural imperialism imposed by the very institutions that Kant took to be cosmopolitan.

Moreover, these struggles over the past forty years did not always involve the establishment of an independent state through decolonization or secession, although this was common enough from Algeria and Vietnam to the breakup of the Soviet Union. These struggles for "cultural recognition," as Charles Taylor points out, just as often take place within existing constitutional states (including within newly decolonized states, as Fanon predicted), to recognize and accommodate a diversity of cultural identities either in the shared institutions of unitary political associations, as in the United States, or through institutions of legal and political pluralism in multi-ethnic and multinational federations and confederations, as in the European Union.[29] These demands are put forward by indigenous peoples; linguistic, religious, and ethnic minorities; nations within multinational states; and immigrants, exiles, refugees, and multicultural citizens.[30] The aim is not to overturn but to amend the institutions of constitutional democracy, so they will express the cultural plurality of the sovereign people, or peoples, rather than impose the dominant culture's identity while "masquerading" as universal and difference blind.[31] Will

[28] Pagden, *Lords of all the World*, 188.
[29] Charles Taylor, "The Politics of Recognition," in *Multiculturalism*, ed. Amy Gutmann (Princeton: Princeton University Press, 1994), 25–75. This collection provides a good introduction to the politics of recognition or "difference." See also Seyla Benhabib, ed., *Democracy and Difference: Contesting the Boundaries of the Political* (Princeton: Princeton University Press, 1996); bhabha, *The Location of Culture*; and Will Kymlicka, *Multicultural Citizenship: A Liberal Theory of Minority Rights* (Oxford: Clarendon Press, 1995). Said traces the connection between decolonization struggles against cultural imperialism in the Third World and the politics of difference in the First World and Fourth World (Indigenous peoples) in *Culture and Imperialism*, 191–281.
[30] James Tully, *Strange Multiplicity: Constitutionalism in an Age of Diversity* (Cambridge: Cambridge University Press, 1995).
[31] Taylor, "The Politics of Recognition," 44.

Kymlicka writes:

Throughout the world, minorities and majorities clash over such issues as language rights, federalism and regional autonomy, political representation, religious freedom, education curriculum, land claims, immigration and naturalization policy, even national symbols such as the choice of national anthem or public holidays.

Resolving these disputes is perhaps the greatest challenge facing democracies today. In Eastern Europe and the Third World, attempts to create liberal democratic institutions are being undermined by violent nationalist conflicts. In the West, volatile disputes over the rights of immigrants, indigenous peoples, and other cultural minorities are throwing into question many of the assumptions which have governed political life for decades. Since the end of the Cold War, ethnocultural conflicts have become the most common source of political violence in the world, and they show no signs of abating.[32]

Since these struggles against five hundred years of imperialism are only forty years old, it is too early to say if they will be effective or simply mark the transition to a third phase of imperialism. Nevertheless, they have manifestly challenged the purported cultural impartiality and universality of constitutional states and federations in practice, and the response in theory has been "urgent" critical reflection on the "imperial setting" of one of the most authoritative regulative ideals, the Kantian idea of Europe.

Three cultural aspects of the Kantian idea in particular have come in for criticism: the conception of cultures, the relation of cultures to constitutions and federations, and the procedures that render a constitution impartial and legitimate. I will now survey these criticisms and their relation to the earlier tradition of a critical Enlightenment *ethos* in order to show how they give rise to a changed understanding of the idea of Europe.[33]

RETHINKING CULTURES

As noted earlier, the fourth feature of the Kantian idea of Europe is a background philosophy of world history. This philosophy of history ties all five features of the Kantian idea together into a comprehensive worldview.

---

[32] Will Kymlicka, ed., *The Rights of Minority Cultures* (Oxford: Oxford University Press, 1995), 1.

[33] In order to focus on cultural imperialism, I set aside the important question of whether Kant's idea of federation challenges or legitimates economic imperialism. (The answer seems obvious enough.) It is worth noting that Kant was aware of and sought to arrest aspects of military imperialism. See Preliminary Articles 3, 5, and 6, *Perpetual Peace*, 108–10.

In *Perpetual Peace* and *Idea for a Universal History with a Cosmopolitan Intent,* Kant lays out his version of the stages idea of world-historical development. All societies are located on hierarchically arranged levels of historical development. Western European nation-states with their emerging republican constitutions, commerce, inchoate federal relations, enlightened self-seeking, competitive motivation of "unsocial sociability," cultivated civilization, and, finally, intimations of a single and universal "culture" and "morality" are closest to the highest stage, yet only halfway there:

> We are, to a high degree, *cultivated* beyond bearing by all manner of social convention and propriety. But we are a long way from being able to regard ourselves as *moral*. For the idea of morality belongs to culture; and yet using this idea only in references to semblances of morality, e.g. love of honour and outward propriety, constitutes mere civilization.[34]

All other societies, with their lower political, economic, and cultural ways, are described and ranked from the standpoint of the European level. The stage that European societies are approaching—of independent nation-states with republican constitutions and one culture and morality in a federation—is universal and cosmopolitan. It is the end-state to which all others are tending in due course, the level of the development of all the capacities of the human species, and the level of perpetual peace.[35]

As the processes of colonial rule and commerce spread around the globe from the European nations, "which will in all likelihood eventually give laws to all others,"[36] they stimulate the lower societies to "progress" in such a way as to shed their primitive institutions, cultures, and "different kinds of historical *faiths*," which were appropriate to their lower stage of development.[37] These societies either develop into independent states or become incorporated in the European colonies, which develop into independent nation-states. Cultures tend to be relative to the underlying stage of political and economic development. "Barbarism" and "savagism" appear at the inferior, hunter-and-gatherer stage; "civilization" and "refinement" at the superior, commercial stage. The motive of unsocial sociability, which drives the development of human

---

[34] Kant, "Idea for a Universal History," 36.   [35] Ibid., 36–9 (theses eight and nine).
[36] Ibid., 38.
[37] Kant, *Perpetual Peace*, 125 note. For Kant there is no religious or moral pluralism. There is only one religion (and one morality) "valid for all men in all times." The variety of faiths historically can "be nothing more than the accidental vehicles of religion and can only thereby be different in different times and places."

capacities through individual competition for "honor, power, or property, to secure status among his fellows," appears to emerge at the transition from shepherding to agriculture and initiates the "first true steps from barbarism to culture." Kant continues:

Without those characteristics of unsociability...man would live as an Arcadian shepherd, in perfect concord, contentment and mutual love, and all talents would lie eternally dormant in their seed; men docile as the sheep they tend would hardly invest their existence in any worth greater than that of cattle; and as to the purpose behind man's creation, his rational nature, there would remain a void.[38]

Antagonisms among competitive individuals within crude political organizations have the unintended consequence of constructing the foundations of a "perfect civil constitution." In the same way the antagonism of war among political organizations leads unintentionally to the development of federations:

Through wars, through excessive and never remitting preparation for war, through the resultant distress that every nation must, even during times of peace, feel within itself...[men] are driven to make some initial, imperfect attempts; finally, after much devastation, upheaval, and even complete exhaustion of their inner powers, they are driven to take the step that reason could have suggested, even without so much sad experience, namely, to leave the *lawless state of savagery* and enter into a federation of peoples.[39]

This "course of improvement" can be discerned first in the history of "the constitutions of the nations on our continent" from the Greeks to the present, and then used as a guiding thread to clarify and predict the "the national histories of other peoples."[40] The reason why the process began in Europe, spread from Europe, and will reach its goal first in Europe is the superiority of the "national characteristics" of Europeans over other races:

The inhabitant of the temperate parts of the world, above all the central part, has a more beautiful body, works harder, is more jocular, more controlled in his passions, more intelligent than any other race of people in the world. That is why at all points in time these peoples have educated the others and controlled them with weapons. The Romans, Greeks, the ancient Nordic peoples, Genghis Khan,

---

[38] Kant, "Idea for a Universal History," 32.
[39] Ibid., 34. Compare *Perpetual Peace*, 121. The "lawless state of savagery" underlined in the quotation refers to international relations but also to the hunter, gatherer, and fisher stage of development (*Perpetual Peace*, 122 and note).
[40] Ibid., 38.

the Turks, Tamurlaine, the Europeans after Columbus's discoveries, they have all amazed the southern lands with their arts and weapons.[41]

This worldview is, as Said explained, the "vocabulary of classic nineteenth-century imperial culture." It is "imperial" in three senses of this polysemic word. It ranks all non-European cultures as "inferior" or "lower" from the point of view of the presumed direction of European civilization toward *the* universal culture. It legitimates European imperialism, not in the sense of being "right" (which Kant roundly denies) but in the sense that it coincides with nature and history and the precondition of an eventual just national and world order. Finally, it is imposed on non-European peoples as their cultural self-understanding in the course of European imperialism *and* federalism. Fanon's patriotic plea to the Third World to avoid the imitation of Europe is presumably directed at all three senses. Decolonized peoples must not fall into the comprehensive identity given by this scheme and thereby continue imperialism by other means of dependency. They must refuse it by exploring alternatives and so become independent.

The first challenge to Kant's idea came from one of his former students, J. G. von Herder (1744–1803). In *Ideas on the Philosophy of the History of Mankind* (1784–91), Herder defended cultural pluralism.[42] He argued that "each culture contains its own unique and incommensurable truth or worth, and as such could not be subordinated or elevated as inferior or superior to another."[43] Kant reviewed Herder's work and reasserted his view that all cultures can be ranked relative to a developmental logic and a normative apex. In a particularly revealing passage of the review (which reasserts the thesis of the *Idea for a Universal History*), Kant asks

---

[41] Kant, "Observations on the Feeling of the Beautiful and Sublime," in *Race and the Enlightenment: A Reader*, ed. Emmanuel Chukwudi Eze (Oxford: Basil Blackwell, 1997), 64. Kant wrote this in 1764, twenty years before the *Idea for a Universal History*. However, nothing in the latter text (or in *Perpetual Peace*) repudiates or contradicts his earlier view on national characteristics. The whole tenor of the text is complementary to it (see especially 38–9). He also continued to write on the racial superiority of Europeans in 1775 (*On the Different Races of Men*) and 1798 (*Anthropology from a Pragmatic Point of View*). For an introduction to Kant's views on race and national characteristics, see Eze, *Race and the Enlightenment*, 1–9, 38–70.

[42] Johann Gottfried Herder, *Ideen zur Philosophie de Geschichte der Menschheit* (1784–91), translated in part as *Ideas on the Philosophy of History of Mankind*, trans. T. Churchill (New York: Bergman Publishers, 1800).

[43] Eze, *Race and the Enlightenment*, 65. Compare Charles Taylor, "The Importance of Herder," in *Philosophical Arguments* (Cambridge, Mass.: Harvard University Press, 1995), 79–99.

rhetorically:

Does the author really mean that, if the happy inhabitants of Tahiti, never visited by more civilized nations, were destined to live in their peaceful indolence for thousands of centuries, it would be possible to give a satisfactory answer to the question of why they should exist at all, and of whether it would not have been just as good if the island had been occupied by happy sheep and cattle as by happy human beings who merely enjoy themselves?[44]

Herder's work challenges two features of the Kantian idea: the presupposition that all cultures can be ranked relative to a European norm and that they all develop (once they come into contact with the more civilized nations) toward that apex. Herder also presents an alternative attitude of cosmopolitanism as cultural pluralism: the presumption that all cultures are of intrinsic worth and that they have their own histories. In the long term Herder's cultural pluralism called into question the attitude of European cultural superiority informing the Kantian idea and helped to foster an outlook of cultural pluralism. This outlook is expressed in early-twentieth-century anthropology, the respect for non-European cultures that began to emerge during decolonization, and the more recent demands of multiculturalism. As Taylor suggests, the demands of multiculturalism rest on the "premise" derived from Herder that "we owe equal respect to all cultures." This is understood as a "presumption" that cultures are of "equal worth":

it is a starting hypothesis with which we ought to approach the study of another culture. The validity of the claim has to be demonstrated concretely in the actual study of the culture.[45]

Notwithstanding, Herder did not question another feature of the stages view of cultures and constitutions: the idea that each nation has one culture and that it is independent, separate, and internally uniform. Indeed, Herder may be said to have put the idea of a national culture on a new and influential footing. The more recent critics of cultural imperialism have accepted Herder's presumption but challenged his "billiard-ball" picture of cultures. They have argued that the culturally complex character of decolonizing and First World nations, the tangled and overlapping struggles for cultural recognition in all societies today (mentioned by Kymlicka), as well as the history of cultural interaction and suppression, suggest that

---

[44] Kant, Review of Herder's *Ideas on the Philosophy of the History of Mankind*, in *Kant's Political Writings*, ed. H. Reiss, trans. H. B. Nisbet (Cambridge: Cambridge University Press, 1970), cited in Eze, *Race and the Enlightenment*, 70.

[45] Taylor, "The Politics of Recognition," 66–7.

cultures are not independent, separate, and internally uniform but over-lapping, interacting, and internally contested or negotiated. Moreover, the multiplicity of cultures does not seem to bear any straightforward relation to constitutional and economic development or to tend to convergence and uniformity. Quite the opposite.[46]

Consequently, cultures should be seen, in the words of Said, as "contrapuntal ensembles."[47] The overlapping, interacting, and internally negotiated character of cultures is expressed as a second presumption—of cultural diversity rather than Herder's pluralism or Kant's monism. Reflecting on the cultural diversity and demands for recognition within the emerging European Union, Jacques Derrida writes that, contrary to both Kant and Herder, "what is proper to a culture is not to be identical to itself." This is not to say that cultural identity is not important or "not to not have an identity" but "to be able to take the form of a subject only in the difference with itself." There is, Derrida suggests, "no culture or cultural identity without this difference with itself."[48] This second presumption is, like the first, a working hypothesis, an attitude one takes to culture, not a preconceived idea to which reality must correspond. When approaching a culture or any demand for the acknowledgment of a culture, one should ask three questions. Are there other cultures or, recalling Fanon, other activities of cultural discovery and invention that share the same geographic space and deserve mutual presumptive respect? Is the culture in question constituted temporally by interaction with other cultures? Are there others who share the culture in question yet contest the way it is articulated and expressed by spokespersons claiming to speak for all?[49]

What are the differences between the attitude toward cultures in the two presumptions of cultural diversity and in Kant's idea of Europe? The first and most obvious difference is the attitude of presumptive respect for cultural differences in contrast to the presupposed attitude of cultural superiority (of Europeans). The second presumption suggests that a citizen or a people will be the bearer of more than one culture, of multiple

---

[46] For Herder's view that cultures are separate and incommensurable, see Anthony Pagden, *European Encounters with the New World* (New Haven: Yale University Press, 1993), 172–81. The change in the understanding of cultures as overlapping, interacting, and internally negotiated is summarized in Michael Carrithers, *Why Humans Have Cultures: Explaining Anthropology and Social Diversity* (Oxford: Oxford University Press, 1992), 12–33.

[47] Said, *Culture and Imperialism*, 52.

[48] Jacques Derrida, *The Other Heading: Reflections on Today's Europe*, trans. Pascale-Anne Brault and Michael R. Nass (Bloomington: Indiana University Press, 1991), 9.

[49] For these three questions, see Tully, *Strange Multiplicity*, 1–29.

cultural identities, and that this diversity is better approached as activities of cultural discovery, invention, reimagination, and contestation in agonic relation to the powers of cultural imposition and assimilation than as a diversity of fixed cultural formations—more Dionysian than Appollonian.[50]

The third difference is the understanding that culture is closely related to identity. Kant understood this as well, but he saw cultural identity, except at the highest stage, as something superficial and irrelevant to one's identity as a citizen. One's identity as a citizen is defined in the First Definitive Article in terms of a metaphysical and universal theoretical identity, toward which the species is tending, of autonomy: the capacity of rational agents to direct their lives reflectively in accordance with universal principles. In contrast, cultural identity is seen as an important aspect of one's "practical identity." The appropriate acknowledgment of and respect for one's practical identity is now seen as relevant to one's identity as a citizen. "Practical identity" refers to the aspects of citizens' identities that "matter" to them. It is the answer to the question "Who are we?" or the "structure of strong evaluations" in accord with, and against, which humans live their lives.[51] In an influential and representative analysis, Christine Korsgaard describes practical identity in the following way:

The conception of one's identity in question here is not a theoretical one, a view about what as a matter of inescapable scientific fact you are. It is better understood as a description under which you value yourself, a description under which you find your life worth living and your actions worth undertaking.... Practical identity is a complex matter and for the average person there will be a jumble of such conceptions. You are a human being, a woman or a man, an adherent of a certain religion, a member of an ethnic group, a member of a certain profession, someone's lover or friend, and so on. And all of these identities give rise to reasons and obligations. Your reasons express your identity, your nature; your obligations spring from what that identity forbids.[52]

---

[50] For one important attempt to work out the implications of this second difference, see William E. Connolly, *The Ethos of Pluralization* (Minneapolis: The University of Minnesota Press, 1995).

[51] For these ways of characterizing practical identity, see Michel Foucault, "The Subject and Power," in *Michel Foucault: Beyond Structuralism and Hermeneutics*, ed. Hubert L. Dreyfus and Paul Rabinow (Chicago: University of Chicago Press, 1982), 210–13; Charles Taylor, *Sources of the Self: The Making of the Modern Identity* (Cambridge, Mass.: Harvard University Press, 1989), 3–101; and David Owen, *Maturity and Modernity: Nietzsche, Weber, Foucault and the Ambivalence of Reason* (London: Routledge, 1994), 64–216.

[52] Christine Korsgaard, *The Sources of Normativity* (Cambridge: Cambridge University Press, 1996), 101.

Fourth, the awareness that the jumble of cultural aspects that make up one's practical identity matter to one's sense of self-worth has led to the argument that these cultural aspects require a level of mutual respect in one's society in order to live the sort of life of self-directed agency presupposed by Kant. John Rawls forcefully argues that self-respect must be seen as a primary good of a liberal society; self-respect requires a threshold of mutual acknowledgment and respect of citizens' practical identities (or practices of identity formation and reformation).[53] Forms of cultural disrespect (such as racism, sexism, or the *a priori* ranking of citizens' cultures as superior or inferior in the Kantian scheme) and misrecognition and nonrecognition of cultural differences (such as the suppression and assimilation of minority cultures and languages) are serious forms of oppression and injustice, Anthony Laden argues. They undermine the conditions of self-respect required for free and equal citizenship.[54]

These four differences mark the fairly widespread transition from and repudiation of the conception of cultures in the Kantian idea of Europe to the recognition of the problem of cultural imperialism and the exploration of the two presumptions of cultural diversity, not only between the so-called First and Third Worlds, but within European and North Atlantic societies themselves. This change in outlook is in part the achievement of the critical Enlightenment attitude and, in particular, Fanon's contribution to it. Nevertheless, one could agree that this is a change in the understanding of cultures from Kant's idea of Europe but deny that it entails any change in what is essential to the Kantian idea: the concepts of constitutions and federations. It is to this that we now turn.

RETHINKING CONSTITUTIONS AND FEDERATIONS

Recall that on Kant's account the constitution of every free and independent nation-state should be the same. The constitution is republican, and this means that it treats each citizen the same, as free and equal. "*Rightful equality*," Kant explains, "is that relation among citizens whereby no citizen can be bound by a law, unless all are subject to it simultaneously and in the very same way."[55] This "idea" of equality gives expression to the principle that all humans are equally worthy of respect because

---

[53] John Rawls, *A Theory of Justice* (Oxford: Oxford University Press, 1971), 440–1.
[54] See the important thesis by Anthony Simon Laden, *Constructing Shared Wills: Deliberative Liberalism and the Politics of Identity*, Ph.D. diss., Department of Philosophy, Harvard University, 1996.
[55] Kant, *Perpetual Peace*, 112, note.

of their status as rational agents with the capacity for autonomy. To recognize citizens are equals in this sense involves treating them impartially ("in the very same way") and, so Kant thought, in a difference-blind manner. It is standardly expressed in individual rights and duties, formal equality before the law, and the principle of nondiscrimination. The upshot of the change in the understanding of cultures is the recognition that humans ought to be respected as equals in their capacity to form, contest, and transform practical identities or identity-related cultural differences as individuals and as members of cultural groups. However, the presumption of the equal recognition and respect for cultural differences, which, as we have seen, seems to follow from recognition of the equal capacity to form such cultural differences, comes into conflict with the presumption of equality as impartiality or difference-blindness, which seems to follow from the equal capacity for autonomy. The tension between these two kinds of equality of respect and recognition, which are both equally well grounded in the values of modern politics, can be formulated in different ways.[56]

The first and most Kantian resolution is to argue that the recognition and respect for cultural differences take place outside the political realm in the realm of "ethics" and "self-esteem," whereas "citizens" are recognized and accorded respect solely under the description of impartial equality: that is, as bearers of identical rights and duties.[57] It is certainly true that many cultural differences and forms of multiculturalism can be treated fairly in this way. Citizens can express and contest many aspects of their practical identities while exercising the rights and duties of impartial equality and fight against various forms of cultural imposition and disrespect by the application of the principle of nondiscrimination, as Jeremy Waldron has asserted.[58]

However, there are many cases where the two aspects of equality cannot be separated into two mutually exclusive categories, where the equal recognition and respect for cultural differences involve some conflict with

---

[56] For this formulation of the debate between Kantians and their critics as a question of the relation between two kinds or aspects of equality of recognition and respect, rather than as equality *versus* difference, see Taylor, "The Politics of Recognition," 41–3.

[57] This is the response associated with Jürgen Habermas in, for example, *Moral Consciousness and Communicative Action*, trans. Christian Lenhardt and Shierry Weber Nicholsen (Cambridge, Mass.: MIT Press, 1995). For an historical account from Kant to the present, see Axel Honneth, *The Struggle for Recognition: The Moral Grammar of Social Conflicts*, trans. Joel Anderson (Oxford: Basil Blackwell, 1995).

[58] Jeremy Waldron, "Minority Cultures and the Cosmopolitan Alternative," *The Rights of Minority Cultures*, ed. Will Kymlicka, 93–122.

the Kantian idea of a constitution based solely on impartial equality. Taylor neatly summarizes the conflict:

These two modes of politics, then, both based on the notion of equal respect, come into conflict. For one, the principle of equal respect requires that we treat people in a difference-blind fashion. The fundamental intuition that humans command this respect focuses on what is the same in all. For the other, we have to recognize and even foster particularity. The reproach the first makes to the second is just that it violates the principle of nondiscrimination. The reproach the second makes to the first is that it negates identity by forcing people into a homogeneous mold that is untrue to them. This would be bad enough if the mold were itself neutral—nobody's mold in particular. But the complaint generally goes further. The claim is that the supposedly neutral set of difference-blind principles of the politics of equal dignity is in fact a reflection of one hegemonic culture. As it turns out, then, only the minority or the suppressed cultures are being forced to take alien form. Consequently, the supposedly fair and difference-blind society is not only inhuman (by suppressing identities) but also, in a subtle and unconsciousness way, itself highly discriminatory.[59]

Such conflicts comprise one of the central problems of the present (as the preceding quotation from Kymlicka highlights). Yet it is difficult to formulate in the terms of the Kantian idea of Europe. As a result, the Kantian idea of a constitution and a federation has been amended in two types of cases.

John Stuart Mill was one of the first to suggest how. He argued that the "a priori presumption" should remain in favor of "impartiality," and "the law" should "treat all alike" except "where dissimilarity of treatment is required by positive reasons, either of justice or of policy."[60] In the first type of case, citizens reason that they cannot exercise the rights and duties of impartial equality (and so participate in the public and private life of their constitutional association without injustice) unless they are allowed to exercise them in ways that recognize and accommodate, rather than misrecognize and denigrate, their cultural differences. The relevant cultural difference may be linguistic, religious, gender-related, ethnic, and so on. This is a challenge, not to the shared rights, duties, and institutions

---

[59] Taylor, "The Politics of Recognition," 43.
[60] John Stuart Mill, "The Subjection of Women," in his *Three Essays* (Oxford: Oxford University Press, 1975), 428–9. In Mill's view, no reasons (of justice or policy) advanced to treat women dissimilarly by subordinating them to men are convincing. Nevertheless, he introduces the proviso that impartial equality can be amended if reasons for dissimilar treatment of some citizens *that does not involve subordination* can be made good. This is precisely what recent feminists, building on Mill, have argued, for purported impartial public norms often embody a male norm.

associated with impartial equality but to the requirement that all exercise
them always "in the very same way."

The "positive reasons" advanced for this "dissimilarity of treatment"
often appeal to the very value of impartial equality that was thought to
entail difference-blindness. If, under the rubric of impartial equality, a
constitution upholds one public language, statutory holidays that coincide with one religion, public practices that uphold a male norm, public
education that upholds one historical narrative, and so on, then the constitution, while treating everyone "in the very same way," does not treat
them "impartially." It is partial to, and serves to impose, one culture and
subordinates and assimilates all others to some extent. To be impartial
the constitution cannot be difference-blind, which is impossible in these
cases, or difference-partial, as it is by upholding one set of dominant cultural differences while pretending to be impartial. Rather, the constitution
must be difference-aware or diversity-aware: that is, it must accord equal
due recognition and respect, in some way, to the respectworthy cultural
differences of all citizens. This is the same structure of argument against
cultural imperialism we saw earlier with Constant and Fanon, but now it
is advanced by the culturally diverse citizens of contemporary societies.
Alternatively, as Kymlicka has argued, the due recognition of the cultural
differences of citizens is a necessary condition of the capacity for autonomy, something impartial equality is meant to secure. In these and other
ways, the idea of a constitution in the Kantian idea has been modified
from within to include, as a matter of justice, the equality of respect for
cultural diversity.[61]

The second and stronger type of case is where citizens reason that the
equal recognition and respect of their cultural identities require different
institutions of self-government: that is, forms of legal and political pluralism that accord with cultural differences by means of devices of subsidiarity, devolution, regional autonomy, federalism, and confederalism within
a larger constitutional association. This demand conflicts with another
principle of a republican constitution according to Kant—the principle
"of the *dependence* of everyone on a single, common [source of] legislation (as subjects)."[62] In multi-ethnic and multinational constitutional
associations, the positive reasons for this second type of dissimilarity of

---

[61] The literature is vast. See, for example, Gutmann, ed., *Multiculturalism*; Will Kymlicka,
Liberalism, Community and Culture (Oxford: Clarendon Press, 1991); and Kymlicka,
Multiculturalism. In this and the second type and case, I set aside arguments that appeal
to the equal respect for cultural differences as a value in its own right.

[62] Kant, *Perpetual Peace*, 112.

treatment have been similar to those advanced by Constant immediately after the publication of *Perpetual Peace*, or they have been analogous to the ones advanced in the first type of case: that participation in the same legislative body in all matters would involve some degree of cultural imperialism. The consequence is that citizens are dependent on more than one common source of legislation (regional, provincial, national, federal) and the powers of these legislative assemblies are not ordered in a single hierarchy. The resulting form of federalism differs from Kant's "idea of federalism": it can occur within as well as among constitutional associations, and it is based on the recognition and respect of cultural diversity rather than on cultural uniformity.[63]

One of the best examples of the two cases (diverse constitutionalism and federalism) is arguably the very organization that was supposed to unfold in accord with the Kantian idea, the European Union. Another example that exposes the limitations of Kantian constitutionalism and federalism is the demand of the Indigenous peoples of the world to free themselves from the internal colonialism imposed on them over the past five hundred years by the former colonies of European imperialism and to govern themselves in their own constitutional associations. As we have seen, the Kantian idea locates these peoples at the lowest (hunting-and-gathering) stage without laws and property and (as in all cases) without a right to challenge the system of laws imposed on them by the European settler states:

A people should not *inquire* with any practical aim in view into the origin of the supreme authority to which it is subject, that is, a subject *ought not to rationalize* for the sake of action about the origin of this authority, as a right that can still be called into question [*ius controversum*] with regard to the obedience he owes it. For, since a people must be regarded as already united under a general legislative will in order to judge with rightful force about the supreme authority, it cannot and may not judge otherwise than as the present head of state wills it to. Whether a state began with an actual contract of submission as a fact, or whether power came first and law arrived only afterward, or even whether they should have followed in this order: For a people already subject to civil law these rationalizations are altogether pointless and, moreover, threaten a state with danger.[64]

---

[63] For the European Union, see Richard Bellamy, "The Constitution of Europe: Rights or Democracy," in *Democracy and Constitutional Culture in the Union of Europe*, ed. Richard Bellamy (London: Lothian Foundation Press, 1996), 153–73. The literature on this second type of case is also vast. See Kymlicka, ed., *The Rights of Minority Cultures* and *Multicultural Citizenship*; Iris Marion Young, *Justice and the Politics of Difference* (Princeton: Princeton University Press, 1990); and Laden, *Constructing Shared Wills*.

[64] Kant, *The Metaphysics of Morals*, 129–30.

Once this is settled, Aboriginal peoples have no appeal for the recognition and protection of their cultures and Aboriginal rights. As we have seen, they face assimilation under the Kantian idea of equality, which decrees their subjection to non-Aboriginal legislative authority in "the very same way" as every other citizen.

Of course, this dimension of the Kantian idea has always been contested by Aboriginal peoples, and they continue to challenge it in the courts and legislatures of Canada, the United States, Australia, and New Zealand, and in international law today.[65] In addition, it was forcefully challenged from within the Enlightenment tradition of constitutionalism by John Marshall, chief justice of the United States, in the early nineteenth century. Like Herder, he repudiated the stages view on which it is based and reasoned that Aboriginal peoples should be recognized and respected as equal: that is, as self-governing nations, equal in juridical status to European nations.

As Marshall wrote in *Worcester v. the State of Georgia* (1832): "America, separated from Europe by a wide ocean, was inhabited by a distinct people, divided into separate nations, independent of each other and the rest of the world, having institutions of their own, and governing themselves by their own laws."[66] Marshall goes on to conclude that the just establishment of non-Aboriginal constitutional states in America requires the consent of the Aboriginal nations acquired through nation-to-nation treaties. His opinion gives rise to a treaty-based federalism between self-governing, co-existing Aboriginal nations and the American (and Canadian) governments.[67]

Thus two central features of Kantian constitutionalism and federalism are abandoned: the difference-blind application of his principle of equality and the principle of citizens' dependence on a single, common source of legislation. Aboriginal peoples are dependent first and foremost on their own legislation, and the source of this legislative authority is not the United States or the Canadian constitution, but the Aboriginal peoples themselves as self-governing nations prior to the arrival of Europeans. Moreover, this line of argument has been extended to question the underlying Eurocentric direction of constitutional and federal development

---

[65] See *The Report of the Canadian Royal Commission on Aboriginal Peoples*, 5 vols. (Ottawa: Supply and Services, 1996), esp. vols. 1 and 2.

[66] Chief Justice John Marshall's opinion in *Worcester v. the State of Georgia*, reprinted in *The Writings of Chief Justice Marshall on the Federal Constitution* (Boston: James Monroe and Co., 1839), 426–7.

[67] Ibid., 435, 445. See Tully, *Strange Multiplicity*, 117–38.

in Kant's framework. A number of scholars have argued that the federation of the United States was influenced not only by European and Atlantic ideas of federalism but also by the federation of the five Iroquois nations. Others have suggested that Iroquois federation and its constitution, The Great Law of Peace, is a better heuristic for global federalism than the Kantian idea precisely because it respects and recognizes cultural diversity.[68]

FROM MONOLOGUE TO COSMOPOLITAN MULTILOGUE

The Enlightenment critical attitude toward the problem of cultural imperialism modified all five features of the Kantian idea of Europe and the world. However, recall the line of argument. Two "presumptions" regarding the equality of respect for cultures gave rise to three questions and four differences with respect to Kant's understanding of cultures. It followed from these presumptions, questions, and differences that Kant's ideas of constitutions and federations should be amended, specifically the ideas that equality always entails difference-blind treatment and that there must be one locus of authority in a constitutional association. These amendments led to the justification of two non-Kantian types of cases: where citizens share the same rights and institutions yet exercise and participate in them in different ways (diverse constitutionalism) and where citizens require a plurality of legal and political institutions (diverse federalism) in order to accord equal respect to the diversity of their cultural similarities and differences.

These rather dramatic changes in the understanding of the principles and practices of constitutions and federations rest entirely on two "presumptions" that the cultural differences in question are worthy of respect. The changes should be accepted if and only if the two presumptions can be made good. We have assumed this for the sake of the argument, but the point of describing them as "presumptions" is precisely to flag that

[68] Robert W. Venables, "American Indian Influences on the America of the Founding Fathers," *Exiled in the Land of the Free*, ed. Oren Lyons (Santa Fe: Clear Light Publishers, 1992), 73–124; Jose Barriero, ed., *Indian Roots of American Democracy* (Ithaca: Aewkon and Cornell University Press, 1988); and Iris Marion Young, "Hybrid Democracy: Iroquois Federalism and the Postcolonial Project," in *Aboriginal Rights, Political Theory and Reshaping Institutions*, ed. Duncan Ivison, Paul Patton, and Will Sanders (Cambridge: Cambridge University Press, 2001). For a careful treatment of the demands for recognition of Aboriginal peoples and the principles of liberal democracy, see Michael Murphy, *Nation, Culture and Authority: Multinational Democracies and the Politics of Pluralism*, Ph.D. diss., Department of Political Science, McGill University, January 1998.

they are open to question. So how is it to be decided if a presumption of equal respectworthiness for identity-related cultural difference is valid, and, if it is, what kind of constitutional or federal recognition is due? The answer to this question marks the final and most important change in understanding of constitutions and federations brought about by the Enlightenment critical attitude.

Kant's answer is that he decides. First, he judged the relative worth of the cultures of the world and ranked them relative to his background Eurocentric philosophy of history. Second, he determined the corresponding essentials for all legitimate constitutions and federations (by means of his "transcendental principle of publicness" that functions like the test of universalization and noncontradiction in morality).[69] The very idea that the question can be answered in this way, monologically and comprehensively, is now challenged as yet another dogma of cultural imperialism.

Take first the question of the validity of the presumption of equal value of a culture or cultural difference. A necessary condition of reaching an impartial answer is that we enter into dialogue with members of the culture in question. Drawing again on Herder and the tradition of cultural hermeneutics that developed in part from his work, Taylor explains why cross-cultural dialogue is necessary:

> we may have only the foggiest idea *ex ante* of in what its valuable contribution might consist. Because, for a sufficiently different culture, the very understanding of what it is to be of worth will be strange and unfamiliar to us. We learn [by dialogue] to move in a broader horizon, within which what we have formerly taken for granted as the background to valuation can be situated as one possibility alongside the different background of the formerly unfamiliar cultures. The "fusion of horizons" operates through our developing new vocabularies of comparison, by means of which we can articulate these contrasts. So that if and when we ultimately find substantive support for our initial presumption, it is on the basis of an understanding of what constitutes worth that we couldn't possibly have had at the beginning.[70]

If Kant had entered into dialogue with members of the cultures he ranked monologically, he could have broadened his horizons and seen the idea for a universal history with a cosmopolitan intent as one background of valuation among many. He could have entered into the difficult but rewarding activity of comparing the worth and public respectworthiness

---

[69] Kant, "On the Agreement between Politics and Morality according to the Transcendental Concept of Public Right," in *Political Writings*, ed. Hans Reiss, 125–30.
[70] Taylor, "The Politics of Recognition," 67.

of European and non-European cultures and their internal diversity in a genuinely cosmopolitan way. This activity could change not only his understanding of other cultures but also his idea of Europe itself.[71]

Citizens are required to accord the appropriate mutual respect to each other's respectworthy cultural differences (for the reasons given above by Rawls). Therefore, it follows that citizens must engage in this kind of intercultural and agonic dialogue. Given the need to test the second presumption of cultural diversity in the course of the dialogue (by asking the three questions), the dialogue is properly called a "multilogue." Such a public multilogue can be thought of as a reformulation of Kant's ideal of "public enlightenment" in the face of cultural diversity. The persons who decide the second part of the question (the kind of constitutional or federal recognition that is due) must engage in the multilogue to determine which cultural differences are candidates for constitutional recognition (that is, are worthy of respect). Yet must all citizens reach agreement on the second part of the question, or can it be decided by a few? The answer given by Kant is that a few can decide questions of constitutional essentials as long as their reasons are "compatible with their being made public" (the test of "public reason"), and citizens on individual reflection are able to give their consent (the test of "external freedom").[72]

However, this monological feature of Kantian constitutionalism and federalism has been challenged from within the Kantian tradition by John Rawls and Jürgen Habermas. Both argue that Kant's monological test of public reason and external freedom is insufficient to ensure impartiality and justification. It is through an actual dialogue in which equal citizens exchange public reasons to reach agreement on constitutional essentials, Habermas explains in contrast to Kant, that partialities can be exposed and overcome, and the form of consent required for public justification can be achieved.[73] The dialogical reformulation of the demands of an

---

[71] For the logic of this kind of intercultural and agonic multilogue, see James Tully, "Diversity's Gambit Declined," *Constitutional Predicament: Canada after the Referendum of 1992*, ed. Curtis Cook (Montreal: McGill–Queens University Press, 1994), 149–99; and Laden, *Constructing Shared Wills*, 260–8.

[72] Kant, "On the Agreement between Politics and Morality," 125; and idem, *Perpetual Peace*, 112 note.

[73] See Jürgen Habermas, "Discourse Ethics: Notes on a Program of Philosophical Justification," in *Moral Consciousness and Communicative Action*, trans. C. Lenhardt and S. W. Nicholsen (Cambridge, Mass.: MIT Press, 1995), 43–116; John Rawls, *Political Liberalism* (New York: Columbia University Press, 1993); Jürgen Habermas, "Reconciliation through the Public Use of Reason"; and John Rawls, "Reply to Habermas," *Journal of Philosophy* 92, 3 (March 1995): 109–31, 132–80.

ideal of public reason and freedom is presented by Habermas in terms of principle D: "Only those norms can claim to be valid that meet (or could meet) with the approval of all affected in their capacity *as participants in a practical discourse.*"[74]

Since citizens begin the public discussion on constitutional essentials from within their various cultural understandings, the two questions (the respectworthiness of citizens' cultural differences and their appropriate form of recognition) are raised and addressed in the same practical discourse:

> The descriptive terms in which each individual perceives his interests must be open to criticism by others. Needs and wants are interpreted in the light of cultural values. Since cultural values are always components of intersubjectively shared traditions, the revision of the values used to interpret needs and wants cannot be a matter for individuals to handle monologically.[75]

This change in the understanding of constitutionalism can be seen as a reformulation of the ideal of public reason in order to place the constitutional rule of law on equal footing with the democratic idea of the sovereignty of the people who impose the constitution on themselves. The thesis that the rule of law and democracy (or self-rule) are co-equal principles, associated in European theory with Locke and Rousseau, became widely accepted in the twentieth century despite Kant's objections to it. A constitution or a federation rests on the agreement of the sovereign people reached through processes of deliberation or what is now called "democratic constitutionalism."[76] A cultural difference is worthy of respect and some form of recognition if it can be shown to be reasonable. It is reasonable if through the exchange of public reasons among free and equal citizens the cultural difference in question can be "made good to citizens generally." In the exchange of public reasons, citizens accept the burdens of judgment associated with freedom and equality in conditions of cultural diversity or reasonable pluralism: the awareness of and

---

[74] Jürgen Habermas, "Discourse Ethics," 66. The role of dialogue in overcoming partiality and securing consent based on conviction is mentioned on pages 66–7. Habermas interprets Rawls's theory here as monological like Kant's. Rawls corrects him on this in "Reply to Habermas" and clarifies his own conception of public dialogue on constitutional essentials.

[75] Habermas, "Discourse Ethics," 67–8.

[76] See Habermas, "Reconciliation through the Public Use of Reason," 126–31; Rawls, "Reply to Habermas," 161–7; and Habermas, "Popular Sovereignty as Procedure," in *Between Facts and Norms: Contributions to a Discourse Theory of Law and Democracy*, trans. William Rehg (Cambridge, Mass.: MIT Press, 1996), 463–90. For Kant's objection that popular sovereignty is self-contradictory, see *Metaphysics of Morals*, 130.

respect for those identity-related cultural differences that are compatible with reaching agreement on a shared identity as citizens.[77]

The changed understanding of constitutionalism, Laden explains, is a matter of rejecting that a conception of citizenship is "worked out ahead of time" based on "supposedly universal principles" and then arguing "that any identities with non-political aspects which are incompatible with this notion of citizenship are unreasonable." Nor can one argue that "complaints about the burdensomeness of citizenship from their perspectives" are illegitimate charges of injustice. Laden starts, "not from a conception of citizenship, but from an ideal of society ordered by a shared will formed through a process of reasonable political deliberation." He continues:

The realization of that ideal involves members of the society coming to construct a political identity they can share despite their other differences. We call that identity citizenship, and try to work out some of its basic features given the role it plays in securing the possibility that deliberation could construct such a shared will. Freedom and equality come in to its characterization in this fashion.[78]

In his early presentation of principle D, Habermas appeared to hold that cultural differences would be filtered out in the course of the dialogue by processes of generalization and role-taking and that citizens would reach agreement on a difference-blind constitution.[79] However, as the critical response to Habermas has shown, this reintroduction of difference-blind equality as the regulative ideal of discourse cannot be sustained. If citizens take into account the culturally different or "concrete" other, as well as the "generalized" other, in the course of their deliberation, as they must, then there is no reason in principle why they cannot give good public reasons for the respect for and public recognition of those differences in diverse forms of constitutions and federations: reasons that are not particular to the members of that culture but are based on considerations of justice, freedom, equality, and nonsubordination that are shared by citizens generally.[80] Furthermore, as Iris Marion Young has gone on to argue, if

---

[77] This paragraph is a rough description of the transformation of Kant's ideal of public reason to bring it in line with Rawls in *Political Liberalism* and Laden in *Constructing Shared Wills*. For situations in which equality (in both senses) is challenged, see Rawls, "The Law of Peoples," in *On Human Rights: The Oxford Amnesty Lectures 1993*, ed. Stephen Shute and Susan Hurley (New York: Basic Books, 1993), 41–82.

[78] Laden, *Constructing Shared Wills*, 338–9.

[79] Habermas appears to modify his earlier view to some extent, perhaps in response to the critical literature. See Habermas, "Struggles for Recognition in the Democratic Constitutional State," *Multiculturalism*, 107–49, and "Citizenship and National Identity," in *Facts and Norms*, 491–516.

[80] See Seyla Benhabib, *Situating the Self: Gender, Community and Postmodernism in Contemporary Ethics* (London: Routledge, 1992), 148–77.

citizens are to treat each other equally in the discussion itself, they will have to recognize that Habermas's *form* of public argumentation is not impartial but culturally particular and thus accept culturally different forms of argumentation. In these and other ways the imperial aspects of the early formulation of principle D have been exposed and corrected. A postimperial and genuinely cosmopolitan conception of the critical exchange of public reasons among free and equal citizens can then become the basis of constitutionalism and federalism.[81]

CONCLUSION

The Kantian idea of Europe and the world is not as cosmopolitan as Kant intended it to be. His conceptions of cultures, constitutions, and federations, as well as the procedures of constitutional legitimation, are partial in one way or another, and as a result they continue cultural imperialism when they are treated as if they were universal. My critical survey was not restricted to this negative, Socratic task of showing that Kant's idea of Europe and the world does not possess the cosmopolitan status it intends to possess. The Enlightenment critical attitude is often criticized for being only negative, for failing to put forward an alternative. In response to this objection, I sought to show how a different way of thinking about and acting in relation to the cultures, constitutions, and federations of Europe and the world has been developed in the course of the two hundred years of criticism. This way of thinking and acting appears to be less imperial and more cosmopolitan, and perhaps more peaceful, than the Kantian idea that it simultaneously respects and challenges.[82]

---

[81] Iris Marion Young, "Communication and the Other: Beyond Deliberative Democracy," in *Democracy and Difference*, 120–35.

[82] This attitude of both respecting and challenging the prevailing forms of thought and action in the present *is* the Enlightenment critical attitude. See Foucault, "What is Enlightenment?" 41.

Contributors

TALAL ASAD teaches anthropology at the Graduate Center of the City University of New York. He was born in Saudi Arabia, spent his boyhood in India and Pakistan, and was educated in Britain where he has lived for most of his life. His most recent book is entitled *Genealogies of Religion* (1993).

ANDRÉS DE BLAS GUERRERO is Professor of Theory of the State and Chairman of the Department of Political Science and Administration of the Universidad Nacional de Educación a Distancia in Madrid. His most recent publications are *Tradición republicana y nacionalismo español* (1991) and *Nacionalismos y naciones en Europa* (1994).

HANS W. BLOM teaches social and political philosophy at Erasmus University, Rotterdam. His recent books include *Causality and Morality in Politics: The Rise of Naturalism in Dutch Seventeenth-Century Political Thought* (1995) and, as editor, Algernon Sidney's *Court Maxims* (1996). He is currently working on editions of texts by Pieter de la Court and Lambertus van Velthuysen. He is acting editor of the series *Studies in the History of Ideas in the Low Countries* and editor of *Grotiana*.

ARIANE CHEBEL D'APPOLLONIA is *maître de conférences* at the Institut d'Études Politiques in Paris. She also is associate researcher at the Centre d'Étude de la Vie Politique Française (CEVIPOF) and executive director of the American Center/ Sciences Po. She has published widely on the politics of European integration and on the history of the Right in Europe. Her most recent publication is *Les racismes ordinaires* (1998).

ELIE COHEN is Director of Research at the CNRS (National Center for Scientific Research) and Professor at the Institut d'Études Politiques in Paris. He is a member of the Council of Economic Advisers at the Office of the French Prime Minister,

Vice President at the *Haut Conseil du secteur public*, scientific adviser to the European Union Cost Program, and a former member of the Board of Directors of France Telecom. His books include *L'État brancardier: Politiques du déclin industriel 1974–1984* (1989), *Le Colbertisme "High-Tech": Economie des Telecom et du grand project* (1992), *La Tentation hexagonale: La Souveraineté à l'épreuve de la mondialisation* (1996), and most recently, *L'Ordre Economique Mondial: Essai sur les authorités de regulation* (2001).

DANIELA ENGELMANN-MARTIN is a Ph.D. candidate in the Department of Social and Political Science of the European University Institute, Florence, Italy.

BIANCAMARIA FONTANA is Professor of the History of Political Ideas at the Institut d'Études Politiques et Internationales of the University of Lausanne. Her books include *Rethinking the Politics of Commercial Society* (1985), *Benjamin Constant and the Post-Revolutionary Mind* (1991), and *Politique de Laclos* (1996). She is also the editor and translator of Benjamin Constant, *Political Writings* (1988).

MICHAEL HERZFELD is Professor of Anthropology, and Curator of European Ethnology in the Peabody Museum, at Harvard University. A past president of both the Modern Greek Studies Association and the Society for the Anthropology of Europe, he has also served as editor of *American Ethnologist*. He is the author of a large number of books on the anthropology of Europe, the most recent of which are *The Social Production of Indifference: Exploring the Symbolic Roots of Western Bureaucracy* (1992), *Cultural Intimacy: Social Poetics in the Nation-State* (1997), and *Portrait of a Greek Imagination: An Ethnographic Biography of Andreas Nenedakis* (1997).

WILLIAM CHESTER JORDAN is Professor of History at Princeton University and former Executive Director of the Shelby Cullom Davis Center for Historical Studies at Princeton. His most recent book is *The Great Famine: Northern Europe in the Early Fourteenth Century* (1996). He is currently at work on a book on Europe from 1000 to 1350 to be published by Penguin Books.

WILFRIED NIPPEL is Professor of Ancient History at the Humboldt Universität Berlin. He has also held positions at the universities of Cologne, Basel, Bochum, Munich, and Bielefeld. He has written widely on the political and social history of antiquity and ancient political theory and on the history of classical scholarship. His most recent publications include *Griechen, Barbaren und "Wilde"* (1990), *Public Order in Ancient Rome* (1995), and, as editor, Max Weber's *Wirtschaft and Gesellschaft, Teilband 5: Die Stadt* (1999).

ANTHONY PAGDEN is Harry C. Black Professor of History at the Johns Hopkins University. Until recently he was Reader in Modern Intellectual History at Cambridge University. He has held visiting positions at the European University

Institute (Florence), Harvard University, The Institute for Advanced Study at Princeton UNED (Madrid), and the Centre for European Cultural Studies at Aarhus (Denmark). His most recent publications are *Lords of all the World: Ideologies of Empire in Spain, Britain and France* (1995) and *La Ilustración y sus enemigos: dos ensayos sobre los origenes de la modernidad* (2001).

LUISA PASSERINI is Professor of History of the Twentieth Century at the European University Institute in Florence. Among her most recent books is *Europe in Love, Love in Europe: Imagination and Politics in Britain between the Wars* (1999, 2000).

J. G. A. POCOCK is Professor Emeritus at the Johns Hopkins University where he taught from 1974 to 1994. He held previous appointments at Washington University in St. Louis and the University of Canterbury in New Zealand. His published works include *The Ancient Constitution and the Feudal Law* (1957, 1987), *The Machiavellian Moment* (1975), *Virtue, Commerce and History* (1985), and the first two volumes (1999) of *Barbarism and Religion*, a series related to Edward Gibbon. He is also at work on a consideration of British history in relation to Europe and beyond.

THOMAS RISSE is Joint Chair in International Relations at the Robert Schuman Centre and the Department of Social and Political Science of the European University Institute in Florence, Italy. His most recent publications are, as editor, with Stephen Ropp and Catherine Sikkink, *The Power of Human Rights: International Norms and Domestic Change* (1999) and, with James Caporaso and Maria Green-Cowles, *Transforming Europe: Europeanisation and Domestic Change* (2000).

PHILIP RUTTLEY was educated at Oxford University and was called to the Bar in 1980. After practicing in EC law in London and Brussels, he served as a UN legal advisor in Rome and then as an EC advisor to the UK Government's Treasury Solicitor's Department. He is a Partner in the EC and WTO department of the international City firm of Clyde & Co. He has appeared in many cases before the EC Courts and has been involved in several WTO dispute settlement proceedings. He has published widely on EC and World Trade Organization issues and is Secretary of the World Trade Law Association.

JAMES TULLY is a Jackson Distinguished Professor of Philosophical Studies at the University of Toronto. He is a political theorist and historian of political thought. His most recent publications are *Strange Multiplicity: Constitutionalism in an Age of Diversity* (1995), co-editor with Alain Gagnon, *Struggles for Recognition in Multinational Societies: Spain, Belgium, United Kingdom, European Union and Canada in Comparative Perspective* (2000), and "To Think and Act Differently," in *Foucault Contra Habermas*, ed. S. Ashenden and D. Owen (1999).

Index

Other books in the series *(continued from page iii)*

Theodore Taranovski, editor, *Reform in Modern Russian History: Progress or Cycle?*

Deborah S. Davis, Richard Kraus, Barry Naughton, and Elizabeth J. Perry, editors, *Urban Spaces in Contemporary China: The Potential for Autonomy and Community in Post-Mao China*

William M. Shea and Peter A. Huff, editors, *Knowledge and Belief in America: Enlightenment Traditions and Modern Religious Thought*

W. Elliott Brownlee, editor, *Funding the American State, 1941–1995: The Rise and Fall of the Era of Easy Finance*

W. Elliott Brownlee, *Federal Taxation in America: A Short History*

R. H. Taylor, editor, *The Politics of Elections in Southeast Asia*

Sumit Ganguly, *The Crisis in Kashmir: Portents of War, Hopes of Peace*

James W. Muller, editor, *Churchill as Peacemaker*

Donald R. Kelley and David Harris Sacks, editors, *The Historical Imagination in Early Modern Britain: History, Rhetoric, and Fiction, 1500–1800*

Richard Wightman Fox and Robert B. Westbrook, editors, *In Face of the Facts: Moral Inquiry in American Scholarship*

Morton Keller and R. Shep Melnick, editors, *Taking Stock: American Government in the Twentieth Century*

Richard Grassby, *Kinship and Capitalism: Marriage, Family, and Business in the English-Speaking World, 1580–1720*

Charles E. Butterworth and I. William Zartman, editors, *Between the State and Islam*

Blair A. Ruble, *Second Metropolis: Pragmatic Pluralism in Gilded Age Chicago, Silver Age Moscow, and Meiji Osaka*

Lightning Source UK Ltd.
Milton Keynes UK
UKOW041443141012

200560UK00001B/93/P